D0734553

Shades of Gray

BORDERLANDS AND TRANSCULTURAL STUDIES

Series Editors:

Pekka Hämäläinen
Paul Spickard

| MOLLY LITTLEWOOD MCKIBBIN

Shades of Gray

| Writing the New American
| Multiracialism

University of Nebraska Press | Lincoln & London

Portions of chapter 1 and the conclusion were previously
published as "The Current State of Multiracial Discourse"
in *Journal of Critical Mixed Race Studies* 1, no. 1 (2014): 183–202.

Library of Congress Control Number: 2018016616

Set in Sabon Next LT Pro by Mikala R. Kolander.

To the memory of my beloved M. and W.

Contents

| Preface

This book is the result of many years of thinking about race and a persistent intellectual desire to grapple with the slippery subject. Examining multiracialism struck me as the best way to work through issues of race, since in order to do so we must address our beliefs, assumptions, and practices with regard to race. In other words, in order to talk about mixed race, one has to be able to talk about race. As a researcher of African American literature, I am specifically interested in blackness and its relationship to whiteness. But the way in which concepts of whiteness and blackness have developed in the United States—and the way the relationship between the two has defined so much about American society—is the reason this book focuses specifically on these two races and on American racial identity in particular. This book is intended to hold the black and white "races" up to the light and understand, via multiracialism, how they are conceptualized and how multiracialism might change those conceptual beliefs. It is, of course, also about how we conceptualize multiracialism in the twenty-first century. The title, *Shades of Gray*, is meant to signal not only the illogic of "black" and "white" categories but also the shades of "gray," or the unclear nature, of the racial binary that has for so long been thought of as definitive.

I discuss black–white multiracialism exclusively because black and white exemplify the most deeply embedded and passionate beliefs about race concepts in the United States. Because of their roots in the origins of the nation and in the very long history of racial slavery and inequality—based specifically on the "color line" between them—black and white offer the quintessential example of how racialism and multiracialism have developed and are understood in the United States. That the relationship between the two categories is still the most politically sensitive and delicately discussed of all racial relationships in the country demonstrates just how central it is to the American consciousness. That said, my focus is not meant to suggest that other racial mixtures or identities are not important or prominent in American history or literature but simply reflects the fact that the black–white binary has had the most significant influence on U.S. culture and is unique in the nation's racial discourse. Furthermore, as most studies of interracial marriage or multiracial identity articulate, a lasting effect of the tragedy of black–white race relations in the United States is that black–white intermarriage is considerably less prevalent than other interracial marriage combinations, and also that black–white couples are disproportionately active in multiracial advocacy.[1] In other words, black–white interracial families and mixed identities are still the most difficult for Americans to accept. It is this history that makes black–white mixture a topic that so readily reveals deeply held beliefs about race in America.

I also focus specifically on American race concepts and ideas about multiracialism—all of which are, of course, culturally specific to the United States. Consequently, I will focus exclusively on American racial discourse and not draw on concepts of hybridity that are so abundant outside America's borders. I want to explore how race functions and is understood within the United States, and this requires a theoretical framework that reflects the nation's thoughts rather than one that reflects how other cultures might reimagine American race practices. The analytical work of *Shades of Gray* is very much tied to the time and place of contemporary America.

Acknowledgments

Paul Spickard is incredibly supportive of young scholars of critical mixed race studies, and I am exceptionally fortunate to be among them. I cannot thank him enough for his extraordinary support, his selfless generosity with his time and energy, his thoughtful responses to my work, and his profound kindness.

I also want to thank my editor, Matthew Bokovoy, who has been remarkably communicative, thorough, and supportive. His faith in this project and his patient guidance have been invaluable to me. My project editor, Elizabeth Zaleski, and my copyeditor, Kenneth Wee, have been a pleasure to work with, and I thank them for their care and expertise.

I am grateful to Jennifer Ho and Carlton Floyd, who have offered helpful critiques of my manuscript, and to Jolie Sheffer, who offered constructive comments on an earlier draft. I appreciate the insight of these scholars as well as their generosity with their time and attention.

I am indebted to Leslie Sanders and Art Redding, who have offered me guidance for many years. I have benefited immensely from their keen minds and support.

Karen Bamford has been a wonderful source of goodwill and encouragement, and I am grateful for her wisdom and friendship.

I thank my brother for his reliable and enthusiastic support.

I thank my spouse for his sharp intellect and unqualified encouragement, without which I cannot imagine having accomplished what I have.

I thank my mother for all of her generous help and unwavering support, both of which have led me here.

Shades of Gray

Introduction
Race and Mixed Race in the United States

While race mixing began well before there were "races" to mix, what is usually meant by European and African race mixing in the United States occurred even before enslaved Africans were brought to North America. Many scholars note that mixing occurred during the Middle Passage and that Europeans who arrived in Africa before the trans-Atlantic slave trade had already begun producing what we might now call "multiracial children" with Africans before the first Africans were forced aboard slave ships. Reaching even further back, others point out that "whites and blacks had been mixing in Africa, Europe, and Asia for eons before Columbus sailed the western ocean, and they mixed in Latin America for a century before either white Englishmen or black Africans came to the Virginia shore."[1] It is interesting, then, that while black–white racial mixture has been a part of American history since the first African was brought to the "new world," this same mixture has been considered *new* generation after generation.

In literature alone, the newness of race mixing is remarked upon over the course of centuries. For instance, Frederick Douglass proclaims in his 1845 *Narrative*, "It is plain that a very different looking class of people are springing up at the south ... from those originally brought to this country from Africa," while in Charles W. Chesnutt's 1900 novel *The House behind the Cedars*, John Warwick insists: "You must take us for ourselves alone—we are a new people."[2] In the 1930s Jean Toomer asserted, "In America, we are in the process of forming a new race. . . . I was one of the first conscious members of this race," while Vera/Greta, in Danzy Senna's 2004 novel *Symptomatic*, claims, "We're a new race. A new people."[3]

The perpetual renewal of race mixing's "newness" is largely a result of, or a response to, shifting perceptions of blackness, whiteness, and race more generally. Race and racial mixing are thought about and defined differently over time, and so both undergo huge shifts in the social imagination. However, because of the United States' historical obsession with race and the separation of black and white, mixture has never posed a formidable threat to either the existing racial hierarchy or the categories of black and white, though it has certainly demonstrated the problematic conceptions and applications of both. That is, while the United States changes the way it thinks about race over time, its changing attitudes toward and understandings of race have always maintained in one way or another a belief in a race binary that has survived centuries of social, legal, and scientific revision. As a result, race mixture has been continually in a position of resistance even though it is nothing new and has not caused an overhaul or dissolution of the black–white binary. In turn, American literature reflects and responds to ideas about race and race mixture as they change, and since race mixture never generated significant change to existing race concepts over time and was itself so infrequently acknowledged, it is little wonder that, a century apart, Chesnutt and Senna would write characters who identify themselves as members of a "new people." Because multiracialism has never successfully altered the conception of black and white throughout American history, it can be seen as a perpetual—though largely ineffectual—threat to the racial binary.

One might rightly ask, then, why this book claims that we are witnessing a "new multiracialism" in the twenty-first century; in fact, many critical mixed race studies scholars decidedly oppose the idea that black–white multiracialism in the current century is any different from multiracialism in the past. Those who assert that contemporary multiracialism offers nothing more than did its iterations in the nineteenth and twentieth centuries often raise concerns that are important when considering some of the claims that multiracial advocates make. Among the skeptics' most vital concerns are the possibilities that, depending on how and what we understand it to be, multiracialism might well duplicate racial caste systems of the past that left white supremacy and the race binary entirely intact, or it could abandon race and in the process abandon social justice struggle. These are not only valid concerns but issues central to any responsible discussion of multiraciality, and they are addressed in chapter 1. They remind us how careful we must be as we think through the complexities of (multi)racial identity. However, they do not foreclose the possibility that we are witnessing a new era of multiracialism—one in which a genuine and socially sensitive challenge is being posed to American race concepts. What *Shades of Gray* works to establish is that contemporary multiracialism is not only arising out of a very different social context than in the past but also offering a different and new set of challenges to monoracial conceptions of blackness and whiteness. Like some opponents of multiracialism, I agree that we must be very careful not to invest in multiracialism as a hybrid category that leaves blackness and whiteness untouched or as an end to race via color blindness. I do not propose that contemporary multiracialism is already dismantling racialism or racism, and I do not see the *category* of multiracialism as disruptive to American race practices. Rather, I hope that this book helps us to think through how being *both* black *and* white—not simply "multiracial"—can alter the ways in which both blackness and whiteness are conceptualized. I also hope to demonstrate that contemporary multiracialism can be black positive and framed in the terms of social justice, and that it can work to unseat the white supremacy that has characterized historical conceptualizations of whiteness.

While we do need to be careful about accepting multiracialism uncritically or praising it as some sort of solution to centuries of racialism and inequality in a naïve or premature effort to achieve a "postracial" society, such caution can translate into defensiveness or even dismissal. I propose that while we need to call out efforts among some scholars and advocates to turn multiracialism into color blindness or some other "end to race," there is rich opportunity to consider carefully what multiracialism can offer us and what writers do offer in their representations of it. If we reorient some of the existing discussion to see black–white multiracialism in its contemporary context—informed by but no longer existing within the first half of the twentieth century—we can notice how the literature often prods us to see multiracialism in a new light. Specifically, I think that contemporary multiracial literature is, for the first time, challenging the monolithic categories that we believe blackness and whiteness to be and the dichotomous way they have historically functioned in the United States. If anything, multiracialism is more about blackness and whiteness than it is about hybridity in and of itself. In other words, this examination of multiracialism and its depiction in contemporary literature proposes that multiracialism is neither simply a third category of hybridity nor a reconstitution of the race binary that sets black and white in opposition. It is only by reading multiracialism as a simultaneous claim of both blackness and whiteness that we can change the views of blackness as a racial sponge, whiteness as racially pure, and hybridity as a separate category that leaves blackness and whiteness untouched as a binary.

Rainier Spencer dismisses the effectiveness of multiracialism's impact on race: "Adopting multiracial identity is not owning oneself; it is merely trading monoracial bondage for multiracial bondage. Race is still race, whether the shackles are monoracial or multiracial."[4] I agree that multiracial identity is as much a racialized identity as monoracial identity. But where Spencer sees this as evidence that multiraciality is not, in fact, doing anything to race, I propose that multiracialness can force us to think through how racialization works and what our race concepts mean. If the prevailing beliefs about race—the "pure" conceptualization of whiteness and one-drop conceptualization of blackness—are tested through black–white multiracialism, then multiraciality is doing quite important and unprecedented work. While passing narratives of a century ago used multiracialism to demonstrate the arbitrariness of the color line, the degree to which they could really challenge beliefs about blackness and whiteness was limited by the time period, when the color line was seen in quite "black and white" terms, helped not a little by de jure segregation and fresh memories of racial slavery. *Shades of Gray* argues that contemporary representations of multiracialism are unlike those of the past because they begin to query how we conceptualize monoraces (that is, blackness and whiteness *as monoracial categories*). So while multiracialism, in its present state, is not "destroying" race, it is making us rethink race in ways that call into question our beliefs about race. It is by rethinking those race concepts that we might, eventually, "break down" race—but we are not at a historical moment where race can logically be "destroyed." Rather, we still need race for reasons of, at the very least, social justice.[5] Whether race in and of itself ever stops being practiced or needed is a related question but really a different conversation than what we are having in critical mixed race studies at the moment.[6] Ultimately, *Shades of Gray* exemplifies Kenneth Warren's observation that "African American literature is the study and contestation of what race had done and is still doing to people"; it is in this spirit—of understanding what race "has done" and examining what race is "still doing" in America—that I offer what follows.[7]

Talking about Race: A Note on Terminology

Because this discussion is an analysis of literary engagement with the social practice of race rather than an examination of the legitimacy of race as a concept, my analysis will use racial terminology with its inaccuracy, shifting meanings, and complicated history in mind. This kind of language helps us understand how labels (and the concepts and ideologies they signify) operate in the particular cultures from which they arise. *Shades of Gray* seeks to engage with the history of race concepts and the resulting terminology without lending them validity; it also seeks to explore the impact of what race has been believed (and is believed) to mean.

The only term I will define in an attempt to be more precise is "racial identity." With this term, I mean to evoke the nature of racial classification as a social practice, avoid the idea that race is inherent or ascribed with certainty, and signal that "identity" is something that can take many forms, originate from various sources, and be altered. I use "racial identity" as a way of noting that racial identity can reflect personal choice or public opinion, can change over time or in an instant, can encompass or resist conventional racial and ethnic categories, might or might not reflect ancestry, and can be performed or thought to require an "authentic" claim. In other words, the phrase "racial identity" is meant to acknowledge that race is a socially developed system of classification and that its labels (and the concepts behind them) are not innate or scientific.[8]

Historical Context: Multiracialism Then and Now

Dichotomous American race concepts began with slavery and have produced not only concepts of blackness, whiteness, and mixedness but also what have become black pride and political solidarity—two of the most important aspects of current multiracial discourse. Because the long history of race and mixture in the United States has produced these beliefs and values that we now grapple with in the twenty-first century, it is helpful to take a moment here to understand that history.[9]

The British colonies treated white indentured servants (who owed their voyage costs) and black Africans (who were first traded to Virginians in 1619) similarly for about forty years until economic pressures divided and ranked them—that is, until white labor diminished (since it was against Christianity to enslave fellow Christians, the indentured had to be set free) and black slavery was adopted in full (since slave labor was deemed necessary and indigenous peoples were so difficult to enslave).[10] The justification of slavery at the time, based largely on racist religious claims, ensured black inferiority, white superiority, and a future in which black enslavement could be continued indefinitely. Kathleen Korgen observes that the first colonists categorized people based on status rather than race (by distinguishing between "servants and masters" and lacking conceptions of "white and black"), and so a distinction had to be made between the races for slavery to work; convincing lower-class whites to see the inferiority of blackness was the cornerstone of this strategy.[11] Korgen also points out that while miscegenation was condemned "even before slavery was an issue," by 1622 the English law that relegated all children to the status of their fathers was reversed in the colonies to ensure that mixed children (most of whom were the offspring of white fathers and black mothers due, in part, to a shortage of white women among the colonists) would follow their mothers' slave status.[12] Once white women began to immigrate in larger numbers, efforts were made to keep white women accessible to white men as wives and to prevent race mixture. For instance, white women were discouraged from marrying black men through a short-lived 1664 law that enslaved them along with their husbands.[13] Laws like these, which condemned multiracial children and their white mothers to indentured servitude—and enslaved free blacks who married whites— were abolished, in part because they actually caused miscegenation when "masters" would encourage or force the coupling of white women and black men to gain decades of bondage from the families. By the end of the seventeenth century, anti-miscegenation laws prohibited the coupling of black men and white women and thus, through matrilineal racial descent laws, worked to keep black and white from mixing officially.[14] Such anti-miscegenation laws reflect a relatively new and developing idea at the time about black and white as a racial dichotomy, with the former firmly subjugated to the latter.[15] Indeed, anti-miscegenation laws in the seventeenth century show a "society in the act of inventing race" in order to strengthen slavery.[16]

Over time, the racial caste systems in slave states changed to accommodate a growing free population: a group that was predominantly multiracial. In the only pre-Revolutionary enumeration of free blacks in the Southern colonies, the "overwhelming majority" of the small number of "free Negroes" were "light-skinned children of mixed racial unions."[17] As centuries passed, free blacks and "mulattoes" formed a separate class in the Deep South and, in fact, were treated relatively well by whites since they were considered a buffer between slaveholding whites and the black masses. In some cases, groups within this (wealthier) class of free "colored" people had more in common with sophisticated, moneyed whites than with any black people. In many instances, in fact, the allegiance of elite groups of free mulattoes to whites was a result of their own family connections to them, since the large number of freed mulattoes in the Deep South was due to wealthy white men taking an interest in and freeing their multiracial families.

As a result of this close relationship between particular groups of mulattoes and whites, mulatto populations participated in anti-blackness at times (as they attempted to separate themselves from blackness), though when defensive white supremacy was reinvigorated—as it was periodically—whites tended to restore a race binary and return mulattoes to categorical blackness.

The lower South behaved more like Latin America and the Caribbean in its consideration of racial classification and its observation of many degrees of blackness/whiteness—behavior that was strikingly different from that of the upper South, where anyone not "pure" white was considered black.[18] In South Carolina, for instance, "the harshest slavery somehow bred the greatest freedom for free mulattoes," and before 1850 "mulattoness did count, real distinctions were made, and the one-drop rule did not always prevail."[19] In Louisiana, the "Creoles of color" also complicated race categories since they enjoyed intermediate status not simply as mulattoes but as a "triracial" and "alternate third identity." G. Reginald Daniel argues that Creoles of color effectively challenged assumptions about the race binary, though the intermediate status they had enjoyed under Spain and France became quite different under the United States after the Louisiana Purchase.[20] The subsequent attempt to make Creoles simply black led the Creoles of color to institute blue vein societies that "challenged the social inequities associated with being designated African American" and to form communities "'outside' the social and cultural parameters of the African American community."[21] However, Creoles, mixed people, and free black people in the lower South made up small groups, relatively speaking, and the buffer mulatto caste was formed along the lines of economic class (as opposed to racial mixture itself). The majority of mixed individuals were enslaved and free mulattoes (or other free "colored" people) without powerful white connections were often poor and considered just as subordinate as "servants, Negroes, slaves, mustees, and Indians" by the governing elite.[22]

As a result of the Louisiana Purchase of 1803 (which spread slavery) and the Slave Act of 1807 (which halted the importation of new slaves), the enslaved were getting notably whiter.[23] However, by the mid-nineteenth century, many states conferred slave and free status based on race: if you were black you were a slave; if you were white you were not. Whites could not be slaves—the idea was repugnant to those who otherwise endorsed slavery. The ironies of such a view abound, including the fact that whites knew perfectly well that their slaves had white ancestry (to the point that some enslaved people looked entirely white) and sometimes were their own relatives. Additionally, whites' own sexual exploitation of black women resulted in a small but conspicuous trade in "fancy girls"—young enslaved people who were mixed or white (in appearance if not in status) and were bought expressly for more miscegenation.[24] The great intellectual effort to justify slavery leading up to the Civil War was built upon the race binary, and as Joel Williamson points out, nowhere did the proslavery argument account for mixed race; nowhere did proponents of slavery based on white supremacy account for the enslavement of white blood. Williamson explains that "in effect by 1850 proslavery thinkers had no choice."[25] Advocates of slavery had already committed themselves to a racial defense of slavery, and thinkers in the 1830s did not know what to make of people with black and white ancestry: "Slaves, by definition, could not be white. The fact that slavery was getting whiter, that in reality many slaves were more white than black, was a fact with which the proslavery argument could not cope. Either it could ignore the problem, which it did explicitly, or it could brusquely dismiss it by applying the one-drop rule to persons in slavery, which it did implicitly."[26] As in the early decades of slavery in the seventeenth century, the nineteenth century's understanding of black and white was based not on any abstract notion of race but on the necessity of explaining slavery. As Williamson argues, "Racism took the shape that slavery imposed. In the world the slaveholders made, Southern whites were not allowed to believe anything about black people other than what served the purposes of slavery."[27]

As slavery underwent extensive attack by the middle of the nineteenth century and white Southerners "closed ranks" in its defense, free mulattoes were "looked upon with increasing suspicion."[28] In the effort to defend slavery in the years preceding the Civil War, communities formerly tolerant of a free "colored" class instead began to consider mulattoes in terms of the taint of blackness encroaching upon their superiority and purity and to reassert the racial binary.[29] Vigilante and surveillance groups sought to punish and expel interracial and mulatto families through terrorism, while some states passed laws prohibiting "any free persons of color from living in the state."[30] The rise of scientific racism in this century helped fuel hostility toward the free mulatto class, and "no longer did many whites view mixed-race people as 'almost white'"—instead, mixed blood was considered a racial category worse than blackness.[31] It did not take long for the one-drop rule to erase the remaining mulatto caste, and by the 1850s and '60s, "any black blood, no matter how remote, made one black."[32] The infamous comments of a grand jury in Virginia summarize concisely the danger of a mulatto category: "No intermediate class can be other than immensely mischievous to our peculiar institution."[33]

The existence of an elite mulatto caste well before the Civil War illustrates how the perpetuation of the race binary was to some extent an accepted fiction. The small groups of sophisticated and wealthy mulatto families had much more in common with slaveholding whites than with the enslaved black population, to the point that some even acquired black slaves of their own. However, after the Civil War, mulattoes dissolved as a separate class or race and became black in both public perception and the sentiment among themselves, though Creoles were an exception to a large extent.[34] The imposition of the one-drop rule was a "tightening of racial boundaries" intended to protect whiteness and white power.[35] This rule, paired with the bitterly hostile brand of racism that flourished during and after the war, resulted in mulattoes generally identifying more with blacks. After emancipation the position of elite mulattoes no longer existed since there was no longer a distinction between free and enslaved status. Lines were drawn along the black–white color line alone, and the sharp increase in violent white supremacy (marked in part by the postwar rise of Anglo-Saxon clubs, including the Ku Klux Klan) meant that poor whites could assert themselves in a way that was formerly impossible. Additionally, former slaveholders eventually sought the alliance of poor whites against the new population of free "colored" people, exploiting the anxiety of poor whites who were eager to reaffirm their superiority in new ways after losing the reliable hierarchy of racial slavery. After the war "colored" people had to face the hatred of a population that had been ruined militarily, socially, economically, and politically. Black emancipation offered a focus for that hatred quite readily. The racism of whites in the South as well as the North taught mulattoes to align themselves with blacks. Simultaneously, anti-miscegenation laws, which in the antebellum era were "a necessary adjunct to slavery," became "the foundation of post–Civil War white supremacy" by "grouping all non-White races in opposition to Whites."[36]

While the one-drop rule was resisted by some former members of the mixed racial tier who mourned their loss of status and made efforts to maintain a racial hierarchy, by the 1920s such ambitions "had faded because those who most desired to be white had passed and slipped quietly into the white world," and the remainder focused on black "racial survival," worrying little about the maintenance of a system that observed gradations of blackness.[37] The strong new political alliance among all "colored" people was bolstered by hypodescent, which ensured that mixture continued to be synonymous with blackness for subsequent generations.[38] By the early decades of the twentieth century, the elite class of mulattoes had become "Negro" and shifted their loyalty to blackness, often using their privilege and education for the sake of black rights. This elite group would help form the NAACP and influence the cultural movement of the Harlem Renaissance. Williamson asserts that a vastly disproportionate number of Negro leaders in the generations after the Civil War were "visibly mulatto," and that many from this group, including both W. E. B. Du Bois and Booker T. Washington, came to dominate black political struggle.[39] In fact, "almost all" of Du Bois's "Talented Tenth" (those who formed black leadership) consisted of individuals with known white ancestry.[40] For instance, Walter White, a president of the NAACP, was himself blond and blue-eyed and had to assure Negroes that he was black. As Naomi Zack notes, mixed individuals "were well regarded by both blacks and whites—blacks made them their leaders, and whites accepted them as black leaders."[41] Thus, despite the elimination of the middle tier of

mulattoes as the buffer between whites and blacks, the members of that
elite group continued to serve as the bridge between white and black.

Notwithstanding the one-drop rule and segregation, both of which
affirmed the race binary, gradations of black–white multiracialism
were counted in numerous census surveys until the removal of such
categories from the federal census signaled an official shift away from
recognizing black–white mixture. For instance, the "mulatto" population was counted in censuses from 1850 to 1890 and then again in the
1910 and 1920 censuses before the category disappeared for good.[42] In
1890 the census included black, white, mulatto, quadroon, and octoroon; although white was still pure and superior, "a person half white
and half black was neither black nor white" officially.[43] Such counting, which was meant to be a reasonably scientific account of clearly
delineated races, served only to reveal that it was quite impossible to
determine race with any certainty. White ancestry could be invisible
in black-identified people, just as black ancestry could be invisible in
white-looking people. Mixture was usually left up to the surveyor to
determine, and the census included certain criteria at various times regarding appearance, community, and lineage to help assign racial categories. The U.S. Census Bureau even undertook research into racial
groups in 1918, the results of which suggested it was likely that three-
quarters of the "Negroes in the United States were of mixed blood"
in 1910 even though only 21 percent of them "were counted as mulattoes by the census, in which visibility was the test. Pure blacks," they
thought, "were on the way to extinction."[44] Thus, racial classification
schemes, even when they attempted to account for mixture, were total-
ly unreliable and had no real method of determining racial classification. Anthropologists in the mid-1920s also determined that physically,
the "New Negro" was a new homogeneous group "neither African nor
European, neither Negro nor Caucasian."[45] This study also concluded
that the "new" population of black people was largely mixed black-
white-Native. (It goes without saying that all conclusions about race
groups and their degrees of so-called mixedness or purity depended
on particular methodologies and classifications that were inherently
biased.) When mixture was removed from the census in 1930, the U.S.

Census Bureau helped "to create a simply biracial America" as "the entire Negro population became lighter" and all shades, fractions, and degrees simply counted as black.[46] The courts were no better able to determine legal racial classification with certainty; many legal cases regarding race classification took into consideration appearance, ancestry, economic status, social rank, and the opinion of the community as to one's race, while state after state sought to legally define race in terms of fractions. Often, racial identity boiled down to whether one "acted like" and was "treated as" a white or black person. Apparently white people were informed in court that they were actually black, and people who were visibly "colored" were granted legal whiteness. The acknowledgment, from slavery to Jim Crow, of "white niggers" or "white Negroes" highlights the difficulty the United States had in successfully classifying and keeping separate white and black.

However, this is not to say that the country did not work hard to maintain the color line. In the early to mid-twentieth century anti-miscegenation laws were still in place in many states in an attempt to keep black and white "blood" separate, and interracial sex and marriage were regulated in the majority of the country through these laws—as well as through custom and lynching. Several racial-minority groups were named in anti-miscegenation laws, which worked not to prevent intermarriage between all groups but to prevent intermarriage with whites. These laws, in other words, were "equally" applied to everyone but were usually phrased in ways that specified it was marriage between whites (especially white women) and other groups that was illegal in order to protect the purity of the white race.[47] As some anti-miscegenation laws were abolished, new laws were created so that interracial relationships validated in some states were invalidated in others. This attempt to stem the spread of human and civil rights continued well after the 1948 United Nations Declaration of Human Rights prohibited limitations on the right to marry based on race. In the fifties, the courts in Virginia—the state perhaps most dedicated to anti-miscegenation statutes—asserted that the state's anti-miscegenation laws reflected Virginia's goal "to preserve the racial integrity of its citizens" and to "regulate the marriage relation so that it shall not have a mongrel breed of citizens."[48] The Virginia Supreme Court stated that anti-miscegenation laws merely reflected appropriate "racial pride"[49]—the same white supremacist pride that was apparent in the state's eugenics-inspired Racial Integrity Act of 1924, which was "the most draconian miscegenation law in American history."[50] It is significant in no small measure, then, that it was in Virginia that what is considered the final legal victory of the civil rights movement took place. The *Loving v. Virginia* case of 1967 struck down all remaining anti-miscegenation laws in the United States and, as Peggy Pascoe argues, initiated the multiracial movement when the couples finally able to legally wed after the *Loving* case began forming support groups for the first federally protected interracial families in the late seventies.[51]

Importantly, marriage rights were essentially the last civil right addressed because the issue was so "explosive to whites" in that segregationists and other white supremacists were convinced that intermarriage with whites was the ultimate goal of black people agitating for racial equality.[52] Additionally, "most civil rights activists believed that fighting segregation and disenfranchisement was more important than trying to change laws and customs prohibiting personal relationships across the color line."[53] While racial integration among their membership was important to many civil rights groups, interracial sex was still a major concern for groups like SNCC (Student Nonviolent Coordinating Committee) and CORE (Congress of Racial Equality), which generally attempted to prevent it within their organizations and keep it out of the public's gaze when it did occur.[54] The potential of interracial relationships to derail civil rights efforts made the topic risky—in the midcentury, even liberal pro-integration whites were uncomfortable with and unprepared to accept the logical extension of civil rights to matters of interracial sex and marriage. In the second half of the twentieth century a large proportion of whites opposed interracial marriage, but so too did many black people.[55] The militant black nationalism of the 1960s and '70s opposed interracial relationships, especially between black women and white men—in large part because black nationalism was so invested in black masculinity. The racism that had fueled the dichotomous understanding of race and that had, in turn, forced all "colored" people into one oppressed group in the past, was transformed with the black power movement into racial pride and strength. However, black nationalism also led to the questioning of black racial authenticity and loyalty within the heterogeneous black race; it also shared with white supremacy an intolerance of interracial relationships and interracial identity. Embracing black pride meant that multiracials should identify with their black heritage exclusively, and so where multiracial people had struggled in the past with not being white enough (to fulfill the demands of paranoid guardians of whiteness), they now faced not being black enough (to fulfill the demands of black nationalists). The census, so often the measure of social opinion about race in the United States, reflected the dominance of the one-drop rule in the minds of whites and blacks: it ascribed monoracial categories in the 1960s by assigning children of interracial couples to the mother's race and in the 1970s by adopting Statistical Directive No. 15, which forced everyone into four official races (White, Black, Asian and Pacific Islander, and American Indian and Alaskan Native) according to whichever category "most closely reflects the way their community sees" those of mixed race.[56] And because of the prevalence of hypodescent, the "community" has generally viewed multiracials as "monoracially black."[57]

The civil rights movement (and the gay/lesbian and women's liberation efforts that occurred shortly thereafter) gave rise to an era of individual rights in both legislation and social thought that, in turn, permitted new personal freedoms that would affect racial identification. For instance, Williamson claims that interracial marriage, which had occurred so little during segregation, increased 63 percent in the sixties, and the *Loving* decision is widely acknowledged as initiating an additional increase in interracial marriage (since it enabled existing couples to wed legally across the country).[58] While the spirit of the one-drop rule never disappeared, civil rights and integration encouraged the formation of new ideas surrounding racial and cultural identity. Korgen argues that multiculturalism paved the way for mixed-race individuals to consider themselves bi- or multiracial for the first time. The result, she says, "is that biracial Americans no lon-ger have an obvious racial identity" the way they did when the one-drop rule legally defined all multiracials as black.[59]

Though it could be argued that the one-drop rule was the dominant understanding of race at the end of the twentieth century (and perhaps still is), the 1990s marked a significant shift in racial discourse with-in the United States. The publication of *Time* magazine's special issue on multiraciality in 1993, called "The New Face of America," is often cited as a major event in this shift. Although it has been criticized by many scholars of multiracialism for its treatment and understanding of mixed race, the magazine did offer a very public declaration that race heterogeneity was becoming a familiar reality and significant cultural topic.[60] Foundational publications in that decade by Maria P. P. Root (*Racially Mixed People in America* in 1992 and *The Multiracial Experi-ence* collection in 1996) and Naomi Zack (*Race and Mixed Race* in 1993 and the *American Mixed Race* collection in 1995) provided the touch-stones for the newly emerging discussion of mixed race. The multiracial movement was also in full swing during the nineties and played a key role in what could be considered the defining moment of the contem-porary era of multiracial discussion: the revision of the U.S. census.[61]

In 2000 the census was altered to allow respondents to select as many categories as they personally felt applied to them and included an "other" category, which could be checked or filled in with what-ever racial identity the respondent preferred to articulate.[62] Certainly hybridity and heterogeneity have not completely taken over racial dis-course in the United States, but monoracial identities (or even homo-geneous mixed identities like mulatto, quadroon, and octoroon) can no longer be said to dictate racial classification in the United States the way they once did.[63] It might appear that self-identification (which began only in the 1980 census) could absolve the government of re-sponsibility for defining race or classifying individuals. However, it is important to remember that self-identification had to fit ready-made categories, and so when multiracial people articulated their belonging to more than one group, census takers followed orders to count them among whatever racial group their mother belonged to or whichever race they listed first. David Theo Goldberg remarks that "the democracy of self-naming is underpinned by the authoritarianism of imposed identity and identification. Those resisting literally become the 'new Others.'"[64] Historically, then, there is a gap between how citizens self-identify and how they are counted.[65]

The census change in 2000 was both vehemently opposed and heartily supported, and for the most part the concerns raised by the census revision are still being debated. Generally, those who argue for and against changing the way the United States categorizes and considers black–white mixture can be broken down into two major groups: one that wants multiraciality to be recognized in some official capacity and one that views change in the way blackness is classified as a threat to African American group pride, racial solidarity, civil rights, and political empowerment. These two major camps of the multiracial-census debate offer meaningful and important arguments regarding racial identity, and their dialogue (which I discuss in chapter 1) illustrates the complexity of the current thinking about racial identity. Even when we consider the census not as an opportunity to express a personal sense of identity but as a political gesture with profound social effects, multiracial advocates of various stripes can be just as politically strategic as black civil rights activists.

This brief history of the development of blackness and mixedness in the United States is intended to help orient subsequent discussion. When considering the views of contemporary theorists and literary critics, it is helpful to understand how this history informs the contemporary conceptualization of race. For instance, it is important to keep in mind the status of mixture, including the mulatto caste and the workings of hypodescent in past centuries, in any consideration of whether the twenty-first century is, in fact, doing something new. Similarly, it is essential to recognize the momentous social change of the twentieth century when considering the importance of (multi)racial identity as both a private and a public issue, as well as its relationship to the formations of family, its relevance to issues of classification, and its connection to black-nationalist sentiment.

Ultimately, the history of the development and growing acceptance

of multiracialism reminds us that mixture is not remotely a new phenomenon, but that multiracial identity has evolved significantly over
the centuries and since the final decade of the twentieth century in particular. Peggy Pascoe's *What Comes Naturally: Miscegenation Law and
the Making of Race in America* and Renee Romano's *Race Mixing: Black-
White Marriage in Postwar America* suggest that the most momentous
shift in the latter half of the century was the change from thinking of
interracial families in terms of social health (and the need for public
regulation) to considering marriage and family as individual rights (and
private matters). Pascoe's and Romano's substantial histories articulate
the evolution not only of legal arguments and laws but also of public
opinion; as Romano explains, the idea that "interracial marriage was
a personal [issue] rather than a[n] issue for political debate . . . was the
most radical of the reactions to the southern defense of segregation."[66]
Considering the fact that anti-miscegenation laws were from their very
inception calculated to deny black people access to rights and power (through denying legitimacy, the rights that come with it, and the
wealth and power that might come with rights) and to ensure both the
purity and privilege of whiteness, it is perhaps most striking that the
growing recognition of multiracial identities is occurring at the same
time that the social acceptance of overt expressions of white supremacist sentiment is shrinking. I maintain that it is specifically this legal and
social evolution toward a more politically progressive society (in rhetoric if not much in fact) that has made the twenty-first century an unprecedented moment in which to express multiracial identity—which
is not to say that political progress resides necessarily in multiracialness
but rather in the fact that (non–white supremacist) multiracial identities are possible. As Paul Spickard observes, the "increasing acceptance
of intermarriage over the past three or four decades, together with the
rise of the multiracial movement," has meant that now "more than at
any other time in US history, most Americans seem comfortable with
the idea that people who are identified as members of different races
should know each other, mix socially, and perhaps marry when they
choose to do so. This is new in the current generations of adults. So, too,
there is a new openness on the part of a lot of people to consider the

constructed quality of racial identities and the contingent nature of racial affiliations."[67] Those claiming a multiracial identity are faced with a more receptive audience in the contemporary era than ever before— an American public more likely to both observe an individual's freedom to self-identify and respect unconventional racialization than in the past. The individualism associated with civil rights—which drastically reshaped the legal, political, and social landscape of the United States during the civil rights movement and other liberation movements of the sixties and seventies—has altered how subsequent generations respond to matters of self and identity. As Spickard points out, for instance, interracial relationships and racial mixture are far from new; what "is new in the last decades of the twentieth century and the first decades of the twenty-first" is not mixture itself but rather "that we are beginning to see those people as mixed." He goes on to state,

> We are also beginning to see racial mixing, mating, and marriage as normal, not aberrant—as part of the core experience of being Americans, not as something epiphenomenal. That is a huge change, but it is as much a change of consciousness as it is a change of demography or social behavior. This change of consciousness is built on the positive social value attached to interracial socializing that arose out of the Civil Rights movement. In that sense, it is a change of social etiquette. . . .
>
> . . . In addition, as the stigma that once attached to interracial mating has abated, more and more people who know they possess multiple ancestries have come to embrace that multiplicity. Many of them, probably most, still think of themselves, and are perceived by those around them, as monoracial people, White or Black or whatever. But they no longer so freely ignore their multiplicity. And a rapidly increasing number of people have come to identify themselves as racially multiple.[68]

Moreover, while multiracial identities were accepted historically, they usually fit into white supremacist racial hierarchies whereas they now seem, for the first time, to be considered (by many, though certainly not by all) apart from such hierarchies. Put another way, what sets contemporary multiracialism apart is that it is not being articulated within a white supremacist hierarchy (as in the past) but rather in a way that repudiates it. While I am not suggesting that multiracial identities are *causing* a decrease in white supremacy or other racist ideologies, I argue that multiracial identities are being expressed in unprecedented ways because of the increasing intolerance of overt racism and the steady increase in sensitivity to issues of race and equality. While American multiracialism is certainly still informed by centuries of racism and racialism, it has never before been claimed in a society that, in its public discourse at least, values racial equality so highly. In the contemporary moment, when black pride is expected and white supremacy is ostensibly reviled, multiracialism can be represented in ways that were impossible for earlier individuals and writers.

Literary Context: Representing Multiracialism Then and Now

In order to understand how new the representation of black–white multiracialism is in literature since the late 1990s, we must understand how multiracialism has been represented in the past. *Shades of Gray* argues that contemporary writers are building upon the rich history of African American depictions of multiracialism to reflect the changing realities of the twenty-first century.[69] Most important to this discussion is the fact that throughout African American literary history, black pride and black solidarity have been valued consistently. However, where this pride and solidarity translated into an embrace of black monoracial identity in the past, it now exists alongside multiracial identity.

While the one-drop rule, which forced all people with "one drop" of black "blood" into one group, did its intended work of oppressing a huge number of people, it also galvanized and solidified black identity in response to such oppression. Consequently, African American literary history exhibits a characteristic proliferation of black pride in the face of white supremacy. Interestingly, literature depicting mixture has tended to either affirm the one-drop rule by asserting blackness as the only viable racial identity for those who could otherwise claim whiteness or resist the one-drop rule by revealing its constructed and unrealistic nature. Both strategies work to challenge white supremacy and, while in opposition at times, are often employed simultaneously. That is, even if blackness is critiqued as an imposed racial identity, racial pride is essential to counter the racism that imposed it originally.

There is an abundance of excellent scholarship on multiracialism in slave narratives and the literature that followed, especially "passing novels" of the late nineteenth and early twentieth centuries, a fact that reminds us that multiracialism is an ever-present feature of American life and literature. Critiques of the color line were par for the course in slave narratives and novels, which worked not to assert multiracial identity but rather to undermine whites' faith in the color line as a barrier between white and black. This resulted in critiques of racial enslavement and, subsequently, of segregation and other forms of racialized oppression. Certainly, memoirs of formerly enslaved people often used multiracialness to demonstrate the illogic and malleability of racial identity under a system of racialized slavery. Similarly, the passing narratives that followed used multiracialness to expose the illogic of racial categories and the discriminatory laws they anchored.

Passing narratives of the nineteenth and early twentieth centuries also often adopted the "tragic mulatto/a" character (originated by white abolitionist Lydia Maria Child) but altered the figure from one envious of whiteness to one proud of blackness.[70] Earlier texts, like William Wells Brown's *Clotel; or, The President's Daughter* (1853), used passing as a way to critique racial slavery by identifying the horror of white enslavement to (largely white) readers. In texts like Brown's, the "tragedy" of racial mixture translates to the tragedy of the exploitation and abuse of white-looking women; however, the "tragedy" of the mulatto/a is also represented as a matter of racial betrayal. In fact, black solidarity becomes a matter of life and death in some texts, such as Frank J. Webb's *The Garies and Their Friends* (1857) and Charles W. Chesnutt's *The House behind the Cedars* (1900), in which characters who choose to pass for white rather than proudly inhabit black identities suffer intense racial loneliness and die of broken hearts. Though scholars are discussing the tragic mulatto/a figure in rather nuanced ways of late, what is apparent in the frequently used plot point of blackness-or-death for the mulatto/a is that racial ambiguity is intolerable.[71] Indeed, the black–white mixed character in such texts can be read as a metaphor for the refusal of American society to adequately address black–white mixture.

The fact that the tragic mulatto/a figure captured the American literary imagination explains in part why it is still referenced by so many twenty-first century writers; like a sore that will not heal, the tragic mulatto/a is replicated even today by some who cannot escape its shadow. However, the tragic mulatto/a also helped spur the literary convention of affirming the importance of black solidarity and black pride. Certainly, the racial ambiguity of mulatto families in nineteenth-century novels illustrates the irrationality of racial classification, thus questioning both the race binary and the racial foundation of slavery. But where the mulatto's whiteness might in one case demonstrate the absurdity of the race-based justification of slavery, the mulatto's blackness might in another case be used to claim the need for racial solidarity to combat continued racism. In Frances Harper's *Iola Leroy; or, Shadows Uplifted* (1892), for instance, characters choose to abandon the white privilege made available to them and opt instead to embrace black identities and contribute to black political struggle. Indeed, the point of Harper's novel appears to be that mulattoes must embrace their blackness and recognize the injustices of racism for the sake of all black people. Both James Weldon Johnson's influential *The Autobiography of an Ex-Colored Man* (1912) and Walter White's *Flight* (1926) convey the sentiment that passing for white will leave multiracial figures spiritually and emotionally bereft and reinforce the notion that only in affirming a proud black identity can multiracial figures find meaning, purpose, and satisfaction in their lives. Additionally, texts like White's epitomize a common trend in late nineteenth- and early twentieth-century multiracial literature: the assertion of the blackness of mixed characters in a narrative's subscription to the one-drop rule. Whether a mulatto/a character dies from the emotional and psychological effects of "pretending" to be white or can find belonging and purpose only amid a black population, these novels embrace the one-drop rule as a racial system by insisting upon the personal and public need for racial solidarity. That virtually all African American passing narratives affirm black solidarity, paired with the fact that such narratives were extremely popular, demonstrates how important this sentiment was in the twentieth century. Novels like Nella Larsen's *Passing* (1929) and White's *Flight* suggest that the black population will protect passers if only for reasons of racial solidarity and revenge on white America. Others consider passing a betrayal and suggest that black loyalty trumps the personal gain of passing. In Jessie Redmon Fauset's *Plum Bun: A Novel Without a Moral* (1929), for example, characters learn that the personal benefits of passing for white are greatly outweighed by the political and emotional benefits of black racial loyalty.

Such sentiments of black solidarity essentially dominated twentieth-century representations of mixture until multiracialism went out of vogue in the mid-century. By the middle of the twentieth century, passing plots and multiracial identity concerns were essentially entirely replaced with stories that probed the effects of racism on all kinds of black people and affirmed a new interest in black identity and history. With few exceptions, such as Fran Ross's *Oreo* (1974), multiracialism and passing plots were abandoned after the Harlem Renaissance. However, with the great social and political changes of the mid- to late twentieth century came a resurgence of multiracial literature. The new awareness and understanding of the effects of racial discrimination that arose in the late twentieth century initiated an increase in life writing about the horrors of the early and mid-century color line.[72] More important to this discussion is the fact that young writers—including the children of some of the first legally wed interracial couples in the United States—also began publishing essays, autobiographies, and fiction that depicted late twentieth-century multiracial experiences.[73] In the work of many of these authors, the echoes of the tragic mulatto/a and passing plot are evident and the interest in black pride and solidarity has only grown stronger, to the point that it is taken for granted as a chief concern of the protagonists. Many writers today use literary history as a reference point but not as a model. The contemporary authors whose work *Shades of Gray* analyzes, including Danzy Senna, Rebecca Walker, Emily Raboteau, Rachel Harper, and Heidi Durrow, depict a new generation of black–white multiracials—one in which black racial shame and betrayal of black community are unthinkable, racial equality and black empowerment are obviously necessary, multiracialism is no longer reduced to a choice between black and white, and multiracial identity is explored without the burden of de jure racial hierarchies and the responsibility of fighting them. While these narratives do not suggest that black–white multiracial subjects are in any way free of American history or its racisms, they do depict an era in which multiracialism is no longer automatically an abandonment of blackness in favor of white privilege. They represent an era in which interracial families can be formed out of love and intention (rather than exploitation or deception), and monoracialism is expected or required less (for the purposes of black political struggle, for instance). These are important differences between the literature since the 1990s and the literature written in the contexts of enslavement and de jure segregation. The fact that multiracialism went largely unrepresented between the Harlem Renaissance and the late nineties reveals that multiracialism was really not a topic of social concern in that half-century gap; that it is now "in vogue" suggests there is a fresh need (and opportunity) for conversations about and representations of contemporary multiracialism in both the literary and social spheres. *Shades of Gray* argues that the new social consciousness of the twenty-first century has made it possible for writers to revisit multiracialism and write new representations of multiracial identity. Specifically, this book seeks to demonstrate that contemporary authors are writing multiracial identities that allow black pride to coexist with mixed-white identities and are both black *and* white rather than "mulatto." In this way, contemporary writers are challenging in new ways the meanings of both "white" and "black" as categories and diverging from the literary history of "passing" and the "tragic mulatto/a."

Critical Context: Current Literary Scholarship

It is noteworthy that the few books of literary criticism on contemporary representations of black–white multiracialism all focus on blackness. While this focus is not problematic in and of itself, it can become problematic because of the ways it shapes not only *what* is being discussed but *how* it is being discussed.

Sika A. Dagbovie-Mullins's astute *Crossing B(l)ack: Mixed-Race Identity in Modern American Fiction and Culture* (2013) is chiefly interested in how blackness can coincide with multiracialism. She explains that her book details "the ways in which biracial subjects who negotiate racial borders claim multiple identities while remaining especially connected to blackness."[74] Dagbovie-Mullins's stated goal is to trace what she calls a "black-sentient mixed-race identity," which "intimates a mixed-race subjectivity that includes a particular awareness of the world, a perception rooted in blackness. It suggests a connection to a black consciousness that does not overdetermine one's racial identification but still plays a large role in it."[75] That is, Dagbovie-Mullins's focus on "black-sentient mixed-race identity" is primarily an effort to consider how mixedness can be a black-positive identity. (I share her interest in relating a "black consciousness" to multiracial identity, though I focus on the intersection of racial identity and political orientation and argue that people can claim mixed *racial* identities and black *political* identities simultaneously.) Dagbovie-Mullins is concerned with how multiracialism and blackness are positioned as dichotomous categories in popular culture, and her goal is to mitigate the prevailing language of separation in popular multiracial discourse in order to better conceptualize a black–mixed racial identity.

In *The Souls of Mixed Folk: Race, Politics, and Aesthetics in the New Millennium* (2011), Michele Elam also concentrates her criticism on the relationship between multiracialism and blackness through what she identifies as a "black mix focus"; as she says, *The Souls of Mixed Folk* consists of "critical mediations on black mixes."[76] She employs the "post-soul" aesthetic of Bertram Ashe and Trey Ellis and explains how the cultural texts she examines do not "replace blackness" with "biracialism and biculturalism" but instead "prompt a deeper investigation and expansion of it."[77] She borrows Ashe's term "blaxploration" to articulate her own approach: to explore how new writers and artists are "engender[ing] a generous blackness that reconciles pre–civil rights and post-soul conditions" through hybridity.[78] Elam argues that this "blaxploration honors a hybridity that is 'in service to' and 'on behalf of' black needs and ends," and that her work examines how contemporary cultural production "suggests ways that mixed race studies, aesthetics, and politics can be understood [as] allied alongside this sense of mulattoesque blackness."[79] Overall, Elam's primary concerns are with refuting the twentieth-century view of multiracialism as pathological and the late twentieth-century celebration of multiracialism as a new and progressive solution to America's race problems. Elam's work addresses the stereotypes of multiracials as "outcasts" and "trailblazers" and uses contemporary cultural production to find a middle ground. *Shades of Gray* instead focuses on how literary representations depict the functionality of multiracial identity and how multiracialism is actually affecting the beliefs about and practices of the race categories of black and white. Additionally, Elam is hostile toward multiracialism and considers it potentially dangerous. She is rightly concerned, for instance, that multiracialism is viewed as an end to or the transcendence of race itself; however, her opposition to this sentiment tends to shape her discourse into one suspicious of multiracialism (in public discourse, at least) and protective of blackness (in the face of misguided multiracial activism).[80]

Like Dagbovie-Mullins and Elam, Ralina Joseph focuses entirely on multiracialism's relationship to blackness in *Transcending Blackness: From the New Millennium Mulatta to the Exceptional Multiracial* (2013). Joseph draws a distinction between the labels of "mixed race," which she considers a racist betrayal of blackness, and "mixed race African American," which she considers a multiracial adaptation of blackness; black–white multiracialism is thus framed exclusively within the context of how it affects blackness. Joseph reads contemporary representations of multiraciality as anti-black and, consequently, uninterested in social justice. Joseph mistrusts multiracialism, viewing it as an escape from or abandonment of blackness for the privilege and power of whiteness (much like how "passing" was viewed in the early twentieth century). She argues that "contemporary black–white representations do not go beyond . . . the umbrella metaphor of black transcendence" and that "ultimately, mixed-race African American representations—and by extension the

subjectivities of multiracial African American individuals—continue
to be delimited by the racist notion that blackness is a deficit that black
and multiracial people must overcome."[81] Joseph's primary argument is
that contemporary literature depicts two types—the "tragic mulatta" or
the "exceptional multiracial"—and thus that representations either perpetuate the tragedy historically associated with black–white mixture in
the former or propose "transcending" or abandoning blackness in order to "succeed" in the latter. That is, she proposes that blackness is either distained as something sorrowful or desired only for its ability to
be overcome. She states that "blackness is not seen as a positive part of
a multiracial identity" in contemporary representations of black–white
multiracialism and that multiracial identity is actually an enactment of
white supremacy.[82] She argues, for instance, that "because [of] the popular conception that race means black, the end of race must mean the
end of blackness. Whiteness, imagined as pure, invisible, and promise-
laden, remains prized as the savior for multiracial African American
figures from blackness, presented as sullied, hypervisible, and tragedy
filled."[83] Ultimately, Joseph views anything but black monoracial identity as a desire for whiteness and betrayal of blackness. In contrast, I argue that blackness is a desired and important part of multiracial identity
for reasons of black pride and black political solidarity, and that blackness is a source of pleasure and positivity for multiracial subjects. Reading multiracialism as inherently anti-black or "assimilationist" not only
makes multiracial identity unacceptable politically and psychologically but also accepts the continued practice of monoracialism without
question. The potential result of such an approach is an academic and
practical stalemate because it proscribes intellectual exploration of multiracialism and strips multiracial subjects of their agency to explore their
identities beyond what is ascribed to them according to any particular
schema or ideology. Rather than revitalizing the past pathologization
of multiracialism or accepting the continued dominance of monoracialism, a productive approach would be to challenge the thinking behind or concepts resulting from both traditional monoracialism and
traditional multiracialism, to force us to think about race in potentially transformative ways.

Ultimately, while Dagbovie-Mullins, Elam, and Joseph take different approaches to the subject of contemporary black–white multiracialism (and its representation in contemporary cultural production),
all three focus on multiracialism as it affects blackness. While this is
an important issue to address, considering multiracialism exclusively
as a version of blackness automatically limits how we can discuss race
concepts or assess multiracial identity. Indeed, critics like Elam and
Joseph, who view multiracialism with suspicion, do so largely because
of a focus on blackness in isolation (from other races) and a defense
of blackness from the erasure that they see multiracialism enacting
on blackness. In other words, if multiracialism is considered only in
terms of not being monoracially black, then the discourse surrounding multiracialism will necessarily be narrow.

Like the books by these three authors, *Shades of Gray* also examines
the relationship between multiracialism and blackness. However, I focus on how multiracialism affects the conceptualization of blackness
as a race *category* rather than on how multiracialism can be a modification of a monoracially black identity. While I agree with Elam's assessment that "blackness [has] a distinct, powerful, and troubled status
within the study of mixed race" and "continues to have one, intrac-
tably, within broader U.S. racial politics," I use chapter 3 of *Shades of
Gray* to consider multiracial identity not as an *adaptation* of blackness
but as an identity that inherently troubles our beliefs about blackness
as a race.[84] But perhaps most significant here is that while Dagbovie-
Mullins, Elam, and Joseph take different approaches to black–white
multiracialism, they all overlook the fact that multiracialism affects
both blackness *and* whiteness. This is not to say that it is not important to consider how multiracial identity affects black pride and
solidarity—indeed, this is a major concern of chapter 3. But to consider blackness to the exclusion of whiteness means that we miss the
opportunity to examine whiteness at best and risk repeating old habits of treating race as nonwhite at worst. Seeing black–white multiracialism exclusively as a modification of black identity both ignores the
equally significant race category of whiteness and frames the discussion in ways that limit the perception of multiracialism's critique of

race concepts. In order to really discuss black–white multiracialism as a whole, it is necessary that we examine whiteness as a category and, in doing so, avoid traditional patterns of talking about race as a non-white concept or about multiracialism only as a modification of blackness. It is absolutely essential that we address whiteness and blackness in equal measure; by doing so, we can see multiracial identity as a potentially disruptive conceptualization to *both* categories and can avoid seeing it simply as an attack on black identity. In fact, by refusing Joseph's willingness to read race as blackness, we can perform the vital work of changing historical habits of viewing race as nonwhiteness and move toward the necessary act of racializing and changing the category of whiteness. As chapter 2 of *Shades of Gray* demonstrates, multiracialism must affect whiteness in order for it to affect race. It is only by doing this work—by using black–white multiracial literature to re-examine both blackness *and* whiteness—that multiracial literature can affect change to (beliefs about and practices of) race. Overall, *Shades of Gray* offers a comprehensive discussion of the blackness and whiteness that contribute to black–white multiracialism and how multiracial identities are shifting discussions of hierarchical identity formations onto more thoughtful and equitable ground.

Writing the New American Multiracialism

Literary scholar Paula Moya explains that because writers both represent and interpret the world around them, their "literature can provide us with an important source of knowledge about the pervasive cultural ideas (or ideologies) through which individuals apprehend their world(s)."[85] Thus while a lot of important work on multiracialism is being done by philosophers, sociologists, psychologists, historians, legal scholars, cultural studies scholars, and many others, literary criticism offers its own rewards when it comes to sociocultural criticism. As a work of literary criticism that engages with an interdisciplinary field (critical mixed race studies), a primary goal of *Shades of Gray* is to pay close and detailed attention to the texts themselves so that we can best see how they perform their work. The ultimate goal of *Shades of Gray* is to demonstrate what contemporary writers are doing and how they are doing it—in other words, how contemporary literature is contributing, as a body of work, to multiracial discourse. Consequently, each chapter engages with the scholarship of the field to help contextualize and ground its literary criticism in the "world" of the literature itself before devoting considerable attention to particular texts.

As Moya argues, "a good work of literature can . . . help readers understand" how identities "actually *matter*" in terms of their processes of formation and importance in lived experience.[86] Therefore, I have chosen particular texts to examine in depth and across chapters—namely, Danzy Senna's *Caucasia* (1998), Rebecca Walker's *Black White and Jewish: Autobiography of a Shifting Self* (2001), Emily Raboteau's *The Professor's Daughter* (2005), Rachel Harper's *Brass Ankle Blues* (2006), and Heidi Durrow's *The Girl Who Fell from the Sky* (2010). These first-person depictions of late twentieth-century coming-of-age experiences of identity formation address contemporary black–white multiracialism in sophisticated and complex ways and offer, I believe, the best representation of the "good work[s] of literature" produced recently. The concerns they hold in common have helped shape my thinking and the structure of this book; that is to say, I have allowed contemporary literature to show me what it is doing with multiracialism (rather than tried to find texts to support preconceived notions of multiracialism). I examine the texts by Senna, Walker, Raboteau, and Harper across numerous chapters to consider as fully as possible how each takes up and offers us ways of thinking about the myriad aspects of contemporary multiracial experiences and identities. It is by thinking through how multiple texts address the same issue and how the same text addresses multiple issues (rather than thinking about texts and/or issues in isolation) that we can best grasp the broader project of multiracial literature. These four texts in particular stand out as doing a great deal of work with contemporary black–white multiracialism in sophisticated ways. They offer an appropriate selection of texts to demonstrate what I think are trends moving multiracial discourse and representation forward. Durrow's text, which I focus on in chapter 4, is discussed alone because her text does a kind of work in multiracial discourse and offers a kind of depiction of multiracialism that are both, I think, unique at the moment. While the works of Senna, Walker, Raboteau, and Harper offer nuanced and productive explorations of multiracial identities and experiences, Durrow's offers an interesting departure from other texts in that she prioritizes multiethnic identity over multiracial identity and thus explores both in helpful ways. Through these five texts, I hope to establish that contemporary writers, as a group and as individuals, are changing social understandings and literary depictions of multiracialism and helping to shape twenty-first-century discourse about and representations of multiracial identity.

Chapter 1 focuses on perhaps the most central of questions: How readily does American society accommodate multiracial identities or changes to traditional race concepts? The chapter begins by assessing the vital arguments and problems—both popular and scholarly—of multiracial discourse. As part of this discussion, I critique current multiracial theoretical scholarship and multiracial advocacy, as well as expose the strengths and weaknesses of contemporary multiracial discourse. Subsequently, I analyze how writers respond to public and academic discourses in their representations of multiracialism and examine the extent to which public perception plays a role in racial identity formation within the texts. Here I adapt the pervasive academic discussion of how racial identity is formulated through social context and the views of others to an analysis of literary narratives. In the works of Harper, Raboteau, Senna, and Walker, black–white multiracial figures often do not have a definitive concept of their own racial identities to assert and they struggle to decide how to self-identify (or whether to self-identify) within a society so burdened with American race history. These characters are also often (mis)recognized racially and must decide to what degree they will accept or challenge how others see them. This scenario of (mis)recognition reveals in the observer a desire to categorize yet an inability to see or categorize mixedness. In this sense, the scenario also reflects the legacy of dichotomous race labels in general. Additionally, multiracial characters are faced with the burden of identifying verbally or allowing themselves to be seen in certain ways. The second of these options—to submit to the gaze of others—leads to the external assertion of a racial identity over the character and raises issues about the claim and/or performance of mixedness, whiteness, blackness, and even other identities to which they are linked through assumptions based on appearance or culture rather than ancestry. In allowing their identities to be guided by assumptions about group membership, multiracial subjects reveal a desire to belong to a socially accepted category (rather than to claim one and explain themselves) or at least a discomfort with the lack of a label that others will understand. This chapter examines how public opinion about racial classification and the public perception of mixture affects multiracial individuals as they come of age in the contemporary United States. This chapter's discussion explores how multiracial figures have unprecedented freedom to self-identify but have to do so within a particular social context that is slow to change yet changes continuously. Ultimately, while those of mixed race can assert racial identity in contrast to or to coincide with public perceptions of race, this chapter asserts that racial identity is usually an ongoing negotiation.

Building on this discussion of the difficulties surrounding concepts of mixture and racial classification in American society, chapters 2 and 3 explore the complexities of black–white multiracial negotiations of the traditionally monoracial categories of whiteness and blackness. Chapter 2 takes up the theoretical framework of critical white studies in order to address how whiteness has been conceived of racially (as pure, monolithic, unracialized, invisible, and defined against nonwhite otherness) and how contemporary literature is attempting to racialize and diversify whiteness to enable it to mix with blackness. The chapter also explores how the performance of whiteness—by both racially white and racially mixed characters—helps call attention to the "construction" of whiteness as a racialized identity. This discussion of whiteness also addresses how ethnic Jewishness and Hispanicness diversify and racialize whiteness and thus complicate the black–white binary. Chapter 2 argues that by making whiteness racialized and heterogeneous, contemporary writers are making whiteness capable of being incorporated into a multiracial identity. Here I focus on Walker and Senna exclusively because they offer texts so ripe with possibilities. Walker divides her time as a child and adolescent between her father's Jewish community, Latinx friends in the Bronx, and her mother's black community in San Francisco; her assessment of her racial identity is largely invested in politics and class. For Senna's protagonist, who is forced to "pass" for both black and white/Jewish at different times in her life, racial identity is as much a question of culture and community as it is a question of appearance. In neither text is whiteness a simple identity to inhabit; rather, it produces conflicted emotions and provokes behavior that undermines the power and so-called purity of the racial category.

Chapter 3 addresses the relationship between multiracialness and blackness and examines the ongoing scholarly discourse surrounding identity politics in order to explore the complicated choice between a monoracially black identity and a multiracial identity that includes blackness. Given the historical practice of hypodescent, blackness has always absorbed whiteness, and monoracial black identity has developed essential black pride and solidarity. Consequently, mixed figures must articulate an antiracist identity if they are to assert a specifically black *and* white identity, but asserting such an identity remains difficult because of the lingering use and spirit of the one-drop rule. Since most of the texts depict characters with not-black-enough appearances, they complicate the ability to claim blackness successfully in traditional ways. The texts negotiate this problem of claiming identity by circumventing tradition and exploring new ways of understanding and embodying blackness. My discussion analyzes how, in Harper, Raboteau, Walker, and Senna, blackness is always sought but frequently elusive because of the complexity of American racial and identity politics—especially with regard to black solidarity. The characters invest black identity with phenotype, culture, politics, and justice; in each case they desire blackness but what they want blackness to be varies. This chapter argues that monoracially black and multiracially black identities are not straightforward or easy for many mixed figures and that, in many ways, claiming blackness is as difficult as claiming whiteness for multiracials in twenty-first-century America.

Chapter 4 diverges from the preceding chapters to examine Durrow's representation of a protagonist who asserts her multiracialism not through her racial identity but rather through her ethnic identity. Within the critical framework of discourses of identity formation and ethnic identity, this chapter examines how notions of inheritance and family affect the embodiment of ethnoracial identity and explores how Durrow's novel works to question whether race (in the phenotypical sense) and ethnicity (in the cultural sense) must mirror one another or might sometimes be considered independently. When the protagonist opts to accept a monoracial (black) identity but insists upon being recognized as multiethnic (Danish and African American), she poses a challenge not to the race practices of the United States (like contemporary multiracial literature often does) but rather to the ethnoracial category of African Americanness itself and the traditional view that race and ethnicity are synonymous. In this sense, Durrow's novel adds to what other writers like Senna, Walker, Raboteau, and Harper are doing and complicates further the (multi)racial discourse of the new millennium by broadening the use of multiracialism to examine, independently of one another, factors that contribute to notions of identity and classification.

These chapters illustrate that contemporary multiracial literature is beginning to define not only what race *is not* (clearly dichotomous categories), as earlier literature did, but also what it *can be*. If a significant characteristic of multiracial literature in the past was the fight against being defined, contemporary texts might instead be characterized as doing the defining. The greatest shift is with regard to who is in control of the process of definition; earlier literature emphasized the ironies and damage of social and legal views regarding race and classification, whereas more recent texts explore the relationship between social and individual classification. If the choice used to be between accepting or defying legal or social racial classification, it is now more about how one might define one's own identity while negotiating social attitudes about race. Certainly, many multiracial people born after civil rights continue the practice of identifying as monoracially black, but for those who choose to explore multiracial identities this option has never before been so possible. A consequence of change in American society is the simultaneous change in American cultural production. African American authors (who identify as mixed and/or monoracially black) are using literature to explore what the new era of multiracialism might offer and writing new representations of multiracialism into the American literary landscape.

| Chapter One

"What Are You, Anyway?"
The Social Context of Racial Identity

In her autobiography, *Black White and Jewish*, Rebecca Walker proclaims, "I am not tragic," and thereby signals her refusal to adhere to the "tragic mulatta/o" script that has haunted narratives of black–white mixed race since its nineteenth-century conception.[1] This sentiment is not unusual in either literary or social circles: writers are asserting a new literary tradition that refuses to adhere to conventions that make race mixing both personally and socially damaging; at the same time, the multiracial movement continues to push for legal, social, and political recognition of multiracialness as something valid. Much as civil rights, black power, and over a century's worth of African American writers before these movements worked to transform the taint of blackness into pride, the multiracial movement and contemporary writers work to shift the perception of mixedness from destructive marginality to affirmed validity. As Elizabeth Atkins Bowman declares, "We are demanding recognition and respect. . . . We are replacing 'tragic' with 'triumphant,' and bringing this mulatto taboo out of the closet."[2]

Contemporary writers, including Walker and Bowman, are addressing the issues that surface in multiracial discourse and engaging with the broader American social context in which they are writing. Ultimately, these texts are engaging with and contributing to a changing social atmosphere in which multiracial identity is being conceived in new ways. However, the "recognition" that Bowman proclaims is complicated by a number of political, social, and historical factors as well as contentious academic and activist multiracial discourses. Contemporary representations of multiracial subjectivity reflect the particularities of historical American racial practices and engage with the recent and current changes to such practices. In order to understand what contemporary narratives of multiracialism are doing in the broader national conversation about race and identity, it is essential to grapple with the new opportunities and inherent limitations of current discourse.

Personal Choice, Public Good: The Politics of Multiracial Identity

While they may have things in common, post–civil rights black pride and late-century multiracial affirmation display a critical difference in the relationship each has to racial classification. Specifically, black pride and black nationalism employed traditional racial categorization for political unity, whereas the multiracial movement challenges the same racial categories in and of themselves. In the nineteenth and twentieth centuries hypodescent made mobilizing black peoples a relatively straightforward task because social and legal blackness was inherited and ascribed so readily. Although discussions about black pride and black nationalism certainly included debate about authenticity, the one-drop rule meant that there was little question of whether one was white or black, since blackness could and did include mixed ancestry and all shades of color. The efforts of multiracial organizations, however, are significantly different, and the basis of group unity is considerably less clear. Whereas black nationalism worked for political gains within the existing racial classification system (that is, mobilized all officially "black" peoples), multiracial activists work toward changing the system itself for a group that has none of the historical, racial, or cultural similarities that brought black people together in racial pride and political solidarity. Though some activists argue for multiracialness as its own category and cultural group (based on shared experiences of mixture as the common ground that brings people of various racial and ethnic backgrounds together as a group), it is nonetheless a category that has few of the unifying factors of black pride, such as African American history and hypodescent.

Given that racial identity has always been linked to both phenotype and a history of shared experiences as a race, multiracialness poses a problem as a racial identity because it possesses neither. Or, at least, multiracialness does not exhibit shared phenotype or history as obviously as do existing racial groups (some argue that ambiguous racial appearance and common experiences among multiracials and their families are ingredients for group formation). Without a discernible group, multiracials are faced with the challenge of forming a convincing group or claiming racial identity as individuals. In *Bulletproof Diva*, Lisa Jones queries the tendency among certain multiracial activist groups to consider multiracials a "community" in and of themselves. Jones argues that assuming commonality among multiracial people risks reaffirming monoraces as isolated and singular (or not already diverse), and she objects to the suggestion that having multiple backgrounds creates a new culture of plurality: "Shouldn't we ask what makes biracial people a community? What holds us together other than a perceived sense of our own difference from the ethnic mainstream? Consider if the Mexican-Samoan kid in San Diego has the same needs as the black-Jewish kid from New York's Upper West Side? Maybe politically as people of color, but do they share a definitive mixed-race culture? And if they do, should we call it 'biraciality' or should we call it 'American culture?'"[3] Unlike many activists who consider multiracial identity and the shared experiences and concerns of multiracials a foundation for community, Jones resists the notion of multiracial community because she thinks multiracialness is not distinct from the political community of "people of color" or the heterogeneous culture of the nation.

Some multiracial advocates assume that multiracials share identity and community more often among themselves than with monoracial groups. In fact, the stance of such advocates is that a sense of belonging to one or more of one's monoracial heritages is somehow undesirable or even wrong—that one's multiracialness is what ought to be embraced;

that it is unique and no longer the sum of its parts but an entirely new identity. But while multiracials might find they have shared experiences and can identify with one another on the basis of mixture (regardless of what kind of mixture), multiracials might just as likely (or more likely) find they share experiences and culture with those who identify monoracially. Some advocacy groups view the shared experiences of multiracialness as community and identity forming and disregard the fact that, generally, children are socialized by monoracial parents with clear links to monoracial groups. Thus, claims of multiracial community can overlook the connection multiracial children often have to the racial/cultural/ethnic heritages of their monoracial parents and ignore the multiracial person's link to those specific heritages in favor of a generic "multiracial" heritage. The desire for a multiracial label and/or the desire to form a group identity tends to erase the (mono) racial cultures and histories from which multiracialness originates.

Ultimately, the notion that multiracialness produces a group identity is continually debated; while some argue that "multiracial" is a specific identity, many multiracials identify with their specific backgrounds and not simply with the *fact* of their mixedness.[4] These multiracials argue that it is not hybridity or mixedness that is recognized per se but rather the racial/ethnic groups with which people identify, no matter the number. Multiracialism is technically recognized by the American government whenever someone chooses more than one race on the census, but since multiracialism is recognized as a diverse combination of races rather than as its own race, and since multiracialness is seen as a personal choice (that is, whereas blackness is ascribed, multiracialness is chosen as a category), multiracialism is a much less stable political umbrella than blackness. The difference, then, is that the civil rights movement made claims for all who were considered black, whereas it is unclear whether the strategies of multiracialism activists can produce such an easily identifiable group, if they can identify a group in the first place.[5] Proclaiming multiracialness is thus complicated by the fact that heterogeneity within multiracialness is much more difficult, if not impossible, to turn into a homogeneous identity the way blackness can be/has been, since variation is the point

of multiracialness. Consequently, multiracialism is much more difficult to classify than monoracialism, and multiplicity can be articulated and understood in any number of ways—including monoracially.

The alternative to proclaiming a multiracial group identity is to proclaim an individual identity. This can range from simply selecting more
than one box on the census to naming combinations as racial identities (such as Tiger Woods's "Cablinasian").[6] Essentially, classification
is a matter of what one has to choose from: either one from a list (that
may include "multiracial") or one or more from a list (which recognizes multiraciality as *more than one* race rather than as *a* race). The former option offers the apparent safety of recognizable groups but limits
people to one group only; the latter offers specific belonging to multiple groups without a single label (or, as in the case of Woods's "Cablinasian," a label for only one person and thus a label unrecognizable in
social practice). Many scholars identify the danger of the individualism
inherent to multiracial identity, usually citing the threat posed to the
sociopolitical strength and/or protection of nonwhite groups if multiracials were to abandon monoracial groups.[7] Frequently, this objection
to a multiracial category assumes that multiracials will flee nonwhite
groups for whiteness and conflates multiracialness with whiteness.[8]

While john a. powell seems to make such an assumption, he also
usefully points out the political and moral responsibility involved in
identity. According to powell, while the argument that we should be
allowed to identify ourselves appeals to "our ideology of individualism," it is dangerous because "we all may be individuals, but none of
us are just individuals" who can identify in isolation.[9] Eileen Walsh
agrees that a too-narrow focus on the individual can end up doing
more harm than good. She explains that while monumental legal
battles related to interracial marriage and transracial adoption relied
on an individual's right to choose a spouse or to be raised in a loving
home, such a focus on individual rights "cannot achieve the systemic
elimination of racial hierarchies."[10] Walsh argues that apparent equality within multiracial families at the level of individuals often leads to
overly optimistic views that social equality across gender, class, and
race at the level of groups is growing simultaneously.[11] She also argues

that "unless the Multiracial Movement shifts its attention away from asserting the rights of individuals, . . . its enduring legacy will be to sustain existing hierarchies, albeit along a color continuum instead of through a fictional race dichotomy."[12] Similarly, Heather Dalmage claims that "white supremacist society will not be challenged by moving the discourse to the level of the individual."[13] Instead, she argues, "We must acknowledge historical contexts, systemic or institutional injustices, and interlocking discourses that perpetuate injustice" by maintaining engagement with historically oppressed racial groups.[14] Walsh's and Dalmage's comments identify a very real threat, since the shift toward individual rights and away from the protection of historically oppressed groups provides a springboard for conservative efforts to abolish affirmative action (as discrimination against individuals) and even racial data collection (as a violation of individuals' privacy).

However, although arguments about the need to recognize the growing practice of identifying with multiple races on the one hand and to observe continued white supremacy and historical oppression against groups on the other tend to be polarizing, they need not be. Multiracial identity is certainly not, as numerous scholars argue, always aligned with whiteness against blackness, and one can articulate a multiracial identity while maintaining black political solidarity. It is also important to remember that while group identities are critical for maintaining existing race concepts and thus existing civil rights protections, individualized identities have the potential to disrupt the racial ideology that upholds the troubling system of categorization that was built upon and continues to feed racism. Consider, for instance, that while the binary homogenizes black and white experiences, so too does multiraciality as a race/category (that is, as a group identity it homogenizes multiracial experiences). Consequently, individualized multiracial identities pose the greatest challenge to homogenizing, monolithic race concepts. Binary/monoracial and multiracial categories are constructed using the same method; in this sense, multiracialism as a group identity offers less of a challenge to "race" than some propose. While individual racial identities are just as constructed, if a challenge is being mounted against how race has been and is still used in American society—especially with regard to dichotomous race concepts and the notions of purity and exclusion that accompany monoracialism—then individualizing (multi)racial identities in ways that resist the conventions of group identity may offer a way to question race practice. It is not just multiraciality itself but also how heterogeneous experiences and, often, unique identities are expressed that contributes to political resistance. So, while group identities are necessary to combat white supremacy (and thus remain essential tools in American culture), individual identities are necessary to challenge race as a method of classification and, more specifically, to begin to change how Americans see and treat people. Ultimately, this means that individual racial identities threaten group identities by challenging the basis of group categorization through race. But the fact that no rational argument can propose that the United States is remotely near ceasing the practice of racialist thinking means that multiraciality can be seen as a contributor to the discourse on race and racism in the United States instead of a threat to racial political struggle. While group and individual identity formations seem like two separate projects in this sense, it is possible to pose a challenge to conventional racial thinking while maintaining civil rights; this seems to be the goal of most scholars—even, or especially, those who argue for one identity option against the other. It is ultimately a question of *how*, not *whether*, individual and group multiracial identities are theorized and practiced.

What We Mean When We Talk about Race:
The Problems of Language in Multiracial Discourse

The discourse surrounding what multiracialism is and what it does to the practice of race in the United States offers a productive and helpful way to work through the consequences of group and individual identity and enter into a discussion of how contemporary writers are taking up (multi)racial identity. In order to understand how identity might be formed, defined, or employed, we must understand what such identity is believed to be and do, as well as how it is theorized and debated. Multiracialness is, in the most straightforward sense (and as the vast majority of current discourse assumes), when a person claims more

than one ethnoracial heritage, most often through parents of different groups. Multiracialness is also an acknowledgment of belonging
to more than one monoracial group (just as any monoracial identity is
a social acknowledgment of belonging to a single monoracial group)
regardless of how one identifies. The opportunity to identify as multiracial arises out of a political history that has brought about an abandonment of enforced hypodescent for the purposes of racial oppression.
However, multiracialism must still engage with that history and the
continued struggle for racial equality or risk reaffirming the racial ideology it purports to challenge. As often as multiracialism is argued to
be breaking down racial hierarchies, challenging race categories, and
combating discrimination, it is also accused of doing the opposite.

The most apparent obstacle slowing multiracial discourse is the
vague language that the conversation employs. Any thorough discussion of race must critique how race itself is used as a concept and term.
A vigilant critical approach is essential because while advocates, politicians, and academics alike seem to agree that race is a social rather
than scientific system, biology tends to creep back into the discussion
(and has even been reinvigorated by the popularity of genetic ancestry testing).[15] The incorporation of biological language is often the
result of carelessness and a lack of critical thought rather than any genuine proposal that race is biological—or strictly biological, at least.[16]

Many commentators argue that race is not "real" in a biological
sense, while others argue that race is not "real" because it is socially
constructed. Still others point out that biology is irrelevant to lived
experiences of race and that social race difference needs to be recognized in the interests of social justice and/or historical and cultural
usage.[17] The problem is that critics do not address the essential debate
about what "race" means and proceed to discuss race without clarify-
ing how they understand the concept. As Joshua Glasgow explains in
"On the Methodology of the Race Debate: Conceptual Analysis and
Racial Discourse," "The ontology of race . . . is often driven by the
semantics of race, as the race debate frequently takes this tack: if racial terms purport to refer to natural—specifically, biological—kinds,
then race is not real (since there appear to be no biological races); but

if racial terms purport to refer to social kinds, then race might be real (on the premise that social kinds can count as real). Thus the race debate hinges on what racial terms purport to refer to."[18] The problem then arises: Does a given commentator think of race as a social or biological kind? Does race exist or not exist if considered biological? Does race exist or not exist if considered social? The distinction is usually not evident, and the ensuing lack of clarity leads to untidy arguments that seem to suggest that if racial classification is not based on biology our discussion of "race" (as a generic term) is unnecessary and we ought not to consider race at all. Because some commentators are not clear about what they mean by "race," they quite frequently appeal in one instance to biological kinds and in another instance to social kinds without observing that their use of "race" is inconsistent. Ultimately, this means that a significant portion of discourse on racial classification is unclear and thus not especially helpful. And because debates about multiracialism rely on such discourse, the central questions of multiracial discourse—whether, how, and why multiracialism might be recognized—are weighed down to a great degree.

Perhaps the most essential question of multiracial discourse is what "multiracial" is thought to reference. At its most basic level, multiracialness renders blackness and whiteness, as well as other racial categories, "impure" in that any race can be claimed in any quantity or manner; that is, multiple races can be claimed simultaneously, so a person can be black *and* white, where before, blackness and whiteness were mutually exclusive in legal and social terms. However, it is dangerous to consider multiracialness as a new reality as opposed to a new way of thinking about race. Certainly, "race mixing" has always existed and races have never been "pure." After all, racial categories were developed in an effort to classify and group individuals for particular objectives. While beliefs about what a race consists of may be changing, the fact of diversity or mixture within racial categories is unchanged. However, defining that diversity usually leads to trouble; because the category of blackness has historically included any and all racial backgrounds mixed with blackness, many critics propose that multiracialness is unnecessary or redundant as it is an identity that includes blackness. However, these critics make the mistake of ignoring the difference between identifying as monoracially black, which collapses multiple racial backgrounds into one racial category, and identifying as multiracially black, which explicitly acknowledges blackness as well as other racial heritages.

The problem of conflating multiracialism and blackness is also related to recognizing the social meaning of these (social) race categories. That is, critics frequently argue about the *genetic* diversity of the *social* category of blackness. By far the most prolific and frequently cited academic who takes up the problem of biology in discussions of race is Rainier Spencer, and it is worth tracing how his arguments trip up discussions of multiracial identification. In "New Racial Identities, Old Arguments," Spencer observes that the so-called "bi-racial baby boom" of recent decades has produced people no different from the "average Afro-American child (who possesses a significant African, European, and Native American admixture in his or her ancestry)."[19] He therefore sets out to counter "the notion of post-1967 black/white multiracial persons as being distinct from Afro-Americans."[20] Spencer is concerned that multiracial activists risk reinscribing conventional notions of race—especially blackness—as something pure and consequently, to Spencer at least, as something biological.[21] In fact, Spencer is convinced that the multiracial movement is misguided: "Afro-Americans, the most genetically diverse people in the United States, are effectively placed together in a single biological black box in order to provide half the ingredients for creating multiracial children—children who are in fact no more the result of population mixture than they themselves are. Far from dismantling the race concept, it is cemented all the more firmly in place through multiracial ideology and the relentlessly uncritical coverage granted by the popular media."[22] The primary problem with Spencer's analysis is that he makes the mistake of using biological concepts of race while trying to debunk what he views as biological arguments made in support of multiracialism. Recognizing the "purity" of black and white need not rely on biology. The social practice of making everyone fit into monoracial categories has a connection to biology, like everything racial in the United States. But biology was simply invoked during a particular time period to prop up the social practice of race, and it is a matter of social purity when everyone is relegated to one race and not permitted to identify as multiracial. The fact that mixture has been socially acknowledged in the past (with the "mulatto" class, for instance) and then was no longer observed (replaced with a black–white binary) demonstrates the social rather than entirely biological construction of race and racial purity. Socially, one had to be either white or black; as blackness was assigned to those who had black relatives, people with black-identified ancestors had black identities. Now, since blackness is not necessarily ascribed through black relatives or claimed monoracially, one's racial identity can be different from one's parents' because the social system of racial identification has changed. Indeed, the scenario of a child of a black parent (or even black parents) identifying as multiracial exemplifies racial identity as a social system, as does the monoracially identifying child of one white and one black parent.

Spencer himself makes race biological by claiming that multiracial people are, in fact, no more genetically diverse than their black parents and relies on notions of biological mixture to dismiss multiracialness as a social identity. Similarly, in *Challenging Multiracial Identity* Spencer argues, "The idea of multiracial identity depends absolutely on biological race. There cannot even be a conception of multiracial identity absent the clear and unequivocal acceptance of biological race. After all, we are talking about the biological offspring of (allegedly) differently raced parents."[23] He explains further, "They need nothing else but to be known as the biological children of their socially defined parents in order for the multiracial label to be affixed. Here we see a major inconsistency of multiracial advocacy—what is for the lack of a better term a bait-and-switch—for the racial criterion is thereby switched invalidly from social designation to biology in the cases of supposed first-generation children."[24] Again, multigenerational multiracial identity undoes his argument (in the case of a child of two black-identified parents who claims multiraciality because of a nonblack ancestor, or a child of two white-identified parents who claims multiraciality because of a nonwhite ancestor). Furthermore, Spencer never makes clear how the child's race is any less social than the parents'. In the case of a child of at least one black parent, the child could choose to be monoracially black (or white) but could also choose a multiracial identity. That multiracial identity was not available as a choice for (or at least was not chosen by) someone's parents does not make multiracial identity biological for a new generation, as Spencer seems to argue. Spencer sees black identity as socially derived but for some reason does not see multiracial identity similarly.

However, though Spencer gets caught in the trap of biological concepts of race at times, his concern that biological race is being used as grounds for multiracialness is well founded. Many commentators of various disciplinary (and racial) backgrounds voice concern over the risk of reifying biological race concepts in an effort to distinguish difference for current generations. Susan Graham, the founder and executive director of Project RACE, is one of the most high-profile targets of this criticism, in part because her position allowed her a voice in Congressional hearings on census reform. Graham campaigns for a "multiracial" category to be added to the census and argues that her children are "half" black even though she relies on the unlikely assumption that her husband's blackness is "pure."[25] As numerous commentators note, her attitude reflects, ironically, a subscription to hypodescent and monoracialness with regard to her husband yet a rejection of both when it comes to her children. While her comments could make sense were she to present her husband as black identified and her children as multiracial identified (rather than as biologically pure or mixed), her other public statements suggest that she is more than likely relying on biology.

Graham's "letters from the director" on the Project RACE website are characterized by contradictory statements that most often concern the distinction between social and biological race concepts. For instance, in several letters she states that race is socially constructed, argues that multiracial identity is about how one chooses to identify, and insists that racial self-identification ought to be accepted by others. In "Is Obama Multiracial?" she explains that despite his white and black parents, Obama cannot be seen as multiracial if he does not identify himself that way: "Although we could argue that he truly is multiracial, we won't; we don't. It's not how we see him or how anyone else sees him that matters, it's how *he* sees himself that matters." Yet in "Is This President Obama's Post-Racial America?" she states, "We have our first multiracial president, Barack Obama, and even if he does self-identify as black, he cannot deny DNA." Similarly, in "The Obama Racial Identity Factor and Saving Multiracial Lives," she argues that "Barack Obama can call himself black, white[,] magenta, green, or whatever he wants, it really does not matter socially. However, genes are genes and his genes are multiracial. Barack Obama has a white mother and a black father, and to categorize him as only one race *medically* is just wrong, inaccurate." Her evocation of DNA, genes, and medical science demonstrates an explicit appeal to biological race. Her statements would make more sense if she were proposing that *identity* is a matter of personal choice and social practice whereas *race* is a separate, biological thing, but biology seems to be at the root of her schema.

Similarly, in her commentary on health care, Graham insists on the need to recognize the genetic difference of multiracial individuals, arguing that they are at risk of under- and overdosing because drug trials do not determine dosages for multiracial people. She argues that people who identify monoracially (like Obama) are putting multiracial lives at risk because genetically, multiracials have different medical needs. She asserts a genetic difference between multiracials and monoracials in such statements but also clearly contradicts her interest in self-identification and her proclamations of race as a social construction.[26] Furthermore, when a nurse wanted to test her child for sickle cell anemia because it is common among black populations, Graham objected, arguing that race is far too difficult to determine. It seems the nurse had done precisely what Graham wants—she identified Graham's daughter's black genetics and thus tested her for a disease carried in higher numbers among black people—yet here Graham suddenly abandons her insistence that racial genetics are critical in medical care. Overall, many of Graham's arguments break down because she prioritizes identifying her children (and all multiracial people) as "multiracial" rather than as embodying multiple monoraces. She argues that multiracialness is genetic, that Obama is genetically multiracial, that her children and others seeking medical care need medical care tailored to *multiracial* biology, yet is uninterested when the *monoracial* genetics of her children are used to inform care. It is unclear what she imagines her children's multiracial genes to be if not those genes inherited from their white mother or black father.

Ultimately, Graham's inconsistent use of biological and social concepts of race reflects an obvious lack of critical deliberation, which many argue is characteristic of advocacy groups such as her own Project RACE.[27] But her inconsistencies also reflect the fact that she is more concerned with the multiracial designator than with actually engaging with the issues surrounding racial identity. Her organization's website states, "Multiracial people should have the option of recognizing *all* of their heritage. 'Multiracial' is important so that children have an identity, a correct terminology for who they are. 'Other' means different, a label that no person should bear." However, in "The Real World" she proposes "the addition of the classification multiracial to the five basic racial and ethnic categories without further breakdown. In other words, multiracial children would only check multiracial and not be forced to list the race and ethnicity of their mothers and fathers."[28] Her priority is self-esteem and a sense of personal validation and belonging, all of which are certainly important factors in people's lives. But her belief in freedom of choice when it comes to identity and in the celebration of all heritages dissolves in the face of her overriding belief in "multiracial" as a racial identity. Though she supports Tiger Woods in "The Problem with the 'Mixed' Label," saying that "Cablinasian" is "creative and meaningful for him," she reveals her insistent push for one identifier: "For the rest of us, let's stick with the term *preferred by our community*—'multiracial.'"

The Implications of Mixture: How Multiracialism Affects Race

While Graham's insistence upon "multiracial" as the only acceptable possibility for a racial category is problematic on several fronts, her arguments emphasize the need to recognize multiplicity in some way. Multicultural theory is founded on the principle of recognition and argues that a lack of recognition is a form of oppression. Many scholars who work in ethnic or multicultural studies incorporate this principle,

and some multiracial scholars agree that the recognition of race mixture is indeed important to one's sense of oneself as being legitimate
or valid. However, how multiracialness is recognized is no simple matter, and there is great divisiveness regarding how to socialize multiracial children and how multiracial identity ought to be articulated
and understood. Indeed, as this discussion has demonstrated, there
is still a lack of agreement regarding what multiracialness is. In sort-
ing through how we might think about what multiracialness is, and
in working through the concept of multiplicity in racial identity, it is
helpful to also consider what multiracial identity is believed to do to,
or what purpose it serves in, the social practice of race.

A lot of early scholarship and ongoing advocacy makes claims
about multiracialness bringing about a breakdown in race. Naomi
Zack argues, for instance, that "the facts of racial mixture, namely
the existence of individuals of mixed race, undermine the very notion of race, which presupposes racial 'purity.'"[29] Elsewhere she argues
that "if individuals of mixed race are granted a separate racial identity, then all of the myths of racial purity and stability break down
because there is then such a large universe of possible races that the
historical contingency of any group's racial identity becomes transparent."[30] However, the "fact" of mixture does not inevitably challenge
racial purity as Zack's comments suggest. Creating a "separate racial
identity" does not cast doubt on existing race concepts because, as
Rainier Spencer points out, it will simply "reify explicitly those other racial categories on which it necessarily would depend for its own
existence."[31] Or, as Naomi Pabst argues, "it risks reinscribing the very
modes of classification it seeks to critique by establishing an additional category of belonging with its own dominant narratives, its own
questions of belonging, its own issues of authenticity and essentialism, and its own policings and regulations" just like existing categories do.[32] In fact, the appeal to mixture as a threat to race or racial
purity is not as straightforward as some would argue. "Pure" race is
not necessarily threatened by race mixture, particularly when mixture is recognized as a separate category—essentially, as a race. Black
and white can be pure while black–white (whether called "mulatto,"

"multiracial," or "gray," as Zack proposes) poses no threat to the ideas of pure monoracial categories.

Mixture does not automatically challenge beliefs about what monoracial categories are or mean. But if multiracial identity is understood as belonging to more than one monoracial category as opposed to being its own race, it can begin to challenge beliefs about monoracial categories if they are assumed to be incapable of blending in one identity (as opposed to one body). That is, a claim to both blackness and whiteness as separate racial groups begins to challenge the purity of whiteness especially, whereas claiming blackness and whiteness as a new race (in some formulation of multiracialism) does not. After all, hybridity does not necessarily dissolve ideas about distinct races or pure races. To borrow Spencer's use of color as an analogy, green does not make yellow or blue disappear. The only thing green really challenges is a belief that yellow and blue cannot be mixed. It only makes sense to claim that multiracialism challenges existing race concepts if it is believed that the races cannot be crossed—and this would seem a rather groundless charge to make since even white supremacists have argued for centuries that mixture is an abomination, not that it is impossible. Rather, it is in racial identities that claim belonging to multiple monoracial groups that beliefs about those monoracial groups might potentially break down; since blackness mixed with whiteness has always equaled blackness and not-whiteness, black-and-white confounds the understanding of blackness as mixed and whiteness as unmixed.

This point applies just as readily to arguments that take the opposite view from Zack. For instance, Michele Elam argues that in choosing more than one race on the census, respondents think they are challenging the homogeneity of race categories. She says they are mistaken because existing American races are "mixed" and therefore "there is no purity to overturn."[33] While monoracial identities might not be "pure" in terms of ancestry, regardless of whether we consider "race" a biological or social kind, accepting only monoracial identities (that explicitly exclude identifying as additional races simultaneously) does effectively reinforce notions of homogeneity. If in practice you are *either* white *or* black then you are not white *and* black. In order to accept monoracial identity based on Elam's argument, one would have to accept that all monoracial categories are already mixed and, most important, assume that the public also views those monoracial categories as multiracial. However, while it could be argued that the American understanding of blackness might be taken for granted as incorporating other races, the argument that the American understanding of whiteness is similarly taken for granted as mixed with other races does not seem likely. Notably, Elam herself touts the inherent mixedness of Latinx and black Americans as evidence for why multiracialism is unnecessary but never suggests that whiteness is similarly mixed.[34] Indeed, the historical social practice of whiteness and blackness has maintained strict separation: the one-drop rule defines blackness as specifically not-white and whiteness as specifically unmixed. Consequently, being able to identify as more than one race does offer a challenge to a kind of "purity" or homogeneity—specifically, of identity rather than biology—associated with monoracial classifications.

As the preceding discussion suggests, a major problem when discussing whether multiracialism has the capacity to begin to challenge the practice of race itself is whether multiracialism is thought of as a separate race category or as a different sort of racial conception. Part of the worry over confirming existing racial concepts through a multiracial category is that doing so would reinforce the practice of classification and retain the historical racial hierarchy. As Heather Dalmage argues in *Tripping on the Color Line*, "A multiracial category and an officially recognized community would create greater divisions, and society would not necessarily be pushed to think more critically about race and racial identities. Whites could just recategorize this group of racially mixed people and, with calm certainty, once again see themselves as superior."[35] Similarly, Abby Ferber argues, "An analysis of the construction of race and white supremacy reveals that the Multiracial Movement's revolutionary potential lies in its threat to racial essentialism. Attempts to reify multiracial identity as simply another racial identity classification will neutralize that threat and instead contribute to maintaining the hierarchical classificatory system."[36] Or, as Rainier Spencer argues, "The practical price of establishing a multiracial category would be the loss of all the corrosive, subversive, theoretical energy inherent in the multiracial idea—resulting in what, in other venues, has been called collaboration or co-optation."[37] Though Spencer distinguishes between theoretical and practical applications of multiracialism and thus does not subscribe to the official recognition of multiracialness in any form, his comment reflects what concerns a lot of multiracial discourse: multiracialism has a distinct potential for unsettling, challenging, and perhaps revolutionizing the practice of race in the United States, but whether such potential is achieved depends on how the United States goes about recognizing multiracialism and how multiracials go about articulating their identities. Susan Graham's call for "correct" labels subscribes to the idea that official classification is somehow accurate and that multiracialness deserves a label as accurate as monoracial categories. Consequently, she unwittingly implies, in opposition to her own explicit predictions, that multiracialness poses no threat to existing systems of classification or racial categories.

As Dalmage's, Ferber's, and Spencer's comments point out, multiracial identity must be conceived of in a new or contrary way rather than simply fit into current practice if it is going to trouble the way race is considered in the United States. As these scholars and others observe, conceptions of multiracialness as a race (that is, as a racial category on par with monoracial categories) duplicate the thinking behind the monoracial categories rather than challenging them. For many commentators, the conception of multiracialism as a race reproduces historical scenarios in which mixture was observed as its own race without posing a threat to the white supremacist racial hierarchy or existing beliefs about whiteness or blackness. In fact, many skeptics of the multiracial movement worry that (once again) recognizing mixture risks a return to the color hierarchies of the nineteenth century. For instance, Suzanne Bost is unconvinced by commentators, like Maria Root, who posit that multiracialism combats the racism involved in keeping up the color line. Bost worries that such attitudes risk repeating the historical fascination with mixture that has always led back to binary thinking and white supremacy.[38] In "The New Multiracialism,"

Mary Texeira claims that "the mixed-blood category under discussion is merely the mulatto, quadroon, mestizo, and so on in a new guise."[39] Naomi Pabst makes a similar observation: "If American racial pathologies remained deeply entrenched when 'mulatto' was on the U.S. census pre-1920, I wonder why so many hopes are being pinned on a multiracial census category now. And looking at the Caribbean and South Africa, it becomes equally clear that formalizing a hierarchical tier for mulattoes, 'half-castes,' 'colored,' or 'grays' does nothing whatsoever to undermine dichotomous systems of domination, whether ideological or institutional."[40]

What Texeira, Pabst, and others identify is a need for a shift in ideology rather than in racial labels. Ultimately, approaching multiracialness differently than in the past is essential for a growing number of multiracial theorists. For instance, G. Reginald Daniel argues that we must shift our understanding away from Eurocentric and radical Afrocentric understandings of race that reinforce dichotomous race concepts and "static" race identities. A new understanding of multiracialism, he argues, could "potentially forge more inclusive constructions of blackness (and whiteness)" that could, in turn, "provide the basis for new and varied forms of bonding and integration" and better reflect the wide set of variables that shape identity.[41] If we understand the past and avoid duplicating its mistakes, we can allow the past to inform current and future theorization of multiracial identity. Such a critical examination of (multi)racial identity has the potential to work toward broader goals of equality and perhaps eventually a society that no longer needs race.

Black and White or Color Blind? Multiracialism and Civil Rights

The critical approach necessary for the socially responsible reformation of race concepts is not taken up by a significant number of multiracial advocacy groups and politicians. A considerable amount of multiracial advocacy argues that because of racism, inequality, and the personal implications of racial identity, race should cease being the guiding method by which Americans are categorized. These multiracial advocates proclaim to be working to free American society of

its racist and racialist past, but the way in which they plan to go about
it is highly problematic since they call for an abolition of officially recognized race rather than progress toward social equality. Given that
the abolitionist strategy is based on policy reform rather than social
justice, it would remove the racial structure in society without removing the racial ideology behind it—and most scholars take care to warn
against abolitionist sentiments for this reason. In fact, the current prospect of multiracialism "undoing" conventional race concepts should
be considered the demolition of the subscription to hypodescent, *not*
the demolition of beliefs about race as a social system of categories.[42]
Some theorists posit that much abolitionist advocacy originates with
well-meaning yet misguided white parents (usually mothers). The argument is that these parents simply have an unrealistic assessment of
race and race relations in the United States and consider a color-blind or
raceless society the best thing for their multiracial children or, in some
cases, an easier solution than taking on the complex history and politics of racial identity.[43] But, as john a. powell points out, the problem
with the color-blind stance is "in assuming that the major race problem in our society is race itself, rather than racism," and so efforts are
misdirected in a way that is ultimately more damaging than helpful.[44]
Or, as Peggy Pascoe warns, color blindness needs to be seen "not, as it
is popularly constructed, as the celebrated end of racism but as a racial
ideology of its own, one that can, like any racial project, be turned to
the service of oppression."[45]

As scholars like these argue, the "deliberate nonrecognition of race
erodes the ability to recognize and name racism and to argue for such
policies as affirmative action, which rely on racial categories to overturn rather than to enforce oppression."[46] Thus the very real threat
of abolitionism is evident in the conservative backing of such efforts.
During the census debates of the 1990s, Republicans, Newt Gingrich
most notable among them, supported a multiracial category because
it would mean that social support as well as legal protection for nonwhite groups could be suspended in a "color-blind" society. In California, Ward Connerly proposed a state bill that would eliminate
"racial identity" by making it illegal for the government to ask for such

information. His "Racial Privacy Initiative" was geared toward doing away with affirmative action, which his colleagues at Adversity.net explain is "'racial preference discrimination' (i.e., *reverse discrimination*)!" The website for Connerly's own organization—the American Civil Rights Institute—explains, "The days of racial set-asides are over. Citizens demand their government treat each of us fairly and equally regardless of race, ethnicity, color, gender, or national origin." In his memoir *Creating Equal: My Fight against Race Preferences*, Connerly terms affirmative action "racial preferences" and asserts that it is a discriminatory "regime of systematic race preferences" that "put[s] the government back in the same discrimination business it had been in" during school segregation.[47] Both Gingrich and Connerly strategically aligned themselves publicly with multiracial advocates who were lobbying for a multiracial category. This conservative support signals the very real possibility that multiracial identity may be—or is being—appropriated for an attack against civil rights efforts and antiracist initiatives. Moreover, this conservative interest in multiracialism also undermines claims that multiracial identification is a step toward equality or the natural "evolution" of civil rights, as is often argued.

The desire for color blindness or racelessness may be well intentioned, but the prolific scholarship that evaluates and condemns color blindness serves to illustrate the necessity of maintaining an agenda of social equality within multiracial activism.[48] Scholars use opportunities to critique color-blind initiatives in order to reaffirm the necessity of formulating multiracial discourse in tandem with, rather than in isolation from, issues of social justice. Eileen Walsh explains it well in "Ideology of the Multiracial Movement: Dismantling the Color Line and Disguising White Supremacy?":

> If the Multiracial Movement is to succeed in eliminating race and the racial hierarchy, it must adopt and promote an antiracist, social justice agenda. Disappearing race from the vocabularies and consciousness of academics, policy makers, and the citizenry prior to dismantling the structures of inequality that persist not only puts the cart before the horse, it also serves to render white privilege invisible—a most

dangerous proposition with a long legacy. Ignoring the ways in which race has been constructed as an essence, as well as marker for white group privilege, allows the mischief of race to remain hidden insidiously in our institutions while individuals, distracted from ferreting out injustice, delight in the belief that color no longer matters.[49]

The scholarship that takes color-blind activism to task emphasizes the difference between approaching multiracialism as an issue of antiracist political awareness and progressive political engagement and, conversely, offering an ahistorical treatment of multiracialism as an elimination of race/racism through color blindness.

However, progressive political engagement is not entirely straightforward either. While the Right works to eliminate the official recognition of race and thus discard hard-won civil rights protections, some members of the Left work to maintain the status quo in the interest of civil rights but at the cost of multiracial identity. For these commentators, civil rights can best be protected through exclusively monoracial identity; for this reason, they view multiracialism as both an ideological and a political threat to black solidarity. These monoracialists accuse multiracial "race traitors" of being anti-black and abandoning blackness for the benefits of whiteness. Certainly this hostile rhetoric is not characteristic of most civil rights groups and activists, but some scholars do approach the issue by arguing that blackness has always absorbed mixture and therefore that multiracial identity is redundant and ought to be discarded in the interest of black solidarity. The possibility of multiracial identity coexisting with black solidarity is not discussed; instead, political loyalty is aligned with racial identity, and in this instance multiracial is not black. In the same way that ahistorical treatments of multiracial identity ignore black history and the continuing legacy of white supremacy in contemporary American race practices, attacks on multiracial identity as a wholesale abandonment of blackness ignore the changes in American society that might permit an articulation of multiracial identity in a new way. That is, historically, "passing" usually required that blackness be discarded in favor of whiteness, and mulatto classes did fit into the white supremacist color hierarchy. However, the American social context is very different now than it was then. While colorism has survived well in contemporary America, multiracial identity is not necessarily tied to the claiming of white privilege and the betrayal of blackness as it had been in the past. Naomi Pabst argues,

> Mixedness is cast as—among other things—inauthentic, irrelevant, tragic, and a site of unmitigated privilege within blackness. All of these assumptions serve to curtail a serious treatment of interraciality and the taking seriously of mixed-race subjectivity, and as such, they reify long-standing taboos around mixed-race subjectivity as a social location and as a site for critical excavation. Even the fact that this topic is so often met with loud proclamations of the inherent blackness of mixedness or the inherent mixedness of blackness effectively paralyzes further, more probing discussion of mixedness and blackness as converging, coconstituting signs.[50]

The declaration that "everybody is mixed" is problematic because it does not take into account differences that occur over time. For instance, Susan Graham's argument that historical figures like Langston Hughes ought to be taught as icons of multiracialism ignores the historical and political context in which Hughes himself could identify (and be identified) only as black while acknowledging his mixedness.[51] As insightful, recent work on figures such as W. E. B. Du Bois, Jean Toomer, and Nella Larsen emphasizes, it is essential to consider the very real and complex implications of the sociohistorical moment on (multi)racial identity.[52]

In much the same way, critics who suggest that "mixedness is mixedness" regardless of social context ignore the changes that have occurred up to and including the contemporary moment. Kimberly DaCosta argues that "in referencing the tangled genealogies of blacks and whites decades and generations removed, these critics treated racial mixedness as an entity whose meaning is the same regardless of historical change, social context, or individual experience."[53] And as Pabst further argues, the mixed-is-black argument implies a refusal to engage

in discussion or thought regarding racial identities. She states that
such an argument is "a silencing device":

> It is often put out there in order to curtail further discussion about in-
> terraciality, as if nothing else of significance can or should be said about
> it. Some people, especially academics, seem to think that the only val-
> id thing to be said about racial mixing is that "everybody is mixed."
> Proclamations of universal mixedness can be helpful as they debunk
> "purity," removing the stigma of being mixed and also in emphasiz-
> ing, rightly, that the phenomenon of hybridity is widespread. But on
> the other hand, this emphasis takes the salience and the meaning out
> of mixed race matters. . . . To say that everybody is mixed overstates
> the similarity among people. This in turn prevents us from being able
> to talk about what makes us who we are and the differences between
> us that make a difference.[54]

The urgency with which critics work to defend blackness against the
possible threat of multiracialism (as it has traditionally been recognized) is understandable. However, their opposition valorizes the single-
minded protection of existing systems of civil rights enforcement and
ignores new propositions. As Kim Williams explains, the rapid decline
of blackness as the majority minority has more to do with immigration
trends than with multiracialism.[55] Thus, the dogged maintenance of
protections that were set up in the 1950s and '60s, when the American
racial makeup was very different, and a general defense of civil rights
through a discourse of population or monoracial classification alone
are not likely sustainable regardless of whether multiracial identity is
ever acknowledged. In any case, the potential threat of multiracialism
to civil rights is not a threat of multiracialism per se but of how that
racial construction is used—for instance, whether multiracial identity is an acknowledgment of black and white ancestry or whether it
is used to argue for an end to African American identity. Ultimately,
just as commentators must ensure that their activism and arguments
maintain and further social justice struggle, they must also ensure
that their efforts for social justice do not exclude the possibility of a
simultaneous articulation of multiracial identity.

As this discussion demonstrates, a vigilant and open-minded critical approach is vital for working through issues of multiracial identity.
Much as the oppressive one-drop rule was embraced by black Americans and turned to their advantage in demanding civil rights, multiracialness might easily be shaped into something that multiracial activists
and commentators might never have intended. For some, the risks
outweigh the potential benefits; for others, these risks must be taken
to begin overhauling the way Americans understand race. However,
as many scholars argue, American society will have to deal in some
fashion with a growing number of Americans who want to identify
multiracially, like it or not. The issue at the heart of the demand for
multiracial recognition is how (and perhaps whether) the recognition
of multiracialness on an official level will translate into recognition
on an ideological level. While a lot of activism necessarily focuses on
political change and official classification issues, the abundance and
diversity of personal narratives by multiracial people (in anthologies
but also, anecdotally, in academic work) suggests that the social perception of race is a primary site of concern. The official classification
and social perception of race shape and are shaped by one another; for
both, a major challenge is the deep-rootedness of monoracialism in
American racial practice on every level. As I hope to demonstrate in
my analysis of the literary depictions of multiracialism, having identity recognized and understood is a multifaceted yet essential challenge.

Questions of Classification: The Significance of Social Recognition

While racial classification in the United States has relied on self-
identification since the late twentieth century, and multiracialness has
been a legal option since the 2000 census (via the "choose one or more"
instructions), there is a difference between official race classification
and the social practice of race. This difference is not a contemporary
issue: for those who passed as white in the nineteenth and twentieth
centuries, for instance, the difference between how they were classified (as black) and recognized (as white) troubled white supremacist
society immeasurably. The difference between the current situation
and historical situations is that passing depended on appearance to

guide social perceptions of race. That is, black-looking people could rarely pass unless they could convince others that certain physical attributes were nonblack. Currently, individuals are ostensibly given the choice of how to identify themselves regardless of appearance. However, whether the public will accept whatever identity is proclaimed is another question.[56] A shift has to occur for society to accept whatever a person chooses to be rather than ascribe race according to social perception or existing group identities. Individuals with similar appearances or ancestral backgrounds might well identify differently depending on their childhood experiences, the makeup of their families, the attitudes of their parents, their locations, their friends and social circumstances, their political persuasions, and so on. Even siblings might identify differently despite being socialized similarly. Potentially, the way a multiracial subject wants to identify may not be recognized or respected in the general public or even by other multiracially identified people. And despite the government's endless revision of the census and reliance on self-identification, it nevertheless remains unclear the extent to which the state will recognize multiracial identities. Yet change is certainly possible, and modifications to the observation of race both legally and socially have occurred throughout American history. How multiracialness might affect change and what might be changed are the central questions in advocacy and scholarship. These questions and the ensuing debate help inform my analysis of literature that is exploring and responding to the possibilities of this historic moment of shifting race practices.

Now that hypodescent and the one-drop rule are not legally imposed, people are asked to self-identify as they wish, and individuals' self-identified racial classifications are increasingly accepted in society, it is apparent that the process of racial identification is unlike what it was before. Multiracial individuals—as well as those with ambiguous appearances—are left with the burdens and opportunities of locating themselves within the racial spectrum. That the racial spectrum still embodies the long and troubled history of race concepts in the United States and that individuals continue to find race ascribed to them by others reveals the complexity surrounding what might otherwise appear to be a (relatively) simple matter of choosing a racial identity. For multiracials in an apparently freer society, racial identity continues to be something negotiated, something flexible, and something that requires justification. The fact that multiracial literature has in recent decades included a large number of coming-of-age stories emphasizes that identity is something that is formed over time and is dependent upon how people are socialized.

For a number of observers, multiracialness as a race (that is, as a standalone category) is a danger not only because it collapses difference into sameness (by creating an identity based only on the fact that those to whom it applies fit nowhere else) but also because it reinforces the notion that race can be contained within boundaries that can be officially articulated. That language is a significant factor in multiracial discourse is evident in the lengthy debate and testimony regarding labels that occurred in Congress when it was deliberating census revisions in the 1990s. The importance of language is also apparent in the fact that the Office of Management and Budget decided not to include "multiracial" on the federal census, while organizations like Project RACE still advocate aggressively for adding the category to government forms. A lack of language can be freeing but also difficult for those who want to be recognized and/or recognizable. Language can also codify and make static something that many want to keep in flux, and the debate over language itself offers transformation—perhaps as much or more than a label might—as the nation considers and reconsiders its racial history and future. Alternatively, Maria Root argues that language that continually changes is itself potentially transformative since ideology adapts to such alteration. She argues that "language is important to the whole issue of race relations" and that there is a need "to develop a language to negotiate the frontiers of the borderlands."[57] She further states that changes to how race is understood and used "can be accomplished by taking concepts people are familiar with and transforming them. The fact that race is a social construct, the meaning of which changes in location and over time[,] suggests that it is still malleable. The multiracial dialogue inserts the confusion that may be necessary to accomplish flexibility and complexity for deeper structural change."[58]

The concerns about recognizing multiplicity are certainly complicated and far reaching. How is one, after all, meant to identify oneself? Root's "A Bill of Rights for Racially Mixed People" suggests that one approach is for multiracials to maintain complete control over individual identity in a way that frees them from conforming to any social expectations regarding race:

> [Resistance]
> I have the right
> not to justify my existence in this world
> not to keep the races separate within me
> not to be responsible for people's discomfort with my physical
>   ambiguity
> not to justify my ethnic legitimacy
> [Revolution]
> I have the right
> to identify myself differently than strangers may expect me to identify
> to identify myself differently than how my parents identify me
> to identify myself differently than my brothers and my sisters
> to identify myself differently in different situations
> [Change]
> I have the right
> to create a vocabulary to communicate about being multiracial
> to change my identity over my lifetime—and more than once
> to have loyalties and identify with more than one group of people
> to freely choose whom I befriend and love.[59]

However, while Root's "Bill of Rights" alleviates the obligation of having to account for one's mixedness, it does not address what is invested in the request to identify or whether such a request is a permissible one. Nor does Root address the responsibilities or obligations that might accompany one's rights.[60] Her "Bill of Rights" asserts, perhaps necessarily, only that the multiracial individual is under no obligation to identify in any particular way(s) and so does not address whether group identity or labels are important or necessary for either multiracials or broader society.

While Jayne O. Ifekwunigwe responds to Root enthusiastically, applauding the assertion that multiracials ought to be able to identify as they choose and change that identification as they desire, she also sees value in labels. She argues in *Scattered Belongings* that there is a practical purpose for labels and terminology, saying that her research reflects "the fact that 'mixed race' people themselves as well as parents, caregivers, practitioners, educators, policy makers, academics and curious lay people are all hungry for a uniform but not essentialist term that creates a space for the naming of their specific experiences without necessarily reinscribing and reifying 'race.'"[61] Root seems to agree on the importance of language beyond the level of individuals' needs when she explains in *The Multiracial Experience* that "self-designations are important vehicles for self-empowerment of oppressed people" and that "labels are powerful comments on how one's existence is viewed."[62] Significantly, neither Root nor Ifekwunigwe proposes the possibility of refusing to identify (or name) oneself or what that might do. Harry Wolcott argues, "The human approach to experience is categorical . . . what we don't label others will, leaving us at their mercy. We are better off to supply labels of our own and to be up front about the identifications we seek"; yet the lack of consensus over group identity ("multiracial" or not) and individual identities (whether individualized racial terms can be accepted) suggests that it is not as simple a matter as categorizing or being categorized.[63] How labels might function is as critical as who creates them; as Trinh T. Minh-ha argues, there is a great degree of political power invested in that creation. Trinh proposes that one may "re-nam[e] to un-name" and thus grant the political power of identification to those who have had an identity imposed on them by others.[64] In her tongue-in-cheek "The Mulatto Millennium," Danzy Senna identifies the problems (and dangers) of naming and proposes a list of endless possibilities, including Standard Mulatto, African American, Jewlatto, Mestizo, Gelatto, Cultural Mulatto, Blulatto, Negratto, Cablinasian, Tomatto, Fauxlatto, Ho-latto, and finally, for those who might not fit into any category, Postlatto.[65] Ultimately, naming race is always a fraught task because it is such a political act, and as Senna points out, names are always going to encounter resistance since racial labels are socially derived and socially practiced.

Desire for terminology is a common theme in multiracial literature and commentary, but such a desire is not easily satisfied since what is being signified is so unstable and is dependent on such a complex social and political history. Elliott Lewis, for instance, identifies the difficulty in labeling something when its meaning is dependent on social thought alone—social thought, one might add, that has recognized black and white primarily as a binary. In *Fade: My Journeys in Multiracial America* (2006), Lewis explains how the lack of words to describe race in a way he considers accurate was an impediment for him as a child and that his subsequent search for appropriate language has been fruitless. He is troubled by his inability to "figure out what to call [him]self" for a "long time" and describes a situation where, in the small rural town to which he and his mother have moved without his father, a shopkeeper asks him if his father is white.[66] The shopkeeper's question reveals his own discomfort with Lewis's ambiguous race and his own desire to be able to identify Lewis's racial background in a way that makes sense to him. Lewis does not know how to respond because to him, black and white seem inapplicable to his family members; the way he understands race is unlike how the shopkeeper understands race. In a sense, his response embodies the irony of the perceived need for racial labels in order to know who or what people are and the impossibility of really possessing that knowledge with or without labels:

> I knew by now that my parents thought of themselves as black. Why couldn't I just say, "No, my dad is a black man," and be done with it? I suppose my hesitation had to do with what I figured was the intent of Mr. Lee's question. Describing my father as a black man doesn't convey the right mental picture in terms of a physical description. Mr. Lee knew what my mother looked like. Now he was fishing for some genealogical explanation of why I turned out looking the way I do, an outcome in his mind was more likely if my father were white. What I really wanted to communicate to him was that my dad, like my mother, looked like me. There was no mystery here; we all had similar complexions. But at that moment, I didn't have the words. . . . Once again, the intertwining of race, color, and ancestry had rendered me

speechless. I had no vocabulary to respond confidently or effectively to questions about my mixed and matched family.[67]

The fact that Mr. Lee asks for the racial identity of Lewis's father but Lewis cannot understand if the shopkeeper is asking for the label his father uses (black) or the way his father looks (not particularly black) suggests that labels are always going to be circumstantially relative.

When his mother explains that his father's birth certificate identifies him as a 'mulatto' and then explains what a mulatto is, things begin to make more sense to Lewis: "Hearing my father had been labelled 'mulatto' somehow seemed to reconcile the conflict between his light appearance and my parents' sense of being legally black. It was just the kind of vocabulary I could use to handle such racial questions in the future."[68] Lewis learns, however, that it is not the easy label he was looking for and notices years later that his father's death certificate identifies him as "black": "So there it was. Dad was born mulatto. He died black. And he would by no means be the last in the family whose identity would change between cradle and grave."[69]

Furthermore, Suki Ali notes that "although language or terms in common usage may change, meanings may well not," and those meanings may be as racist in new language as they were in older language.[70] The most productive strategy, particularly for the present discussion of literature, is the recent assertion of some sociologists that "researchers studying racial identity development need to shift their gaze from the racial label that individuals use to the process by which they have come to adopt that label as a racial self-understanding."[71] It is not any label itself but how a label is arrived at, negotiated, or avoided that is critical in this examination of multiracial literature.

The desire to label seems to reflect the perceived need to have a public identity. But the external public pressure to identify oneself and the political significance of "re-naming to un-name" often conflict. We see these sociological challenges at play in countless narrative representations, such as Lewis's *Fade* and Carolyn Meyer's young adult novel *Jubilee Journey* (1997). For Meyer's protagonist, Emily Rose, the conflict between her parents' label for her and the label others prefer to ascribe to her becomes most apparent when she travels to the South and encounters different cultural norms regarding racial identity. Taught to call herself "double" rather than "half," as in *"twice as much history, twice as much culture, twice as much of everything that counts,"* Emily Rose learns when she goes to Texas that her "doubleness" and her family label of "café au lait" simply are not accepted in the South.[72] Emily feels odd saying "white people" and "black people," as if the the two groups are distinct from her identity, but soon her understanding of race as mixing ("coffee with milk") is challenged: when she attempts to identify herself as "biracial" and a blend, a black Southerner retorts, "You think being a half-breed makes you one bit less black? . . . Maybe up in Connecticut you can say you're double—whatever that means—and you can get away with telling that to those Yankees who believe just about anything. But around here you are *black*, Emily Rose. Black just like everybody else."[73] The history of racial classification in the United States cannot be forgotten, and in the South the one-drop rule appears to be far too ingrained for Emily Rose to assert a new concept of racial blending. When her older brother Steven begins to date a white girl, the daughter of an openly racist man, her mother warns him against the relationship: "Marissa is white. You're black. . . . [They] don't like the idea of a black boy and a white girl together."[74] Emily Rose wonders, *"How come Mom didn't say 'You're double,' like she always does at home? Did that all change when we came here?"*[75] Meyer's text demonstrates the flexibility of race in that Emily Rose and her siblings can be mixed at certain times—and significantly, in certain places—and monoracial at other times and in other places. However, Meyer's novel also highlights the difficulty of asserting one's personal sense of identity to those who refuse it and combating race concepts that have dominated American history since before the United States existed. Additionally, Emily Rose's experience suggests that while she is interested in discovering "what it means to be *me*," her identity has relied upon the perceptions of others thus far, both in terms of how she is mixed (ascribed by her parents) and how she is black (ascribed by her grandmother and peers).[76]

As Meyer's text demonstrates, the numerous challenges to racial identity formation among multiracial individuals often stem from the expectations and beliefs of others. Though racial identity is intensely personal and reflects how people feel about themselves, these feelings are shaped by—and indeed, result from—their experience in the world. R. L'Heureux Lewis and Kanika Bell argue that "personal attributes and categorical memberships overlap within the cognitive frameworks of the individual" and ultimately take into account context *and* individual agency in the "structuring of an individual's identity."[77] As Root's "Bill of Rights" and Meyer's literary representation of Emily Rose's experiences suggest, racial identity is a personal identity, but it is also one that has to engage in broad social contexts and bear the brunt of the views of others, be they family members or strangers, monoracialist or multiracialist.[78] In *Bulletproof Diva*, Lisa Jones articulates the kind of interrogation many multiracials experience:

> *Who are you, what are you, where are you from, no, where are you really from, where are your parents from, are your grandparents American? Are you from here, what's your background, what's your nationality, where do you live? Are you black, are you white, do you speak Spanish? Are you really white, are you really black? Are you Puerto Rican, are you half and half, are you biracial, multiracial, interracial, transracial, racially unknown, race neutral, colorless, color-blind, down with the rat race or the human race? Who are you? Where are you coming from? Who are your people?[79]*

These kinds of questions consistently dog those of ambiguous race and reflect the social pressures that accompany multiracialism. Racially ambiguous people are asked to identify themselves, but their self-naming is an arduous task because of a number of factors, including the desire to belong or be accepted as however they label themselves and the lack of vocabulary available to label themselves with in the first place.

The exasperation evident in Jones's remarks also signals the invasiveness of such interrogation as well as the regularity with which it occurs. Additionally, the question, "What are you?" often reflects not just an invitation to self-identify but also an expectation or even demand that racial classification be articulated in particular ways. In *Post Black: How a New Generation Is Redefining African American Identity*,

Ytasha Womack explains not only how frequently she is asked "What are you?" but also the frequency with which her answer is met with disappointment or even accusations of dishonesty depending on the desires or beliefs of the person asking the question. Her account emphasizes how this ubiquitous question is often less about respect for multiracials' individualism or personal freedom to identify themselves and often more about onlookers' desires to have things explained to them in ways they understand. In other words, the question often reflects not the rights of the multiracial person but the perceived rights of the person posing the question. Womack explains: "Randomly asking 'What are you?' has got to be one of the most ignorant questions on the planet, and yet perfect strangers at bus stops feel they have a constitutional right to know."[80] Indeed, the fact that answers are not always accepted suggests that even though the question implies that multiracials can control their own identities, multiracials do not always have the freedom to self-identify as they wish. As Ralina Joseph explains, her efforts to identify herself overtly as multiracial have not assured her that her personal identification choices will be respected: "I learned that racialized choice, a key value of the multiracial movement, was not an option for most, while racialized conscription . . . was."[81] Certainly, it is this kind of paradox that tends to characterize the interaction of multiracial figures with the social environment—and much of this social interaction comes in the form of interrogation regardless of whether a multiracial figure's identity is questioned directly.

Indeed, social interaction and the resulting formulations of identity are dependent on several important factors. Since racial identity is dependent upon social context, the variables of time, place, and population shape how identity is perceived by others and how a subject self-identifies. While all of the texts in this discussion are representing the time of the late twentieth and early twenty-first centuries, we see that the location of multiracial subjects and the people they are surrounded by directly affect the ways multiracial identities are articulated, embodied, and understood. The overlap between place and identity and the shifting of both as multiracial subjects live their lives reflect what social psychologists have demonstrated about the social context of identity. The "What are you?" question, for instance, embodies the particularities of the local culture and the beliefs of the person(s) asking the question. As Hazel Rose Markus explains, "Who you are at any given moment depends on where you happen to be and who else is there in that place with you."[82] Markus's research supports the claims of many scholars of multiracialism that "identities are always in flux," and she explains that as social context changes because of geographical movement or the passage of time, identities "are continually formed, expressed, changed, affirmed, and threatened in the course of everyday life."[83]

Here I will turn to close examinations of the texts by Raboteau, Harper, Walker, and Senna to demonstrate the commonality of such experiences and to consider what their representations in literature help us understand about contemporary multiracial identity.

Racial Insufficiency: Emily Raboteau's *The Professor's Daughter*

In Emily Raboteau's *The Professor's Daughter*, the protagonist Emma remarks repeatedly that "What are you?" is "not an everyday question, but one [she gets] asked every day," and that her response is not to offer a racial label for herself; instead, Emma says, "I just tell them what color my parents are, which is to say, my father is black and my mother is white" (2, 27). She uses her parents to make herself understandable, though her efforts fail anyway since people "don't usually believe [her]" and instead insist, *"You look _____ (fill in the blank) Puerto Rican, Algerian, Israeli, Italian, Suntanned, or maybe Like you Got Some Indian Blood, but you don't look like you got any Black in you. No way! Your father must be real light-skinned"* (2). Similarly, on her first day at college, Emma's new roommate admires her attractive brother, understands that he is black, and then looks at her, "perplexed": "She was looking at me funny. 'So what are you anyway?'" (21). Two days later, someone comes to her door saying he is looking for Emma:

"Is she your roommate or something?"

"No—I'm she. I'm Emma."

Karim looked confused. "Oh. There must be some kind of mistake or something. I'm supposed to be Emma's culture counselor. Through the Af-Am Center?"

"Well, that's me," I said. "I mean, I'm Emma."

He stared at me for a moment. "All right, then. So, I'll see you around." We shook hands and he never spoke to me again. (21–22)

Her blackness is not enough for the counselor or for those who insist she does not appear to have any black ancestry. Her appearance remains the central focus of her ambiguous identity since she continually finds herself in circumstances where people begin to question "what" she is once they see her.

Though she never tries to label herself or insist upon being recognized in a particular way, Emma nevertheless discovers that no identity she is willing to embody is acceptable to those around her. Professor Lester, her father's colleague and a prominent black figure in the novel, argues in his newest book on biracialism,

> There can be no life on the hyphen. The "mulatto" cannot be both black and white just as he cannot be neither black nor white. These terms are mutually exclusive and mutually imperative. In the hyphenated psyche, an internal choice must be made to privilege one of two warring selves. Black-White. Pick one! Or this choice will be made hard and fast by the external world. (22)

Professor Lester articulates the common stance that the United States is a monoracial society and that only one race may be declared, and if it is not then one or another will be imposed nevertheless. But what the novel demonstrates is that society is just as likely to exclude someone like Emma from both categories as it is to force her into either. Though her preference is blackness, Emma has little success convincing anyone of her blackness (that is, being recognized or acknowledged as black by others), and it seems unlikely that she would have been accepted as white any more readily had she chosen to identify as such.

For instance, when she meets her (white) boyfriend's grandmother, who knows nothing about her racial background, the woman asks, "What color is she?" and demands that Emma be removed from her presence (258). Just as Karim finds Emma's blackness suspect, her boyfriend's racist grandmother finds her whiteness suspect.

Like Lisa Jones, who is asked if she is "really" black or white and endures repeated challenges to her Americanness, Emma is asked if she is "really American," because of her ambiguous race. The resistance to seeing her as black, white, or some version of a combination is clear when the "races" other people suggest she might be are as much nationalities as they are racial or ethnic groups (*"Puerto Rican, Algerian, Israeli, Italian"* [2]). It seems, then, that if Emma is not unambiguously white or black she must not be from either (or any) of the conventional American races. By "othering," by making foreign those who do not fit into the binary, observers can avoid acknowledging the mistake of their assumptions about race or the evidence that race is not dichotomous and thereby prevent a new way of identifying race from being articulated. Emma's alcoholic boyfriend focuses his insults on her racial ambiguity when he gets drunk; he calls her a "stuck-up whiteniggerbitch" and thereby strips all value from any racial identity Emma might claim. Indiscernible race has left Emma feeling "unfinished" and "halfway something and halfway something else, without definition" (254, 261).

When Emma is identified as a member of a distinct racial group, it is ironically a group that is officially white in the United States but has been considerably socially "othered" since 9/11. A week following the terrorist attacks in New York City, someone assaults Emma "outside the subway": "A maniac who mistook me for an Arab, chucked a beer bottle at my head, and told me, in expletive terms, to get out of his country. I remember his eyes, how they were looking through me at something else that wasn't there. This wasn't the first or worst time I was mistaken for an Arab" (262–63).

Once again, her appearance dominates others' perceptions of her, and it is only when she goes to Brazil, where "everybody there looked like some permutation of her," that she is able to make sense of her experiences (270). She comes to the conclusion that there "wasn't any-thing wrong with her head, but rather something wrong with her coun-try" (271). She explains, "It made me invisible. I couldn't feel my body there [in the United States]" (271). The novel concludes with Emma in the process of psychic healing after the trauma apparently caused by her lack of a distinct race in the United States. In Brazil, Emma "[dis-covers] herself in a new language"—not only in Portuguese, literally, but in a culture where she is not a racial anomaly (275).

It is Emma's inability to fit into American society that offers the most poignant critique of American race practices. As Michele Elam observes, Raboteau's text resists the traditional European bildungs-roman structure, which typically traces an individual's estrangement or dislocation from society to a conclusion in which the individual is reconciled with his or her society.[84] The inclusive "socialization" that Elam says characterizes the conventional bildungsroman is evasive for Emma, who is not "incorporated" into her society by the end of the novel.[85] Indeed, the impossibility of racially "fitting in" in her native country makes Emma's estrangement from the United States a conse-quence not of her own pathology but, as she indicates herself, of the pathology of the country. It is the country that has harmed and re-jected her. Emma's lack of "incorporation" into American society is not a subversive act on her part but the act of exclusionary race prac-tices on the part of her nation. Because race is socially derived, the only societies where she can "fit in" are those that do not overburden white-and-black mixture with centuries-old skepticism and painful-ly acute examination.

Racial Unbelonging: Rachel Harper's *Brass Ankle Blues*

Like Raboteau's novel, Rachel Harper's *Brass Ankle Blues* begins with the multiracial protagonist's racial identity being challenged. Harp-er's prologue identifies the interrogation of ambiguous race as the central focus when Nellie says that she tells her father, at age seven, "I want to grow up to be invisible" (1). She reads Ellison but has the "opposite problem":

People see me wherever I go, remember me places where I haven't been. They follow me with their eyes, their questions. They ask me things I haven't even asked myself.

"What are you, anyway?"

A bullfrog, a butterfly.

"I mean, where are you from?"

Boston. One fifty-one Tremont Street. My mother's womb.

"Your parents? Grandparents?"

New York. Minnesota. A Brooklyn brownstone. The Blue Ridge Mountains. A sod house in Iowa. A dairy farm.

"But what's your nationality?"

I'm American.

". . . Is that it?"

And German, Irish, and English. Cherokee, Chippewa. African. (Sorry, I don't know from where.)

"You all those things?"

Yes.

"You don't look black."

Do I look white?

"You look different, like no one I've ever seen."

I look exactly like myself. (1)

The lack of quotation marks in Nellie's responses emphasizes the way in which others' questions about her identity force their way into her psyche. Her words are not simply a verbal response to her questioner but also reflect personal and private thoughts and feelings. Encounters with those who would doubt her and make her account for herself cause Nellie to develop a hyperawareness of her race.

Like Lisa Jones and Raboteau's Emma, Nellie's racial ambiguity leads observers to question her nationality and her blackness. Just as Emma must endure the racist attacks of whites who mistake her identity, so too must Nellie; when a man fails in his attempts to abduct her, he calls her a wetback, "hating [her] with the wrong slur" (78). But Nellie is also misrecognized by those who would claim her: when she and her cousin Jess get a ride from some Spanish speakers while hitchhiking, the people say goodbye in Spanish and leave some of their homemade food with the girls. When Jess expresses surprise, Nellie explains, "It happens to me all the time. Especially in New York City, where all the Puerto Ricans think I'm one of them. When I was a kid this guy in a museum thought I was his niece and wanted to take me home. My mother had to get a security guard involved" (55). Similarly, when Nellie meets a young man in the park who is "exactly [her] color," he asks her if she is Sioux. Nellie misunderstands: "Sue? . . . No, my name's Nellie" (71, 73). When he explains her mistake, she says, "I'm mixed, black and white. But my great-grandfather was half Chippewa"; he tells her she looks like his pretty "half-breed" mother (73). Significantly, whenever she is claimed rather than simply rejected as Other, those who claim Nellie always claim her as a race "of color." Never do whites claim her as one of them. When Nellie finds solace in sameness, it is always with the qualification that she is still an Other to whites. When Dallas, the young Native American man, takes her to Dairy Queen, Nellie assesses their situation: "I like the fact that everyone knows we're together. They also think we're the same. I can see it in their eyes, the way they stare and then look down at their feet" (82). However, the fact that she is "passing as an Indian" means that her satisfaction in fitting in is still limited by racism and reflects the fact that she has not found a way to be entirely accepted by "mainstream" white society. That is, she may have achieved belonging in Nativeness but she has not achieved belonging in whiteness. She can fit into a group, but that group is itself marginalized in American history and culture. When the only table the pair can find has no umbrella and is next to the garbage, Dallas's joke reveals the legacy of racism in the United States that people who look anything but white will always have to combat: "'Come on,' he says, leading me back to the table. 'It's the colored section'" (82). Ultimately, then, while Nellie might sense belonging at times, it is never found within whiteness.

Throughout the novel, Nellie continually yearns for a sense of belonging, but belonging either requires "passing" as something she feels she is not or eludes her entirely. When her cousin Jess jokes, "You integrate every town you walk through," Nellie responds, "Are you kidding? I'm not even integrated myself. The only time I feel black is in a room full of white people, and the only time I feel white is in a room full of black people. And unfortunately, I'm never in both rooms at the same time" (242). On the one occasion when Nellie does finally feel her difference disappear, it is significant that she and her cousins have covered their skin and hair with mud after a trip to the quarry on a rainy day. Even then, she feels not racial belonging but an erasure of racial difference in "the freedom of invisibility" under "the shield of mud, the cloak of a brown mask": "When we all stand next to one another, I finally feel like I belong, like I'm no different from my cousins. In this moment, we are the same color, with the same thick locks of tangled hair, the same clumped and crackled skin, the same grotesquely distorted features. We are all monsters" (199–200). The fact that Nellie and her cousins have to become a "real freak show" in order for her to feel belonging suggests the doubt Nellie has about her own validity and that of her family (199).

However, the quarry episode is also simply a period of bonding between cousins and is as much an aid to Jess, a white cousin who has been estranged from her extended family, as it is to Nellie, who has grown up with her cousins and spent every summer of her life with them and the rest of her mother's family. Nellie sees the power of family in forging a sense of inclusion and ultimately decides that she and her father ought to take in Jess when she is abandoned by her parents. Though Jess is not a blood relative of Nellie's father and Nellie's parents are divorcing, Nellie considers herself, her father, and Jess "family" and assumes they share responsibility for one another.

Nellie also sees herself not as a monstrous and illegitimate figure but as someone who has the potential to connect difference. Though she articulates how she does not feel at home with whites or blacks, she does wonder if she is capable of bringing the two together instead of fitting into either group: "If a child can integrate a family, does that family then integrate the town, that town the state, that state the country? If so, we are on our way to a blended world, where people like me not only exist, but are held in high regard, becoming the bridge that connects separate islands, a steel frame built to sway or expand with the changing weather, but never to crumble and fall" (242). Just as Raboteau's novel identifies American society as the source of Emma's "depression" about her racial ambiguity, Harper's novel suggests that it is the "separate islands" of American race concepts that leads Nellie to feel lost. But Nellie's poem in her *Notes on Interracial Relationships* suggests that it is possible to transform the judgmental gaze of others into something self-affirming:

> I am not a mule.
> I am not a.
> I am not.
> I am. (234)

Like Emma, Nellie works toward shrugging off the social attitude that she is something negative ("I am not a mule."), something that requires a label ("I am not a."), or something invalid ("I am not."); instead, like Emma discovering herself in a "new language," Nellie articulates herself in language that she chooses herself ("I am."). Instead of allowing hateful ("I am not a mule.") or exclusionary ("I am not a. / I am not.") language to reduce her worth or isolate her, she reduces that language into something positive and affirming, and something that does not require group membership—she simply is: "I am."

Racial Dislocation: Rebecca Walker's *Black White and Jewish*

In her autobiography *Black White and Jewish*, Rebecca Walker finds that her race troubles other people and that other people tend to hold her responsible for their confusion. During Walker's first year of college, a "WASP-looking Jewish student strolls into [her] room through the fire-exit door," drunk and casually "twirling a Swiss Army knife" between his fingers. He asks her, "Are you really black and Jewish?" and then wonders, "How can that be possible?" The racism involved in his apparent comfort with his own "possibility" as a white and Protestant looking Jew while questioning her "possibility" as a black Jew is something Walker notices even if he does not. His interrogation of her identity is unwelcome, like his invasion of her room, and Walker makes her "rage" clear when she holds his knife threateningly and tells him, "in a voice [she] want[s] him to be sure is black [that] . . . he'd better go." However, welcome or not, the student has forced her to "prove" her blackness and question herself. She sits "for quite a while in the dark" and asks herself, "Am I possible?" (Walker, *Black White and Jewish*, 25).

This question haunts Walker to a great extent, and while her text is in part a struggle to answer the question, it is also an expression of a desire to avoid it. Being able to define herself is something she cherishes but also a task she finds oppressively huge: "Freedom can feel overwhelming. I would not trade it, but sometimes I want to be told what to do. I want to know constraints, boundaries. I want to know the limits of who I am. Tell me what I cannot do. Let me master myself within articulated limitations. Without these, I feel vast, out of control" (4). Like Raboteau's Emma, who feels "unfinished" and "without definition," Walker feels a sense of being in "limbo" and is weary of having to account for herself:

> I am more comfortable in airports than I am in either of the houses I call, with undeserved nostalgia, Home. I am more comfortable in airports than I was in any of the eight different schools where I learned all of the things I now cannot remember. Airports are limbo spaces— blank, undemanding, neutral. Expectations are clear. I am the passenger. I am coming or going. I am late, on time, or early. I must have a ticket. I must have identification. I must not carry a weapon. Beyond these qualifications, I do not have to define this body. I do not have to belong to one camp, school, or race, one fixed set of qualifiers, adjectives based on someone else's experience. I do not have to remember who I, or anyone else, thinks I am. (3–4)

Walker finds locating herself racially an arduous task because of the requirements and expectations embedded in classification. She is aware that she is meant to be the bridging of a racial binary, that her parents wanted her to represent the equality they sought politically. She is the product and proof of the "interracial defiance" of the sixties, but with the rise of black power her family is "suddenly suspect" and her father is "recast as an interloper" though he works as a lawyer for the NAACP (60). Walker reflects on her family's situation: "The . . . problem, of course, is me. My little copper-colored body that held so much promise and broke so many rules. I no longer make sense. I am a remnant, a throwaway, a painful reminder of a happier and more optimistic but ultimately unsustainable time" (60). Walker's parents "return to the life that was expected," to what is "familiar, safe": her father marries a "nice Jewish girl" he grew up with and her mother begins a serious relationship with an old college flame from an HBCU (116–17). Her parents, and the society they created her in, have returned to the status quo. Her choice, then, is to identify herself as a "remnant" of a time gone by, and thus something that cannot fit into contemporary society, or else reidentify herself as something that can fit.

She can identify what she is *not* and what she *was*; she proclaims, "I am not a bastard, the product of a rape, the child of some white devil. I am a Movement Child. . . . I am not tragic" (24). When her father tells her the story of her birth, she recognizes that she did, indeed, perform the function she was meant for:

> A nurse walks into Mama's room, my birth certificate in hand. At first glance, all of the information seems straightforward enough: mother, father, address, and so on. But next to boxes labelled "Mother's Race" and "Father's Race," which read Negro and Caucasian, there is a curious note tucked into the margin. "Correct?" it says. "Correct?" a faceless questioner wants to know. Is this union, this marriage, and especially this offspring, correct? . . . A mulatta baby swaddled and held in loving arms, two brown, two white, in the middle of the segregated South. I'm sure the nurses didn't have many reference points. (12–13)

It is as much her parents' love, and in particular her white father's devotion to her black mother and to their baby, as it is Walker herself that is being questioned in the Mississippi hospital. Interestingly, Walker comments, "I am surely one of the first interracial babies this hospital has ever seen" (13). While she appears to be claiming herself as racially "new", it is more likely that what she claims as new about her interracialness is that it is something intentional and welcomed for reasons of love and equality. Her whiteness is not being ignored or treated as sinister as it had been before for babies like her; rather, her whiteness is part of the point of her. She is not tragic, as she claims repeatedly, yet her text seems to ask, What is she?

The way Walker negotiates racial belonging throughout her memoir is seen to a significant degree in how she has to move back and forth between her divorced parents every two years. Walker is unable to establish much in the way of roots since she must move so frequently and rarely moves back to the same house or neighborhood she left. She has to cultivate a sense of unbelonging to ease the pain of impermanence; she uses a "process of forgetting" to erase "almost all of what [she's] come from": "I'm only in the present, driving up to the airport, waiting still on the escalator as it carries me closer to the gate. I'm an amnesiac because if I weren't I'd be feeling all that loss, all that tearing away, and who wants to feel that?" (163–64). But her unbelonging is not just about place—it is also about race: her shifts are between homes but also between races. She moves "from place to place, from Jewish to black, from D.C. to San Francisco, from status quo middle class to radical artist bohemia," and it is "like moving from planet to planet between universes that never overlap" (117). She has to continually reinvent herself for each new situation, learning the speech patterns, popular culture preferences, clothes and make-up norms, and social hierarchies and dangers of each group of racialized peers she has to insert herself within. She explains that in every new situation she performs what has become her routine: "I heighten the characteristics I share with the people around me and minimize, as best I can, the ones that don't belong" (184–85). She is both a "foreigner" and a "translator," doomed, it seems, to be outside of or in between ethnoracial identities (213, 212). She may be the "Jewish American Princess" at a Jewish summer camp but "a Puertorriqueña, a mulatta, breathed out with all that Spanish flavor" with her Latinx friends in the Bronx, or a black girl defined by her "respect for elders, impatience with white-girl snottiness, [and] the no-shit tough attitude" she learns from black friends in San Francisco (200, 180). But in each situation she is not entirely legitimate: she is too black for the white Jewish kids, unable to "get it quite right, never get[ting] the voice to

match up with the clothes"; she is too white for the black kids who
tease her for saying "like" and asking if they have heard the new Police album; and she is too middle class to have her Latinx friends from
the Bronx "up the hill" to her father's apartment in a Jewish neighborhood (180, 268, 205).

The fact of Walker's physical movement between two very different families makes tangible her continual negotiation of her racial
identity. Having to reinvent herself in place after place is juxtaposed
with her travels—alone and with her mother—where the pressure to
identify herself is relieved. She finds the same racism, confusion, and
avoidance that she feels in the United States when she goes to Greece,
England, Ireland, Spain, France, and Holland. But, like Raboteau's
Emma in Brazil, Walker finds that she feels different in places like Jamaica, Mexico, and Bali than in the United States:

> In these places where many of the people have skin the same color as
> mine and where I am not embroiled in the indigenous racial politics
> of the day, I get a glimpse of a kind of freedom I have not experienced
> at home, where I always seem to be waiting for a bomb to drop and
> where I feel I am always being reminded of the significance, for better
> or worse, of my racial inheritance. In the race-obsessed United States,
> my color defines me, tells a story I have not written. In countries of
> color I feel that I am defined by my interactions with people. (304)

For Walker too, though race is largely about culture (which she has
to adopt in order to fit in), her color is a significant factor in her identity; she also feels that others identify her based on her appearance.
Her cultural similarities are undoubtedly greater to anyone in the
United States than to those in a foreign country, yet her appearance
makes her less responsible for accounting for herself and proclaiming a cultural identity when she is in "countries of color" (304). Her
racial identity, then, bridges a culture gap in another country much
more readily than her cultural Americanness can bridge an American race gap. In the "race-obsessed United States," Walker is made to
"feel" her races, to feel her parts instead of her whole, whenever people who identify monoracially "point out something in [her] that they

don't want to own in themselves" and then attribute to another racial background (305).

She wonders, too, about her ancestors and whether they could accept her and love her as part of themselves. She considers her oldest known maternal ancestor, May Poole, who was a slave, and her paternal great-grandmother Jennie:

> I cannot help but wonder if either of them could have fully claimed and embraced me. If as an anonymous child I walked up to Grandmother Poole unannounced she might have cared for me, might have extended herself for my well-being, but wouldn't she also see the lightness of my skin as a sign of danger, the evidence of brutality? Wouldn't part of her heart necessarily then, out of self-preservation, close to me? And if I were to happen upon my great-grandma Jennie, my hair bushy and my skin brown, wouldn't she ignore me, or shoo me away like a bothersome fly, like a little nigger child in her way, a child of one of the tenants in the Harlem apartments she owned with her husband, a child whose parents owe rent? (151)

She knows that her racial histories complicate her identity and notices that the same imagined concerns of her slave ancestor arise again, seven generations later, when her black relatives identify certain "cracker" mannerisms in her as a child (84). Similarly, the imagined racism of Walker's paternal ancestor is repeated in her grandmother, who has disowned her father for his marriage to an African American and who refuses to acknowledge her mother (16). Additionally, she knows that her extended family has inaccurate ideas about her, that she is "an empty screen for their projections" (74).

Walker's deliberation over whether either of her ancestors would recognize her as family reflects Kimberly DaCosta's discussion of the "racialization of the family" and the "familization of race" in "All in the Family: The Familial Roots of Racial Division." DaCosta argues that interracial families were pathologized in American history, and thus multiracials are only now beginning to "make visible relationships that are often not assumed by others."[86] In her discussion of the motivations for and functions of the one-drop rule, DaCosta notes that "what is often forgotten are the ways in which the logic of hypodescent is aimed at preventing the formation of family ties across racial boundaries. For according to the one-drop rule, it is impossible for a black woman to give birth to a white child, yet a white woman can bear a black child."[87] In other words, racial classification practices force parents and children into different groups and thus make parent–child bonds less recognizable and families more difficult. DaCosta's observations regarding the historical obstruction of familial relations across racial lines in American society are reflected in both Walker's interest in family belonging and Nellie's reliance on family relationships in Harper's novel. Nellie quite readily enjoys kinship across race and finds it critical to her sense of self, whereas Walker lacks such unhindered kinship and finds that her racial identity and psychic well-being suffer as a result.

The ways in which Walker is made to feel her difference emphasize the great degree of influence others have on her sense of personal identity. For many years, her identity and sense of herself have been shaped by others' desires. For a long time, she admits, "I tell people whom I think will be shocked about my Slavic, Jewish ancestry. I get a strange, sadistic pleasure from watching their faces contort as they reconsider the woman who was more easily dismissible as Puerto Rican or Arab. On the subway, surrounded by Hasidim crouched xenophobically over their Old Testaments, I have to sit on my hands and bite my tongue to keep from shouting out, 'I know your history!' I don't feel loyalty as much as an irrational, childlike desire to burst their suffocating illusions of purity."[88] But she also subsequently admits that all she wants is "to be recognized as family," that all she seeks is ethnic, racial, and cultural belonging.[89] That she characterizes ethnoracial group inclusion as being "family" identifies how personally affected she is by the degree to which others accept and recognize her. Her responses to those who do not suspect her ancestry reveal the extent to which she spends her life reacting to the way others see her and the hurt she feels at being excluded. Ultimately, her autobiography is a prolonged effort at defining herself and coming to terms with how she has been shaped by the desires of others and her resistance to those desires.

However, she ultimately concludes that whatever the formulation of her racial identity, it cannot be a simple allegiance to a particular racial group. Her "people," she explains, can only be hers—she cannot be one of theirs. She feels she is inherently set apart—not because she refuses any group but because other people cannot perceive her as one of them:

> I was never granted the luxury of being claimed unequivocally by any people or "race" and so when someone starts talking about "my people" I know that if we look hard enough or scratch at the surface long enough, they would have some problem with some part of my background, the part that's not included in the "my people" construction. It's not that I am not loved and accepted by friends and family, it is just that there is always the thing that sets me slightly apart, the "cracker" lurking in my laugh.
>
> And then there is the question of how I can feel fully identified with "my people" when I have other people, too, who are not included in that grouping. And this feeling I have, of having other people too, is in effect even when the other people under consideration do not claim me.[90]

While Walker might be able to claim her own version of "my people," she knows that her people are not "my people" to one another, that her white "people" would not claim her black "people" and vice versa. Even her own legitimacy as part of any group might be questioned at any time since the "my people" construction is as much about exclusion as inclusion, and Walker will always embody something that "my people" might want to prohibit. As if to prove her right, Julius Lester states in his highly critical review of her book that "Rebecca Walker seems to be unaware that she is laying claim to an identity few Jews would say she has a right to."[91]

The tentativeness of Walker's racial identity illustrates the balance that so often must be struck between the personal feelings of a multiracial individual and the effect of the perceptions of others. In a sense, Walker's autobiography articulates both the difficulty of being identifiable and the pressure to be identifiable because of how others

observe her. As she says elsewhere, multiracial people are not themselves "broken" but instead "have only held the fractured projections
of others, innocently imbibing harmful judgements that were not
[their] own."[92] Looking back on her life in *Black White and Jewish*, she
finds it "jarring" to recognize that for "most of [her] life" she was "defined by others, primarily reactive, going along with the prevailing
view."[93] She acknowledges that she has since taken the power to articulate her identity away from others but admits that her identity is
still shaped by forces beyond her control. She wonders when Americans will be free of "the cultural or personal narrative we've inherited or devised."[94] Indeed, she asserts that she is "thought of as a traitor
and misfit, a poser and malcontent," and that a "lifetime" of it "takes
a toll" emotionally and psychologically.[95] She argues that if multiracial people are able to get out from under the pressures that society
and other people bury them under—if they can "survive" the "battle"
of racial classification—they can "embody a different tomorrow."[96]
Her own solution, her own ability to "exit the tragedy" that is her racial mixture (in the eyes of others), has been to refuse to be obsessed
with race. She insists that her salvation—not from her racial mixture
but rather from what others think about her mixture—has been to
"become the director of the movie and not just the passive screen" of
others' "projections."[97]

Racial Adaptability: Danzy Senna's *Caucasia*

In Danzy Senna's *Caucasia*, Birdie Lee is assumed to be various races
that she feels she is not and is doubted when she tries to claim a race.
Like Harper's Nellie, Birdie is mistaken for a member of an observer's own group when she disappoints a man on a plane for not being
the fellow South Asian he was so pleased to have found (Senna, *Caucasia*, 323). When Birdie is living as a Jewish girl with her white mother, her neighbor and landlady thinks she looks "classic" and "Italian,"
while the landlady's son calls Birdie "Pocahontas [. . .]. Because [she]
turn[s] all brown in the sun. Like a little Indian" (165, 164). Birdie's white
grandmother values her for her whiteness even though Birdie objects
to being identified as such, but her blackness is not particularly evident

and thus is not readily accepted by observers. On the only occasion when she is alone with her black father without her older and darker sister, Cole, her difference—or lack of blackness—leads strangers to assume that she and her father do not belong to one another, that their being together is "incorrect," as Walker might say. Strangers at the public gardens get the police, who in turn never question the assumption that Deck, her father, ought not to be with Birdie: "All right, brotherman, [. . .] Who's the little girl?" (50). They refuse to believe that she is his daughter even after she tells them Deck is her father and subsequently ask her if he has molested her—the one circumstance they seem to consider might explain why the two are together. Their interrogation makes her feel her difference from her black father and the need to defend who she is: "I felt sick and a little dizzy. I wanted to spit in the cop's face. But my voice came out quiet, wimpier than I wanted it to. 'No, he didn't. He's my father' was all I could manage. I wondered what my sister would do. I figured she wouldn't be in this situation in the first place, and that fact somehow depressed me" (51). Though the episode in the public gardens is an extreme case, it is in no way an isolated one. When, on another occasion years later, Birdie has to explain that her father's sister is her aunt, the police are reluctant to believe her: "I hadn't seen that double-take since I had last been with my father—that look of skepticism mixed with embarrassment. The look had once been followed by 'Oh, she must be adopted'" (285). Birdie notes how, when she and Cole were children, "the eyes of strangers flickered surprise, sometimes amusement, sometimes disbelief, when [her] mother introduced [them] as sisters" (24).

Her parents do little to clarify Birdie's race since they argue over her identity and are themselves inconsistent in identifying her. When Birdie was young, Deck would "joke with his friends that Cole and [she] were going to be proof that race mixing produced superior minds," but when he leaves his wife he insists that she send their two daughters to an Afrocentric school (22). When Sandy claims that it "makes sense" for Cole, who is dark, but not for Birdie, since she "looks like a little Sicilian," Deck retorts, "Cut this naïve, color-blind posturing. In a country as racist as this, you're either black or you're white. And no daughter of mine is going to pass" (23). Yet whenever he has the girls Deck focuses only on Cole, trying to teach her about blackness and help her develop a racial consciousness, but ignores Birdie when she tries to participate and shows keen interest. His insistence, then, that his daughters are black in a black-and-white society is not put into practice in the way he raises his girls.

Furthermore, despite his rejection of passing, Deck takes Cole while Sandy takes Birdie when they leave Boston separately, with the understanding that Birdie will have to "pass" for white in order for Sandy to escape whatever danger she may be in. When Birdie finally finds her father again years later and tells him, "I passed as white, Papa," he replies, "There's no such thing as passing. We're all just pretending. Race is a complete illusion, make-believe. It's a costume. We all wear one. You just switched yours at some point. That's just the absurdity of the whole race game" (334). He argues that race is "not only a construct but a scientific error along the magnitude of the error that the world was flat," and that when the mistake is discovered "it'll be as big as when they learned the world was, in fact, round. It'll open up a whole new world. And nothing will ever be the same again" (334). He also explains his theory of the mulatto as the canary in the coal mine of American race relations and proposes that his daughter's generation is the first to survive, "a little injured, perhaps, but alive" (336). While she thinks he is right, she is outraged: "You left me. You left me with Mum, knowing she was going to disappear. Why did you only take Cole? Why didn't you take me? If race is so make-believe, why did I go with Mum? You gave me to Mum 'cause I looked white. You don't think that's real? Those are the facts" (336). Her father's perspective is one rooted in his academic pursuit of race theory and reflects his knowledge that black and white are both part of a social system and the reality of American race concepts. But Deck's perspective throughout the text also demonstrates his own shifting opinion from an early interest in multiracialism to a dedication to black power to an eventual interest in breaking down American race concepts and the practice of racial classification. He can offer Birdie no consistent concept of race nor help shape her own sense of racial identity in any way that is not continuously transitional. Her outrage even when she agrees with him reflects the fact that Birdie finds the shifting meaning of race frustrating and, more important, that changes in how her father or society thinks about race cannot undo the effects of a previous race concept. Her father spends whatever time he has with his daughters trying to educate them about race, but all he has taught Birdie is that race cannot be concrete and so cannot offer her the stable identity she struggles to find.

Birdie's mother is no different from her father. Sandy tells her, "It doesn't matter what your color is or what you're born into, you know? It matters who you choose to call your own" but seems to contradict her own opinion that race can be a choice when she insists that Birdie's appearance makes the Afrocentric school less suitable for her than for Cole (74). In the past, when Birdie was young, her mother insisted on homeschooling both girls to keep them "safe from the racism and violence of the world" (22). While she might have included Birdie simply because she was already homeschooling Cole, Sandy seemed to consider Birdie in the same racial terms as her sister. When Birdie explains her understanding of black power, she says, "All I knew of it was that my father agreed with it, my mother and her friends supported it," which suggests that to some degree at least, Sandy sees Birdie as black and wants her to identify as such (31). But Birdie also notices that after she and Sandy have been apart from Cole and Deck for a number of years, her mother behaves as though Cole were her "only black child" and Birdie her white one (233). Like Deck, Sandy seems to be inconsistent in what she teaches Birdie about race and her own identity. At times, Sandy's behavior reflects her own attachment to blackness and her sense that her choice to link herself to blackness is something that must be accepted as valid. She insists that her daughters be treated the same and have the same experiences as children but, like Deck, allows her children to be divided into the race binary when she and Deck part ways. When she is away from Cole and Deck, part of what Sandy mourns is her loss of blackness, and so Birdie learns that her mother does not see her in the same way that she sees Birdie's sister.

Like Deck, Sandy changes her views of race over time and in doing

so hampers Birdie's efforts to develop a consistent self-identity. While
Sandy supports Deck's early interest in black power on political grounds,
she grows to question it and consider it hypocritical (considering his
initial marriage to her and his willingness to leave his daughters to be
raised by their white mother). She insists that Birdie take on a Jewish
identity and deny her blackness to keep them safe, since she is convinced that the FBI will be searching for her as someone traveling with
a black daughter. However, her willingness to let Birdie identify as
white for so long without ever demonstrating concern about Birdie's
distance from black people and culture or Birdie's inability to publicly identify herself as black suggests that she does not consider Birdie's blackness as something essential to her daughter's sense of self or
overall well-being. Like Deck, Sandy has offered Birdie inconsistent
guidance regarding race and racial identity. Birdie is left not knowing if her mother really considers her white or still considers her black
but in hiding. Though Birdie knows she does not want to identify as
white, her life with her mother in New Hampshire only makes it more
difficult for her to determine how to develop her own racial identity.

Perhaps most indicative of Birdie's indeterminate racial identity
is the fact that she carries not the "black" name her father wanted
("Patrice, as in Lumumba") or the "white" name her mother wanted
("Jesse, after her great-grandmother, a white suffragette") but the race-
free name of Birdie—her sister "had wanted a parakeet for her birthday and instead got [her]" (17). Since Birdie is not even her legal name,
she is, in fact, nameless: "My birth certificate still reads, 'Baby Lee,' like
the gravestone of some stillborn child" (17). Yet it is "Birdie" that she
claims, along with the indefinite identity that comes with the name.

When she goes west in search of her sister, Birdie also goes in
search of her own racial identity. She is tired of having a white identity ascribed to her and of being seen as white, but her efforts to claim
blackness (at the Afrocentric school) have been no easier. With either
race, she has been at the mercy of other people's perceptions, and all
she really desires is the ability to define herself. Like Rebecca Walker and Raboteau's Emma, Birdie finds comfort in seeing herself in
others rather than having others judge her. In California, where she

goes to locate her father and sister, Cole asks Birdie to stay with her and attend Berkeley High, telling her, "If you ever thought you were the only one, get ready. We're a dime a dozen out here" (351). The fact that Cole points out their ordinariness in California emphasizes the importance of how racialized bodies are perceived. If Birdie is one of many, there will be less pressure to explain herself and fewer interrogations of her identity. Though Birdie has yet to articulate how she identifies herself, she finds solace in the fact that she is one of many. When she sees a school bus full of young people, Birdie is transfixed by a "cinnamon-skinned girl with her hair in braids": "She was black like me, a mixed girl" (353). Her assessment of the girl not only suggests that Birdie has yet to form the vocabulary to identify what she feels she is but also demonstrates that she is not anything that anyone else has called her. It is significant that the only time Birdie feels capable of recognizing herself is when she has stripped herself of any ascribed or imposed identities and distanced herself from both her parents' opinions about her racial identity. In a way, Birdie has inhabited black and white identities constructed for her, and by the novel's conclusion she has shrugged off both and seems prepared to begin her own process of identity formation relatively free of the demands of others.

However, Birdie does not simply find her racial group in multiracialness the way she could not in whiteness or blackness. Rather than recognizing her sameness in any particular color or racial ancestry, Birdie does so specifically within the terms "black like me . . . mixed." Having noticed throughout her life that she does not look like her sister, Birdie recognizes upon their reunion that she and Cole have also had different experiences of race. Having used her sister to validate her blackness (at their Afrocentric school) or her memory of Cole to maintain a connection to blackness (when she is "passing" for white), Birdie seems to realize that she is able to recognize her own blackness apart from Cole. Birdie realizes, "I had believed all along that Cole was all I needed to feel complete. Now I wondered if completion wasn't overrated" (347). "We were sisters," she says, "but we were as separate in our experiences as two sisters could be. I had to face this, if I could" (349–50). As Hershini Young notes, the end of *Caucasia* "highlights deep fracture lines that belie any myths of sameness," and, indeed, Birdie's recognition of her sameness among those who are not identical as a race but are similar in their ambiguity suggests that community and belonging occur within a context of shared heterogeneity rather than shared homogeneity.[98] In the novel, Birdie imagines herself at Berkeley High "with a medley of mulatto children, canaries who had in fact survived the coal mine, singed and asthmatic, but still alive." Then she thinks of Samantha and feels "a wave of sadness": "I wondered what would happen to her."[99] Samantha—the first person Birdie recognizes as "black like me" because of her mixture—is, significantly, the person Birdie talks to before she flees New Hampshire in search of Cole.[100] Though Samantha reminds her of Cole, the person Birdie has most wanted to be like throughout her life, Birdie also recognizes the differences in their situations. She remarks, "I didn't want to be black like Samantha. A doomed, tragic shade of black. I wanted to be black like somebody else" or, it seems, black like Samantha but *somewhere* else.[101] Birdie's ability to find some promise of comfort in Berkeley, where mixture is common and therefore identity options broader, reminds her that Samantha has no such freedom in how she identifies in New Hampshire. Ultimately, the novel suggests that social context is perhaps the most critical factor in racial identity formation.

Virtually all contemporary narratives of multiracialism, including those of Raboteau, Harper, Walker, and Senna, imagine or remember childhood experiences and include comparisons of location. These common characteristics emphasize how racial identity develops through a process of socialization and life experience, depends on place and time, and begins well before individuals are even capable of the critical thought necessary for personal reflection on identity. In American history those who opposed race mixing have claimed, "What about the children?" and those who enacted laws or other barriers to interracial relationships or offspring have appealed, "It's for the sake of the children." Such concerns suggest that these children will not belong or feel whole and will instead be damaged. They also suggest that the actual source of the "problem" of mixture resides in those vocalizing their displeasure rather than in multiracial children themselves. For well over a century, sociologists, psychologists, and public figures have written about multiracial individuals in a way that asserted that not fitting into ready racial categories was a "problem" for those individuals and for (rather than of) American society. In fact, academic and popular discourses occasionally pathologize multiracialism even now.[102] However, even if American society in general has moved beyond expressing concern over the fate of multiracial children, the same signals are conveyed in a troubled gaze, a well-meant query, or a mistaken assumption. The society that questions black-and-white identity is the society that makes multiracials feel their mixture and the "correctness" of "black" and "white" categories. It makes multiracialism something that has to be legitimized within or asserted against prevailing attitudes. While monoracial and one-drop understandings of race are certainly changing in American society, contemporary writing suggests that conventional understandings of race still influence the formation of racial identities to a huge degree. The efforts of contemporary writers to depict both multiracial experiences and multiracial identities demonstrate that while multiracial self-affirmation is being explored and built within texts, and social adaptation to contemporary race concepts is occurring, neither affirmation nor adaptation transpires in a vacuum. In fact, the two act in concert.

Together, Harper, Raboteau, Walker, and Senna identify the long-standing problem of racial classification within the context of contemporary notions of race mixing. As Kobena Mercer notes, the construction of a new racial identity is no easier than the construction of old racial identities was: "Identities are not found but *made*; . . . they are not just there, waiting to be discovered in the vocabulary of nature, but . . . have to be culturally and politically *constructed* through political antagonism and cultural struggle."[103] Multiracials must work within and without existing race concepts as they incorporate aspects of conventional race categories into or discard them from whatever identity or identities they choose. That multiracials can identify differently in different situations, change their identities over time, and claim more than one identity simultaneously reminds us that identity is something that is entirely socially dependent. Identity is at once po-litical and personal, always responding to a social context. But this is old news. What has changed is the social context in which American racial identities are being negotiated, and though there is unprece-dented freedom to self-identify in the United States today, that free-dom can never be unlimited—it can only be as free as society allows.

| Chapter Two

Wonders of the Invisible Race
Negotiating Whiteness

The negotiation of whiteness in contemporary narratives of black–white race mixture takes up two related historical and literary problems. First, whiteness has been normalized to such an extent that it is not racialized, and second, racial passing has been a matter of abandoning blackness and pretending to be white. The way that hypodescent has governed American race concepts has meant that blackness has been a marker of race, whiteness has lacked a marker, and blackness has been considered the totalized race of anyone with any black "blood." However, contemporary writers effectively racialize whiteness by positioning multiracial subjectivity as something that includes and challenges whiteness. Since multiracialness inherently resists monoracialism, the choice for multiracial figures is not the older literary one of accepting what they "really are" (black) or "passing" for what they "are not" (white) but rather one of how they will incorporate whiteness and blackness into a racial identity that may be highly individualized. In contemporary literature whiteness is not only made a legitimate part of identity but also portrayed as heterogeneous. Whiteness was a "trick," or inauthentic, in passing novels of the nineteenth and early twentieth centuries. However, contemporary literature reflects a changing perception of whiteness: it can include blackness. Or, rather, whiteness can still exist in the presence of blackness where it really

could not before. Ultimately, the representation of multiracialism requires this kind of revision of whiteness since, as Carol Roh Spaulding observes, "no matter how mixed one's ancestry, racial identity in
American literature is most influenced by a character's status in relation to how the narrative defines 'whiteness.'"[1]

This shift in the social thought and literary representation of race
is certainly not free of the issues that troubled the public and literary
discourses of past centuries. Questions of white supremacy and racial hierarchy, black racial solidarity and pride, and the longevity of
the one-drop rule continue to arise in contemporary literature and
current discussions of race concepts. The ostensible choice of claiming whiteness is still associated with appearance and social attitudes
about race—especially those views on the purity of whiteness. However, contemporary literature is newly articulating a multiracialness
that includes whiteness. Older works did not hide the white ancestry
of black characters—in fact, such ancestry was usually the basis for a
character's ability to "pass" for white—but the stranglehold of hypodescent and the political need for racial solidarity still positioned racial identity as a choice: one was either black or "passing" for white. In
passing novels, characters never had the opportunity to claim a non-
monoracial identity (that is, a "multiracial" identity) or a racial identity
of two monoraces (that is, both black *and* white). Today, hypodescent
is not necessarily the requisite method of classification and black racial solidarity is articulated differently: one can identify politically
with their "minority" race and also racially as both black and white.

These changes, both social and political, have shifted simultaneously with literary representations of black–white multiracialism. This
transition is a result of the racial, gender, and sexual liberation of the
latter half of the twentieth century, which fostered appreciation for
self-identification and challenged the boundaries of normalized identities. Articulating multiracialness has meant racializing and diversifying whiteness in much the same way that blackness has been treated in
American racial-classification schemes. In redefining whiteness, contemporary multiracial literature imagines black–white race mixture
in a way that it has not been imagined before. The interest in passing

and tragic mulatto/a figures, which arose during and after slavery and preceded civil rights, had waned by the mid-twentieth century. For new generations that were born after civil rights and into some of the first legally sanctioned interracial families in the United States, multiracial identity is possible in unprecedented ways. Accordingly, multiracialism offers uncharted literary territory. In the texts examined here, whiteness is revealed to be as diverse and racialized as blackness and thus just as accessible to multiracial figures. As these texts demonstrate, whiteness can exist alongside blackness rather than being absorbed into it according to the one-drop rule.

Contemporary scholarship in various disciplines examines how whiteness developed historically as an unracialized race in the United States. As Toni Morrison argues in *Playing in the Dark*, whiteness is assumed to be "'universal' or race-free."[2] She observes that whiteness is so normative in the United States that it is taken for granted and considered the generic standard against which everything else is racialized. Whiteness has been specifically formulated, since its nationalist and nativist inception, to lack markers of race, culture, and ethnicity; the absence of anything that identifies whiteness means that anyone who exhibits anything nonnormative is a race, is nonwhite, is something "other." "Ethnic food" (including "white-ethnic" food) could not be labeled as such in the United States, for instance, if it were not defined against the white American nonethnic nonrace. In a conception of whiteness as the normative "us" against the nonnormative "them," American whiteness is understood to be invisible. Part of the success of this kind of generic whiteness is the fact that it is taken for granted as such. As Abby Ferber argues, "We are not used to thinking about whiteness when we think about race. Books and courses on race usually focus on the experience of racial minority groups, the victims of racism."[3]

Even when "hybridity" is recognized, whiteness generally remains intact and dominant as differences are assessed. In his work on multiculturalism, for instance, Homi Bhabha articulates this method of white dominance in recognizing hybridity. In "The Third Space," he explains that even an "endorsement of cultural diversity" corresponds to an effort to "contain" that diversity. Bhabha states, "A transparent norm is constituted, a norm given by the host society or dominant culture, which says that 'these other cultures are fine, but we must be able to locate them within our own grid.' This is what I mean by a *creation* of cultural diversity and a *containment* of cultural difference."[4] Though he is discussing "multiculturalism" more broadly, Bhabha's comments support this discussion's contextualization of whiteness as a form of dominance that seeks to keep itself out of the mix. Whiteness can observe and even appreciate other races (or cultures, as Bhabha states) but it seeks to define others, viewing them within a normative white framework and protecting whiteness from the "multi" of the multicultural or multiracial. It is its dominance in American culture and its conception as somehow race neutral that insulates whiteness from incorporation into multiracialism. Whiteness stands on its own but is overwritten when combined with nonwhiteness.

Even the discipline of white studies is, ironically, not free of the problem of deracializing whiteness. The description on the back cover of Mike Hill's *After Whiteness: Unmaking an American Majority* states, "As each new census bears out, the rise of multiracialism in the United States will inevitably result in a white minority." The use of the census as proof that multiracialism is on the rise and whiteness is on the decline suggests an uncritical acceptance of what, who, and how the census counts, and gestures toward the ways in which notions of whiteness (and nonwhiteness) are made official and institutionalized. This statement is problematic, however, because it seems to accept the lingering attitude that whiteness is pure and, consequently, that increased multiracialism means whiteness is disappearing. If mixture is synonymous with the end of whiteness, multiracialism is failing to change the way we think about race.[5] The strength of conventional white American race concepts is remarkable, as Habiba Ibrahim's otherwise sound analysis of Danzy Senna's *Caucasia* illustrates. In "Canary in a Coal Mine," Ibrahim comments that darker-skinned sister Cole is "unlike the racially unfettered" Birdie, who is herself "black but white-appearing."[6] Since the novel itself explores whiteness as a racialized identity as much as if not more than it does blackness,

Ibrahim's comments miss the position offered by the text. Rather, her comments suggest her own underlying assumptions that Birdie is "really" black (which reinforces the one-drop rule) and that by looking white Birdie is lacking race. Ibrahim also then accounts for blackness specifically and analyzes the meeting point of only blackness and "biracialism"; whiteness is, yet again, absent in a discussion of race.[7] Similarly, Michele Elam argues that multiracial identity poses no challenge to monoracial categories (which she assumes are traditionally understood to be homogeneous) because "racial homogeneity . . . [has] never existed"; however, her evidence rests upon her assertion that Latinx and African American populations are "mixed."[8] Like Ibrahim, Elam ignores whiteness as somehow extraneous (rather than essential) to multiracialism. In fact, both critics seem to be overlooking whiteness rather than consciously excluding it; if this is the case, it is certainly strong evidence of the way whiteness has been taken for granted as unracialized in American culture.

The goal of white studies in recent years has been to notice the whiteness that has gone unnoticed for so long to racialize that which has done the racializing yet avoided being racialized itself—and it is a call that contemporary multiracial literature has answered.

The Development of American Whiteness and the Role of Critical White Studies

Because blackness and whiteness have been conceived of in terms of opposition, it is not surprising that the diverse and ever-changing white race has developed as monolithic and exclusionary. The economic interests and racism that helped define blackness and mixedness throughout American history were similarly at play in the development of whiteness. As Valerie Babb notes in *Whiteness Visible: The Meaning of Whiteness in American Literature and Culture*, the first European colonists characterized themselves in terms of nation, religion, and status initially, but *"English, Christian, and free"* would eventually serve as the foundation for whiteness in what would become the United States.[9] Throughout the history of the European presence in North America, religion, class, and nationality would shape how society organized itself along racial lines. And so, as Matthew Jacobson outlines in *Whiteness of a Different Color: European Immigrants and the Alchemy of Race*, "the eighteenth century's free white persons became the nineteenth century's Celts, Slavs, Hebrews, Iberics, Latins, and Anglo-Saxons, who in turn became the twentieth century's Caucasians, as popular recognition of consanguinity of racial difference fluctuated in response to national, regional, and local circumstances."[10]

Though the white racism that would characterize the founding and history of the United States was taken to the "New World," it took a great deal of time to develop in what would become the trans-Atlantic colonial powers. Well before Europeans left Europe to occupy the Americas, differentiations were primarily considered according to geography and culture; groups that we would now identify as white were once considered separate races.[11] Babb notes that even in chronicles of early European exploration, such as those from England, Norway, Spain, and Portugal, "the absence of a privileged white norm is evident" at least for a short while.[12] As David Roediger states in *Towards the Abolition of Whiteness*, Norwegians "did not spend a great deal of time and energy in Norway thinking of themselves as white."[13] Perhaps not surprisingly, when whiteness was noticed in Europe it was as a result of immigration. Roediger points out, for instance, that in British cities with large numbers of migrants, natives sought to develop a sense of their own whiteness and did so largely in contrast to blacks.[14] But overwhelmingly, racial difference was neither a matter of color nor acknowledged as whiteness and nonwhiteness early on. Racism existed in Europe but not within the same framework that the formation of whiteness would provide in the United States. According to Roediger, English anti-Irish oppression was "racism rather than ethnic prejudice" and Italian anti-Sicilian, European anti-Gypsy, and European anti-Semitic oppression "involved a kind of race-thinking" according to some researchers.[15] If, as many scholars of whiteness propose, we consider whiteness not in terms of color but as a way of thinking and seeing and as an embodiment of power and privilege, then the racism between what we might now term European ethnic groups "deserves consideration in accounting for the development of a sense of [racial] whiteness among immigrants to the US."[16] Indeed, "according to nineteenth-century popular wisdom and anthropological science, the Irish were Celts, a particular race separate from and inferior to the Anglo-Saxon English" in the early United States as they were in Britain.[17]

European—or, more specifically, British—attitudes toward racial or ethnic groups certainly shaped attitudes in what would become the United States. Differences between British stock and other European immigrants were noticed both in terms of what we might now call ethnicity (for instance, language and culture) and what we might now call race (for instance, "complexion" and other physical attributes). For example, in 1751 Benjamin Franklin objected to the influence of "aliens" and the cultural and racial threat they posed to Anglo Americans, though legislators at the time paid less attention to differences of whiteness because of the all-consuming problem of slavery and the differences between whiteness and blackness.[18] The competing goals evident in Franklin's scenario—of asserting Anglo-Saxon whiteness as the only true whiteness and promoting a broader concept of whiteness in opposition to exploited nonwhites—epitomize how whiteness was cultivated in America. Ultimately, whiteness in the United States developed out of the dual efforts to justify white supremacy and to define and build a nation and its people accordingly.

English racism was alive and well in North America as the descendants of the colonists strove to assert their Americanness. American nationalism was connected to race and class, since the descendants of the English differentiated between themselves (Protestant, white, wealthy) and newer immigrants whom they forced into "dirty" jobs and neighborhoods in a way that maintained racial differences along caste lines. Although the Irish would serve as a prominent target for racism along with immigrants from European and Asian countries and Jews of any nationality, the English first denigrated indigenous and Mexican peoples.[19] Charters established among the colonies in the early decades of the seventeenth century juxtaposed the "barbarous" and "savage" inhabitants of the New World to the "pious" English in much the same way that the Declaration of Independence would in

1776.[20] As Jacobson points out, though "colonial documents do not use the word 'white'," between "the charters of the early seventeenth century and the naturalization law of the late eighteenth, the word 'white' did attain wide usage in New World political discourse and it was written into an immense body of statutory law," as well as into the Articles of Confederation (though not the Constitution).[21] The naturalization law of 1790 did employ the word "white" and limited citizenship to "free white persons"[22]—a restriction that was kept in place "for over a century and a half, remaining in force until 1952."[23] At the time of the law's passage, Congress debated "whether Jews and Catholics should be eligible" and considered the law "too inclusive rather than too exclusive, and nowhere did [legislators] pause to question the limitation of naturalized citizenship to 'white persons.'"[24] The early conception of "universal suffrage" after passage of this law and until the mid-1850s was in fact an appeal for "adult white male" suffrage; the "abolition of economic barriers to voting by white men" meant that the "first enlargement of American whiteness" was to poor white men, who "could be welcomed into the definition of American, as long as they could be defined as white."[25] The requirement of whiteness (and maleness) for citizenship and the intertwining of origin, class, whiteness, and religion inscribed the developing caste system and "Americanness" with a particular conception of (privileged) whiteness. Indeed, as Ruth Frankenberg argues, whiteness still "has a habit . . . of sliding into class and nationality all the time."[26]

Social historians point out that those who work together and have class in common tend to relate to one another and potentially unite in their shared goals through social struggle. But while there was some kinship between blacks and other poor workers in the United States, this bond was tentative and short-lived. White ethnics tended to see their similarity to blacks in the social hierarchy and in their consequent living and working conditions as something to avoid; for many "not-yet-white" and "not-quite-white" groups, reaching for whiteness held great appeal.[27] Despite social recognition of a black–Irish "parallel," the Irish, in particular, "stoutly supported the proslavery Democratic Party,"[28] staunchly opposed fighting for the emancipation of black slaves during the Civil War, and violently attacked African Americans during the draft riots in New York during the war.[29] While white ethnic groups suffered oppression that has been likened to that of black Americans, they sought to distance themselves from rather than unite with blacks and thus grope their way out of the social hierarchy that placed them only remotely above blacks.[30] In fact, by the end of the nineteenth century American whites were ranked and "degenerate families" of poor—though racially Anglo-Saxon—whites were at the bottom of the white hierarchy (close to nonwhites) because of their poverty and consequent social inferiority.[31] "Not-yet-white" groups strategically adapted the stereotypes white Americans used to identify them by deflecting these stereotypes onto blacks.[32] Part of becoming white in America, then, was learning and employing anti-black racism in order to join the ranks of those who would oppress poor and/or "ethnic" whites in a homogenizing white solidarity.

Roediger argues that "the very claiming of a place in the US legally involved . . . a claiming of whiteness," and so virtually all Europeans joined the descendants of the English colonists in claiming their American whiteness by the twentieth century.[33] Whiteness was equated with nationality in order to turn arguments over immigration from the question of who was foreign to the question of who was white. During the labor unrest of the early twentieth century, ties to the white American nation formed the common ground on which to divvy up jobs and other resources and displaced the anti-immigrant argument that had pitted foreignness against nativeness. The shift to whiteness hurt the "native" black population as much as it benefited European immigrants, of course. As Roediger observes, nativists had frequently and favorably "compared the long-established Black population with the newcoming immigrant one as an argument to curtail the rights of the latter. Abolitionists made the same comparison to buttress the case for African American freedom. Blacks at times used their long-established tenure in America to argue that they should be protected against 'invading' Italians or Chinese or at least placed on a par with the immigrants."[34] For instance, Booker T. Washington famously advocated employing African Americans over new immigrants in his

Atlanta Exposition speech of 1895. Furthermore, Washington's efforts to train the black population in trades at his Tuskegee Institute draw attention to the way that a significant portion of black Americans were less a threat to wealthy ruling whites than they were to ethnic and poor whites struggling to prosper. And just as powerful wealthy whites sought the racial loyalty of poor whites during and after the Civil War in order to maintain white supremacy and guard against black empowerment, poor immigrant whites sought to exploit their place in the American system of white racial protection and advantage in subsequent decades.

With the rise of whiteness as the chief characteristic of American-ness, "nativeness" evaporated as a route for the advancement of the black population. The shift from racial groups ("German in America" or "Polish in America") to white ethnic groups ("German-American" or "Polish-American") reveals how whiteness became both universal and American. Instead of being German or Polish immigrants, white ethnics sought to assimilate into the national category of American; yet instead of being German or Polish racially, they sought assimilation into whiteness. And, as Roediger explains, "In the Irish case this seeking of whiteness involved constructing a pan-white identity in which Irish Americans struggled to join even the *English* in the same racial category. In Ireland, it goes without saying, there was little talk of the common whiteness uniting Anglo-Saxon and Celtic peoples."[35] Jacobson maps the "ascent of monolithic whiteness" through the eugenics and immigration policies of the end of the nineteenth century and beginning of the twentieth century, and argues that homogeneous whiteness was solidified in the twentieth century through the "authority of modern science" and its "Caucasian" label.[36] This new racial alliance meant that "the new-coming Irish would help lead the movement to bar the relatively established Chinese from California, with their agitation for a 'white man's government' serving to make race, and not nativity, the centre of the debate" after the Civil War.[37] It also meant that, sixty years later, the "despised newcoming internal migrants, the 'Okies,' would similarly seek to establish their claims as more fit to be Californian than long-established Californians by turning to questions of race" and wrongly arguing that Chinese and Japanese people had less to do with the founding of the state than they, non-Californians but white Americans, had.[38]

The rise of whiteness as the defining characteristic of Americanness dissolved the previously recognized racial differences of newly white immigrants and their descendants into a homogeneous race despite heterogeneous ethnicities. But this tradition of racial practice, and the practice of nationalism in particular, has also transformed the way white Americans form their racial identities. Put simply, one's white-Americanness is one's defining identity, and any ethnic heritage that might tie a person to another country (or formerly, another race) is diminished in the face of homogeneous American whiteness. Charles Gallagher argues in "White Racial Formation" that a unifying white racial identity has taken the place of formerly observed ethnic differences. In fact, Gallagher states that "ethnic identity has all but vanished" in the contemporary era and "after generations of assimilation, only whiteness is left as an identity with any real social or political import. The decline of ethnicity among later-generation whites has created an identity vacuum, one that has been at least partially replaced by an identity grounded in race."[39]

Like many other scholars, Gallagher claims that it is the loss of ethnic identity and consequent identity politics that "has made whiteness a visible racial identity."[40] While some scholars do not trace the visibility of whiteness to a loss of ethnicity as Gallagher does, many do discuss how the politics of the last decades of the twentieth century have made whiteness (along with maleness and heterosexuality) a marked (and thus noticed and addressed) category. Sociologists Stephen Cornell and Douglas Hartmann argue in *Ethnicity and Race: Making Identities in a Changing World* that ethnic difference is recognized as much less of a distinction than it once was. Cornell and Hartmann suggest that the colloquial understanding of white ethnic groups is primarily a matter of recognizing ancestral origin "as what sets [ethnicities] mostly clearly apart and accounts for whatever distinctive cultural characteristics remain."[41] In other words, difference depends only on the lingering cultural influence of immigrant family members or the knowledge of distant immigrant ancestors and is no longer a defining characteristic of identity the way race is now. In the twentieth century, then, ethnic difference (or heterogeneity within whiteness) diminished in favor of a homogeneous white American race. Differences within whiteness dissolved in the face of a unifying white racial identity that was constituted in opposition to the black race. Many academics argue that the observation of white ethnicity is now frequently a symptom of white supremacy, which manifests in a reaction against affirmative action and other equalizing measures that some whites see as having become discriminatory against whites. Some also argue that this new interest in white ethnicity is a symptom of white guilt, which manifests when whites "selectively resurrect ethnic family history to create a rather ahistorical record that equate[s] the experiences of their ancestors with the experiences of blacks."[42] Overall, scholarship suggests that these and other scenarios exhibit an attempt on the part of some whites to downplay the continuing effects of white supremacy and racism through angst or defensiveness.

This contemporary reclaiming of white heterogeneity emphasizes the way American whiteness has historically developed through a homogenizing process that absorbed multiple racialized peoples into one category. For instance, Babb maps the creation of a white race through claims, at different periods, of Teutonic, Anglo-Saxon, and Nordic origins, which satisfied "a desire for racial history and antecedents, even if this imagined past was in direct conflict with the multiple ethnicities, languages, physical appearances, cultures, and class statuses that formed the actuality of American existence."[43] While this process of homogenization similarly grouped other diverse peoples into American races—such as black, indigenous, and, in the late twentieth century, Asian, Hispanic, and Arab—it effectively managed to disguise whiteness as a race because whiteness was the norm by which "others" were racialized. As Margaret Andersen explains, "Whiteness is an unmarked category against which difference is constructed. Hence to be white is to be not-black and blackness is created out of the vantage point of white identity."[44] Linda Schlossberg discusses this concept of how whiteness has been considered "unmarked" whereas black-ness and other races are "marked" in comparison.[45] Schlossberg argues that to be unmarked

> is to occupy a position of privilege, in which the subject hides behind an apparent transparency. White individuals, for instance, are in a constant state of passing as having no ethnic or racial identity at all, as having "nothing to say" about race, or as somehow existing outside the volatile world of "racial tensions." Indeed, white racial identity seeks to make itself visible only when (as in the case of White Aryan Resistance or the KKK) it perceives itself as being under siege financially (from Jews) or sexually (from blacks), or when the ability of people of African American racial heritage to pass as Caucasian calls a white person's own seemingly unblemished whiteness into question.[46]

American whiteness is so dependent upon its generic characteristics for its definition that those who speak a language other than English or practice a faith other than Christianity are frequently made non-white (and, in a conflation of whiteness and Americanness, such non-whites are simultaneously deemed not-American).[47] As Babb argues, "The devices employed in creating white hegemony are for the most part devices of exclusion. They articulate not necessarily who or what is white but rather who or what is not white. As such, they reveal the fundamental paradox of whiteness: the persistent need of nonwhite-ness to give it form and expression."[48] It is this exclusion, this measure of whiteness against nonwhiteness, and in particular this lack of acknowledgment of whiteness as a self-sustaining and independently defined race, that has shaped concepts of whiteness as a generic race in the United States. Furthermore, as Frankenberg points out in "Mirage of an Unmarked Whiteness," the "invisibility" of whiteness is a rather suspicious assumption: "The more one scrutinizes it . . . the more the notion of whiteness as unmarked norm is revealed to be a mirage or indeed, to put it even more strongly, a white delusion. The next interesting question is, then, what is the nature, the character, and the origin of this delusion, and when and how does its opposite, the marking of whiteness come about?"[49]

Indeed, the assumptions about whiteness that she argues have characterized the perception of whiteness even in academia are those that Frankenberg and others have begun to examine closely. White studies researchers and literary critics have argued in recent years that the acceptance of whiteness as invisible must change and that a critical eye must be cast upon whiteness. As Frankenberg herself points out, an acceptance of whiteness as a silent, generic category effectively reinforces white hegemony: "The phrase 'the invisibility of whiteness' refers in part to moments when whiteness does not speak its own name. At those times . . . whiteness may simply assume its own normativity. It may also refer to those times when neutrality or normativity is claimed for some kinds of whiteness."[50] Consequently, she argues, "naming 'whiteness' displaces it from the unmarked, unnamed status that is itself an effect of its dominance."[51] Or, as Coco Fusco says, not challenging the "construction" of whiteness and its normative power "redouble[s] its hegemony by naturalizing it."[52] Critical white studies scholars continually assert the necessity of scrutinizing whiteness in order to better recognize how race and racism operate, as well as help raise awareness about and combat white racism and racial inequality. Many academics, like Ferber and Schlossberg, point out how both race and racism have traditionally been relegated to nonwhites as their territory and problem; these commentators stress the absolutely critical need for race and racism to be located as a "white problem." Ashley Doane points out in "Rethinking Whiteness Studies" that "a growing body of research suggests that whiteness is a 'hidden identity'; that is, that it does not generally intrude upon the everyday experiences of most whites."[53] So, commentators argue, unless white people see themselves as racialized and engage with the functioning of race and racism in the United States as something as relevant to them as to black people, American racial discourse cannot really change. And, as scholars increasingly claim, unless this recognition and discussion of whiteness goes beyond observation to deal with racism and engage in antiracist strategies, it will acknowledge white privilege without critically analyzing it. Racial injustice will remain unchallenged and unaltered as a result, and both mainstream

American discourse and the attention of whites will isolate and return to whiteness itself.

In the past, the normative quality of whiteness has been perpetuated by the prolonged literary conception of whiteness as pure and generic. More recently, literature and literary criticism has begun adopting a critical approach to whiteness.[54] Like whiteness scholars and Morrison, who argues for the necessity of making the "unconsciousness" of whiteness conscious, Babb argues for the necessity of considering cultural production with an awareness of white normativity.[55] Babb states that racialized others have been viewed through the lens of whiteness and that whiteness itself must be considered in similarly racial terms:

> Rarely do we consider that notions thought to have no racial content often do. It can be argued that Innocence, Freedom, and Individualism, concepts frequently used to characterize American culture and commonly deemed universal, are racialized through implicit exclusion. When cultural representations of American Innocence are predominantly figured through Huckleberry Finn or Shirley Temple, they come to embody a race as much as an idea. Similarly, when Freedom and Individuality are personified through Annie Oakley, John Wayne, or Ronald Reagan (as both actor and president), they too become associated with a particular racial group. When such characterizations are consistently repeated over long periods of time, as they have been in the United States, notions having no specific racial content become racialized. This process weds the racial to the universal, allowing the latter to disguise the former.[56]

However, the "invisibility" of whiteness and the accompanying assumption that whiteness is a generic nonrace are being pointedly challenged in twenty-first-century multiracial literature.

Contemporary writers—at least those who write about multiracialism—are beginning to do just what Babb, Morrison, and others argue is necessary. While whiteness has been taken for granted traditionally, narratives of multiracialism now call into question conventional concepts of whiteness. Though earlier novels, particularly of passing, also posed a challenge to accepted notions of whiteness, the critiques within these texts were necessarily limited by the historical moment in which they were published.[57] Earlier texts had to combat slavery, segregation, and other severe and conspicuous impediments to racial equality, whereas contemporary writing reflects a much different set of concerns regarding race and racial identity. In addition to the monumental human rights gains of the 1960s, the shift in social thought and political action since the 1970s has allowed a generation to renegotiate identity or, in fact, negotiate it for the first time. Though blackness is certainly still often claimed as a monoracial identity, there is now the opportunity to claim whiteness and blackness (and any other ethnoracial group) simultaneously. Although the one-drop rule is alive and well in contemporary American civilization, and it certainly dictates how some recognize race in themselves or in others, it seems to be taken for granted less often without the legal enforcement and denial of civil rights that went with it in generations past. And while the loosening grip of the one-drop rule on racial practice affects monoracial black identity, it simultaneously affects concepts of whiteness. Whiteness is no longer in binary opposition to blackness, and the terms of whiteness itself are being challenged and transformed in contemporary culture. Consequently, whiteness becomes as racialized as blackness in multiracial narratives as figures explore the possibilities of this new era of self-definition and multiracial identity.

A Kind of White: Danzy Senna's *Caucasia*

While texts like Rachel Harper's *Brass Ankle Blues* and Emily Raboteau's *The Professor's Daughter* do not conspicuously racialize whiteness beyond disregarding hypodescent, or diversify whiteness beyond making it co-exist with blackness, Danzy Senna's *Caucasia* makes it apparent how acknowledged black–white mixture does both of these things.

Throughout the novel, the protagonist struggles to locate herself within blackness and mixedness and repeatedly identifies a feeling of invisibility or disappearance when she bears no markers of blackness either on her body or in her company. As a child, Birdie is intrigued at the possibilities of not being seen when she witnesses an argument through a crack in a door: "I . . . felt a thrill of anonymity, invisibility, all of a sudden."[58] The possibilities of being anonymous and invisible are new and broad. Though her "invisibility" is due to literally not being seen because she is hidden, it foreshadows her experiences throughout the novel as she battles invisibility that is racially inscribed. Her initial thrill as a young child is short-lived and as she gets older she begins to doubt the genuine benefit of invisibility because of what one loses—a doubt that will grow when she does "pass" for nonblack only a few years later.

As children, Birdie and her sister develop their own language centered around an imaginary world called Elemeno, and it forces Birdie to consider the drawbacks rather than the benefits of anonymity:

> The Elemenos, [Cole] said, could turn not just from black to white, but from brown to yellow to purple to green, and back again. She said they were a shifting people, constantly changing their form, color, pattern, in a quest for invisibility. According to her, their changing routine was a serious matter—less a game of make-believe than a fight for the survival of their species. The Elemenos could turn deep green in the bushes, beige in the sand, or blank white in the snow, and their power lay precisely in their ability to disappear into any surrounding. As she spoke, a new question—a doubt—flashed through my mind. Something didn't make sense. What was the point of surviving if you had to disappear?[59]

The chameleon-like Elemenos' ability to blend into any surroundings (or go *blank* white) and thus disappear bothers Birdie because she senses that, as someone who wants to associate herself with blackness but finds doing so difficult because she looks so much more white than black, she does not want to be overlooked or unrecognized. Moreover, she does not want her identity to become illegitimate for the very reason that it is fluid and malleable; that is, she does not want her mixedness to become invisible (in monoracial identity) just because it can and so readily has in the social world. As Michele Hunter argues in "Revisiting the Third Space," Birdie "challenges the notion that people of mixed heritage must retreat into the familiar terrains of invisibility.

Instead, she intimates that 'the Elemenos' have a place of their own."[60] While Birdie does not, in fact, consider that Elemenos "have a place of their own" in that their "place" is claimed only by disappearing into camouflage rather than asserting some kind of identity of their own, her discomfort with the Elemenos' strategies suggests that, for her at least, invisibility is not a viable response to racial ambiguity.

Birdie's invisibility is not simply the result of her mixedness going unperceived, though. Having her whiteness perceived alerts Birdie to the way her whiteness erases her difference from it (that is, erases her blackness). Initially, her whiteness appears to be, in the tradition of passing narratives, a generic identity that offers her the anonymity she does not have when she is recognized as black or multiracial. In a very real sense, her whiteness overwrites her blackness and can therefore be viewed as a lack of race (a lack of blackness or some "race"); however, the fact that her whiteness carries with it hypervisibility in many situations helps bring attention to it as a race. While her whiteness is often identified in opposition to blackness (and so whiteness racializes the blackness as different), such as when her father is harassed by the police for being with what onlookers see as a white girl or when a school secretary insists that Birdie and Cole be bussed to different schools according to integration policies, her whiteness is also racialized under the gaze of those usually being racialized by normative whiteness. At Nkrumah Academy, the Afrocentric school Birdie and Cole attend when their parents separate, a boy throws a spitball at Birdie and hisses, "What you doin' in this school? You white?"[61] All of the children stare, awaiting an answer, but Birdie has no response: "I tried to think of something to say."[62] Under the gaze of an entire class of monoracially identified black children, in a space where black is the norm, Birdie's whiteness becomes a starkly racialized difference. Just as blackness has historically been identified through its exclusion from whiteness, Birdie is excluded from blackness. She requires Cole to persuade her classmates that she has any claim to blackness, and without her sister she has no method of convincing them. Through the act of exclusion, Birdie's "white skin pushes her out of black communal acceptance and into a (white) space where Cole is not," and thus Birdie is made "other" to blackness.[63]

Birdie's father similarly excludes Birdie from blackness when he discards his interracial family and former interest in mixedness in favor of the newly popular black power ideology. He dedicates himself to educating his black-looking daughter, Cole, in racial awareness, but ignores Birdie. As she is throughout her story, Birdie is acutely aware of how she is being marginalized from blackness, and thus made to feel her whiteness. Birdie tries to flaunt her cultural blackness for her father, parroting his lectures back to him and answering his questions when Cole is unresponsive, but he does not take her seriously. Instead, he "flashed me a fierce look of bewilderment, then burst into laughter as he ruffled my hair, as if he had just discovered I could talk when he pulled the string on the back of my neck."[64] The fact that he has trained Cole (and consequently, the eager-to-prove-herself Birdie) to see white-black interracial couples as "diluting the race" (as Birdie puts it) makes it all the more clear that Birdie's white appearance matters considerably, especially in comparison to her sister's convincingly black appearance.

While Birdie's nonblack appearance results in Deck's unthinking neglect, it fosters his new black girlfriend's pointed animosity. Carmen is especially chilly toward Birdie specifically because she is not black enough. Around others, Carmen teases that Birdie is "Cole's little sister, even if she doesn't look like a sister" but "when we were alone, I sometimes I thought I saw her looking at me with muted disgust."[65] Birdie knows that her family members "had all been going through our separate changes for a while" and "moving in different directions" but she states, "Carmen was the icing on the cake, so to speak. Others before had made me see the differences between my sister and myself—the textures of our hair, the tints of our skin, the shapes of our features. But Carmen was the only one to make me feel that those things somehow mattered. To make me feel that the differences were deeper than skin."[66] Carmen's ostracism of Birdie is so intense that, despite Cole's attempts to compensate, even the normally oblivious Deck notices. Birdie is made to feel her whiteness and so stays away when Cole visits their father and his girlfriend. Birdie's exclusion is made even greater when Cole returns full of admiration for

Carmen: "As she spoke, I saw the new life in my sister's face, as if she had found some reflection of herself in this tall, cool woman. I felt heavy with grief."[67] Birdie mourns because she knows Cole has embarked on an exploration of her blackness that Birdie has been taught cannot include her because of her whiteness. Although she attempts to participate in the cultural blackness of her father's teaching and what she and Cole glean from *Ebony* about black dialect and fashion, the fact that Cole's interest in Carmen stems from their own mother's inability to deal with her hair and Carmen's knowledge about black beauty secrets alerts Birdie to those qualities of blackness that she can never achieve no matter how much Cole vouches for her. The fact that Cole finds a "reflection of herself" in Carmen but not in Birdie and that Deck apparently sees himself represented in Cole but not Birdie reinforces Birdie's growing awareness of her own distance from blackness and, consequently, proximity to whiteness.

If being around black people is largely what racializes Birdie's whiteness, then it follows that when she and her mother "disappear" into white America, Birdie's whiteness disappears too.

Sika Alaine Dagbovie argues in "Fading to White, Fading Away" that "Birdie's body becomes erased under the white gaze when she passes for white."[68] It is only among whites that she can become unraced because whites take their whiteness for granted—especially in New Hampshire where, at least in Senna's novel, there are very few nonwhites against whom to notice whiteness. (There are only two visibly black or mixed students in the town's high school, in fact, and their racial difference is extraordinarily visible and readily acknowledged among observers.) As Dagbovie also notes, "Because Birdie self-identifies as a black person, or at least as one more black than white, her racial passing feels to her like a vanishing."[69] Certainly Birdie describes her entrance into the white mainstream with a white-only identity in the language of loss:

A long time ago I disappeared. One day I was here, the next I was gone. It happened as quickly as all that. One day I was playing schoolgirl games with my sister and our friends in a Roxbury playground.

The next I was nobody, just a body without a name or a history, sitting beside my mother in the front seat of our car, moving forward on the highway, not stopping. (And when I stopped being nobody, I would become white—white as my skin, hair, bones allowed. My body would fill in the blanks, tell me who I should become, and I would let it speak for me.)[70]

The fact that Birdie is with her sister and their (black) friends playing in a black neighborhood and in the next instant is a "nobody" suggests that Birdie is "somebody" when she is in the midst of black community. Birdie's "disappearance" requires her to banish her blackness, but whiteness offers no substitute. Instead of actively taking on a white identity at first, Birdie simply allows others to perceive her as white by letting her body "speak for me." Her body, capable of being racialized in multiple ways, is a blank passport in the racial landscape of the United States. She "disappear[s] into America, the easiest place to get lost."[71] She does not want to deny her blackness but has to stop actively using it to identify herself since "the FBI would be looking for a white woman on the lam with her black child."[72] Her metaphoric "disappearance" is specifically a result of a white monoracial identity since she and her mother are unnoticeable as white but would be noticeable as nonwhite. In other words, she becomes racially unmarked as white and is absorbed into the unracialized norm where only nonwhiteness is made visible.

The passivity that accompanies her whiteness suggests that while Birdie has an identity and the agency to formulate it when she is able to articulate her blackness and mixedness, outside of that context and specifically within the context of white America, Birdie loses that agency. Once an identity is imposed on her, through the anonymity of whiteness among whites who take her race for granted and through her mother's control over her new identity, Birdie begins to feel inauthentic and, in the tradition of passing novels, feels as though she is constantly performing an identity she feels she does not actually embody. The fact that her whiteness does not feel sufficient to Birdie (since she never stops mourning her blackness once she "disappears") and that whiteness is recognized (and thus marked on her body) by others when she has spent her life resisting being seen as white draws attention to the way whiteness is being racialized. Whiteness is not universal nothingness to Birdie—it is a highly racialized identity that she struggles with in one way or another throughout her life.

Caucasia draws further attention to how whiteness is racialized through Birdie's gaze. Trained through her life experience to be hyperaware of whiteness, Birdie notices the whiteness of others and how that whiteness is racially and ethnically encoded. One of the early instances of how Birdie recognizes whiteness occurs when she and her sister and mother visit her grandmother. Sandy has, throughout her adult life, recognized the privilege and abusiveness of her wealthy WASP family, which traces its lineage proudly to Cotton Mather.[73] She has also recognized the plight of the poor and racial minorities and worked as a community and political activist for the rights and needs of the disadvantaged and disenfranchised. Her marriage to a black man and refusal to be a part her mother's life reflects her philosophy: "It doesn't matter what your color is or what you're born into. . . . It matters who you choose to call your own" (Senna, *Caucasia*, 74). Sandy believes that her politics can separate her from the racial identity that her mother calls "her world" and that her mother demonstrates when she gives Cole a Golliwog doll and shows interest only in Birdie and Birdie's unblack appearance (83–85). The fact that Sandy has to consciously select an outfit that is acceptable to wear to her mother's when they go to ask for money and that she anticipates and forces herself to tolerate her mother's constant criticism and unequal treatment of her daughters proves that Sandy has indeed separated herself from her mother's conception of whiteness. Though her mother will always see whiteness in skin, that she also sees Sandy's weight, the children's manners, the children's education, and their overall lifestyle as objectionable suggests that whiteness represents more than white skin. In a way, class is one of the earliest indicators in the novel that whiteness is not homogeneous. And the more variable and diverse whiteness is depicted to be, the more obviously it can be recognized as racial.

Perhaps the most conspicuous instance of Birdie's recognition of

whiteness as an ethnoracial identity is when she and her mother go on
the lam and use the cover of normative social standards. When Birdie
becomes Jesse, her mother also changes her own identity from Sandy
Lee to Sheila Goldman. But this identity is not a shift in name only
for Sandy just as it is not a shift in color only for Birdie. When Sandy
transforms into Sheila, she transforms the cultural markers that signify her mother's kind of whiteness and the kind that her prospective
landlords want to see. Sandy puts both her and Birdie's identity shifts
in the language of passing: with Birdie "simply relabelled as white,
no one would ever suspect the truth. We'd be scot-free, she told me, a
couple of new people overnight" (109). In "re-labelling" Birdie white
rather than black–white, Sandy loses the racial link to those she had
"chosen to call her own" and thus breaks the ties to blackness that have
marked her. Birdie notes that without Deck and Cole (who have no
way of cutting their ties to blackness), she and her mother need only
"re-label" and rename themselves to make blackness disappear: "The
two bodies that had made her stand out in a crowd—made her more
than just another white woman—were gone; now it was just the two
of us" (109). As Sandy tries out new names for herself, she entertains
"'trailer park names' that she thought fun for their white-trash flavor"
but this is not the kind of whiteness she needs to "pass" for, and it is a
photo of a wedding announcement in a newspaper that inspires Sandy's decidedly upper-crust assumed identity (109). Birdie recounts, "It
was a face that jumped out at me. She was blond, and looked the way
my mother might have looked if she had more control over her appe-
tite, if she had never met my father, if she had stayed in Cambridge,
gone to Radcliffe, married a doctor" (109). The woman is, it turns out,
an admissions officer at Wellesley College—in other words, a guard-
ian of the white American aristocracy. She is what Birdie thinks her
mother would have become had she not been so politically engaged
or the wife of a black man—in other words, what Sandy would have
been had she stuck to "her world" as her mother suggested. Birdie
notices that almost immediately she sees her ordinarily unpredict-
able and odd mother in a new light: "She looked different already, in
those few seconds as Sheila. She looked sensible, the kind of mother

I had seen before on television but never known. The kind who lived in the suburbs of Boston and drove their kids to soccer practice and ballet lessons and painted still-life portraits on weekday afternoons. She looked mild" (110).

Sandy's manipulation of her apparel, behavior, language, and body makes her a convincing member of the privileged (white) class. Before long, Sandy has lost seventy pounds and "now she was the woman her mother always wanted her to be—willowy, fragile, feminine, a shadow of her former self" (123). And the woman her mother always wanted her to be is also the kind of woman her white elitist landlords in New Hampshire want her to be. The language of performance is prominent in the scene, both in terms of Sandy's playacting and her costume: "She wore khakis and a white V-neck sweater, her feet in Keds. We had bought the clothes just a few weeks before, in preparation for moments like these. It was paying off. I had never seen my mother so appropriate. Loose strands from her bun brushed against her pale cheek" (127). Her act is convincing as Walter and Libby Marsh ask her "inconsequential questions" that Birdie can see are "a way of proving that she spoke their language. They smiled knowingly at her" (127). Birdie senses that they see in her mother "a tall, statuesque, blue-blooded woman in her mid-thirties, the delicate etchings of sorrow beginning to creep out from her sapphire eyes" and that they interpret as signs of her caste belonging her "bony nose, her blue eyes, flickering, nervous" and her "educated voice" (127, 128). Birdie intuits their mental process: "They heard her accent, so like their own, and knew she would do just fine. Never mind that thin, glowering, dark adolescent by her side, they thought. They saw a woman and a child. No man? No problem. They knew she was one of them" (128).

However, we are reminded that it is an act and that the kind of whiteness they adopt is still dangerous when Sandy later warns Birdie against the Marsh family, saying, "Stay away from those rich fucks across the woods. Hear me? They're just like my own goddamn family—the kind of liberals who would like to see me fry. Remember that" (140–41). She even trains Birdie "how to spot a real Wasp from a fake one" and explains that she is "talking about liberal Wasps. Not Republican ones.

And they might as well be two different races" (130). Sandy then creates a list of the qualities of "A Real Wasp," which stipulates that "the harder a Real Wasp tries to reject his social caste"—by, for instance, "marrying a Jew or a Negro"—"the more authentically Waspy he becomes" (132). Despite fitting the description (apart from her curious, and perhaps intentionally self-excluding, use of the masculine pronoun) and "grudgingly admit[ting]" that she is technically a Wasp "at least by birth," Sandy does not count herself among authentic Wasps (131). Instead, she determines that the Marshes are "Real Wasps" and that she can "pass" for one successfully. When she needs to convince them that she is "one of them," Sandy does perform convincingly. She casually mentions that the family's stable and horses would finally give her daughter the "chance to ride" and agrees that her daughter would "have to start thinking about boarding school at some point" when the Marshes warn, while "imitating the New Hampshire accent," that at a certain age "the locals start acting like locals, if you know what I mean" (127, 126).

Sandy's performance as a kind of white helps direct attention to the ways in which whiteness is inflected by class, education, racism, and expectations for normative gender and sexuality. The fact that Sandy is, in every way American race concepts function, white herself and yet has to "pass" and perform to satisfy the expectations of the "white liberals" that Birdie's parents have taught her to mistrust suggests that whiteness is no more readily accepting than the blackness into which Birdie has to work so hard to convince her schoolmates in Boston to admit her. In Senna's novel, whiteness functions much like blackness—as something that can be performed, embraced, and disowned—and the novel invites the reader to recognize that whiteness is as much of a "race" as blackness. Birdie can be mixed and yet resist whiteness in favor of blackness (that is, she can be comfortable with the blackness of her mixedness but uncomfortable with the whiteness of her mixedness when it is singled out). In much the same way, Sandy can embrace her (cultural and familial) blackness and resist or at least qualify her whiteness as a matter of phenotype, not political identity. Sandy's performance for the Marshes and constant tirades

against white racism and white politics despite her own racial whiteness ultimately maintain whiteness as something "other," something
she keeps at arm's length and observes critically. And in this way, Sandy racializes whiteness in the same way that whites "other" and thereby racialize nonwhites.

Unlike Sandy, who acknowledges her whiteness but manipulates
it, Birdie considers her whiteness as something that impedes her embodiment of a more genuine racial identity. Birdie actively keeps herself distanced from her white identity out of a desire to keep alive the
hope of being reunited with her sister and of simultaneously recon-
stituting her blackness in a multiracial identity. Birdie thinks, "The
less I behaved like myself, the more I could believe that this was still a
game. That my real self—Birdie Lee—was safely hidden beneath my
beige flesh, and that when the right moment came, I would reveal her,
preserved, frozen solid in the moment in which I had left her" (198–
99). Birdie's feelings about her "real" or authentic self that includes
blackness and about the fraudulence of her monoracially white identity duplicate the conventions of passing narratives. Her discomfort
with the ongoing, blatant racism of whites (who do not know she is
"really" black) around her also echoes earlier passing plots. But the
fact of her desire differentiates her from the protagonists of earlier literature. Birdie does not "pass" to free herself from economic, material, political, and social oppression in a self-conscious decision to cut
herself off from her family and community as in traditional passing
novels. Rather, she "passes" because she is too young to be permitted a choice not to and agrees to participate to save her mother's life.
Furthermore, she agrees to "pass" with the heightened awareness that
her whiteness is only a temporary identity (that she does not actually want to perform and will discard at the earliest opportunity). She
is so emotionally and psychologically bereft while "passing" that she
ultimately abandons her monoracially white identity and her mother along with it. Her "return" to black family and black/mixed identity again mirrors earlier passing plots, but what sets her apart from
the traditional passing heroine is that instead of simply satisfying her
own need for racial solidarity in favor of having others perceive her

and treat her as white, Birdie does not actually want to be recognized as white at any point in time.

Being treated as white requires that she be privy to the frequent and casual racism of her white friends and other members of the community and that she be unfriendly to the black/mixed students at school. In a conventional passing plot, this would be the price one had to pay for membership in the white race and the benefits that come with it, but Birdie neither seeks nor finds benefits and, furthermore, desires no membership in monoracial whiteness. Rather, she is vigilant about resisting the "transformation" into a monoracially white person that her "passing" threatens to bring about (232). While she is driving back to New Hampshire from New York with her mother, her mother's boyfriend, and her best friend from school, some black teenaged boys throw a rock through their windshield. Birdie is simply embarrassed: "I didn't want the teenagers to think I belonged with these white people in the car. It struck me how little I felt toward Mona and Jim. It scared me a little, how easily they could become strangers to me. How easily they could become cowering white folks, nothing more, nothing less" (223–24). The fact that she does not include her mother as "these white people in the car" the way she specifically includes Mona and Jim demonstrates that she and Sandy have some kind of connection to blackness even though they look like Mona and Jim. Her comments also reveal how unpleasant it is for Birdie to be seen as white—especially under a black gaze. For Birdie, racial identity is not simply a personal sense of self; it is defined by and defines her interaction with other people and, consequently, her sense of place in the world.

These situational differences between Birdie's circumstances and the conventional passing circumstances further emphasize how the novel racializes whiteness. Birdie is not simply discarding her blackness and, for lack of a "race," becoming white once she and her mother have to maintain social relationships in New Hampshire and thus uphold specific identities. Rather, she characterizes whiteness as a role she has to play and constantly evaluates whether she is performing the race convincingly. For Birdie, it is not simply a matter of not showing signs of her blackness, of her nonwhiteness, of her race; rather, she attempts to exhibit the racial signifiers, the qualities that have come to represent whiteness. The fact that her mother also "passes" for a kind of white and identifies the kinds of whiteness—whether it be the Marshes' or her mother's liberal elitism, "trailer park white trash," or her own boyfriend's "honky ass" behavior—to which she feels she does not belong helps to reinforce the notion that whiteness is as much the result of social conventions as blackness.

Birdie's resistance to whiteness and her constant and conscious desire to be a part of blackness does not presuppose that she wants to claim a monoracial black identity or in any other way divorce herself entirely from whiteness. Rather, it is the specific kind of whiteness, the kind her grandmother represents and her mother performs, of which Birdie wants no part. Instead, Birdie wants to formulate her own multiracial identity that includes the kind of whiteness that can blend with her kind of blackness. It is clear that her grandmother's whiteness decidedly does not mix even before Birdie returns to Boston with the hope of finding her sister, who she is convinced has returned to the United States. But once back in Boston, Birdie has to exploit the material opportunity of privileged whiteness as her literary passing predecessors do and ask her grandmother for the airfare she needs to go to California. Yet Birdie refuses to play along and satisfy her grandmother's desire to see her as white. Her grandmother calls Birdie's situation a "terrible fate" and insists, "It was doomed from the start. Tragedy in the making. Your mother should have stuck to her world" (311–12). But Birdie responds, "Oh, please. I'm not in the mood for this Victorian crap. You and all your ancestors are the tragedies. Not me. You walk around pretending to be so liberal and civilized in this big old house, but you're just as bad as the rest of them. This whole world—it's based on lies. No wonder my mother left. I mean, it stinks" (312).

Furthermore, Birdie also rejects *any* kind of whiteness that requires her to deny her blackness. The more time she spends in New Hampshire, the more she feels whiteness encroach upon the blackness she has kept hidden within herself, the blackness she feels she possesses but cannot exhibit. Reflecting on her time in New Hampshire, Birdie notes, "My father had said white liberals were a disease. At least you know what you're dealing with in an overt racist. But a liberal was more slippery. You could lose yourself. There was something to that argument. I had become friends with Mona and all the little racists. That way I would always know I was living a lie. Better them than someone who would smile in my face and make me believe I was at home" (231).

But even among white racists, Birdie finds that her performance of the kind of whiteness that she expects will always remind her of its artificiality is slippery in a different way: "It had come so easily to me. I had become somebody I didn't like. Somebody who had no voice or color or conviction. I wasn't sure that was survival at all. They say you don't have to choose. But the thing is, you do. Because there are consequences if you don't" (349).

Her choice, consequently, is to find her sister, the symbolic link to her blackness and mixedness, and begin a process of forming a racial identity that she will like. Her choice exhibits her agency in defining her own identity and demonstrates the deliberate decision she has made to abandon a white monoracial identity. She realizes when she is back in Boston that she misses her mother, her white friends, and the horse she rode in New Hampshire, and admits: "The missing scared me. It made me feel a little contaminated. I wondered if whiteness were contagious. If it were, then surely I had caught it. I imagined this 'condition' affected the way I walked, talked, dressed, danced, and at its most advanced stage, the way I looked at the world and at other people" (280). This "condition" of whiteness is what she consciously decides to cure herself of, and her desire to claim a multiracial identity is not simply a default but what she chooses for herself.

Instead of being surrounded by whites, Birdie seems prepared to stay with Cole in California where, as Cole states, multiracial people are "a dime a dozen" (351). Birdie will now be submerged in a society where her mixedness is relatively normal and where she will feel no need to proclaim blackness (as she did in Boston) or whiteness (as she did in New Hampshire). She looks at a school bus full of a diverse group of young students and sees them as "utterly ordinary." On the bus she sees "a cinnamon-skinned girl with her hair in braids": "She was black like me, a mixed girl, and she was watching me from behind the dirty glass. For a second I thought I was somewhere familiar and she was a girl I already knew. I began to lift my hand, but stopped, remembering where I was and what I had already found. Then the bus lurched forward, and the face was gone with it, just a blur of yellow and black in motion" (353).

Though Birdie has never described her own skin as cinnamon colored or brown, her comment does reflect her ongoing recognition of herself in the dark skin of others. She recognizes herself in the girl but also recognizes her as Cole before she remembers "what [she] had already found." She sees both herself and her sister in one person's appearance in a way that demonstrates how racial identity can transgress phenotype. Just as she sees her sister—"cinnamon-skinned, curly-haired"—as her own reflection as a child, and sees Samantha, the black–white multiracial student in her New Hampshire high school as "the color of cinnamon" and racially similar to herself, Birdie sees the girl on the bus as "black like me" and "mixed" (5, 192). If, as Michele Hunter argues, "in all cases, recognition is motivated by desire," then Birdie's ability to see herself in darker multiracial girls suggests that her multiracial identity is something she recognizes in herself regardless of appearance, labels, or social convention.[74] The fact that she sees similarities between herself and other girls like Cole and Samantha (who do not look like her) indicates that multiracial identity is something she perceives in ways other than phenotype. Birdie also understands that, like blackness and whiteness, mixedness is not monolithic, and she is ready for the first time in her life to define her own racial identity in a way that makes sense to her.

Birdie's struggle to identify her mixedness and, indeed, to be able to embody it freely works to racialize whiteness because race becomes a question of how to identify black and white wed together rather than to discern how blackness or whiteness exclude each other. The ways in which whiteness is also inflected by class and culture further racialize whiteness since Birdie and her mother consider whiteness critically, taking little for granted and refusing its "universal" and normative hegemonic power. For the better part of the novel, Birdie and her mother are "passing" for what they *are* (racially white) but also what they *are not* (monoracially and monoculturally white), and the examination of whiteness as a "constructed" identity forms the focus of much of the text.

Separate or Synonymous? Complicating Whiteness with Jewishness

Senna's scrutiny of whiteness is made even more rigorous by the fact that Sandy invents a dead Jewish man as a husband for herself and father for Birdie. Since the creation of whiteness in the United States (or simply whiteness as American) involved bridging ethnic and racial divisions into a heterogeneous white category, the inclusion of Jewishness in mixed-race texts complicates the black–white opposition and racializes whiteness by attending to the ethnic diversity within the racial category. Furthermore, the continued social confusion over what Jewishness constitutes—a race, an ethnicity, a culture, a religion—makes Jewishness a useful addition to contemporary black–white multiracial literature. In the vast majority of contemporary texts about multiracialism that make whiteness anything more diverse than the American norm, it is Jewishness that does the diversifying. Rosellen Brown's *Half a Heart* (2000) follows the efforts of a Jewish woman to find and reconnect with her black daughter; when he tells his life story about growing up black in America in *The Color of Water* (1996), James McBride focuses on his mother's Jewishness; Lisa Jones accounts for her mother's Jewishness when she explores her black/mixed racial identity in *Bulletproof Diva* (1994); and Jewishness is a critical aspect of Jane Lazarre's account of her life raising children with her black husband in *Beyond the Whiteness of Whiteness* (1996), to name just a few. Lori Harrison-Kahan points out in "Passing for White, Passing for Jewish" that the incorporation of Jewishness in contemporary representations of black–white race mixing serves to "challenge existing theories of mixed race identity that rely on binary configurations" in that Jewishness "simultaneously signifies whiteness and racial otherness" and thus demonstrates the "plurality of whiteness."[75]

Despite the fact that other races and ethnicities assimilated into the white American race much more quickly, Jews did not assimilate until the anti-Semitism of the mid-twentieth century subsided after World War II when "the same folks who promoted nativism and xenophobia were eager to believe that the Euro-origin people whom they had deported, reviled as members of inferior races, and prevented from immigrating only a few years earlier were now model middle-class white suburban citizens."[76] In much the same way that "Asian" dissolved the differences between Japanese and Chinese Americans in the twentieth century after those differences allowed for the internment of the former during the Second World War and the anti-immigration laws that barred the latter from the United States for decades, new racial conceptions diminished Jewish difference. The newly accepted Europeanness of Jews evaporated much of the perceived racial difference that had enabled the segregation and other discriminatory practices leveled against Jews before the war and the turning away of Jewish refugees fleeing the Nazis during the war. While other "not-yet-white" groups joined the white American race even as black Americans remained racialized and thus separate, Jews effectively moved from being likened to blacks to being likened to white ethnics. Although anti-black racism was replicated in racism against Irish, Czech, and Polish immigrants as well as Jewish immigrants, non-Jewish ethnicities had an easier time assimilating as white, and Jewish people were grouped loosely with black Americans in terms of caste.[77] As David Roediger notes, in the early twentieth century "nativist folk wisdom that held that an Irishman was a Black, inside out, became transposed to the reckoning that the turning inside out of Jews produced 'niggers.'"[78]

However, while historians trace the cooperation and mutual efforts of Jewish and black peoples over the course of the twentieth century and especially during the civil rights activism of the mid-century, most state that the relationship between Jews and blacks was "vexed" (as Roediger puts it) in part because of a complex set of problems related to politics, activism styles, economics, legal strategies, and color-based discrimination, among other things. In the general population, whiteness came between Jewish and black allegiance since, as Cheryl

Greenberg observes in *Troubling the Waters: Black-Jewish Relations in the American Century*, "almost all Jews were white people. Not only could many Jews therefore 'pass,' but social and economic opportunities were often based on skin color rather than on ethnicity or religion. Thus Jews' color and their job skills facilitated mobility into entrepreneurial positions, and into white-collar work generally by the 1940s and '50s, while most African Americans remained trapped at the bottom of any occupational field they were permitted to enter at all."[79] Additionally, by the thirties and forties "upwardly mobile Jews in the North" had joined white flight away from African Americans "while keeping their jobs, stores, and other real-estate investments" in black neighborhoods and, as incomes rose, Jewish businesses and Jewish housewives hired black help.[80] Consequently, "precisely at the time that Jewish and black civil rights organizations began to reach out to each other, Jews had also become landlords, rental agents, social workers, teachers, employers, and shopkeepers in black communities. For the masses of blacks and Jews, then, relations took place in interchanges where Jews generally held greater power."[81] Greenberg is careful to point out that the general black–Jewish relationship was a complex one but, like other historians, argues that a breakdown in that relationship did occur in large part due to the effects of racial difference.

Despite the complicated relationship between Jewish and African American people, the similarities they share help contextualize the contemporary use of Jewishness in black–white multiracial literature. In "Passing Like Me: Jewish Chameleonism and the Politics of Race," Daniel Itzkovitz maps the stereotype of Jews as changelings. This image of Jews means that while a black passing for white is considered a traitor, a Jew's "skill at blending into his surroundings is attributed to both 'tradition' and 'instinct.' His chameleonism is thus culturally and naturally determined; the 'natural place' of the Jew is in passing."[82] Itzkovitz explains how anti-Semitic Americans found Jews troubling because Jews so readily seemed white in appearance and culture. His analysis indicates that the paranoia regarding Jews passing is similar to the paranoia regarding blacks passing since the inability of racist whites to tell the difference between themselves and the persons they want to be distanced from might cause doubt about the actual existence of a difference or the superiority of whiteness. As Itzkovitz says, "Distinctions between Jews and the white Americans who were opposed to them were clearly elusive, and it was not simply Jewish performativity but the slipperiness of Jewish difference—the fear that behind the performance there was no 'authentic' kernel of difference—which made the situation so vexing."[83] Just as the lack of a stable linguistic or racial signifier in Jews upset white supremacist beliefs in difference, so did the light skin of some blacks, or "white Negroes."[84] It is because of this common experience of being suspected of "passing" that Jews have appeared in literary depictions of black–white passing. Itzkovitz points out that Charles Waddell Chesnutt's *The House behind the Cedars* (1900), James Weldon Johnson's *The Autobiography of an Ex-Colored Man* (1912), Walter White's *Flight* (1926), Jessie Fauset's *Plum Bun* (1928), Nella Larsen's *Passing* (1929), and Fannie Hurst's *Imitation of Life* (1933) "all feature Jews whose movements into mainstream American culture resonate with the struggles of their passing African American characters."[85] Itzkovitz argues further that African American passing novels use the "slippage from Jewish to white American" to ironically juxtapose the relative ease with which a Jew might "pass" against the betrayal of one's "true" race and the inevitable sorrow that "passing" meant for Negro characters.[86]

Passing for Jewish: Danzy Senna's *Caucasia*

In contemporary narratives Jewishness echoes the historical and literary relationships between black and white. In Senna's *Caucasia*, Jewishness racializes whiteness by drawing attention to ethnicity within the category but it also draws attention to Jewishness as something more akin to blackness than whiteness. In doing these seemingly contradictory things, Jewishness functions to emphasize the muddiness of racial waters. Even at the moment Sandy conceives of Birdie as a "half-Jewish" and "half-white" girl, the ironic contradiction is clear. This racial identity that has Sandy simply replace blackness with Jewishness is meant to unmark Birdie's blackness (and gain the racially unmarked Birdie acceptance into unraced whiteness) but it

simultaneously marks Birdie anew with Jewishness. Sandy first suggests that Birdie can take on any white ethnic identity such as "Puerto Rican, Sicilian, Pakistani, Greek," but she ultimately decides that
"Jewish is better."[87] Though Sandy feels it necessary to assign a non-
"universal" white ethnoracial identity to Birdie in order to account
for her darker hair and any other signs of nongeneric whiteness, the
fact that Jewishness has a history of being associated with blackness
is also part of Sandy's strategy to soften the blow of "passing." In fact,
in a very real sense, Jewishness becomes a stand-in for blackness when
blackness is too dangerous a marker; Jewishness offers a disguise for
blackness in place of a generic whiteness that would obliterate blackness. Having raised her daughters to embrace black pride and having
spent her life fighting against the hegemony of white America, Sandy tries to reassure Birdie that she is not being disloyal or risking real
"invisibility" among rural, "universal" whites in New Hampshire:
"She . . . liked to remind me that I wasn't really passing because Jews
weren't really white, more like an off-white. She said they were the
closest I was going to get to black and still stay white. 'Tragic history, kinky hair, good politics,' she explained. 'It's all there.'"[88] Sandy
even makes her imagined husband approximate Deck in his mind
and body by making him a gifted academic and giving him a "Jew-
fro" like Deck's own. The similarity is not lost on Birdie when she
tries to imagine her new father, the "esteemed classics professor and
so-called genius," but keeps "coming up with a lighter-skinned version of [her] own father, seated in his office beside a mountain of
books."[89] In addition to her insistence that Jewishness is "not-quite-
white," to borrow Roediger's phrase, Sandy says to Birdie of her Jewish father, "[He] was pretty much an atheist even though he wanted
you to know your history, your heritage. For him, Judaism was more
like a cultural thing."[90] Thus Sandy suggests that Jewishness is partly racial (not white, not black) and partly cultural (a history and heritage). To Habiba Ibrahim, Sandy's characterization of Jewishness as
highly ambivalent indicates the multiple ways one inhabits an identity.[91] Nonetheless, it also demonstrates how identity itself can encompass more than any singular or strict formation. By aligning herself

with blackness despite having no black racial ancestry, by "calling it her own" and then instructing her daughter that she is not "really" passing as Jewish despite lacking Jewish ancestry, Sandy signals her belief that ethnoracial identity can largely be a matter of choice, that it is certainly not a simple matter of appearance, and that it is a politically charged decision since, through blackness and Jewishness alike, Sandy resists "Real Wasp" whiteness for both herself and her daughter.

However, Birdie also admits, "Mostly my Jewishness was like a performance we put on together for the public," and in private her marked race—blackness or Jewishness—essentially ceases to exist.[92] She wears a Star of David but indicates that it is the only sign of her Jewishness since she otherwise "looked like [she] was changing into one of those New Hampshire girls" because she "talked the talk, walked the walk" and "only looked away into the distance, [her] features tensing slightly, sometimes a little laugh escaping" when she hears the "inevitable" racial slurs "nigga, spic, fuckin' darkie."[93] Though Birdie does not herself subscribe to the kind of racist "othering" that the whites around her use to unracialize themselves, she does ultimately erase her marked whiteness and become "unraced" white. When Birdie suffers anti-Semitic racism at the hands of teenage boys who throw pennies at her and call her a "fuckin' kike," she feels "a pang of loyalty toward [her] imaginary father and touche[s] the [Star of David] necklace" but within moments answers her girlfriends' questions about her Jewishness by saying that she is "not *really* Jewish" because "you have to have a mother who is Jewish" according to "the religious law or something."[94] She subsequently removes her Star of David and, while she does not discard it, leaves it in a drawer where it will not be seen. When she runs away from New Hampshire and her white identity she takes very few belongings but does take the Star of David along with her Negrobilia box of mementos of blackness, which is the only connection she still has to her father, sister, and blackness. Her decision to keep mementos of both of her marked identities indicates that even when they are not seen or publicly acknowledged, racial identities can remain a part of a person's private sense of identity. But according to Harrison-Kahan, Birdie's multiple shifts in identity call into question "whether it is possible to be 'really' anything."[95] She argues that "when the layers are peeled away, [Birdie] is like a Russian doll with an empty center. These layers of identity are most evident when biracial Birdie passes for a Jew who passes for white."[96] Harrison-Kahan's suggestion that Birdie's "empty center" is the result of the sheer number of her identities or the frequency with which she shifts them indicates an uneasiness with the legitimacy of identities that change. In other words, if repeated shifting threatens to make one empty, then "real" identity requires stability and longevity. Though it seems clear that Birdie desires a multiracial identity that includes blackness, the novel never does conclusively identify Birdie. It is certainly possible that Birdie's repeated shifting of identities (from ambiguous race to black, to half-Jewish half-white, to unmarked white, to some kind of mixture) is indicative of the lack of authenticity of any of her identities until she comes to rest on the possibilities of black–white multiracialism. But her shifts might also (and not necessarily instead) illustrate the way in which race is malleable and "constructed." If, as many critics of African American literature propose, conventional passing plots essentialize race by making blackness a "true" identity and whiteness an "untrue" identity, then Senna's passing novel imagines race as unessentialized and "constructed." Whether Birdie is "trying out" options before choosing one of any number of legitimate possibilities or is testing the possibilities to find the single identity that is "real" for her, she deconstructs conventional notions of race because the identity she chooses is a blend of blackness and whiteness. She does not "return" to a blackness that excludes whiteness, and she only finds whiteness illegitimate when it requires a denial of blackness. Rather, she finds that both are a part of her and that together they form her racial identity. As Kathryn Rummell observes in "Rewriting the Passing Novel," the fact that Birdie has spent her life being defined by other people and chooses at the novel's close to self-identify (as "mixed") is critical in that it diverges from the path of earlier passing narratives in which 'drawing one's own boundaries' was not possible.[97] It also acknowledges a different racial landscape in the late twentieth-century United States.[98] Even though Senna duplicates some aspects of conventional passing plots, *Caucasia* does not reinforce the black–white race binary or existing race concepts. Ironically, it is largely due to the fact that Senna draws attention to whiteness *as a race*—as something that is as diverse and racialized as blackness—that her novel succeeds in undermining whiteness *as a race* or at least as the kind of race that cannot be heterogeneous and coexist with blackness. The novel's final image of the "blur of yellow and black in motion" that Birdie sees herself within evidences the futility of attempting to separate races or guard the color line.[99]

Racial Fluency: Rebecca Walker's *Black White and Jewish*

Like Birdie's negotiable and frequently changing identity, Rebecca Walker's "shifting self" in her autobiography *Black White and Jewish* helps to identify the heterogeneity of racial identity. If, as Birdie's, Emma's, and Nellie's experiences suggest, the body cannot be relied upon as a signifier of racial identity, Walker's name offers one way of learning how she might identify herself. At first she signs letters with her birth name, Rebecca Grant Leventhal, but even as a child she adds her mother's name and signs "Rebecca Grant Walker Leventhal" (Walker, *Black White and Jewish*, 30, 34). By the end of high school, she explains, "I decide to move Leventhal to the more obscure middle position in my name and add Walker to the end, privileging my blackness and downplaying what I think of as my whiteness. After all, why should my father get all of the credit? Why should that line, that clan of people who have been so resistant to my birth, be allowed to claim the young woman I have become?" (312). Walker wants a named matrilineal and racial bond: "I want to be closer to my mother, to have something run between us that cannot be denied. I want a marker that links us tangibly and forever as mother and daughter. That links me tangibly and forever with blackness" (312). Her father "suggests that [her] choice has something to do with [her] own anti-Semitism, with wanting to distance [herself] from the Jewish in [her]" (313). Walker is furious and considers his response "obliviousness" to her "reality"; however, what she says is not particularly unlike her father's suggestion in that she is trying to distance herself from, as she says herself, "what Jewishness has become" (313). She wants her name to reflect her blackness and considers it a political choice. She feels her father "has seemingly stopped caring about all things racial and political and has settled into a comfortable routine commuting from Westchester and going to lily-white Little League games in pristine suburban ballparks," and thinks, "I do not see how I fit into his life, or that I want to" (313). Her comments reflect an association of Jewishness with money and complacency and an association of blackness with transgressive politics and personal strength. Her comments also reflect the ongoing debate throughout her text about whether she feels she is or can choose to be Jewish and whether Jewishness is whiteness. Ultimately, Walker identifies with Jewishness initially but disidentifies with it when she feels it has become too unmarked, too mainstream, too much like the generic white American race that deracializes itself and holds itself apart from racial politics, to paraphrase Linda Schlossberg. Hers is not really a desire to separate herself from Jewishness (since she admits that as an adult she maintains an interest in Jewish culture) but to separate herself from the whiteness she feels "Jewishness has become." Walker's sense of "what Jewishness has become" maps the historical shift of Jewishness from "other" to whiteness and indicates the coinciding danger to blackness as white hegemony makes whiteness one homogeneous force against which she must assert herself as a multiracial subject.

Walker does depict Jewishness as some form of marked whiteness. As a child, her paternal grandmother reminds her not to forget her nonblack otherness, telling her to always remember that she is Jewish no matter what her parents say; whiteness might be erased by her "copper," "caramel," and "brown" skin, but Jewishness is not (16, 275, 207). When Walker is a very young child, her father sits on the porch "with the rifle and the dog, waiting for the Klan to come," and sits up all night with his law partners playing poker at the house with a "rifle leaned up against the wall behind" him because, she deduces, "the Klan must have left one of their calling cards: a white rectangle with two eyes shining through a pointed hood, THE KLAN IS WATCHING YOU in red letters underneath"; such scenes serve as reminders that even without his black family, Walker's father would be the target of white racism and violence (14, 21). While Lori Harrison-Kahan argues that "in this context, Mel Leventhal is not white," Walker's narrative is not that definitive.[100] For Walker's father to be "not white" in this context, he would have to be targeted as a Jew; if the Klan is terrorizing the family for the more likely reason that they are interracial (and thus are tainting the white race), then the Klan is, in fact, ascribing whiteness to Leventhal. However, if Walker's father is anything like Birdie's mother and has chosen to liken himself to those he "calls his own," then the "otherness" he embodies is partly chosen (black) and partly unchosen (Jewish); either is a threat to white supremacists. Regardless of the Klan's perception of her father, Walker sees the terrorist organization's interest in her family and, indeed, her family's existence itself, as partly the result of her father's Jewishness because she ascribes to his Jewishness his interest in those suffering under the oppression of unmarked white society, as well as his devotion to herself and her mother.

Leventhal's Jewishness/otherness does not last in his daughter's estimation, though. Frequent stories of the love and affection she shares with her father illustrate Walker's reliance on and admiration of her father early in her life. Other women seem able to stand in for her mother—woman after woman cares for her and after all that "there is still another woman who mothers me"—but her father is irreplaceable and no other figure steps in to father her. However, once her parents separate, her parents reverse in her esteem (Walker, *Black White and Jewish*, 40). Walker notes before her parents split up that a moment she shares with her father is the last "when [they] will not have to speak to be connected. When just being in his presence is all [she] need[s]" (51). Subsequently, she aligns herself with her mother—significantly, a figure of sorrow and betrayal. She recognizes the pain her father is causing her mother, and since Walker feels "an instant affinity with beings who suffer," the admiration she has for her father as a defender of "beings who suffer" and as someone who willingly suffers himself for the sake of those beings is transposed onto her mother, someone he has now caused to suffer (306). Walker revokes the intimacy she had with her father and reconstitutes it with her mother:

I feel the ether of my spirit meet the ether of hers and become all tangled up. As I fall asleep I do not know where she starts and I begin. I do know that my mama is hurting and that what I have to give to stop that hurting is myself: my arms, my warmth, my little hands on the side of her face. I no longer am only for myself, but now I'm for her, too. I must be strong. I learn how to forget myself, to take my cues from her, to watch carefully so that I can know what to do. (56)

The willingness of her father to face the scorn of his family and the violence of white supremacists because of his devotion to his wife and child lead Walker to associate him with "otherness" and the force of opposition to white oppression. But when he gives up his family and, eventually, seems to lose interest in both his daughter's blackness and the political struggle of African Americans, Walker comes to associate him with the very white hegemony she resists. She no longer wants to be separated from her mother to go live with her father, and what time she spends at her father's house she spends "waiting for [her] mother" (88). Instead of continuing to identify with her father's Jewishness/otherness, which Walker sees as something of a betrayal or at least something she cannot trust, she chooses to identify with her mother's blackness, to give herself (to blackness) to stop the "hurting." As a child, then, Walker develops the practice that dictates the rest of her life story—namely, to identify with those she perceives as needing help and disidentify with those who do not. As she states, she empathizes with "beings who suffer, whether they are [her] own, whatever that means, or not" (306). Consequently, she "identifies" with "the legacy of slavery and discrimination" in the United States and the "legacy of anti-Jewish sentiment and exclusion" as well as the "internment of Japanese-Americans during World War Two" and the "struggle against brutality and genocide waged against the Native Americans in this country" (306–7). Her interest lies in defending those at the mercy of any social hierarchy that leaves them without power, and so when she perceives her father transitioning from a position of resistance to a position that allows him to enjoy the hegemonic power of mainstream America, her sentiments transition as well.

However, the shift Walker perceives in her father is to a great extent projected onto her stepmother, whom she often blames for her father's supposedly lagging interest in racial equality and in raising a racially aware child. Walker admits, "I'm convinced if it wasn't for her my father would still be mine and would listen to me and would tell me to be proud of who I am, that I was born for a reason and that being black and white is better than being just one thing and screw people who can't deal" (218–19). What appears to be her nostalgic love for her father motivates her to assume that it is her stepmother alone who is interested in investing in the middle-class American dream—which Walker identifies in her father and stepmother's case as "the Jewish dream"—of living in the suburbs with a Volvo and a couple of kids and going to "see the romantic comedy playing at the local uniplex" once a week (206). She condemns the move to Larchmont—"[It] is some kind of plot my stepmother has concocted to kill me, to wipe away all traces of my blackness or to make me so uncomfortable with it that I myself will it away"—and thereby indicates that she has come to consider Jewishness a threat to her blackness (206). Walker's perception of her father's new lifestyle as something deplorably mainstream and her assumption that it is a specifically Jewish pursuit make apparent how she considers Jewishness an erasure of blackness and the political activism blackness represents to her: "She and I are doing battle for my father's soul, me with my brown body pulling him down memory lane to a past more sensual and righteous, she scratching the dirt off pale Jewish roots I didn't know he had" (207). But the Jewishness that Walker is so critical of is essentially conflated with whiteness, and it is the whiteness of her Jewish family that she perceives as such a threat. As Harrison-Kahan argues, "Juxtaposed with blackness, Jewishness loses its status as a minority identity because of its ability, at least in some contexts, to offer the appearance of conformity with the dominant culture," and so "Walker disidentifies with Jewishness on the grounds that it is passing into whiteness . . . [and] repudiates her Jewishness based on her need to disidentify with power and instead align herself with otherness."[101]

The years Walker spends with her father and stepmother convince her that her Jewishness is not really genuine and that it poses a threat to her blackness. That she does not entertain the notion that she can be Jewish and still retain blackness reflects her fear, like that of Birdie, that she is being transformed or swallowed up by whiteness, as well as her belief that her blackness is not welcomed into Jewishness. Just as the two black students at Birdie's New Hampshire high school avoid each other to prevent drawing attention to their blackness, Walker and the only other black kids at her Jewish summer camp "don't talk much": "It is like if we talk to each other everyone around might notice that we are black, and neither of us wants that" (Walker, *Black White and Jewish*, 173). At the camp, Walker is constantly trying to "will [her] body into some kind of normal posture, into some semblance of ease and comfort to disguise [her] feelings of not belonging," and to a great extent her sense of exclusion from the group is racial (178). But her blackness cannot be held entirely responsible for these feelings. In part, her feeling of unbelonging is potentially the result of her desire *not* to fit in because she despises so much the degree of privilege she sees in the other kids. Her unfailing inclination to identify with the oppressed is usually tied to class (which is in turn tied to race), and at the camp she falls into the familiar role of critiquing the power structure of the social hierarchy, commenting that there are "plenty of girls at camp I don't like at all" because they are "so rich they think they are better than me" (178). She makes friends and jokes with them about "what a 'Jap camp' Fire Lake is": "It means something repulsive, gauche, flashy, and yet secretly we are proud to be Japs, to think of ourselves as spoiled by Daddy's money and Mom's overprotectiveness" (179). As if to compensate for her affectation of "the appropriate air of petulant entitlement" as a "Jewish American Princess" (Jap), she claims that she can "never get it quite right" or "shake free of [her] blackness" (179–80). While her blackness no doubt invites racism and discrimination, Walker also uses it as a way of refuting the "petulant entitlement" associated with wealth and whiteness/Jewishness that she is ashamed of having enacted. Similarly, when she visits a wealthy

Jewish friend's home, Walker is embarrassed at the way Allison speaks to her Latina maid, Maria. The typical racial and class formation that allows a wealthy white girl to hold power over a middle-aged non-white woman predictably makes Walker uncomfortable: "I feel closer to Maria than I do to Allison, like I should call her Mrs. Somebody and I should go with her to the kitchen or wherever she's walking to, and not stay back here in the fancy front rooms with Allison" (210). But Walker does stay with Allison and listens to her friend discuss her fine house and upcoming bat mitzvah. Again, as if to compensate for having participated in what she finds objectionable and reassert her identification with those who lack power and privilege, Walker bad-mouths Allison to her poor, Latina friend Theresa, saying that "Allison wouldn't last five minutes" in Theresa's neighborhood "with her uppity attitude" (212). Walker identifies herself as "the translator, the one in between, the one serving as the walkway between two worlds" because she does not wholly identify herself as a part of her father's white/Jewish middle-class world (212). If she were entirely white/Jewish, she would be incapable of translating that "world" for others and would be unable to transition between it and her black/Latinx "world."

It is this resistance to assimilating into her father and stepmother's class (and thus, to Walker, race) that leads Walker to befriend and identify with the poor racialized minorities in the Bronx. Walker's comparison of her life with her father and his family in Riverdale (before they move to Larchmont) to her social life with her Hispanic friends in the Bronx demonstrates how race and class intersect not only in everyday American life but in Walker's own racial consciousness:

> My father and stepmother live just in Riverdale, but I live in Riverdale and the Bronx. Riverdale to me means Nanny and the Liebermans and shopping down on Johnson Avenue for challah for Friday-night dinner, to go with the chicken soup my stepmother makes. It means a little store that sells OshKosh overalls to my stepmother for my two-year-old brother, Ben, her firstborn son. It means walking around with my stepmother, this Sephardic-looking Jew who calls me her daughter around people who never question.

The Bronx means saying hello respectfully to Mrs. Colón when I visit Loída or César. It means Dominican boys from JFK High School, Zulu Nation and Afrika Bombaataa, and fast girls getting pregnant young. The Bronx means being ready to fight. It means walking around with my friends Sam and Jesús and Theresa and Melissa and being seen as I feel I truly am: a Puertoriqueña, a mulatta, breathed out with all that Spanish flavor. A girl of color with attitude. (200)

She later claims she hates Larchmont and hates "that everybody is white": "When I walk down the street people look at me funny, as if I don't belong" (208). When she is alone with her little brother and sister in Larchmont, she overhears a woman marveling "at what a young but capable nanny" she is and on other occasions is asked if she is "the baby-sitter, the maid, the au pair" (230). Her ongoing sense, whether accurate or not, that her father might "like to relax and enjoy his assimilated all-white family without the aberration, the dark spot in an otherwise picture-perfect suburban life" reflects how out of place she feels and why she might prefer to go to the Bronx and be where she can embody an identity as a "girl of color with attitude" (230, 200).

The racial diversity within Walker's description of the Bronx includes conspicuous references to African American culture, and so the community is depicted as one that is as much "of color" as it is strictly Hispanic.[102] Her experience in the Bronx and her ability to be included there reflects the heterogeneity she locates in communities of racialized minorities. Adding to the complexity of her community's formulation is the fact that Hispanicness, like Jewishness, is both white and nonwhite. Within such a community "of color" with links to marked whiteness, her marked and mixed race—as well as her coinciding interest in allying herself against white power—are made possible. She is "more comfortable at Theresa's house than [she is] at [her] own" and only at Theresa's does she find something she can "fit into."[103] The fact that her father does not fit into her friends' neighborhoods while she does illustrates the degree to which Walker links race and class, as well as her conscious decision to identify with those who

are unlike her father. Unlike her performance of Jewishness, which
Walker repeatedly characterizes as unsuccessful, her performance as
Hispanic—or at least as non-Jewish and/or nonwhite—is convincing,
in large part because she is proud of her Hispanic identity but feels
guilty about her Jewishness. When her father takes her to the building where a friend lives, "he is the only white person around as far as
the eye can see":

> He asks in that same way [as he has before], Are you sure you'll be
> okay? And I think to myself that *I* am going to be fine, but will he? I
> belong because my skin says I do, because people don't question me,
> don't look at me and think of all the wack shit that white people do.
> They don't assume I have money or that I don't respect them. I can
> walk like I know, I can cock my head to one side and look at someone
> like they better step off, but my father? I worry that he's just another
> white man walking down the street, an easy mark.[104]

Harrison-Kahan rightly argues that Walker's "specific identification
with Hispanic identity is as much rooted in a class consciousness as an
ethnic one."[105] Yet Walker also embraces Latinx identity when she lives
with her father because it much more closely approximates blackness
than does whiteness/Jewishness. Certainly she finds wealth and privilege objectionable, but since class and race always intersect so intensely,
Walker also finds whiteness (which she sees as wealthy and privileged)
objectionable and identifies with the poor, nonwhite / highly racialized
folks who happen, in her social circle, to be Latinx. If a Jewish identity
offers Senna's Birdie an approximation of blackness (at least for a short
while), then a Latinx identity offers Walker the next best thing when
she is apart from her black San Francisco community.

Just as Walker finds that her blackness makes it difficult to also be
Jewish when she is at summer camp with Jewish kids, so does she experience difficulty allowing Jewishness and Hispanicness to coincide.
She finds it easy to discard her Jewishness and slip into the world of
her Latinx friends, but transplanting Hispanicness into her Jewish
world does not work well. When Theresa comes to stay at her apartment, Walker comments,

It's strange having Theresa at my house since it's always been the other way around, I'm always the one going into her world, she's never coming into mine. She seems out of place in my room, and even more so sneaking downstairs in the middle of the night to eat the rest of the Entenmann's chocolate chip cookies hidden in the bottom drawer of the refrigerator. It's a bit of a shock to see Theresa in a kitchen that's well lit and full of shiny white Formica. She looks different juxtaposed against it, faded, haggard, and slightly green. I notice the concealer caked under her eyes, her long pink nails, her fake-looking blow-dried hair.[106]

Walker's observations indicate that when she is in her Jewish home she sees her Latina friend with Jewish eyes. And to Walker, Jewish eyes require a critical downward cast. The sensual richness and beauty Walker usually finds in Hispanicness become artificial, dull, and grotesque when "juxtaposed against" the bright and (not insignificantly) white kitchen. Moreover, just as Walker finds Jewishness difficult to embody because of her blackness, she finds that her Hispanic identity is made difficult by her Jewishness. Walker notes, "There isn't anything else in the whole apartment that looks or sounds or smells like my friends' houses, that would prove that I am of color, that I am who I say I am outside of these walls," her own belongings aside.[107] The way she collapses "of color" signals the way she considers all "color" in contradistinction to whiteness and Jewishness and quite decidedly identifies as "of color." In this way, her Latina identity would appear to be more "authentic" than her Jewish one since she so often conflates Jewishness with whiteness. But her comment that she lacks proof of who she says she is when she is in her father's apartment suggests that when her body is contextualized by the signs of middle-class stature, her racial identity "of color" and/or Latinx is thrown into doubt. She makes class and race synonymous and, in doing so, reveals the process by which she makes Jewishness white. Instead of recognizing what she finds objectionable about her father's lifestyle as the effect of class privilege, she recognizes it as an embodiment of Jewishness. According to Harrison-Kahan, "By substituting race for class instead of considering the ways that race and class are intertwined to create specificity, Walker makes an historically dangerous association, conflating the 'middle-class world' of her father's new family with Jewishness" and, as several critics argue, negatively stereotypes Jews.[108] Indeed, Walker seems to scapegoat Jewishness because she does not critically examine what Jewishness means to her.

In identifying with the working class and objecting to the material pursuits and privilege associated with the middle class, Walker erases the markedness of Jews as an ethnoracial identity. She subsequently positions Jewishness as synonymous with whiteness and thus in opposition to the marked ethnoracial groups that reside in the Bronx. Though it is only a brief scene, it is significant that when she reads *The Diary of Anne Frank* Walker does not simply have compassion for Anne but identifies with her intensely. Walker explains, "I become her. . . . [and] I feel something I have never felt before. I feel terror and loss."[109] She even has nightmares "about the Gestapo coming up the stairs and into [her] room."[110] Walker is capable of identifying and indeed is inclined to identify with Jewishness for the very reason that it is not simply whiteness. When she considers Jews as the victims of white oppression she certainly does not conflate the two racially. But in her narrow experiences with Jewishness as strictly upper-middle class, Walker loses the capacity to empathize with or otherwise liken herself to a group that enjoys so much privilege. Though she does have poor white friends when she lives with her mother in San Francisco, the fact that their whiteness is juxtaposed against the poor black population of Walker's school and neighborhood means that her situation holds a vitally different racial dynamic. In the context of living with her mother, Walker's identity is black, and so she does not feel guilt or shame about friendships with white girls the way she does when she lives with her father. In New York, her friendships with white girls occur when she is identified as Jewish, and she consequently feels it necessary to compensate for her position in relation to underprivileged nonwhites. Ultimately, Walker's text mimics the historical shift of Jewishness from marked otherness to unmarked whiteness. But in American society Jewishness has developed into a marked whiteness and has in effect made whiteness more obviously diverse, and therefore made it more difficult to argue that a "universal," un-racialized whiteness exists. Whether Walker mimics this social situation as well is debatable. Harrison-Kahan argues that Walker "ends up overlooking the multiplicity of Jewishness itself," for instance.[111] On the one hand, Walker certainly collapses Jewishness into whiteness and considers race in the broader terms of color. But on the other hand, she is careful to call her memoir *Black White and Jewish*, which suggests that she does see her multiracialness as something more nuanced than the simple white–black binary. It might even be possible to interpret her title as pointedly acknowledging the difference between Jewishness and unmarked whiteness since she includes no comma between "black" and "white." Reading her title in this way, Walker is "black–white" and "Jewish." In other words, she recognizes her black–white mixture according to conventional monoracial race concepts but adds "Jewish" to complicate that dichotomous understanding of her identity.[112]

Walker and Senna go about it differently, but both writers challenge the normative power of whiteness in ways that diversify and, consequently, racialize whiteness. In order to assert multiracialness and break down the boundaries around race concepts, a good deal of multiracial literature aims to make race more fluid and malleable. In an apparent contradiction, whiteness also has to be considered in the same terms as any other race in order to racialize it like any other race. However, these strategies of multiracial literature are not inconsistent because whiteness is not considered a race in the conventional terms of monoracialness and purity. Rather, multiracial literature makes apparent how whiteness is as heterogeneous as blackness and thereby demonstrates the absurdity of imagining that the one-drop rule actually guards the whiteness of whiteness. As these texts illustrate, whiteness can exist in the presence of blackness just as readily as it has traditionally been absorbed into blackness and erased. By refusing to recognize whiteness as a blank, unracialized norm, and by refusing to obey the one-drop rule, these texts emphasize how multiracial identity is not a new race but rather a new way of thinking about race.

Indeed, multiracialism in the literary imagination is not simply a reification of racial division as a result of claiming both white and black but an exploration of multiracial identity that manipulates and begins to break down historical race practices. Naomi Pabst notes this shift in literary representations of whiteness in relation to mixed race: "As testified to in the expanding literature on black/white mixed subjectivity, it is (increasingly) possible for black and/or mixed-race subjects to identify as white without having to pass. This whiteness is provisional, and subject to eternal qualification and dispute, but possible nevertheless."[113] Such claiming of whiteness does not employ the identity politics of earlier literature, in which whiteness was set in stark opposition to black solidarity. As Pabst notes, the argument that mixture is a capitulation to whiteness or a desire to be white "is nothing other than a policing mechanism that regulates and homogenizes blackness. It maintains the hegemonic ineluctability of the black/white binary, it reestablishes black and white as discrete categories, and it upholds race and racism."[114] Recent literary production acknowledges traditional race practices in which whiteness is diversity made homogeneous whereas blackness is at once homogeneous and heterogeneous (as one race that acknowledges its mixture), but writers challenge this tradition directly instead of accepting it. Contemporary writing disputes the racial binary by depicting whiteness as diverse and capable of mixture and blackness as a less simple catchall category than has been accepted in white culture (as chapter 3 will discuss). Ultimately, contemporary literature resists the opportunity to simply fit multiracial identity into accepted American race tradition and instead begins to pull loose the threads that hold it together.

| Chapter Three

"Black Like Me"
Negotiating Blackness

The value of black pride cannot be overstated in its role of providing hope, dignity, and political strength to a population that has long existed within a racist white supremacist nation.[1] After centuries of American history that have consistently made it difficult to be anything but black (via hypodescent) and made black pride the most effective tool for combating white racism and discrimination, it is understandable why an African American might prefer that those with black ancestry identify themselves similarly. Certainly, racial solidarity is the chief objection to multiracial identity in contemporary discourse about multiracialness. Many commentators argue that multiracialism poses a potential threat to the continued struggles of African Americans by reducing the numbers of African Americans or distracting black multiracials from being wholly committed to African American causes. While this may be a problem in relation to some multiracial individuals (as well as some white multiracial-activist parents), for many Americans who identify as black–white, their multiracial identification does not detract from their black pride or their commitment to black political struggle. Even if hypodescent is no longer enforced, its effects remain. That is, the legacy of the one-drop rule—black pride—is undiminished for many who identify as multiracial even if the rule itself no longer legally dictates how they identify themselves.

Furthermore, if it is the case, as Renee C. Romano contends in *Race Mixing*, that mixed children born before the 1970s were raised to identify as black whereas mixed children born in and after the 1970s have been frequently raised as multiracial, and if it is the case, as many commentators worry, that the (white) leadership of multiracial advocacy groups is leading new generations away from identifying as black, then it is important that contemporary literature is imagining multiracialness as containing black pride and respect. Danzy Senna asks a deceptively simple question of multiracial advocates: "Why is it so important for many mixed people not to be defined as black?"[2] These sentiments are worked through in her writing and that of her peers; as a group, contemporary writers affirm rather than avoid the blackness of multiraciality. As Sika A. Dagbovie-Mullins points out in *Crossing B(l)ack*, the black consciousness of so many contemporary literary characters "offers possibilities for identity that remain historically grounded in blackness without being [monoracially] imprisoning."[3] In this sense, the texts explored in this chapter depict figures who embrace black pride but find alternatives to the monoracial blackness that such loyalty necessitated in the past. In so doing, they demonstrate that past racial practices are insufficient to encompass contemporary multiracial identities.

I will be using the phrases "black political struggle" and "black political allegiance" throughout this discussion. These phrases are meant to evoke the political orientation that supports a progressive, antiracist, social equality agenda. As Manning Marable points out in his discussion of Clarence Thomas, it is a mistake to assume that all black people will exhibit this kind of "black political allegiance." Marable argues that in our post–civil rights era, in contrast to the Jim Crow era, black "racial identity doesn't tell us anything significant about a person's political beliefs, voting behavior, or cultural values."[4] Marable's comments are helpful in complicating the black–nonblack political opposition that some black monoracialists seem invested in. As I, like Marable, am interested in challenging the conflation of racial identity and political orientation, my approach is not unlike that of Tommie Shelby. In *We Who Are Dark: The Philosophical Foundations of Black Solidarity*, Shelby proposes "a conception of black solidarity that is not only, or even primarily, concerned with questions of identity, but that urges a joint commitment to defeating racism, to eliminating unjust racial inequalities, and to improving the material life prospects of those racialized as 'black,' especially the most disadvantaged."[5] Shelby's interest in separating politics from identity reflects his study of black nationalism and the way in which identity has come to stand in for political stance. It is this conflation of identity and political allegiance that can dominate objections to multiracial identity, stifle the examination of multiracialness itself, and evade meaningful discussion of solidarity across differences of racial identity. I agree with Shelby when he says that "it is possible to dispense with the idea of race as a biological essence and to agree with the critics of identity politics about many of its dangers and limitations, while nevertheless continuing to embrace a form of blackness as an emancipatory tool. . . . This approach shifts the focus away from questions of social identity as such and toward the various dimensions of racial injustice."[6]

In other words, instead of seeing identity as the site of one's political allegiance or a sign of one's interest in social justice, we must stop considering black political solidarity as necessarily tied to racial identity. As Lisa Lowe argues, depending too much on one particular facet of identity—what she terms an "exclusive cultural identity"—means that we might not perceive other shared qualities between people and therefore might not form potential alliances. That is, using race as an "exclusive identity" not only makes identity rigid and ethnoracial identity a dominant identity (as opposed to class, gender, sexuality, nationality, or age, for instance) but also makes it difficult for people to consider themselves or others outside the confines of such identification. As Marable points out, it leads us to make false assumptions about people's political commitments. Angela Davis—who had to make a famous choice between groups in which her race stood for all (the Black Panthers) or nothing (the Communists)—proposes that political commitment is most effective when it bases "identity on politics rather than the politics on identity."[7] In this vein, my discussion explores how multi*racial* identity might readily coincide with black *political* solidarity.

Credible Blackness: The Politics of Black Identity

Ironically, those who might like to identify as black are frequently challenged for not being black enough in appearance or culture.
Some argue that while whites might question white-looking people
who call themselves black, "in the black community it's just accepted," since "historically, only the black community has taken in the offspring of miscegenation."[8] Or, as Sika A. Dagbovie-Mullins observes,
"Throughout American history, hardly anyone challenges the location
of multiracial people as black."[9] Others point out that if blackness is
not particularly apparent, one's assertion of blackness will not necessarily be accepted by either whites or blacks. Elliott Lewis argues in
Fade, for instance, that it is a mistake to assume that "black-white biracial children are best served by adopting an all-black identity start-
ing at an early age," because so many children of ambiguous race
or light skin are not accepted readily or automatically by other children or other "members of their minority race."[10] Similarly, in "Light,
Bright, and Almost White: The Advantages and Disadvantages of Light
Skin," Margaret Hunter explains that "light skin is associated with
Whites, assimilation, and a lack of racial consciousness, thus leaving
some light skinned people to feel unwelcome in their own communities."[11] Having light skin, Hunter argues, often produces a sense of
lacking "authenticity" or not being "Black enough" and makes some
feel "like outsiders, unaccepted, or even pushed out of their own communities and community organizations based on skin tone."[12] Darker
people "are more likely to be seen and accepted as legitimate members of their ethnic groups, are less likely to have their group loyalty questioned, are more likely to be perceived as 'racially-conscious,'
and are less likely to be accused of trying to assimilate or 'wanting
to be White'"; many light-skinned African Americans, "especially if
they are multiracial, report feeling excluded."[13] For instance, describ-
ing her situation as a child at an Afrocentric school at a time when
her parents subscribed heartily to Negritude, Danzy Senna expresses feelings of "inadequacy." She recalls, "I faced a conundrum that
many mixed people face: The black community of those heady times

told me I'd better identify as black, but that I would never be black enough. It was the ultimate double bind."[14]

The impact of appearance on identity is almost overwhelming for some—including Senna's, Raboteau's, and Harper's protagonists—and emphasizes the degree to which the body is still of the utmost importance when it comes to asserting "who" or "what" we are. Tru Leverette explains that for black (and multiracial) women, in particular, the body still shapes social identity:

> Historically, those on the lower end of hierarchies have been associated with the body—women as opposed to men and people of color as opposed to whites. We may see ourselves outside of or beyond our bodies, but society typically uses our bodies, especially if we are relegated to the bottom of the hierarchy, as points of reference or even as maps of our identities. The identities we establish for ourselves may be at odds with the meanings inscribed on our bodies; thus, our identities may "disappear" because of social forces that locate our identities through cultural interpretations of bodies. . . . Our bodies may play tricks on us; they may lead people who "read" them to conclusions other than those we intend, all unsettling possibilities—certainly so for those whose bodies seemingly are in contradiction with their self-defined identities, as is sometimes the case with those of mixed race.[15]

For many multiracial figures, the issue of appearance can come to dominate their senses of self—not only because the body can demonstrate identity more easily than an explanation (as we will see, the protagonists struggle with ambiguous appearances and the coinciding problem of not knowing how to describe their identities) but also because the body can decide identity for a person and, in particular, act as visible proof of one's blackness. As Leilani Nishime explains, we commonly understand "the materiality of the body as the primary element deciding race" even if we can ostensibly choose our racial identities.[16] Thus, she says, "We experience race as a transcendent fact, a truth written on the body. . . . Race happens in that moment when the viewer considers it."[17] It is this problematic "moment" in which the body is seen and its race determined that troubles multiracial figures so intensely—not only because it precludes an opportunity for them to self-identify but because they judge their bodies to be too insufficiently black to be "seen" in the ways they want to be seen.[18]

In rather stark ways, this newer need for darkness is a reversal of colorism, which developed throughout slavery and into the twentieth century as a hierarchy that valued lightness over darkness. Though colorism is certainly still prevalent in American culture, as studies like Maxine Thompson and Verna Keith's "Copper Brown and Blue Black: Colorism and Self Evaluation" demonstrate, the politically engaged literary world resists such a deeply rooted devaluation of blackness. Indeed, one of the characteristic features of contemporary literature is a refusal to consider blackness a taint; instead, it celebrates blackness without reservation. If anything, black power and civil rights have solidified and augmented the black pride that has always characterized African American literature to the extent that nothing but uncompromising pride in blackness is the norm.

However, pride does not eliminate the problem of acceptance. Black pride and solidarity are highly valued, particularly within the African American population, and black history in the United States contains countless figures who looked white or not particularly black but claimed blackness out of solidarity and were accepted as such. Yet, white–black mixture can still be viewed with suspicion even when a person wants to identify as monoracially black. Lisa Jones notes in *Bulletproof Diva* that she has as little regard for African Americans who "might find 'evidence' of [her] white parent reason to question [her] racial allegiance" as she has for whites who "might wonder why [she] would choose to identify as 'fully' black when [she has] the 'saving grace' of a white parent."[19] Furthermore, proclaiming a black identity and having that black identity accepted by either whites or blacks are very different things. As Naomi Pabst points out, contrary to Jones's insistence that in America she is considered black, Jones is "often described in the media and elsewhere as 'mixed,' as 'black and white,' as 'half-Jewish, half-black,' to name only a few of the commonplace circumlocutions employed to qualify her black identity. She herself lamented in a *Village Voice* article that during her national book tour to promote *Bulletproof Diva*, she was 'biracialized to death.'"[20] While multiracialism does not necessarily exclude one from blackness since identification is so varied, to Jones, being identified as biracial is an explicit effort to avoid recognizing her as black. Similarly, in "Passing for White, Passing for Black," Adrian Piper, a "white-looking individual of African ancestry," recounts how one of her white professors questioned her claim to blackness with "a triumphant smirk," stating, "Miss Piper, you're about as black as I am."[21] Piper admits that "the accusation" of not really being black "was one [she] had heard before, but more typically from other blacks."[22]

This kind of scenario, of having one's claim to blackness questioned, is evident in virtually all contemporary narratives in one form or another and arises over and over again in the multitude of autobiographical accounts that make up a sizeable portion of widely read work on multiracialism. Consequently, if Jones's claim that the "evidence" of her whiteness is enough to cast doubt on her blackness is also the case for many individuals, this is highly problematic not only for individuals' admittance into ethnoracial groups but for individuals' psychological states. For instance, in *The Black Notebooks*, Toi Derricotte dwells on the fact of her lightness and how it has affected her attitudes toward others as well as others' treatment of her. She explains, "Skin color causes certain problems continuously, problems that open the issue of racism over and over like a wound. These openings are occasions for reexamination. My skin keeps things, literally, from being either black or white."[23] She also discusses how the lack of a sign of her blackness (such as black skin) means that she has to identify herself verbally to inquisitive onlookers and how she wishes she could avoid this situation: "I feel a pang of desire that I should have a cross, a star, some sign of gold to wear so that, before they wonder or ask, I can present a dignified response to the world's interrogations."[24] Derricotte's anxiety about the need to identify herself verbally, together with the added pressure of knowing that she will be taken for white if she chooses not to correct others' perceptions, amounts to an almost crippling psychological burden at times.

The experiences of those who do not look especially black in a conventional way, whether they identify as monoracially black (like Jones and Derricotte) or multiracially black (like the dozens of contributors to collections like Lise Funderburg's *Black, White, Other*) demonstrate just how difficult claiming blackness can be. As I have discussed earlier, the prominent and vocal critics of multiracialism argue against it in part because American blackness is inherently multiracial, has always incorporated multiple racial ancestries (African, European, and Native, in particular), and has always been the racial category that could include virtually any ethnicity or race that is mixed with blackness. However, their insistence that the umbrella race of African American is inclusive, or that it inherently absorbs mixture, is called into question when those who want to claim blackness and have known ancestry upon which to base their claims are interrogated or doubted by African Americans themselves—often *because* of mixture.

The dual challenge of asserting one's black pride and claiming an identity that includes blackness when one's blackness is not apparent is not a new problem. In the twentieth century doubt has been cast on the "authenticity" of African Americans who do not have particularly black bodies as well as African Americans who do not exhibit whatever values and behaviors have been deemed black in any given circumstance.[25] This has hardly been made easier with time and is complicated by contemporary identities of mixture. For some, declaring a multiracial identity is a matter of black pride but also a matter of respect for both parents, as in, "I'm composed of two different races and I choose to value each of those. . . . It's not as though I'm going to write off my mother's race for the convenience of pleasing somebody else's view of what I should or should not be doing."[26] For others, like Lisa Jones, choosing to identify as black need not exclude whiteness or her white parent. She explains, "I don't deny my white forebears, but I call myself African American, which means, to me, a person of African and Native American, Latin, or European descent" and thus confirms that her (white) mother is an essential part of her life.[27] In her language, black is a monoracial term but one that names a multiracial concept (or racial identity). Similarly, Danzy Senna makes it clear that she identifies racially as black while simultaneously acknowledging her additional racial heritages: "I . . . identify myself as black. I don't see it in contradiction with my white and Mexican ancestry. Nor does it negate these other parts of myself. I have come to understand that my multiplicity is inherent in my blackness, not opposed to it. To be black, for me, is to contain all colors."[28] Senna also explains that her choice of a black identity was motivated by the racism she witnessed growing up and is a declaration of racial solidarity.[29] For both Senna and Jones, then, "black" or "African American" might mean to them what "multiracial" might mean to someone who identifies as such, with regard to race mixture at the very least but perhaps even in terms of a politically black-oriented multiracial identity.[30] In this identification as multiracial but with black political allegiance, multiracial identity and the black solidarity of African Americanness exist together. Like the literature that preceded them, contemporary multiracial texts exhibit pride in blackness and focus on negotiating blackness in relation to mixture and identity formation. Rather than having to choose between blackness (and racial pride and loyalty) and whiteness (and being a race traitor) as in the past, multiracials can now formulate an identity that exhibits allegiance to black pride without the black monoracial identity that traditionally accompanies it. If multiracial identity is as much about a personal sense of self as it is about a public label, multiracial literature explores the terrain of maintaining the political significance of blackness as well as the personal desire for blackness just as it explores the public and private reasons for identifying as multiracial.[31]

The marriage of the personal and political requires extensive negotiation. Public identities are not always easily achieved through self-identification, and multiracial figures often internalize doubt when it is cast upon their identities. The trauma or anxiety that possessing questionable/questioned blackness evokes in Derricotte and others suggests that one's personal sense of self and public acknowledgment of that self generally need to coincide. In many cases, appearance is the stumbling block for this sense of validation or confirmation of blackness. For Nellie in Rachel Harper's *Brass Ankle Blues*, Emma in Emily Raboteau's *The Professor's Daughter*, and Birdie in Danzy Senna's *Caucasia*, the lack of a convincingly black body means that others do not readily recognize them as black and leads each of the girls to look at herself critically. Each of these protagonists desires a blacker body and thus an unambiguous link to blackness. To them, a more typical black appearance is a more acceptable kind of blackness. The question is not only why they feel insufficient but why they seem to have a specific idea of what sufficient blackness is. This impulse among the characters demonstrates how a particular set of norms has been assimilated by these American girls and how blackness is sometimes less accepting of diversity than some would argue—at least when it comes to appearance. The girls who question the blackness of their bodies really never question their African Americanness (in terms of cultural and historical location), but in various ways they question their blackness in terms of race. It is telling that all three struggle so much with blackness and experience a painful sense of not belonging, of being insufficient, of being black yet other within blackness. As Pabst explains in "An Unexpected Blackness," "You hear it said about a particular type of black person all the time: he or she is 'not really black.'"[32] But she points out that this is a contradiction: "I've never seen a white person or a person of color with no ties to blackness get told that they're 'not really black.' This means that you have to be black by some definition in order to be 'not really black.' And this means that even if your blackness is in question, your blackness is not in question. That is to say that the designation 'not really black' bolsters and underscores your black identity at the same time that it marginalizes you from blackness."[33] As a result, Pabst observes, "All at once you belong and you do not belong, you are simultaneously an insider and an outsider. You are black and yet your blackness is different, unusual. Yours is an unexpected blackness. And this means that in some people's eyes, yours is an inappropriate, inauthentic blackness."[34] Indeed, Pabst argues in "Blackness/Mixedness" that the "regulation" of blackness leads to "the exclusions and hierarchizations of blacks within the category of blackness" in ways that suggest that "interraciality and transculturalism are locations within the sign of blackness that are rendered 'invisible, untenable, and/or fraudulent.'"[35]

However, contemporary multiracial literature also focuses on how mixedness complicates one's claim to blackness regardless of appearance. Cultural whiteness (including anything from fashion to speech) and knowledge of white ancestry are often as relevant to one's claim of blackness as the body. In Rebecca Walker's autobiography *Black White and Jewish*, as well as in the novels of Harper, Raboteau, and Senna, nonbodily signs of whiteness pose a threat to blackness. In a reversal of the way hypodescent might erase whiteness, Walker, Nellie, Emma, Birdie, and Cole find that their blackness is questioned because of cultural signs of whiteness. Indeed, the "cultural artifacts" of "being down," which may be exhibited in makeup, clothes, hairstyle, dance style, musical taste, vernacular, and so on, reflect what Pabst calls the "premium placed on 'look relations' in the realm of black authenticity."[36] She cites Paul Gilroy's assessment in *Against Race* that style or fashion in particular is increasingly instrumental to "multicultural blackness" and concludes that "the ways in which signifiers of blackness have increasingly less to do with the racialized body proper and more to do with what that body is adorned with" means that "these mandates around wearing one's blackness on one's sleeve constitute an intensification and an expansion of the myriad ways that cultural integrity can be performed and regulated."[37] As Gilroy explains, "the unclothed body is not considered sufficient to confer either authenticity or identity" even for certain types of blackness independent of mixture, and so "clothing, objects, things, and commodities provide the only entry ticket into stylish solidarities powerful enough to foster the novel forms of nationality found in collectivities like the Gangsta Nation, the Hip hop Nation, and, of course, the Nation of Islam."[38] Gilroy's argument about black expression and identity is helpful when it comes to multiracial claims of blackness; as he says, blackness is not always "written into or even onto the body" and so at times, "blackness emerges as more behavioral" and "cultural."[39]

Ultimately, each literary figure must decide or discover whether blackness and mixedness can coincide; Pabst argues, "In the United States, despite the loud lip service paid to the idea that any amount of black African ancestry makes you black, and despite all the reminders we hear about how all black people are mixed, being racially ambiguous and/or having a non-black parent pretty much guarantees that some people, indeed many people, are going to call your blackness into question."[40] Pabst further argues, in fact, that the paradox of the one-drop rule—that mixture is simultaneously made "fully black" and yet only "one-drop" black—characterizes black–white multiracial subjectivity. She explains that "black/white mixed subjects are, more often than is acknowledged, just as soon interpellated into either side of the mixedness/blackness coin. . . . And if anything distinguishes a reflexively mixed-race social location, it is precisely this constant, aggressive, and often inconsistent interpellation."[41] At issue, consequently, is how multiracial figures respond to this kind of interpretation of their blackness by others and whether or how self-interpretation affects their subject positions. Also at issue is whether or how multiracial figures adopt or, instead, reshape how others interpret mixture in this blackness/mixedness schema.

The Body as Evidence: Rachel Harper's *Brass Ankle Blues*

Unlike Raboteau, Walker, and Senna, whose stories cover years and even decades, Harper limits her depiction of Nellie to one formative summer of her adolescence. As a fourteen-year-old, Nellie must deal with her parents' separation, her developing gendered and racialized body, and her sexual desire simultaneously, and each of these factors is significant in her efforts to identify herself racially. The first sentence of Nellie's narrative states that when she is only seven years old she tells her father "that [she] wanted to grow up to be invisible" because of the intrusive gaze and questions of those who cannot make sense of her appearance (Harper, *Brass Ankle Blues*, 1). Nellie's awareness of her body as "not usual" has developed over the course of only two years; later in her narrative we learn that a lone conversation with her brothers when she was five is the source of her obsessive concern with color and her understanding of racial identity in terms of appearance:

> I was five the first time I realized I was black. After watching
> *Roots* my brothers and I began to fantasize about slavery. Marcus, always defiant, claimed he would have run off just like Kunta Kinte.

"I wouldn't let anybody own me," he said with the unflinching confidence that only a ten-year-old can muster.

"I don't know . . ." Noah spoke slowly. "I don't think I'd want to be one of the black people." He was almost eight.

"You mean you'd pretend to be white?" Marcus looked shocked.

"But I am white." Noah held out his arm. In all fairness, he was a bit lighter than us.

"No." Marcus shook his head. "Mom's white. We're black, like Dad."

"But Dad's brown," Noah said. "Uncle Bobby's black."

"Aren't we both?" I asked.

"Yeah, but all that really means is we're black."

"I don't know if I want to be black." Noah was scratching a scab on his knee.

"You don't have a choice," Marcus said. "None of us do." (6–7)

The confusion the children have regarding the labels "white" and "black" because of skin color is indicative of their youth and consequent lack of experience with American racial classification practices. As the eldest, Marcus is most initiated into the way race operates in the United States and so he instructs his siblings in what he has learned. Marcus teaches them about the one-drop rule and black racial solidarity—first when he responds to Noah's resolve that he is "white" based on his skin color by insisting that to not be "one of the black people" he would have to "*pretend* to be white," and again when he replies to Nellie's query about being both black and white by declaring that "all that really means is we're black." Nellie's subsequent obsession with her blackness suggests that she has taken this lesson to heart, but her desire for blackness is repeatedly put in terms of phenotype with little to no concern for black community or culture.

This scene of Marcus instructing his siblings in the one-drop understanding of blackness leads Nellie not to an affirmation of her black identity but rather to a hyperawareness of how her body fails to exhibit the black identity she has learned she can (and indeed ought to) claim. Nellie worries that her white skin overpowers the strength of the one-drop rule and links her unwillingly to whiteness. Regardless

of what her brother has asserted about the one-drop rule, Nellie's dis-
satisfaction with the lightness of her skin emphasizes that the rule is
not enough for her—it does not erase the whiteness she perceives in
her skin. The conversation is, she tells us, the first and last time she discusses race with her siblings. And since Nellie never mentions whether or how her parents discuss racial identity with their children (but
does tell this story of her realization of her categorical blackness as a
five-year-old), it seems that her reaction to Marcus's lesson is responsible for her adolescent perception of her own racial identity. As a result
of her right and responsibility to claim blackness, she is determined
to be recognized as black; however, this determination is largely invested in her (largely uncooperative) body. While Nellie's lack of interest in establishing a black identity through politics or culture (as
opposed to through her body) might well be the result of her youth, it
does emphasize the way in which racial identity can be considered in
the strict terms of skin or appearance. Though Marcus has explained
that skin tone is, essentially, irrelevant to blackness, Nellie spends her
narrative preoccupied with her appearance and, in particular, her col-
or. In order to be unquestionably black as Marcus insists she is and to
avoid the curious gaze and intrusive questions of those around her,
Nellie senses that her body would have to change and become darker.
She understands that her blackness is not taken for granted and that
if her appearance does not leave her outside of blackness then knowledge of her white mother will. She overhears her father speaking with
his African American aunt about her parents' separation, and his aunt
advises him to "worry about yourself for once, and those mixed-up
kids of yours. The marriage was hard enough on them, but the divorce will be even worse. Now they really won't know who they are"
(15). In a sense, the aunt's insensitive remarks accurately reflect Nellie's
self-assessment and her parents' separation does play a role (though
a smaller one than her great-aunt believes) in her affinity for blackness and disinclination to be associated with whiteness. Though she
seems to know who she *wants* to be, Nellie has yet to feel that she really *is* that person.

Perhaps the greatest irony is that everyone who looks at Nellie—
including her own family—feels that she does not fit anywhere, while
Nellie herself feels sure that she wants to identify as black. Since her
personal sense of black identity is not readily perceived by others, she
is caught between how she is seen and how she wants to be seen. And
because her public and personal identities do not obviously match,
Nellie is hyperaware of her body and its inability to demonstrate the
racial identity she feels. Nellie's maternal cousin Jess puts things most
straightforwardly when Nellie complains about the "racist bastard"
shopkeeper who shadows her while paying no attention to the blond
and white Jess who is, in fact, shoplifting. Nellie insists that "it happens
to black people all the time," but Jess objects, saying, "You can't seriously think that guy was being prejudiced to you. I mean, it's not like
he thought you were black or anything" (57). When Nellie questions
her, Jess responds, "Come on, Nellie, you don't exactly look black. . . .
You're not like a 'real' black person. . . . Look at yourself, you've got
soft, curly hair and the lightest brown eyes I've ever seen. Plus your
face looks more like Grandma Floss's than anyone, if she'd had a really great tan" (57). When Nellie asks, "So just because my mother's
white that means I am?," in a reversal of the one-drop rule, Jess proclaims, "None of y'all are really black. Look at your aunt Frances,
she's barely darker than me. And your daddy's hair is all soft and he
speaks all proper and shit. . . . You know what I'm saying. I grew up
with black people, with black skin and kinky black hair. Those folks
are from plantations, with grandparents who were all slaves. Those
are real black people. Your family's something else. You're all these
different mixed-up things—" (57). When Nellie asks what that makes
her and her family, Jess is at a loss: "There's no one word." "Exactly,"
Nellie retorts, "and until we come up with one, we're black" (58). Despite Nellie's insistence that she and her father are black, Nellie's own
response to the opinion of an onlooker that she is not a "real black
person" reflects her vulnerability. There is "no one word" for what she
or her family is, so "black" is merely a default. Her conversation with
her cousin illustrates the inauthenticity that Nellie consistently fears

others see in her and that she works so hard to combat. But it also reveals that if Nellie had "black skin and kinky black hair" her ancestry might never be questioned. Indeed, if Nellie and her father had
"black skin and kinky black hair," it seems her father's apparently unblack "proper" speech and other cultural markers that signal a lack
of "authentic" blackness would not be so noticeable. If Nellie looked
the part, it might never occur to someone to doubt whether her family is "really" African American on any grounds. For Nellie, then, her
claim to blackness rests largely on what people see in her rather than
what identity they hear her declare. She feels intense pressure to show,
rather than explain, her blackness, and consequently Nellie fosters and
fiercely guards any physical sign of blackness her body can muster.

Before she has even revealed her name, Nellie has confessed that
she is afraid to use too much powdered soap in a rest-stop bathroom:
"I'm afraid if I rub too hard it will wash away all my color" (5). Her
fear of losing what blackness she has emphasizes the impermanence
and insecurity Nellie feels and the tentativeness with which she can
proclaim blackness. But her fear that she might wash away the signs
of her blackness also indicates how invested Nellie is in her skin color.
Her obsessive cataloguing of her skin, how it tans and grows darker
over the course of the summer, and how it compares to other peoples'
skin, paired with her awareness of her father's sudden positive change
in mood when all of his black friends visit for a barbeque—"he seems
to have lost almost ten years since this morning"—demonstrates how
preoccupied Nellie is with her body (241). She notices repeatedly that
her father is surrounded by white people and even asks him if *he* will
be able to be happy away from black community and culture, but she
never considers her own situation as similar to his (278–79). Instead of
noticing her own distance from black people, Nellie cares only about
her skin. Her desire to be close to blackness is heavily invested in her
own appearance and considerably less invested in community and
culture. Her father appears to be all the black community she needs,
though she is alert to *his* needs and desires to be near other African
Americans. In her constant awareness of color, she notices that her
arm has tanned from the sun coming in the car window during the

cross-country trip and "admire[s] the color" (19). Later, once she has darkened in the summer sun at the lake, she observes "the stark contrast between [her] hand and the white leather seat it's resting on," recognizing that she has "never looked so dark" (156–57). She takes such great pleasure in her darker skin that she does not mind the tar that coats her feet after the car catches fire on the highway. She notes that "the bottoms are still black from the melted turnpike. The tar, like color, won't wash off" (53). Her fear of washing off the color of her hands with too much powdered soap informs her unsuccessful attempt to wash the tar off her feet: she is worried that her highly visible hands will lose their signs of blackness but is not worried about losing the color on her feet. Ironically, she fears she can wash away the color people see even as she cannot wash away the black on the soles of her feet, which no one can see and only she is aware of, which indicates again how conscious she is of the visibility of her blackness and how difficult her blackness is for observers to see. Unlike Brer Rabbit, Nellie wants the tar to adhere to her—or at least wants the color it represents to stay in her skin. Ironically, the "tar baby" that sticks to Nellie the more she struggles against it is a *lack* of blackness. But Nellie's desire for the blackness of the tar reverses the contemporary racist connotations of the "tar baby"; in (re)claiming the meaning of the tar as positive, Nellie combats white racism and exhibits her black racial pride. And like the trickster rabbit, who knows where he belongs even if the farmer is unaware, Nellie knows that she belongs in blackness even if her body and those who see it do not connect her to blackness.

Nellie continually demands that her body reflect her personal racial identity and sees her body's refusal to comply almost as a betrayal. When Nellie stares at herself in the mirror she does not see the physical embodiment of what she feels she should look like and wonders, "Who am I?" (17). Her train of thought reflects the hurt her light skin has caused her and she subsequently allows herself to question her legitimacy: she considers the moles that cover her body to be "the mark of miscegenation" and wonders if her "flawed skin is the ultimate sign of weakness, evidence that [her] blood shouldn't be mixing in [her] veins" (18). Having internalized her great-aunt's suggestion

that she is "mixed-up" and does not know who she is, Nellie is aware
of the stigma of being mixed or, more specifically, of not being black
enough. But since her skin is "flawed" because it is too white and not
because black has tainted her, she is cognizant of the irony that her
"imperfections"—her moles—are the blackest part of her skin. She
does not want the "mark of miscegenation," the "flawed skin," the "imperfections" to disappear and reveal only whiteness but rather wants
them to increase until their blackness covers her sufficiently: "There
is a mole on my side so big and black it looks like a tick lodged under
the skin. But the little freckles on my arms and chest, the ones on my
face, look as harmless as Magic Marker dots. I wonder why these imperfections are the darkest spots I have, blackness coming through
as thick raised marks that decorate my body. More come every year
and by the time I die I will probably be completely covered. On my
deathbed I will finally be a black woman" (18). Nellie's overwhelming desire to have a black body also informs her decision about what
she wants her children to look like and, consequently, what sort of
man she would marry. When Jess asks which member of an all-white
band Nellie would most want to marry, she answers unhesitatingly:

> "None of them. . . . I wouldn't marry a white guy."
> "Why not?" She looks shocked.
> "Because then my kids would be white, or mostly white. Why
> would I want that?"
> "But you just said all that stuff about being black."
> "Well, that's because my father's black. It's different if you have
> at least one parent; then the kids are in the middle, a blend of both
> sides. My kids would only have me."
> "And what if they looked just like you?"
> I picture my future child, light brown with soft, dark curls,
> his face a passport into any nation but his own. I shake my head.
> "That's not enough." I look down at my hands, the color not even
> enough for me. (65)

Her plans for the future have not prevented her from finding white
men attractive. Indeed, she is romantically involved with Luke (a white

boy) all summer and she admits to having dated a blond boy in the past. However, her desire for blackness does eventually begin to affect her own sexual desire. Though Luke courts her affections, she is ambivalent toward him and reluctant to pursue a relationship. In stark contrast, the moment she meets Dallas, an indigenous man who looks like her racially, she is immediately attracted to him; upon first seeing him, she proclaims both that he is "probably the most handsome man" she has ever seen and that he is "exactly [her] color" (71). Furthermore, when Dallas blushes, he becomes "a deep red-brown" she herself would "love to be" (73). Like Emma in Emily Raboteau's *The Professor's Daughter*, who loses her virginity to a graduate student from Bombay whom she describes as "brown," Nellie is attracted to Dallas's brownness. Emma notes, "Our skin was the exact same color. I was sure this meant something," and certainly Nellie's interest in Dallas "means something" similar.[42] Her desire for him is unrestrained and she pursues him as doggedly as Luke pursues her. Her persistent comparison of her own skin to others' establishes how drawn she is to dark skin and consequently explains why Dallas is so appealing to her. Conversely, her obsessive comparisons also demonstrate how unlike Luke she considers herself, since she considers herself black (or at least not white), and thus why Luke docs not particularly attract her. When she compares her feet to Luke's, she notices that hers "aren't much darker," but that there is "a saturation in [her] pigment that he doesn't have" (165). She remarks, "They seem to shine, as if my skin were made of copper or brass. As if I weren't quite human" (165). Next to Luke, Nellie is metallic and inhuman, but Dallas looks like her and can also become a color she would "love to be." And when she sees a similarity between herself and Dallas, as well as with Toni Morrison's Sethe, the heroine of *Beloved*, she embraces that similarity and the color it connotes. Nellie takes the bandage off a burn and observes,

> There is a lighter band of skin where the sun wasn't allowed to go, proving just how dark I have become. The scab has fallen off already, and only the new skin is left behind, as smooth and vulnerable as the inside of an eyelid. It will heal eventually, will fill in with color to

match the rest of my arm, but there will always be a mark there. I am
like Dallas now, or Sethe, graced with a permanent scar that makes
me easily identifiable. Soon it will help define me, creating my indi-
viduality as much as the shape of my fingers or the flecks of color in
my eyes. Is this where we find our identities, in the smooth, defiant
flesh of our scars? (217)

Whether it is a scar like Dallas's or Sethe's—two figures "of color" who
matter a great deal to Nellie—or the blackness of her moles, Nellie
welcomes any mark that makes her "easily identifiable" or connects
her to color. Her "new skin" is something that she feels links her tangibly to color. Whether her "new skin" is a scar or a black mole that has
covered her body, it is a skin "of color," a skin that makes her feel—
if not look—black.

Despite lamenting her lack of blackness, the ongoing comparison
she makes between herself and her white cousin Jess makes her aware
that even if she is not black like her father she is not white like Jess.
Whether a racist shopkeeper recognizes Nellie's blackness or Jess's ignorance about attractive, famous black men identifies her whiteness,
Nellie is fully aware that while she might not be black enough for her
own taste she is certainly black compared to her cousin. She notices
at the end of the summer how Jess has tanned: "I'm surprised by how
dark her feet have gotten during the summer, during her time with
me, as if I'm rubbing off on her and slowly making her black" (261).
While Nellie puts her blackness in terms of skin and notices that her
cousin is literally growing darker, Nellie's racial awareness is not limited to skin—at least in relation to Jess. When Nellie's father hosts a
barbeque for his African American friends, Jess says, "We could be
in Virginia right now. The food, the smell of the grill, the people—
it's just like being at home" (241). Racism surrounds Jess in Virginia,
where she knows she could not date a black boy: "My mama would kill
me. Everybody in the town would kill me. It's not worth it" (66). But
Nellie notices "that being in rural Minnesota with a bunch of black
people finally makes [Jess] feel at home" (241). Though Nellie never
considers blackness entirely outside of phenotype, her recognition

that Jess belongs among African Americans, that her own blackness is "rubbing off" on her white cousin, suggests that at least to some degree Nellie recognizes that part of what makes her black is something she cannot find in her skin.

Throughout the novel Nellie has resisted any association with whiteness or her white mother but by the conclusion of the text she admits that she is her "mother's daughter," and comes to accept her intimate links to her mother's family and legacy and thus to her mother's whiteness (282). Once her initial resistance transforms into acceptance and her concern for how others perceive her diminishes, Nellie's anger, restlessness, and inability to trust in other people (other than her father) gives way. Her constant and urgent search for a racial "home" is reflected in the metaphor of her literal home. Thus, when her relentless need to be in flux or motion subsides, she is finally able to rest comfortably in both her own skin and her physical location. When she is offered a ride when out walking she refuses it, saying she's "almost home." She watches the truck pull away, "thankful that [she's] no longer on the road, that [she's] no longer paralyzed by the need to move" (285). Having never "trusted" anyone enough to fall asleep in their presence, she finds she can sleep next to Dallas and let go of the anger that has burdened her throughout the summer. Receiving her mother's postcard suggests that Nellie has remade her family by choosing to live with her father and take in her white cousin Jess, and that her home is finally locatable. After a fire seriously damages the cabin, Nellie has additional rooms added during the renovation to accommodate her newly formed family that includes both black and white members. Just like her home, her identity is remade and reshaped at the close of the summer and the narrative. Furthermore, the agency Nellie shows in reforming and actively choosing what her family will be indicates the agency she has in forming her own racial identity—agency that Marcus's childhood lesson in hypodescent had ruled out. And in forming her identity, Nellie embraces the whiteness she has resisted for so long and identifies herself as "black and white" by the novel's close (286). Instead of accepting or insisting that she is "only" black (according to the one-drop rule), and instead of having to choose (according to the belief that one cannot be both), Nellie can claim both whiteness and blackness.

Ultimately, Nellie recognizes that her body, color, and race are malleable but that this does not preclude having a legitimate identity. She explains that while her color is inconsistent, it is reliably so, and that having an unchanging color is not the only way to proclaim a racial identity:

> There is a color between black and white; sometimes it's a shade of gray but other times it's almost brown, and when the moon is out and the stars are lighting up the sky, it may look silver or even brass. It is a rare tone, a color you won't find on its own, but it can be blended from other colors, from any color that occurs in nature, and sometimes even if there is no color, but just an idea. Created and re-created.
>
> That is my color. (287)

She knows who and what she is and so she is comfortable. Her conclusive statement demonstrates that Nellie has come to recognize that as long as she knows what she is it no longer matters to her whether anyone else recognizes her in the same way. She states that if her color were a road, she would walk "somewhere between the tar and gravel," and that even if her road has no signs and is on no map "it still exists." In other words, she does not require a socially recognized category in order to feel validated. The gaze of others diminishes in importance, and Nellie is satisfied that she is "a girl [who] knows to make herself whole" (287).

Invisible Woman: Emily Raboteau's *The Professor's Daughter*

While Emma in Emily Raboteau's *The Professor's Daughter* considers blackness as culturally derived to a much greater degree than Nellie does, Raboteau's protagonist, like Harper's, spends the majority of her narrative wishing she were more definitively black in appearance. The beginning of Raboteau's novel is, essentially, a discussion of what makes Emma and her brother Bernie black—or not black enough. Emma explains that "when [they] were little, people remarked on two things" about her and her brother: "The first thing was how we got along so well. . . . The second thing was that we didn't look black, although Bernie came closer: fuller lips, darker skin, flatter nose. Still, most people would guess Bengali or Brazilian when meeting him for the first time. Until his voice changed and they heard him speak. Then he would make more sense to them" (Raboteau, *The Professor's Daughter*, 2). In appearance, then, Emma and Bernie do not "look black," and it is only Bernie's speech that identifies him as such. She explains, "[Bernie] took great pains to learn how to talk Black. Street Black. Prophet Black. Angry Black. Which wasn't something you heard a lot of where we grew up" (1). The performance rather than the experience is thus stressed, and Bernie can affect whatever type of black dialect he wishes. The scene is rife with questions of authenticity since Bernie seems to have learned various speech patterns outside of everyday experience. As Emma says, his speech is not something she and Bernie have heard much growing up among predominantly wealthy, white Ivy League faculty, and his (white) mother notices the performance and says, "Talk like yourself, Bernie. Please" (1). Regardless of how Bernie has come to use black speech, it is certainly effective in establishing his blackness. If his skin is not black enough to convince others, his voice is. Culture, then, links him to blackness if his appearance fails to do so at times.

However, culture does not supersede color as a racial signifier. Emma goes on to explain that "in the pooling pudding of genes, [their] mom's side won out in the category of hair":

This is really what makes you black in the eyes of others. It's not the bubble of your mouth, the blood in your veins, the blackness of your skin or the Bantu of your butt. It ain't your black-eyed peas and greens. It's not your rhythm or your blues or your rage or your pride. It's your hair. The kink and curl of it, loose or tight, just so long as it resembles an afro. And ours didn't. That is why when Bernie shaved his head, he started to pass for the whole of one half of what he was. Even more than talking the talk, that was the act that did it for him. (2–3)

Ultimately, Emma is arguing that the body will speak more for one's

racial identity than any cultural signals will. Moreover, she is suggesting that she and Bernie have bodies that possess the critical sign of
nonblack hair and that without this hair Bernie is "passing" for black.
If "talk[ing] Black" invites debate over authenticity, Bernie's own body
becomes as valid a target for the same discussion. In a reversal of the
traditional passing narrative, Bernie is "passing" for black rather than
white; but unlike those narratives in which blackness was the "real"
or "authentic" identity of the passer, Bernie seems to lack a true identity to betray. Emma claims that he is passing "for the whole of one
half of what he was," but the point remains that she never articulates
her own racial identity (which she considers the same as Bernie's) or
insists that mixture is a definitively accurate or "true" race or racial
identity. Therefore, her account of Bernie's identity formation remains
a muddle of desire for blackness, an acknowledgment of mixedness,
and even jealousy that Bernie can "pass" when she cannot. After all,
she would not necessarily be able to "pass" for black even if she shaved
her own head since she would still lack Bernie's more typically black
features and skin as well as his fluency in black speech. She notes
that his speech means that he "makes more sense" to others and that
shaving his head is even more successful in identifying him as black,
whereas she "remain[s] a question mark" (2). Bernie, who is beautiful
and more obviously black with his "gingerbread skin and movie star
eyes" simply confuses Emma's college roommate—she cannot recognize the siblings as family and assumes Bernie is Emma's boyfriend
(106). When the counselor from the African American Center doubts
her blackness, Emma wishes she could point out that a book they are
studying in one of their African American courses was written by her
father's colleague and is dedicated to Bernie (but, in yet another instance of her exclusion, not to her). She wants to tell him that the chapter "on biracialism was inspired by [her] brother" but never works up
the nerve. She even spends "two hours" doing her hair in "the tiniest
braids" but concludes, "It was like he couldn't see me" (22). She cannot
bring herself to articulate her identity and again relies on signals that
can speak for her—namely her brother and, in this instance, her hair.

    While hair matters for both siblings as they mature, Bernie's choice of shaving or not shaving his head (to lose or keep a sign of whiteness) is decidedly less loaded than his sister's experience. Hair plays an important role in Emma's confused relationship with blackness and in the formation of her racial identity specifically because of the complicated politics of black women's hair. When they visit the woman who raised her father in Mississippi, Nanan Zanobia immediately compliments Emma on her hair: "She sneaks her fingers in the back of my hair and she says there's no naps in my kitchen. Dad tells her there's no such thing as good hair or bad hair and Nan Zan says, 'Hush, Bernard Jr. You ain't a woman so you don't know'" (9). That this African American woman admires Emma's hair and even argues over "good" and "bad" hair with Emma's father draws attention to the ironic desire among some black women for this very kind of hair Emma feels is not black enough. Her cousins enthusiastically take up the opportunity to work with Emma's hair in a scene much like one in Rebecca Walker's *Black White and Jewish*, in which Walker jealously admires the hair of one girl who can style hers the way "we all want but that only girls who have hair like Theresa, white-girl hair, can."[43] Of her cousins, Raboteau's Emma notes: "[They] can't keep their fingers out of my hair and the one called Sweetie Pop gets out her coconut hair grease and she's slathering it on and they're all pulling and twisting, yank, yank, yank" (Raboteau, *The Professor's Daughter*, 9). But Emma is unused to the beauty rituals into which her black cousins are initiated, and when it becomes too painful and she asks them to "Stop, please stop," her cousins turn on her. Like Senna's Birdie, who is called "Ms. Thang" and is accused of being "stuck up" and of thinking she is "fine" and "all that just 'cause she got long, stringy hair," Emma's cousins call her "a stuck-up white prissy" and refuse to let her play with them (39, 9). Ironically, her "white" hair is appealing to her black female relatives, but the response to their "black" way of doing her hair turns her from a black woman with "good" hair into a "white prissy" with whom they will not associate. Her hair, then, can threaten her blackness, as Emma has always feared.

The fact that Emma feels insufficiently black is further complicated by the mixedness of blackness. Emma has a white mother and recognizes her mother's race in her own body, but Nan Zan herself bears signs of whiteness. She is "dark as a chestnut" but has eyes "so light blue they were almost white" (30). Yet despite the fact that Emma recognizes signs of whiteness in African Americans, she never entertains the possibility that her blackness is not invalidated by her whiteness. She acknowledges that her brother and father are light-skinned and that she lacks only the minor signs of blackness that they have on their bodies, but she never doubts her father's or brother's blackness and worries only that she is deficient. Emma's early experiences with racial identity and blackness in particular demonstrate how subjective blackness is and how her blackness is something she cannot always see in herself, especially when others do not see it either. Though we never understand how Emma concludes that hair is the authoritative marker of blackness, it seems reasonable to assume that she has learned this through experience. Being rejected as not black enough by peers, being the object of fascination for her black cousins, and observing how Bernie is accepted as black more readily when he shaves his straight hair are experiences that teach Emma that she is lacking in some way.

Other childhood experiences educate Emma about her proximity to blackness and, overwhelmingly, her sense of her racial identity is tied to her brother. She remarks repeatedly that Bernie somehow explains her, saying, "When people ask me what I am, I want to tell them about Bernie because I grew up in his skin. We were a breed of our own" (20). If her ambiguous racial identity makes her feel isolated, her similarity to her brother makes her feel belonging. Even though she admits they don't "look too much alike" ("I always wished I looked like him, but I was only his pale imitation"), she relies on Bernie to make her make sense (106). Bernie has taught her that the two of them are "the same person in two different bodies" and so she grows up with the assumption that she is unfinished and that Bernie completes her (2). She explains, "I've learned that when people ask me what I am, which is not an everyday question, but one I get asked every day, the easiest thing to do is to tell them what color my parents are—just the black and white of it. I *want* to tell them about Bernie. As if he is an answer and not a question himself. As if he made sense to me" (27). Defining herself through Bernie makes her vulnerable because she knows she cannot use Bernie to identify herself to others. She wants to tell inquisitive people about her brother but knows he offers little explanation to anyone else.

Emma's reliance on Bernie is also partly the result of a lack of guidance from any other source—guidance that Bernie is able to access to a greater degree. But while Bernie gets a higher quantity of (specifically black male) mentorship, neither child receives a quality education in black history or subjectivity from their black parent. And even when their father teaches them general lessons about blackness, he never explains things to them. Though Emma seems to understand in retrospect, as a child she has difficulty comprehending the education her father offers. For instance, when Emma is little, Bernie steals some peanuts for the two of them when the family is on a road trip in Utah; when their parents realize what he has done the father demands Bernie return them, but Bernie points out they have already eaten half. Emma recounts:

> Mom says do it anyway because they're not yours and stealing is wrong, and Dad slaps Bernie full in the face and says:
> "NO. *The reason you don't steal is because that is exactly what they expect you to do.*"
> Everyone in Salt Lake City is looking at us. . . . Bernie takes the peanuts back with five fingers on his face and my mother turns to my dad and she says to him:
> "I guess they expect to see you hitting your children too." (4)

Later, when the family is in a restaurant in Arkansas and the waitress refuses to come to their table, Bernie begins to dance and sing. Their father scolds Bernie for "acting the fool" and storms out of the restaurant in protest; Emma does not know why they "don't like" her family, but she knows everyone is staring at them disapprovingly (7). Their father refuses to let his children act out stereotypes and fulfill the racist expectations of those around them, but he never takes the time to explain his feelings or the demands he makes of his children.

Despite insisting to his colleague, Professor Lester, that "[he] will teach [his] son how to be a black man," after Lester infuriates him by taking Bernie to the Million Man March, Emma's father demonstrates no interest in teaching either of his children anything about blackness—gendered or otherwise (17). When Bernie begins to get into trouble and is eventually arrested for suspicious behavior, his father "[takes] his saxophone away and accuse[s] him of trying to be a statistic" (111). Their father says that their paternal line has worked hard to let the next generation do better. "All you have to do is take your crown and wear it," he says, but he refuses to tell his children about the history of his family—and, in particular, that his father was lynched—to help them understand (112).

Without their father's consistent or thorough help with their racial identities, Emma is left without support while Bernie turns elsewhere for guidance. Bernie relies on Lester to teach him about black culture, history, and politics, and Emma relies on Bernie to help explain her. But Bernie returns from the March in Washington and expresses his sense of connection with black people and his black ancestors after whom he is named: "He started telling me how the march felt like ten million. Each man times ten. Like each man had all the weight of all the men that came before him and behind him only it wasn't heavy like a burden. . . . 'We were light,' he told me, 'like we weighed nothing, and we were lifting up. I could feel Bernard One there and he was carrying me and his father was carrying him'" (18). Bernie's account excludes Emma from his experience and reminds her that her grasp on blackness is not being fed by anyone in the way that Bernie's is being developed by Lester. Bernie's experience is also highly gendered and thereby excludes his sister in a separation of black femininity and masculinity. Bernie can feel his paternal line of male ancestors supporting him and connecting him to African American history and can sense the general masculinity and brotherhood of black consciousness at the time, which he describes explicitly. But Emma recognizes that unlike her brother, who continues the paternal line in name and sex, she has no meaningful connection to her black family (in name or spirit) and that her connection to Bernie is not strong enough to extend his sense of belonging to her: "Bernie was my we. I didn't like to hear him talk about other people like he belonged to them. If the Bernards were carrying each other all the way back to the slave ship and past the ocean and beyond the grave, I didn't know where that left me. I didn't know who was carrying me" (18–19). Her suspicion that Bernie does not need her the way she needs him leaves her even more vulnerable; as he learns about blackness without her, she is made different from the person who is supposed to explain her. As a child, Bernie tells her, "I wasn't finished yet when I came. I came too fast and I left some of me behind. That was you. So you came afterwards to finish me up" (2). Emma has thus come to think of herself not as someone similar in racial heritage to her brother or as her own person but rather as some leftover, some remnant of her brother. Her sense of being an incomplete person fosters her tentativeness regarding her racial identity—being an ambiguous person translates into being an ambiguous race.

Emma's utter reliance on Bernie also means that she cannot make sense of herself or the world when she is without him. When they are together as children, Bernie makes Emma feel secure as though she has an identity but he also literally explains her and grants her an identity. For instance, when the siblings share mutual rage and Bernie makes a racket with his saxophone, their mother comes upstairs to quiet him. She asks what is going on and Bernie answers, "We're mad" (106). She replies,

> "About what?"
> "You wouldn't get it," Bernie said.
> "What do you mean? I'm mad."
> "It's not the same. You have to look like us."
> "I look like you."
> "No," Bernie explained. . . . "You have to look like Dad."
> "Oh." Our mom looked injured. (107)

Here, Bernie makes Emma the "us," the "we," that makes her comfortable, and in this case "we" is not white. Bernie identifies them not as a particular race but as unlike their mother and like their father who,

Emma tells us, is quite light-skinned. Though Bernie does not articulate a specifically black or multiracial identity for himself and his sister, Emma can enjoy the sense of belonging to her brother and father and can enjoy having her identity discernable and discerned for her. But when she is without Bernie, she has no one to interpret the world for her or speak on her behalf. When one of her classmates asks her, "What does it feel like to have a black father?" Emma doesn't understand: "It hadn't occurred to me that I should feel different than she did. 'It feels fine,' I answered, but inside . . . I began to wonder" (14). Independently, Emma finds it difficult to answer for herself or to determine how she really feels. When her mother invites all of the girls from her daughter's class to a birthday party, one of her classmates interrogates Emma about one of her guests: "Why'd you invite *her*? . . . Don't you know she's *black*?" (14). The girl sneers a question about the black girl being Emma's friend, and Emma "protest[s]." Her assertion that the girl is not her friend reflects the "truth" since "none of them were [her] friends" but also reveals Emma's desire to separate herself from something her peers hold in such disdain (14). Being compared to someone other than Bernie leaves Emma without an adequate frame of reference, and all she can comprehend as a young child is that whatever "black" is, whatever the despised girl represents, is something she should distance herself from. Her brother challenges her mother's insistence that he "speak like himself" instead of using black dialect and challenges her father's conservatism about black politics and culture, saying that he is afraid of "what he doesn't understand or hasn't already heard" (18). But Emma's reliance on Bernie to speak for her (in every way) means that she is unpracticed in detecting and combating racist sentiment as a child. When her mother takes her to Toys "R" Us to pick out a Stork Baby doll for Christmas, they find the shelves empty. The white dolls are sold out, and while they have lots of the black version they have not bothered to put them out on the shelves. A clerk explains that the store has "got them in storage" and that Emma and her mother can buy one if they like (14). Whether or not she understands that the black dolls are so undesirable that they are not even made accessible to customers, Emma picks up on the negative evaluation of the black dolls and is not sure if she wants a black one when her mother asks her. She can only think that "it didn't seem like they were as good" (15).

While Emma requires and lacks a racial mediator as a child, as a young woman she is more capable of negotiating blackness autonomously. Though the traumatic loss of her brother when she is in university seems to rob her of her connection to blackness, it also liberates her from her dependence on Bernie. After her brother dies from injuries sustained in an accident, Emma gets the rash that used to inflict the two of them together but she gets it on precisely one side of her face. She subsequently writes to Bernie in a journal: "You made me symmetrical. . . . What does your absence make me? An empty shape. A two-faced shape shifter" (123). However, it is possible to read her two halves as a whole. Whether she has incorporated Bernie into herself (instead of being his leftover self) or has simply come to embody the blackness she has always felt was more closely attached to her brother than herself, Emma is finally able to identify herself as an "us" and a "we" without Bernie. When she attempts to walk to the train station from her dorm at Yale and finds herself "through the looking glass" in a housing project, she befriends a young African American man who initially tries to mug her (120). Once he has guided her to the station and apologizes for having attempted to rob her she replies, "Don't worry about it. We get angry sometimes. That's just how we are" (123). The fact that she considers the two of them "we" and that he calls her "girl" and "sister" while she calls him "brother" suggests that the camaraderie and kinship she felt with her recently deceased brother is something she can find with other (black) people (123). It also suggests that the racial identity she invested so highly in her brother is something she can identify in herself now.

Emma's inability to articulate racial identity is related to her family upbringing but it is also caused by her social upbringing in the United States. Her negotiation of blackness has, for the majority of her young life, been at the mercy of her neglectful father and a brother whom she revered. Bernie's death offers no miraculous transformation, and Emma attempts to lose her indeterminate self in an abusive relationship with a white man she considers beneath her. But in

Emma's eventual trek to Brazil, where she finds her body needs no explanation, she recognizes that her tentative hold on a racial identity has not been merely the result of lacking a voice with which to articulate it. Rather, her tentativeness has resulted from the lack of a language with which to speak racial identity and a culture in which to realize it. Her sense that she is "discovering herself in a new language" in Brazil suggests that the confusion she has had growing up in the United States is not necessarily her own fault or that of her family members (275). In fact, the confusing signals from her black family, her parents' lack of guidance regarding her racial identity, the loss of her brother, and the racism she notices among whites can all be read as representative of the lack of social discourse surrounding multiracialism in the United States. She has to go to Brazil where, though it is no utopia, language exists for what she has never heard articulated. In a letter to her father, she says that she loves the Portuguese word "saudade," which means "'missing,' or 'longing'": "You experience saudade for something absent, something gone from you, something stolen or something that left, something close to your heart but far. You feel saudade for the haunting thing that has a hold on you, what blues everything you see. I ran away so you would have the saudade for me. So I could struggle into a name. So I could begin" (275–76). Her longing—for Bernie, for the belonging Bernie offered her, for the belonging that has eluded her—is something she makes an effort to find at the novel's close. That this belonging seems possible in another place and in another language suggests that she can discover what she is and form her own racial identity but also indicates that this process is something she finds unlikely if not impossible in the United States. Her attempts to have Bernie define her, to choose the black or white doll, to proclaim or avoid allegiance to blackness, or to demand that others recognize in her the blackness that they do not see have been fruitless in helping her define herself. She fits no ready category in the United States and her admittance into whiteness and blackness has always come with qualifications. If Bernie represents the racial identity she longs for but can never be (since he is a separate person), then losing him and removing herself from the American criteria for racial identity ultimately free her from race concepts that have always kept her distanced from blackness and from a language that could never accommodate her mixture. Ultimately, Raboteau's text suggests that Emma's kind of blackness finds no home in existing American racial discourse but that Emma herself has the potential to discover a way to articulate it if she can absent herself from American racial ideology.

Black Cultural Identity: Danzy Senna's *Caucasia*

Like Nellie and Emma, Birdie in Danzy Senna's *Caucasia* does not look particularly black and is troubled by the consequent difficulty of claiming blackness. Birdie dwells on appearances much like Nellie and Emma do, but cultural blackness is equally if not more important in Birdie's claiming of blackness as part of her multiracialness.

Like Nellie and Emma, Birdie has black family members who provide a sense of proximity to blackness and who have their own challenges when it comes to claiming blackness. In the same way that Bernie provides Emma with a sense of connection to her racial identity, Birdie's older and darker sister Cole provides Birdie with a tangible connection to blackness. While Cole contextualizes Birdie's racial identity even in private and since Birdie was a toddler, she also provides a very prominent racializing force when they are in public—never more so than when their mother ceases home schooling and enrolls the girls at Nkrumah, an Afrocentric school in the black neighborhood of Roxbury. When they enroll, Cole does not look especially like her sister. In the winter, "when she lost her tan, she would turn closer to [Birdie's] own shade of beige" but when they start at Nkrumah in the early fall, Cole is "honey-colored" (Senna, *Caucasia*, 36). She also has "tight black ringlets" and "kinky hair" unlike Birdie's own straight hair (36). The fact that Sandy has to insist that both girls are to be enrolled in the school and that they are sisters when the receptionist assumes that only Cole will be registering indicates how much more readily Cole is seen as black. Once school begins, Cole is never doubted as black while Birdie is questioned and harassed repeatedly by peers who doubt her blackness. Cole comes to her defense by trying to include her in a jump rope game with her friends, but Birdie knows that she is under much greater scrutiny than her sister, who is accepted as black: "I sat on the sidelines, watching them jump rope because I didn't know how and was afraid to be laughed at. Cole, meanwhile, played along, jumping in the middle of the flying ropes, clumsy as she wanted to be" (38). When some girls begin to bully and threaten Birdie, Cole comes to her defense again, using her age to intimidate the bullies into submission. Once Cole has made it clear that she will protect her little sister, Birdie is simply left alone, but she does not know which is worse, being "harassed or ignored," since neither option grants her acceptance (41).

Cole's experience as a black child is similar to Birdie's in that they are both teased for possessing some sort of inappropriate blackness. However, the critical difference between the sisters' experiences is that Birdie gets negative attention for being insufficiently black looking whereas Cole is ridiculed for taking insufficient care of her black body. She is teased for having ashy knees and called "Miz Nappy" for having "crazy" hair, and she places the blame squarely on her mother when she laments, "Mum doesn't know anything about raising a black child. She just doesn't" (44). Cole includes Birdie in her new ritual of carefully applying lotion to her "elbows, knees, calves, but especially the feet, where the dust could leave such a thick layer that you actually turned white and dry and cracked and old-looking" (41). But Birdie knows that she holds only honorary membership in the "secret club" of lotion use since "the dust didn't build up so white on [her]—just a little bit here and there" (41). Furthermore, Cole's comment that their mother does not know how to raise "a black child" explicitly excludes Birdie. They are not black children; rather, Cole is a singular black child. Though Cole is careful to maintain a close relationship with Birdie and always tries to include her in her black beauty rituals, her comment suggests that while Birdie might have other claims to blackness, her skin and hair are not her chief assets in making such a claim. Cole is right—it was she, not Birdie, who suffered the humiliation of "disapproving glances of the black people on the street" when, as a child, her mother let her "run around with what she called a 'dustball' on her head" that tangled so badly that it began to dreadlock in the back (42). And so even though she tries to claim that "Birdie isn't white. She's black. Just like [herself]," Cole also acknowledges that their racial similarity is not particularly apparent on the level of appearance (40). Cole's experience has taught her that she exhibits physical signs of blackness that her sister lacks.

Much to Birdie's frustration, phenotype dictates how she is racialized not just in public or at school but also at home. Birdie's lack of physical signs of blackness leads her parents to ignore or forget that she has as much black heritage as Cole even if she does not look as black as Cole. While Birdie's parents are inconsistent and do consciously affirm their daughter's blackness at times, at other times they each link black appearance with black consciousness. Though their father insists, "In a country as racist as this, you're either black or you're white. And no daughter of mine is going to pass," he ignores Birdie in a way that reveals how much he invests in appearance and how he sees Birdie as not black enough (23). Invigorated by the newly emerged black power movement, Deck focuses his energies on Cole, trying to instruct her in his race theories. Birdie explains, "He never had much to say to me. In fact, he never seemed to see me at all. Cole was my father's special one. I understood that even then. She was his prodigy—his young, gifted, and black. At the time, I wasn't sure why it was Cole and not me, but I knew that when they came together, I disappeared" (47). Like her husband, the girls' mother works to instill in them respect for blackness while also failing to treat them similarly in terms of racial identity. At one point she acknowledges Birdie as being "half-black" but when Deck insists that she take the girls to Nkrumah, Sandy reveals her own inability to see Birdie as black: "Come off it, Deck. I mean, I guess the school makes some sense with Cole. But Birdie? Look at her sometime, really look at her. Try to see beyond yourself and your goddamn history books. She looks like a little Sicilian" (184, 23). While it is one thing for Sandy to state that Birdie does not look particularly black, it is another to suggest that, consequently, it does not make sense for Birdie to attain an Afrocentric education. Later, after Birdie and her mother have been living as white in New Hampshire and have not seen Cole in years, Sandy says to her daughter, "I used to think that if I could

just learn to cornrow, [Cole] would stay mine. Remember the way her
hair looked that first time she got it done, at Danny's His and Hers, so
tight and gold and pretty? She was a gorgeous child, wasn't she?" (129–
30). Birdie in no way reminds her mother of her black daughter, and
Sandy mourns Cole; in one instance, when she "remember[s] what she
was missing," Sandy exhibits "no spark of recognition, no reaction"
to Birdie's face (133). Birdie explains, "My mother did that sometimes,
spoke of Cole as if she had been her only black child. It was as if my
mother believed that Cole and I were so different. As if she believed
I was white, believed I was Jesse" (233). Without physical signals to remind her parents of her blackness, Birdie is racially marooned when
she is separated from Cole—her one reliable link to blackness. Once
she and her mother go on the lam, the only bodily evidence Birdie has
that she is her father's daughter is the asthma she has inherited from
him, the *"invisible* proof" that she is his daughter (97; emphasis added).
Tellingly, however, Birdie maintains her black-oriented perspective in
spite of—even in part because of—the not-black identity attached to
her apparently nonblack body in New Hampshire.

It is the visible "proof" that seems to most influence Birdie's parents, and while it also influences Birdie (who desires a more black-
looking appearance), the attention paid to "proof" is indicative of her
father's sense of black authenticity. The attention he heaps on Cole
and denies Birdie is the result of his new interest in black power and
his consequent fear that he has betrayed his blackness:

> [Cole's] existence comforted him. She was the proof that his blackness
> hadn't been completely blanched. By his four years at Harvard. By my
> mother's blue-blood family wedding reception in the back of the big
> rotting house on Fayerweather Street. . . . Cole was his proof that he had
> indeed survived the integrationist shuffle, that he had remained human
> despite what seemed a conspiracy to turn him into stone. She was his
> proof of the pudding, his milk-chocolate pudding, the small dusky body,
> the burst of mischievous curls (nappier than his own), the full pouting
> lips (fuller than his own). Her existence told him he hadn't wandered
> quite so far and that his body still held the power to leave its mark. (47)

Indeed, the fact that Cole looks blacker than Deck himself offers him some hope that his blackness is, if anything, growing stronger. His interest in establishing his blackness and in having proof of it drives Deck to educate Cole in his race theories and ignore Birdie, whose body confirms Deck's fears that he has become a race traitor by marrying a wealthy white woman and attending an Ivy League university. The value he initially sees in integration and teaches his daughters that they embody is replaced with black nationalism and racial solidarity. He begins pointing out "'strong black women' as evidence of [Birdie's] mother's inadequacy" and attempts (unsuccessfully) to grow his hair into a "real afro" (276). Like Birdie, Deck does not have "nappy enough" hair and his friends tease him for it. So, like his daughters who each in her own way has to perform blackness convincingly, Deck uses dialect to connect himself to blackness. Around his black friends, he "spoke differently" and "would switch into slang, peppering his sentences with words like 'cat' and 'man' and 'cool'" (9). Their mother "would laugh and say it was his 'jive turkey act'" newly adopted since his discovery of black pride "just a few years later than everyone else" and that he intended "to purge himself of his 'honkified past'" (9). Later, when Deck and Sandy are splitting up, he says they each need to go to where they belong racially—she needs to go back to Harvard while he needs "to go to Roxbury. Find me a strong black woman. A sistah. No more of this crazy white-girl shit." Sandy responds, "Oh my god. Since when do you talk that way? 'A sistah.' Don't blacken your speech around me. I know where you come from. You can't fool me" (21). His attempts to shrug off his own "belonging" to Harvard and dismiss Sandy's Harvard connection as something foreign to him demonstrate how consciously he is trying to form a new racial identity for himself. As Caroline Streeter puts it, "For Deck, Black Power is less about activism than about remaking himself as an authentic black man."[44] Deck's feelings of inauthenticity mean that instead of being satisfied with his appearance, black family and community, black culture, or his own black-oriented work singly or in combination, Deck subscribes to a black nationalist ideology that requires him to disown his own past experiences. His newest form of black pride means that Deck must eliminate what "proof" there might be that he has ever been anything but a black nationalist.

Deck's own attempt to seem more (or differently) black is contrasted with the behavior of Redbone, who "looked almost like a white man, barely a trace of black at all, except for his tight reddish-brown curls" (Senna, *Caucasia*, 12).[45] While Sandy teases Deck and even calls him out when he "blackens" his speech, Birdie's evaluation of Redbone is considerably different in tone. The inauthenticity she ascribes to Redbone suggests that her own father's performance of blackness is unobjectionable in comparison: "His slang was awkward and twisted. It didn't seem to come naturally to him. Even I could see that. It reminded me of an old black-and-white plantation movie my father had forced Cole and me to watch one Sunday afternoon. The slave characters in it had been played by white actors who wore some kind of pancake makeup on their faces. My father had laughed whenever they spoke in their strained dialect. Redbone sounded as if he had graduated from the same school of acting" (13). Deck argues with Sandy that Redbone ought not to be trusted, and he is proven right when Redbone "sells" Sandy "down river." When Deck grows protective of Birdie after Redbone shows her two rifles, Redbone responds defensively. But once he gets nervous, his "blackened" speech changes: "Redbone's voice was different now, nasal. He was no longer speaking in his butchered slang" (14). Deck argues that Redbone "ain't no brother" and supports the allegation by pointing out that no one knows where Redbone has "come from": "He shows up a month ago actin' like he been a revolutionary all his life. But no one knows where you came from, Red, do they?" (14). Deck's assertion that Redbone is not who he says he is simply echoes Birdie's evaluation of the man as a "white actor" in blackface. The attention drawn to Redbone's inauthenticity is related to culture (speech) and political allegiance (black revolutionary politics) but it is also less explicitly linked to his ambiguous racial appearance (and apparently unknown ancestry). Questioning his motives, Deck also refers to Redbone derogatorily as a "half-breed." Similarly, Birdie's instinct that Redbone is malicious is linked to her unfavorable opinion that he is like her grandmother's

"portrait of Cotton Mather, the octoroon dandy"—a symbol of untrust-
worthy whiteness, which Birdie casts as mixedness (92). Redbone's performance of blackness emphasizes that not all claims of blackness are
legitimate even among multiracials. That he is a traitor and that his
blackness is indeed simply a façade in which he has no personal investment validate Birdie's and Deck's suspicions. But the fact that they refer to his multiracialness negatively is troubling because they seem to
demean mixture itself; while Redbone is himself despicable, he is not
so because he is multiracial. However, the fact that he claims blackness
not out of genuine desire or a sense of personal belonging redeems their
characterization of him somewhat (though arguably not entirely) because he reinforces the message that publicly accepted racial identity
must be balanced with a complementary sense of personal identity. Just
as Birdie is uncomfortable claiming a monoracially black identity and
is miserable claiming a monoracially white identity for the very reason
that she has formed a personal racial identity of both (or mixture), Redbone's claim of blackness is condemnable because he is only doing it
in order to betray the very people he asks to accept him as black. That
is, Birdie knows that her monoracial identities are not "authentic" because she does not consider herself monoracial just as Redbone's claim
of blackness (to whatever degree) is not "authentic" because he has no
actual black racial pride or interest in solidarity. Without a sense of racial loyalty and personal belonging, Redbone's blackness is invalidated
by those with a personal investment in blackness, and thus the mixture
that permits him access to blackness is suspect. Conversely, Deck's performance of the kind of blackness he feels he wants to embody is not
depicted as inauthentic because it is accompanied by a deep sense of
political commitment and racial solidarity. Unlike Redbone, who has
appeared out of nowhere and is thus without evidence of his commitment to black community, Deck has an abundance of evidence of his
own commitment.

Birdie is successful in negotiating a black identity to a certain extent, but her success requires extensive "proof" in terms of appearance, cultural fluency, and, not least of all, her sister. Birdie insists that

since she was a baby she has seen her sister as a mirror of herself. Like Raboteau's Emma, who sees herself reflected in her brother Bernie, Birdie relies on her sister to establish her blackness. Without Cole, Birdie has difficulty seeing her own blackness: "There were no curls, no full lips, still no signs of my sister's face in my own. There had been a time when I thought I was just going through a phase. That if I was patient and good enough, I would transform into a black swan" (154). Her desire to transform is realized to a limited extent while she is attending Nkrumah. Cole's initiation into African American beauty practices is also an initiation for Birdie, who welcomes any opportunity to appear more convincingly black. She states that she "learned the art of changing at Nkrumah," that unlike the dress-up games she and Cole played as children, at Nkrumah she does it "for real" and learns "how to become someone else, how to erase the person [she] was before" (53). In addition to using lotion, she wears her hair "in a tight braid to mask its texture" (53). But more than skin and hair, Birdie's transformation into a convincingly black person depends on cultural fluency. This includes getting her ears pierced, wearing "Sergio Valente jeans, a pink vest, a jean jacket with sparkles on the collar, and spanking-white Nike sneakers" (54). Cole has also learned from an article in *Ebony* entitled "Black English: Bad for Our Children?" that she and Birdie "don't talk like black people" (45). She teaches Birdie how to speak in "Black English": "Don't say, 'I'm going to the store.' Say 'I'm goin' to de sto.' Get it? And don't say, 'Tell the truth.' Instead, say, 'Tell de troof'" (45). Soon Birdie practices "how to say 'nigger' the way the kids in school did, dropping the 'er' so that it became not a slur, but a term of endearment: *nigga*" (54). Birdie relies on Cole, then, not only to be a contextualizing black body but also to help educate her in black culture.

Cole's coaching is successful: Birdie admits that "it took a while" but that later that fall her "work paid off." As Kathryn Rummell says, Birdie "must perform well enough for spectators to stop believing their own eyes," and indeed she is successful.[46] Maria, a girl who once bullied her and insisted that "just 'cause she's white she thinks she's all that," approaches her on the playground and says, "So, you black?" (Senna,

Caucasia, 40). Significantly, once Maria acknowledges Birdie's blackness, she tells Birdie, "I got a brother just like you. We're Cape Verdean" (54).[47] This suggests that while Birdie's appearance is suspect, it is not outside the realm of possibility that people who look like her can still be black identified. Once Maria accepts her, Birdie consents to be the girlfriend of Ali, a boy who once threw spitballs at her and accused her of being white, and thus joins Maria's clique of popular girls. Birdie says, "The rest of the school saw me in a new light. But I never lost the anxiety, a gnawing in my bowels, a fear that at any moment I would be told it was all a big joke" (55). Having learned how to fit in by using aspects of culture to mask whatever does not seem black about herself, Birdie articulates the change in her self-perception: "I feel different—more conscious of my body as a toy, and of the ways I could use it to disappear into the world around me" (56). She is no longer an anomaly but blends in as one who at least appears to belong because her difference is no longer particularly visible. Though she desires invisibility at first, she is satisfied with successful camouflage.

But this "disguise" does not entirely please Birdie, who yearns to have a blacker body. Wearing the right clothes, talking the right way, and identifying herself as black all achieve acceptance, but Birdie cannot resist the fantasy she has when Maria curls her hair. When the girls watch themselves in a smoked mirror in Maria's mother's room, Birdie thinks, "The tint of the mirror darkened me, and with my newfound curls, I found that if I pouted my lips and squinted to blur my vision in just the right way, my face transformed into something resembling Cole's" (60). Ultimately, while Birdie fantasizes about lips, hair, and skin that might more closely resemble her sister's, she is satisfied with being accepted as black and being surrounded by black peers. She is disappointed in her body but finds solace in time spent with friends, in black community, and with her sister. Indeed, while she does desire to be more phenotypically black, this desire cannot be dissociated with her desire to be with and close to Cole. In fact, she seems to want to see herself as Cole, specifically, rather than simply as "black." If her sister is her mirror, as she says, then Birdie's proximity to blackness is also largely dependent on her proximity to Cole.

Consequently, when her parents separate the sisters, Birdie is left without the signs and contexts that satisfy her desire to be close to blackness. The problem for Birdie is that her evidence is invisible: she requires her father and sister to be the proof that she has black ancestry, and once they disappear from her life she finds it uncomfortably easy to get lost in the white identity her mother gives her. Before Cole and her father depart for Brazil, Cole gives Birdie the Golliwog doll that Sandy's mother gave her, and which the girls have cherished despite Sandy's objections. Deck and Cole also leave a box Deck has labeled "Negrobilia" to remind Birdie of black things. Ultimately, the box of trinkets offers a substitute for the actual black bodies and culture of which Birdie will be deprived, but it is a poor one:

> My mother scoffed when she saw what was inside. He and Cole had clearly thrown the collection together at the last minute. It included a Black Nativity program from the Nkrumah School, a fisted pick (the smell of someone's scalp oil still lingering in between the sharp black teeth), a black Barbie doll head, an informational tourist pamphlet on Brazil, the silver Egyptian necklace inscribed with hieroglyphics that my father had bought me at a museum so many years before, and a James Brown eight-track cassette with a faded sticker in the corner that said "Nubian Notion," the name of the record shop on Washington Street. That, along with Cole's Golliwog, was all that was left of them (107–8).

Despite its insufficiency, the box of Negrobilia is by default the only blackness Birdie can access, and so it becomes her most prized possession. When they are on the road, her mother dabbles in her own "bastardized" versions of religion while Birdie "practice[s] [her] own form of praying": "I would sit, fingering the objects in my box of Negrobilia, usually humming a little tune (some old, long-gone soul song), while I tried to imagine what Cole was doing at that very moment" (119). Even though Birdie knows the Negrobilia box was assembled carelessly, she cherishes it because it is the only thing that acts as a physical reminder of her sister and father and because it acts as a portal to the blackness she now must deny in everyday life. Without the box, she has no way to be close to blackness culturally or physically. In a kind of reversal

of the briefcase in Ralph Ellison's *Invisible Man*, in which the protagonist carries tokens of American anti-black racism and of which he
cannot rid himself, Birdie carries her tattered collection of random
objects in a dogged attempt to keep blackness real for her. Even symbols of racism, like the Golliwog, offer Birdie a connection to blackness in the absence of the real black body of her sister.

Over time she adds to the box and her additions indicate that the
box is slowly losing the ability to perform its function. The first items
she contributes herself identify connections to black people—first a
postcard from Deck's sister that she finds among her mother's things
and then a photograph of her mother's new boyfriend in Jamaica
with a black woman. But over the years she begins to add things that
"didn't make as much sense" and that she "couldn't explain," like a
crushed baseball card she finds in her school gymnasium and a friendship bracelet her mother's boyfriend leaves in the bathroom (205). The
box starts to become nonsensical to her and reflects how her current
life does not fit into her past life; mementos of her New Hampshire
existence are out of place alongside souvenirs of her childhood in Boston. But it also becomes a reservoir for new tokens that she imagines
connect her to Cole in the present rather than offering only relics of
their past together. She adds the hair of the only black–mixed girl in
her school, who reminds her of Cole, and a page on Candomblé, an
Afro-Brazilian religion, that she rips out of a library book. She wonders whether "Cole practiced Candomblé in Brazil" and imagines her
father's response to the rituals (205). Birdie acknowledges that she does
not know why she stole the page or why she keeps it in the "box of negrobilia" but then answers herself by explaining, "I had wanted a piece
of Brazil, a piece of Cole and my father as they were now, not just the
stale artifacts my father had left me with from that other time" (205–
6). She keeps using the Negrobilia in a sentimental desire to remember
but eventually has to admit that her connection to blackness is fading
and that she fears her blackness is being replaced by her white identity: "The objects in the box looked to me just like that—objects. They
seemed like remnants from the life of some other girl whom I barely knew anymore, anthropological artifacts of some ancient, extinct

people, rather than pieces of my past. And the name Jesse Goldman no longer felt so funny, so thick on my tongue, so make-believe" (161). She uses the Negrobilia to be reminded of her black sister and father and thus of her own blackness; as a result, the Negrobilia serves to remind her that her white identity as Jesse Goldman is only a temporary act. But its ability to act as a racial life preserver in a sea of whiteness is limited, and when the box's usefulness runs its course, Birdie goes in search of what it represents.

Birdie's refusal to let go of the increasingly nonsensical memory box is indicative of the deprivation she feels when she and her mother go into hiding. Birdie's connection to blackness is severely disabled by her location: the places they go, including New Hampshire, where they finally settle, are places where blackness is noticeably absent. Birdie misses black music, which she does not hear except "when by chance it [comes] on the car radio"—something she notes doesn't happen often "in the parts [she and her mother are] driving through" (135). She notices over the years that she is not content with white culture and community and that she longs for black culture and people. She also has to endure the racism of her white friends and others and continually has to bite her tongue when she feels the urge to identify herself as black–mixed.

Birdie's recognition that she is deprived of the black community, culture, and identity she desires is never more apparent than when she is permitted a small taste of diversity. When Sandy, her boyfriend Jim, Birdie, and Birdie's best friend Mona all go to New York City, Birdie describes their entrance into the city as restorative: "Coming into New York was like being brought back to civilization after years on a desert island. I scrutinized the city people with a kind of hunger, eating up their wild styles and furious features, faces that unearthed some part of me that had been buried for so long" (218). In New York, she is treated to the lone opportunity she has had to publicly enjoy black people and culture since leaving Boston. She watches a group of African American and Puerto Rican teenagers listen to music and breakdance, and while she has lost touch with the culture over the years she finds it recognizable and appealing: "The underlying tune was somehow familiar, something I had known once, long ago" (220). This diverse black culture suits her, unlike the culture of her newer white community: "As well as I had adjusted to New Hampshire, I had never quite gotten used to the music, or the fact that people didn't dance. The parties the kids threw all focused on drinking, smoking, and making out. Sometimes I would try to move my body to some Pat Benatar song, or a Rolling Stones classic, and the kids would watch me and laugh nervously, saying, 'She must think this is a disco'" (220).

In New York, she is freed from the customs of rural white New Hampshire and begins to participate: "I clapped my hands, laughing at their expertise, and began to move to the music" (220). Unlike Mona, who is "clearly uncomfortable," standing still with her "hands shoved in her pockets," Birdie is not hampered by either a lack of initiation into or interest in the music and dancing (221). Instead, she is hampered by Mona herself (and the white norms she represents) and wishes "she would get lost": "She felt like a weight I didn't need" (221). Birdie is "ashamed to be seen with her" and edges away from her (221). When Jim and Sandy catch up to the girls, Birdie is embarrassed and resentful of them. She reflects, "It was dawning on me as I watched these kids dance how long I'd been away. Six years. I felt that I had missed some great party and was now hearing about it the day afterward. A lump of disappointment and envy rose in my throat" (221). She wishes that Jim, Mona, and her mother were strangers, "that [she] lived in this kaleidoscopic city, and that [her] name was Chevell" (221).

Though she fantasizes momentarily about being a black girl in the "chocolate city" of New York, her enduring desire is to return to the blackness she already knows. And the biggest threat to the restoration of her black family and multiracial identity is whiteness. The fact that Birdie has to restrain her own impulses, tolerate racism, and ignore the desire to befriend and identify with Samantha (the black–mixed student who reminds her of Cole) means that she is not simply allowing others to perceive her as white but is actively embodying the kind of whiteness of those around her. But Birdie attempts to compensate for her altered behavior with whatever defenses she has left. Chiefly, her self-preservation comes in the form of telling herself that she is not really

Jesse Goldman and that her multiracial family will shortly be restored to her, but it also comes in the form of refusing to let anyone approximate the black people she has lost. Though Sandy's boyfriend makes an effort to be fatherly and familial with Birdie, she guards against allowing him to replace Deck. She maintains her distance from Jim even when she recognizes that she might otherwise want him to be part of her family and that he does possess the qualities of a good parent: "It often struck me in those moments that my own father had never paid this kind of attention to me. But instead of making me warm to Jim, this fact somehow made me angry and more resistant to his efforts" (215). She realizes, when he proclaims that she and her mother are his family, that "his words made [her] feel sad, defeated. The closer [she] got to him, the more foggy [her] memory of [her] father became" (216). She tells him he cannot be her father, that she has a father, and that she and her mother "were doing just fine without [him]" (217). She knows instantly that she has hurt him and she feels guilty. She is tempted to accept him: "I knew how easy it would be to succumb to his gentle silly love, to let him be my father the way he wanted to be. But I couldn't. Something in me resisted" (217). She refuses to become attached to Jim or accept the new formulation of her family because she feels that doing so would mean accepting as permanent the loss of the sister and father she wants to rejoin as well as the absence of blackness and black people in her life. Keeping her life—her identity, her family, her friendships—tentative keeps alive the hope that her original family will be restored.

For the same reasons, the prospect of becoming sexually involved with Nicholas Marsh, the landlords' son, terrifies Birdie. Just as she wants but simultaneously refuses a father–daughter relationship with Jim, she desires but then avoids a serious relationship with Nicholas. In one instance, after Birdie halts their physical intimacy when he encourages her to go beyond what she is comfortable with, Nicholas makes a racist joke and observes that Birdie might look "colored in the right light" (173). Because her white identity necessarily silences her impulse to object, Birdie's anxiety provokes an asthma attack. Nicholas tries to comfort her, telling her, "I was just kidding about you looking colored.

I mean, you don't look it at all. You're— . . . You're pretty. You're gonna look really hot in a few years. I mean it" (174). But Birdie is "stung" by the familiar racism behind the compliment: "It reminded me of my grandmother, when she would stroke my hair and say what a 'lovely child' I was. Even then, her compliments had struck me as sinister, though I hadn't known why at the time. I had known only that Cole was the girl I wanted to look like, [Aunt] Dot was the woman I wanted to look like, and if my grandmother couldn't see their beauty, she must be blind" (174). Where Birdie fears that her friendships with racist white girls threaten her "real" identity, she fears that a sexual relationship with a racist white boy like Nicholas poses the same threat to an even greater degree. She remarks, "I liked kissing him. But touching him felt too real, proof that the game had gone too far. It wasn't Birdie, but Jesse, who lay beneath him" (173). Afterward, Birdie considers her sexuality in relation to Nicholas and thinks that she might "never be able to go all the way with a white boy": "Sex was the only time, outside of the womb, when a person becomes one with another, when two people really melted together, into one body. Allowing a white boy inside of me would make my transformation complete" (231–32). She wonders if she'll stay a "virgin" forever, "never letting anything penetrate [her]" (232)—a distinct possibility, it seems, while she is lost in "Caucasia."

However, despite her belief in her intact virginity, Birdie has had sex. At the women's commune where she and her mother stay for a number of months, Birdie and her friend Alexis play "honeymoon," during which Birdie orgasms (169). The fact that Birdie wonders later "if it was possible for two girls to go all the way" suggests that she does not grasp as sex what she shares with Alexis (173). It is apparent that she understands normative sexuality since that is what she and Alexis pretend they are doing: when she and Alexis role play, Birdie agrees to "be the guy" and holds Alexis down, pretending that she is "the boss" (169). But it is unclear whether she understands that her own sexual experiences with Alexis are actually nonnormative. When she and Nicholas "neck"—that is, when Birdie participates in the normative sexuality that she has rehearsed with Alexis—Birdie is unsure of how to interact with him because Nicholas has taken over the role she is used to enacting herself: "It was difficult. With Alexis I had always been the one on top, the one doing the groping and the grinding, the one doing what Nicholas was doing. I wasn't sure how to act now that I was on the bottom" (172). Although she eventually feels "a slight tingling between [her] legs, the kind [she] had felt with Alexis," she is uncomfortable with Nicholas's touch, the way he pulls her ponytail "rather roughly" and holds "a tuft of [her] hair in his hand," the way his cold hand under her shirt makes her jump (172). Sex is easier and more fulfilling with Alexis than with Nicholas, with whom sexual intimacy is considerably more arduous and less satisfying. Significantly, Birdie says that when the women at the commune shrug off their lives as "Stepford wives" and become "real, roaring, natural women," same-sex desire is "as natural as anything else." Consequently, Birdie says, "It was my mother's affair with Jim, not with Bernadette, that had disgusted me" (299). Birdie's remarks suggest that she finds something unnatural and repugnant about sexual intimacy with men—or, more specifically, with white men.

Birdie's resistance to heteronormative sexuality—and relationships with white boys or men more narrowly—might well be a resistance to the "racial *and* sexual stereotype" of the tragic mulatta, as Lori Harrison-Kahan argues in "Passing for White, Passing for Jewish."[48] But because Birdie's desire for blackness includes proximity to black bodies, especially those of her sister and Deck, it would seem most likely that her distaste for white males as partners for herself or her mother is largely due to her desire to restore (in her mother's case) and perhaps replicate (in hers) multiracial family. Her mother's relationship with another (significantly unracialized) woman is not threatening because the woman does not take the place of her father, whereas Sandy's relationship with Jim does appear to be fulfilling their transformation into a white family with Jim in the husband/father role. Similarly, Birdie's own relationship with a white boy promises a future like Sandy and Jim's—an entirely white future that Birdie wants to resist. Alexis poses no threat to Birdie's desire for a multiracial family since Birdie has yet to envision the possibility of a family centered on a same-sex partnership. And since we never learn Alexis's race and Birdie has trouble even considering their physical intimacy as sex, Birdie sees no threat to her blackness in a relationship with Alexis. Sex with Nicholas, however, might make her irreversibly white because of the racial ramifications she associates with opposite-sex sexual and romantic coupling.

Birdie resists and finds "disgusting" sex with white men for the primary reasons that heterosexual sex with white men is unlike Birdie's own family and makes whiteness more literally a part of the woman's body and psychologically part of her identity. Just as she rejects Jim as a stand-in for her father in her own relationship with him, she rejects him as a stand-in for her father in his relationship with her mother. And her rejection of Nicholas reflects the terror that grows in her over the course of years during which she worries she is becoming one of the white racists with whom she is forced to share her life. In her mind, Birdie links heterosexuality to her own racial identity, and so her racial choice in boys comes to represent her own racial choice. To Birdie, choosing a white male partner is tantamount to giving up her claim to blackness and giving herself entirely to whiteness in terms of both her own identity and the makeup of her family. Ultimately, the more intimate her relationships get as Jesse Goldman, the greater the hold that identity has on her. It is through detachment—emotional, psychological, and physical—that she feels she is able to preserve Birdie Lee.

Birdie's resistance to heteronormative sexuality is, as Harrison-Kahan argues, a resistance to normativity in general—most especially normative identity. She is only comfortable when she can cling to the hope that her life is undergoing change rather than believeing it has already changed. When her mother's relationship with Jim grows dependable, Birdie worries that its constancy means that her parents will not reconcile and she will not get her multiracial family back. Similarly, when her whiteness begins to feel "natural" to her and sex with Nicholas threatens to solidify a white racial identity, Birdie worries that she is not actually going to repair the now-neglected blackness of her former personal identity or reconstitute the blackness of her now-hidden former public identity. When Birdie believes that Samantha, her black mixed classmate, has said to her, "I'm black. Like you," and Birdie is motivated to leave New Hampshire in search of Cole, her departure confirms that she senses her blackness is being overwritten by her submersion into whiteness.[49] She considers her flight as "abandoning parts of [herself] that [she] no longer wanted" and a search for "some part that had escaped [her]."[50]

However, her transition is not one from whiteness to blackness but rather one from a monoracial identity to a multiracial one. If she has had to "pass" for black at Nkrumah and "pass" for white in New Hampshire, her discomfort in each circumstance indicates her lack of a personal monoracial identity. Though she can convince onlookers of her monoracial status in each situation, she is in constant fear of being told her black identity is a "big joke" just as she is miserable when her white identity begins to convince even her of her belonging to whiteness. As Harrison-Kahan argues, "Birdie's decision to run away from 'Caucasia' is motivated by her desire for blackness, as well as her recognition that there is more than one way to be black."[51] As both Harrison-Kahan and Sika Alaine Dagbovie argue, Birdie desires blackness but also desires mixedness. Rather than reinforcing the conventional passing plot, in which a passer "returns" to blackness as his or her authentic racial identity, Senna portrays Birdie as locating herself in a black–white mixed identity. As Dagbovie points out in "Fading to White, Fading Away," Senna allows for blackness and mixedness to exist together in Birdie's desire for blackness and her simultaneous resistance against a black monoracial identity. In "Tragic No More?" Suzanne Jones observes that the black nationalism that Birdie left in Boston no longer dominates when she returns. Indeed, Nkrumah is closed, and its pupils are integrated into the rest of Boston's schools, while Birdie's aunt Dot has traded American race concepts for a spirituality she found in India. Birdie's pursuit of what Jones calls a "future as a mixed black girl" thus shifts to a new political context: Berkeley.[52]

Conjuring the mythology of the frontier, in California, outside the pressures of Nkrumah and New Hampshire where mixture has not been readily accepted, Birdie finds that multiracialism is better established. When she is in Berkeley where, Cole remarks, multiracials are "a dime a dozen," Birdie can more easily match her public identity to her private one.[53] There, normalcy takes on a whole new meaning and is something that will not demand that she compromise her personal sense of racial identity for the sake of rigid public perceptions of race. There, Birdie has available to her a broader public experience of mixedness. But the normativity of multiracialness is not the same kind of homogeneous normativity that characterizes monoracialness. Birdie and Cole have never had an easy time being accepted as racially "identical," but Berkeley provides an opportunity for them to share a racial identity of mixedness without worrying about the "prescriptive sameness" that so often characterizes group membership.[54] While they have had trouble being recognized as the "same" in black groups and white groups, being in the midst of heterogeneous mixedness instead of monoracialness offers them the chance to form similar multiracial identities regardless of their differences.

Writing One's Self: Rebecca Walker's *Black White and Jewish*

Like Senna's Birdie, Rebecca Walker values the culture and community of blackness as much if not more than she does black appearance. Unlike Birdie, Raboteau's Emma, or, in particular, Harper's Nellie, Walker does not spend her narrative wishing her body would become a "black swan," as Birdie says. In *Black White and Jewish*, Walker focuses primarily on her racial identity and the processes by which identity is formed. Though she is black enough in appearance that she is questioned less than Senna's, Raboteau's, and Harper's protagonists, she is not immune to the same sense of inadequacy and indeterminacy that they suffer. It is important to remember, though, that Walker's text takes place over a longer time period and is more informed by adult hindsight than are the novels; indeed, as a memoir, the entire text is retrospective.

Walker is also more concerned with how she is shaped by others' expectations and how she comes to perceive herself than with the intense self-scrutiny that marks the adolescent perspectives of Nellie's, Birdie's, and most of Emma's narratives. While this kind of retrospective point of view is possible in novels, it is much more inherently a feature of autobiography. And indeed, Walker's text is narrated from the perspective of a person who has come to know herself and is reflecting back on how she got to where she is. The coming-of-age novels, on the other hand, each depict a protagonist on a path of self-affirmation and conclude with the protagonist in a position that will allow her to begin to define herself. Unlike the novels, Walker's autobiography proclaims her identity in the title and thereby indicates that her text is tracing her path rather than portraying a search for that path. However, the fragmentation within her narrative also alerts the reader to the complicated nature of her journey. Her text is itself a process of definition. Like her mother, who believes that "the telling of stories" and the "magic ability of words" can "redefine and create subjectivity," Walker uses her autobiography to define what and why she is (Walker, *Black White and Jewish*, 23). The use of "black" in her title and her comment that her mother is "newly 'Black'" at a certain point in time emphasize how racial subjectivities always undergo shifts in meaning and definition (23). Her choice of words and appeal to the history of racial labels remind her reader that her racial identity is subject to change and that her conception of her identity is firmly dependent on time and circumstance. For instance, if "black" (or "white") were not part of racial discourse in the United States, or if "Jewish" had a different meaning, her racial identity as "Black White and Jewish" might be drastically different. That "black," "white," and "Jewish" have all developed and changed over time also reminds us that racial identities will never be static or even authoritative.

In much the same way that she draws attention to the "construction" of race concepts, Walker draws attention to the construction of her narrative. Walker considers the stories her parents tell about her and says that her "job is to listen carefully and let [her] imagination reconstruct the narrative, pausing on hot spots like hands over a Ouija board" (11). This is a duty she assigns herself when she "reconstructs the narrative" of her life, but it is also an invitation to her reader to "listen carefully" and use "imagination." She makes it clear that hers is no objective account but an interpretation of her life, and she leaves open the possibility that consumers of her interpretation might well "pause on hot spots" and interpret for themselves. Her text conspicuously avoids quotations, and so attention is drawn to the fact that she mediates all the voices in her narrative. Her decision to paraphrase indicates how she shapes her story, chooses to tell it, and refuses to give others the authority to speak for themselves as she chronicles her own life. Additionally, her constant jumps in chronology and abrupt introductions of people who matter a great deal to her, without many details to make them familiar to readers, further emphasize that her chief concern is her own subjective perspective. She has decided that what is important to tell readers is how she is affected by someone or something, and she provides little opportunity for readers to get to know most of the characters in her life story for themselves. Her narrative consists of moments and recollections that are rarely contextualized beyond what that instance meant to her at the time, and friends and family members often appear by name only without any accompanying information to identify them or what Walker's relationship to them might be. Ultimately, then, Walker goes to great lengths to draw attention to the fact that hers is a constructed narrative and an exploration of how others have tried to construct (or dismantle) her identity. Her formation of the narrative reflects her formation of her racial identity, and so in both form and content *Black White and Jewish* alerts the reader to the ways Walker has been shaped and shapes herself.

As with the novels, Walker's autobiography focuses narrowly on her race, and like Nellie's, Emma's, and Birdie's, Walker's racial ambiguousness troubles her while she is growing up. Though she is identifiably black in appearance, Walker is as susceptible as Birdie, Cole, Emma, and Nellie are to feelings of wanting to appear more black. In high school, one of her boyfriends has a photograph pasted above his bed that features "a dark-skinned woman lying naked on her stomach with her butt front and center" and it makes Walker feel "inadequate": "I measure myself against the woman in the picture. I can't possibly compete, not just with her easy sexuality and well-toned thighs, but with her undeniable blackness: the dark chocolate skin, the perfectly formed thick behind" (239). Like Birdie, who attributes beauty to the blackness of her sister and Aunt Dot, Walker considers attractive those features she associates with the darker woman in the photograph. Her sense of not measuring up—in color or sex appeal—means that she feels "inadequate" as a black woman. When she accepts and appreciates the way in which the pornography sexualizes the (dark) black

female body and fetishizes the woman's "chocolate skin" and "thick behind," Walker senses she is not "black enough" or at least not as black
as—or the kind of black—she would prefer to be. Like in the coming-
of-age scenario for each of the novels' protagonists, Walker's awareness of her body and sexuality is complicated by her race and gender.

Though bodily evidence of her racial mixture sometimes casts doubt
over her claim to blackness, most of the doubt that Walker encounters
arises because of culture and behavior. In all four texts discussed here,
the narrators are accused of being snobs or something similar by black
girls who resent something about them. The accusers' resentment is often jealousy that exposes the contradictory combination of black pride
and shame. Whether it comes from girls who wish they had straight
hair or those who resent the obvious access to education and material
wealth of those they call snobs, the resentment scratches the surface of a
deep-rooted and long history of racial oppression. When Walker wants
to participate in a school play, the older black girls who run the show
refuse to let her, saying she is "too white" and "act[s] like [she thinks she
knows] everything" (95). On two other separate occasions, schoolmates
beat her or threaten to beat her for being a "yellow bitch" who thinks
she is "better than everybody else" (108, 156). Similarly, when Walker exhibits signs that she feels "entitled to bliss" and learns to, in her words,
"move like I am important and in control[,] [a]s if I, Rebecca, belong,"
two black girls threaten to beat her up for "acting like a white girl" (41).
She explains that it does not occur to her that she is "taking something
away from the other, darker-skinned girls, that [she is] doing something
to them that feels like betrayal" when she gets attention from a "light-
skinned" boy and a "cute Peruvian boy" and answers all the questions
correctly in math class (41).

What she does notice, however, is that when she flees the school for
safety, her white best friend Lena "is nowhere to be found" (41). Friendship with a white girl does not measure up to the racial solidarity among
African American girls, and it is a lesson Walker learns when she befriends black students in high school. Walker notes that she is "claimed
by black girls and meaty football-playing boys while Lena stays true
to her feathered, beer-drinking white friends" (143). Though the two

were best friends and had "grown up together, . . . things get in between [them], things like language and fashion and color" (143). Walker feels as though she must make a choice between claiming whiteness and blackness: "I feel every inch of our separation, miss her every time I choose to go with my black friends instead of with her" (143). She explains that what happens to her friendship with Lena is "more than growing apart": "It is not knowing how to grow together, not knowing how to bring her into the world that is slowly claiming me, marking me, not knowing how to teach her how to walk and talk so that she can fit into my world, not knowing how to let her be her and fit in without doing any goddamn thing" (144). It is not simply color, in other words, but what is associated with color. When Lena is just "herself" she is unable to join Walker's social world. And if Walker only knew how to teach Lena how to speak, act, and dress like her black friends, then Lena could "fit in."

But Walker has a hard enough time fitting in herself and, as in similar scenarios in the novels, her situation is also complicated by race. The harassment on the part of those who doubt her make Walker question her own blackness. She is intimidated by another girl because the girl makes her feel inadequate: "She's a real black girl, and I'm not" (126). While this girl is darker and wears "some purplish lipstick . . . that looks good against her dark skin," lipstick that Walker thinks would "look stupid" if she wore it, her greatest sense of inadequacy is not in regard to her appearance (131). Rather, she takes to heart what they criticize about her: "I'm too serious, too stiff to hit the ball back, to bounce some words across the pavement. They say I'm more like a white girl" (126). Even her own serious boyfriend Michael teases her about "sound[ing] like a white girl": "He tells me that he forgets sometimes that I'm not a real sister. He says this like he's joking, with a big bright white smile, but I don't hear it as a joke" (268). Instead, she says, "I hear it as territory I'm supposed to defend" (268). The defense she mounts is to learn as well as she can how to fit into her black community of poor, tough, racialized youth in San Francisco. Each time she moves back to her mother after two years of having her tough black attitude accepted and respected in New York, Walker has to go through a transitional period of learning what to say, how to dress, what music to like, and whom she should fear. But even when she is in San Francisco and attending Urban (a liberal private school) to avoid the trap of the public school in a black neighborhood (where, she says, tellingly, she learns nothing, and which produces graduates who can only earn minimum wage), Walker has to remain vigilant. At her private school, she is unsurprisingly not in the company of African Americans fluent in lower-class black culture. Instead, she is "surrounded by one hundred or so laughing, skateboarding, coffee-drinking, Hacky Sack-playing, U2 and UB40 listening-to white kids and six or seven wigged-out-looking, trying-to-be-cool-acting brown ones" (264–65). When Walker begins to attend Urban, Michael starts to call her a "half breed": "He says my white comes out when I'm at Urban, when I slip and say *like* every other word or when I ask him if he's heard the new Police record, or if I analyze a movie for too long or with too much intensity" (268). She hides her interest in what her friends might consider "white" things and does not tell them about her white friends. When she goes to New York City for an internship at the Museum of Modern Art, she consciously avoids telling Michael "about all the things that might mark me more in his eyes as the half-breed race traitor I feel I am becoming" (271). The fact that she feels like a race traitor suggests that she internalizes the kind of solidarity her black friends possess, and her repeated accounts of having to hide parts of herself suggest that the kind of racial solidarity her friends share has no room for anything but a particular monoracially black identity. By the time she is finishing high school at Urban, she is "well trained in not breaking the code, not saying something too white around black people, or too black around whites. It's easier to be quiet, aloof, removed than it is to slip and be made fun of for liking the wrong thing, talking the wrong way, being the wrong person, the half-breed oreo freak" (271). Though this affected behavior leads her white friends to call her "*intimidating*" and African American peers to call her "*snobby*," and does not diminish the assertion among her black friends that she thinks she is "better than" and "know[s] more than everybody else," it is at least effective in reducing the doubt cast upon her claim of blackness (271–72, italics in original).

If she cannot be the kind of person her friends consider ideal she can at the very least convince them of her racial legitimacy.

Walker's black pride and racial solidarity lead her to feel she must consciously exhibit blackness and make her hyperaware of her racialized behaviors and tastes, with the result that she spends most of her youth battling a feeling of inadequacy. As chapter 2 demonstrates, since she is so strongly inclined toward identifying with the side of her heritage that suffers the most discrimination and abuse, she struggles most ardently to be accepted among black peoples. Yet while she wants to embrace her blackness, she also wants to embrace the side of her family that is not black; however, she finds that her African American friends and her own African American family take exception to her whiteness. The black pressure to disown her white/Jewish heritage is something she ultimately resists, but it has lasting effects. She admits to being unhappy with her body, which she feels is "too pale, too pasty, not honey-colored, not the glamorous-sounding café au lait" as a consequence of a "racial mix" in which the two sides "have yet to reconcile" (255). But she is also pleased by her sense of rhythm, which she thinks marks her as black and thus identifies her as more black than those without rhythm; she admits to thinking "poor thing" about a "mixed person with no groove, clinging to a rare, luxurious feeling of inclusion, 'the mix just didn't turn out right'" (255). Yet she wonders, "Where does that leave me? Ashamed of one half, grateful for the other? Ashamed one moment, proud the next, my comfort determined solely by context?" (256).

Her feeling of belonging only at the cost of denying her whiteness/Jewishness is not only a source of personal turmoil for Walker but also ironic when she notices how much mixture blackness and other people "of color" possess. One of her best friends in grade school in San Francisco is so different in appearance from her sister that it is "clear" that they "must have different fathers," but neither sister seems to be subjected to the same doubt that Walker endures, and each sister is accepted as black (154). All of her friends in New York are Latinx and she blends in with them readily, but she has to struggle to convince others of her blackness amid the more discerning African American crowd in San Francisco. The absurdity of her situation is made clear when Walker notes, "Even though none of them talks about it, none of them says I'm biracial or mixed or black and white or this and that, the fact is that each of them is half black and half something else close to if not white, and each of them looks like he could be my brother" (238). As a child, she is even envious of how "normal" her friend Sarah's household is when it includes one black and one white parent like her own apparently abnormal family (62). As her autobiography attests, the defining characteristic of Walker's life is the struggle to assert a racial identity that is at the mercy of social norms and other people's beliefs. Though her plight is not her choice, she has to spend her life coping with its imposition.

Having to contend with other people's attitudes about race requires Walker to face not only the judgmental gaze of African Americans who continually test the authenticity of her claims to blackness but also that of the wealthy Jewish community she encounters when she lives with her father. While she continually feels it necessary to prove that she is black enough in San Francisco, she finds that without any effort at all she embodies the tough attitude that means blackness to her friends in New York: "When I ask Jodi or Pam why people are sometimes quiet or reserved around me, they say that I am intimidating, which doesn't really answer my question but gives me a general idea of how I am perceived" (180). She realizes only in retrospect that "intimidating might be another word for black" (180). But her immersion into privileged white society is unlike her social life among other nonwhites in the Bronx, and the only scenes in the book in which Walker is not proud of her blackness occur when she is living with her father and is limited largely (if not exclusively) to the company of privileged whites. The boy she likes when she is a young schoolgirl tells her he "doesn't like black girls," and Walker recalls, "I think, with this big whoosh that turns my stomach upside down and almost knocks me over, is this what I am, a black girl? And that's when all the trouble starts, because suddenly I don't know what I am and I don't know how to be not what he thinks I am. I don't know how to be a not black girl" (69). In her efforts to be what she thinks others want her to be, Walker makes a show of her white stepmother or grandmother when either picks her up from school so that "he will see that I am related to not black girls" (70). However, after lying to her (black) mother to keep her away from her school play, Walker knows she is missing something, that her mother's voice, "the most important voice," can never praise her performance. She says, "Shame sticks to me like sweat" (72). When she is older and her father and stepmother move her to a middle-class Jewish neighborhood, the only black kids in her school are "from the wrong side of the tracks" and are "scruffy, unkempt, ashy" (207). She notices how "the sea of white, rich, Jewish kids . . . studiously avoid[s] them," and after a few weeks she does "the same, averting [her] eyes guiltily when a black kid in patched-up jeans passes [her] in the lunchroom, in the hallway, in class. Not once does a black student say a word to [her] . . . that whole year" (207). Later, she admits she "lie[s] outright that year" to her best friend Lauren:

> She asks me what I am, anyhow. . . . I have no idea how to answer her question, though I know what information she is looking for. What am I? . . . I get really hot. I look at my feet. I wash my hands and begin to hyperventilate.
>
> I'm Spanish, like from Spain, I say, and tear off a paper towel to put a period on it . . . and she never asks me about it again, not even when there is a big article in the newspaper about my mother, lauding her as a big African-American writer and mentioning that she has a daughter, this half-Jewish half-black girl living with her father in Larchmont. (207–8)

Like Raboteau's Emma, who endures the painful lesson of being made ashamed of her blackness when she is given a choice of dolls, and Senna's Birdie, who feels she must endure her friends' racism in silence, Walker must live through the guilt and shame of denying her blackness.

She compensates by trying to be more black in whatever ways she can. And like Nellie and Emma, who both seek color in their sexual partners, Walker seeks a connection to blackness by making love to a black body. In grade school, Walker's desire "to sleep naked next to Malaika" and enjoy "the warmth of [their] bodies flush against each other" seems more a desire to be close to Malaika's blackness than an expression of love or sexual desire for Malaika herself (96).

Echoing her childhood experience of pressing her naked "copper" body against her mother's naked "cherry-brown body," Walker describes her attraction to Malaika in terms of skin: "I like the color of Malaika's body, I like how brown she is, like Mama. When I look at her I feel the deep brown of her skin pour into me through my eyes and fill me up in a place that feels cold and empty, a place that I forget I have until I look at her naked body" (16, 96). The fact that Walker casts herself in the role of "Mommy" and Malaika in the role of "Daddy" reflects her desire for blackness to affect her and put her under its control: "I want to be the one who is touched more, the one who is done to, the one who is told what to do," and the one who is slapped with her father's old leather belt (97). Her desire to be under the control of Malaika as "Daddy" and to be in the role of black femininity also reflects her "decision to disidentify with positions of power," as Lori Harrison-Kahan points out.[55] Like Birdie's homosexual initiation into sex and sexuality, Walker's indicates a resistance to normative identities in terms of both sexual orientation and racial identity. As Harrison-Kahan observes, Walker's initiation into "ostensibly heterosexual desire" occurs when her Chicana babysitter French kisses her to teach her how it is done.[56] Like Birdie, Walker seems to overlook the homosexuality of her early sexual experiences, but the mixture of Latinx, black, white, Jewish, male, and female partners in Walker's life links the issues of race and sexuality (both of which are informed by gender) and demonstrates how resistant Walker is to ready classifications. She never identifies her sexual orientation and resists any dichotomous racial identity, thereby indicating that her identity or identities have to be understood outside of normative labels. Harrison-Kahan argues that the "fluidity" of Walker's race and sexuality and the diversity she experiences in both help explain her "mestiza consciousness" and indeed, Walker's only proclamation of what she "truly" is, is a conflation of ethnoracial concepts: she calls herself "a Puertorriqueña, a mulatta, breathed out with all that Spanish flavor. A girl of color with attitude."[57]

In contrast to her positive experiences with Malaika and relatively emotionally undamaging relationships with black boyfriends, when

Walker falls in love with a white boy in her late adolescence she states that their racial difference, "while not yet a problem for [them], is clearly a problem for everybody else" (Walker, *Black White and Jewish*, 278). Andrew's father has a nightmare in which the Klan comes after him and he "is convinced it is some kind of warning" about his son "dating a nigger" (279). Michael, Walker's steady black boyfriend, responds to her relationship with Andrew first with anger and then with incredulity: "Oh come on, Rebecca, he shouts, his face contorted and indignant. It's bad enough you slept with someone else, but a white boy? And then he's almost laughing. You're leaving me for a white boy?" (279). But, as Walker herself signals, racial difference—and more specifically, Andrew's whiteness—will become a problem for her as well. Walker realizes that whiteness can pose a threat to her relationship regardless of the love she and Andrew feel for each other when one of Andrew's friends uses the word "nigger" in conversation: "The words walked out of his mouth as easily as if he were saying good morning. . . . From my seat at the table they become dumb rednecks, including the one I love, and a wave of nausea . . . comes over me" (287). When Andrew's friends head off to their car high and drunk, and Walker asks if they are sober enough to drive, Andrew reassures her that they drive like that regularly. She reflects, "I feel sick. This image of white boys out of control, drunk and hurling the word *nigger* around, frightens me, reminds me of lynching photographs I've seen. Looking into Andrew's smiling brown eyes I feel a deep uneasiness, like suddenly I'm separate from him and on the other side of a long, treacherous tunnel I'm not sure I'll be able to get through" (288). Similarly, when she is younger and living with her father, she dates Luca, her friend Tina's brother. Tina brings up the fact that some of Luca's friends have been giving him a hard time for dating a "nigger"; he says, "Fuck them," but Tina asks him tellingly, "Did you tell *them* that" (220). His hockey coach even "single[s] him out" and tells him "not to have sex" before a game, but Walker attributes it to "some strange macho bullshit, a guy thing rather than anything to do with the color of [her] skin" (220). Tina is supportive, but Walker feels alone; she recognizes the absurdity of calling her friends from the Bronx to explain that "some hockey-playing boy

from northern Italy dumped me because I am not white" (220). While
her relationships with black men have their own problems—such as the
jealousy of other black women when she dates the sought-after Michael
or her own feelings of insufficiency due to another boyfriend's nude
pictures of a black woman—she finds them comforting. She calls sex
"the salve that coats the wound" and says, "[It] is the sound that drowns
out all the people who don't like black white girls, who don't like white
black girls, who don't like me, the skin on my body having determined
this long before I have even had a chance to speak" (256). But when she
is romantically involved with white men, the salve is mitigated by her
increased racial anxiety. Instead of being filled up "in a place that feels
cold and empty," as she is when she looks at Malaika's body, Walker is
frightened and reminded of lynching photographs when she looks into
Andrew's eyes. Though she realizes that her blackness "means something different in the downtown New York scene," that it "is cool in
a way it wasn't" at her white school in Larchmont or even at her black
high school in San Francisco, she also realizes that coolness is not a
foundation on which to build a relationship (270). In the New York art
community, her blackness is "something that makes [her] hot, special,
attractive, an untasted flavor of the month," and being exoticized offers Walker the opportunity to have her blackness appreciated when
her blackness has for so long been doubted or taken for granted (270).
But the esteem she feels is short lived, and her relationships with white
partners never offer her the solace that the proximity to blackness in
African American partners provides.

Ultimately, Walker wants to align herself with blackness without
identifying herself monoracially but she finds that difficult to do. She
is made to feel that she does not measure up, that her claim to blackness is inherently compromised by her whiteness. She seems to lament
her apparent multiracialness at times, such as when she notices that
in black-and-white photos of herself with a boyfriend she is not black
like him (or, for that matter, white): "In the bottom two Dave is kissing the side of my face, his big black hand pressing against the length
of my pale gray neck" (143). Sometimes she is considered too white;
even her own African American family has difficulty accepting her

without conditions, and she oscillates between wanting to own her whiteness and wanting to shrug it off. At other times she is considered too black and is made to feel either proud or ashamed of her blackness. Overwhelmingly, however, Walker wants her blackness to be noticed and to identify her primarily but does not want her blackness to erase her white/Jewish heritage. She concludes that her belonging to either race is conditional, that at any given time she might not be welcomed into either group. She might just as easily be called a "cracker" by black relatives who associate her with the pain caused by "the insanity, the cruelty, the maniacal culture of racist white people" as she might be called "you folks" by a white school headmaster who tells her there is "no financial aid available" despite her having asked for none (84, 261). She remarks that other people will always see her in whatever way they want and that to "bridge the distance" she has to share parts of herself that others do not know. But she is unsure when and whether to trust others: "Keeping a part of myself held back is what I've done to cope for the last twenty years, opting instead to be partially known, reservedly intimate, I have no idea if I can tolerate what might be a less than accepting response" (48–49).

Her autobiography works to "bridge the distance" and shares her sense of herself without labels and political agendas. She knows that her blackness makes it difficult for her Jewish family to accept her but also knows that black people find her whiteness difficult. When her (black female) partner asks her, "What does it *feel* like to have white inside of you," Walker questions the notion that one can "feel" race and even wonders how one would define whiteness. But she remarks that the only time she "feels" white "is when black folks point out something in [her] that they don't want to own in themselves and so label 'white'" or when she compares herself "physically to darker people and find[s] [her]self lacking" (304–5). Presumably, then, Walker "feels" (some kind of) black the rest of the time and thus can "feel" white or black or Jewish or any combination variously. What her own malleable racial identity ascertains is Walker's belief that she does not have to choose allegiances "in order to know who [she is] or in order to pay proper respect to [her] ancestors" (307). What she wants is to "taste that freedom" that occurs "when we put down the scripts written by history and memory, when each person before us can be seen free of the cultural or personal narrative we've inherited or devised" (307).

With this concluding thought, Walker seems to support Becky Thompson and Sangeeta Tyagi's claim in their introduction to *Names We Call Home: Autobiography on Racial Identity* that "autobiography illustrates why racial identity formation occurs at the intersection of a person's subjective memory of trauma and collective remembrance of histories of domination."[58] Indeed, Walker's identity is formed within the context of her subjective experience of "trauma" as well as her awareness of black, Jewish, and white positions in "histories of domination." Like anyone else's, nothing about Walker's identity is independent of race or racial history, and so her narrative functions as what Thompson and Tyagi identify as typical of "racial identity autobiography"— her "storytelling" acts as a "social conscience" for the society that has shaped her. But, as I have already noted, Walker's autobiography and the novels are doing similar things. To a great extent, Thompson and Tyagi's observations about autobiography are just as applicable to the realist coming-of-age novels of Senna, Raboteau, and Harper. In all four texts, the narrators are explicitly located in a particular national and historical context that is inseparable from their negotiation of racial identity/identities. It goes without saying that each narrator cannot possibly tell her story in a vacuum, that each young woman develops a sense of her racial self specifically in relation to American racial history and ever-changing American race concepts. A critical component of these texts is the fact that their narrators are not simply finding their way along an established route but rather are exploring the insufficiencies of established racial traditions in the United States and questioning how race was and is practiced.

In *Reading Autobiography*, Sidonie Smith and Julia Watson point out that the typical European bildungsroman "culminates in the acceptance of one's constrained social role in the bourgeois social order, usually requiring the renunciation of some ideal or passion and the embrace of heteronormative social arrangements."[59] However, they also point out that the use of the bildungsroman "more recently by women and other disenfranchised persons" has resulted in the "plot of development culminat[ing] not in integration but in an awakening" to the "limitations" of social categories.[60] This lack of "tidy closure" in the texts of nonwhite and/or nonmale writers resists the generic conventions of the bildungsroman and the autobiography, Smith and Watson explain.[61] For Walker, Senna, Raboteau, and Harper, then, the resistance to tidiness and conformity poses a threat not only to the literary forms established by a white male literary tradition but also to the social conventions established by a white- and male-dominated social tradition. If anything, these narrators argue that they do not (and to a great extent, prefer not to) fit into American racial ideology as they find it; these texts argue for and, in fact, begin to effect change in American racial discourse.

The resistance to normativity of any kind—in particular, the racial binary in the works of Walker, Senna, Raboteau, and Harper—indicates a shift in multiracial literature toward conceiving of multiracial identity in a new way. Just as contemporary literature works to counter beliefs that mixedness excludes one from whiteness, as chapter 2 argues, this literature also works to counter beliefs that blackness makes mixedness irrelevant or, conversely, that multiracial identity distances one from blackness. A significant part of recognizing multiracial identity is to resist considering it as something that precludes monoracial pride or solidarity. It is not a matter of considering blackness as mixedness but rather of considering multiracial identity as something that can coincide with an identification with black people and black political allegiance. These texts argue that blackness and mixedness are neither mutually exclusive nor the same. In "The Racial Politics of Mixed Race," Lisa Tessman explains the problem of conflating racial identity with racial solidarity:

> The "where are you from?" or "what are you?" questions encountered by mixed-race people are telltale in an important way: they reveal that the popular show of concern over mixed-race people is about identity, rather than about political loyalty. However, I believe that what frequently may be concealed in the questions about identity are questions of loyalty, for

it is presumed that loyalty is itself determined by identity. The question "what are you?" may *stand for* the unasked, "where does your political allegiance lie?" Suppose one's true concern, however, is with the political questions, such as "will you stand with people of color against racism?" Does a response that comes in the form of an assertion of identity really tell one anything? Does an answer "I'm mixed race" indicate less of a sense of solidarity in the struggle against racial oppression than, for instance, the answers "I'm black" or "I'm a person of color"?[62]

Certainly, racial identity is an indication of political allegiance for some such as Lisa Jones, who specifically identifies her politics through the terms of her racial identity. But investing racial identity with political loyalty is problematic when only black monoracial identity is an accepted signifier for black political allegiance.

What this discussion has demonstrated is that multiracial identity ought not to be automatically dismissed as a lack of interest in blackness or social justice. Contemporary literature reveals that racial discourse must catch up with contemporary multiracial identities and consider multiracialness (or whiteness acknowledged along with blackness in any fashion) as a contemporary identity. This literature demonstrates that multiracial identity is not disloyalty, an abandonment of blackness, an exploitation of whiteness, or a lack of interest in fighting for racial equality the way multiracialness (or an acknowledgment or use of whiteness) often was in the past. It is unity, not division, that these texts establish or at least gesture toward. It is a new recognition of multiracial identity, not a recycled one, that these texts encourage. It is this contemporariness of multiracial identity that is critical.

Another significant aspect of recognizing multiracialness is recognizing the difference between race and racial identity. As chapter 1 discusses at length, if it is going to trouble American race practices, contemporary multiracial theory must avoid duplicating the mulatto caste of the past, which it risks doing by relying on concepts of hybridity that simply constitute new races and fit into the existing system of racial classification. A difference must be recognized (and put into practice) between the flexibility of "identity" (which may or may not coincide with existing racial categorization) and "race" (the simple use of existing race groups or the insertion of a new race group into existing concepts and language), or else multiracialness restores rather than challenges race practice in the United States. For instance, Kerry Anne Rockquemore argues that multiracial identity is a "border identity" that "conceptualizes biraciality as a new and separate category, one that is neither exclusively one race, nor another, but a blending of all an individual's racial backgrounds."[63] While such an iteration of multiracialism proposes an opposition to existing races through a new race category, it is in fact simply a formulation of a new race category because Rockquemore conflates *racial identity* and *race* categories. While multiracialism might be a "new" identity, it is not necessarily a "separate" race category. Unless one identifies as "multiracial" as if it were its own race, mixedness cannot be taken for granted as a separate category.[64] Rather, it is a different identity that crosses categories (or races)—it is an identity that reaches into multiple categories rather than necessarily defining a new race/category. In other words, being multiracial (for instance, black and white) does not mean that one's *race* is "multiracial" the way it would be "black" or "white" for a monoracial person. Rather, multiracialness is the label of a condition or *identity* rather than of a race. One's "race" is still black and white; one's "identity" is some formulation of multiracialness.

However, like "mulatto" did in the past, some more recent racial identities do indeed formulate multiracialness as a new race. These approaches to multiracialism and/or hybridity tend to do this by homogenizing plurality. Paul Gilroy warns against the dangers of such concepts of hybridity in *Against Race: Imagining Political Culture Beyond the Color Line*: "We do not have to be content with the halfway house provided by the idea of plural cultures. A theory of relational cultures and culture as relation represents a more worthwhile resting place. That possibility is currently blocked by banal invocations of hybridity in which everything becomes equally and continuously intermixed, blended into an impossibly even consistency."[65]

Though the argument could be made that multiracial literature sometimes offers a notion of plurality, it is clear that Walker and Senna's, Raboteau's, and Harper's protagonists value their blackness in such a way that they consider themselves racially proud and loyal even while acknowledging their mixedness/whiteness. While sameness matters sometimes to young women simply trying to fit in (and yearning for community rather than racial sameness), none of the texts is ultimately seeking to articulate a homogenizing hybrid identity.

Michele Hunter's reading of Senna's novel in "Revisiting the Third Space" is equally applicable to other texts when she argues that the differences between multiracial figures challenges the traditional juxtaposition of something normal and something abnormal, and that "difference here is no longer tyrannically hierarchical, nor is it oppositional."[66] Hunter employs the notion that, in relation to multiracialness, difference is no longer measured in the homogenizing terms of normative and nonnormative. The unhierarchical and nonoppositional differences among those who fit no norm serve to illustrate the potential mistake of employing a notion of hybridity that might pit mixture against (apparent) purity, duplicate a dichotomy, and support (rather than challenge) racial systems of categorization. Hunter's use of Senna is particularly helpful since Cole and Birdie share the same parents and early upbringing yet look so different from one another and have such vastly different racialized experiences both together and apart. Hunter argues that "theories of difference rely on the either/or model—or, in the case of mixed-race people, *neither/nor*"—and that in comparing and contrasting the experiences of Cole and Birdie as two multiracial girls rather than only positioning multiracialness against monoracialness, Senna "challenge[s] theories of difference which insist on the inferiority of the subordinate party."[67] Hunter argues, "Birdie and Cole's *difference from each other* undoes our traditional notions of differences in which a normative standard oppresses its corresponding deviant," and "the identification that occurs between Birdie and Cole captures an instance of difference" that fails to "uphold any normative standard" by which to judge difference.[68] It is, she explains, an exploration of *"difference from difference."*

Indeed, this difference in difference—or heterogeneity within nonnormative racial identities—is often lacking in theories of hybridity. Gloria Anzaldúa proposes negotiation between the kinds of oppressed and oppressive forces that Hunter identifies, but even when she stands at the "crossroads" or the "border" Anzaldúa still claims the "specificity of a mestizo identity."[69] Hybridity is often theorized as some identifiable category and constituted against a (usually white-Anglo) norm, and such an approach tends to juxtapose plurality with nonplurality in a way that homogenizes both. While this approach to hybridity is useful in other discussions, it is not useful for thinking about contemporary American black–white multiracial identity. As the discussion above demonstrates, it is the relational, to borrow Gilroy's term, that multiracials must negotiate. The relationship between black and white rests in multiracialness; multiracialness is not conceived of in contemporary literature as a blending that results in some new race the way many theories of hybridity conceive of mixture.[70] For instance, the link between La Raza ("The Race") and the plural identities of Latinx and mestiza/o (or even simply Mexican) illustrates this notion of a homogeneous (mixed) racial identity. As Margaret Hunter explains, "The ideology of *mestizaje* [is] a belief system that values the mixture of races and cultures and creates an inclusive and hybrid national Mexican identity."[71] All of these concepts, as well as others such as Creole, seek to name and identify a particular race category that is a combination of (specific) heterogeneous ethnoracial groups. These concepts work to recognize the heterogeneity inherent to the category but to recognize it in a homogenizing and stable identity.

While some multiracial activists might argue for similar goals, most literature does not—at least not quite in those terms. Much of the black–white multiracial literature of the United States (including the works of Senna, Walker, Harper, and Raboteau) does not simply proclaim a mulatta identity or find a comfortable home in hybridity in and of itself. Rather, these writers explore the complicated racial history of blackness and whiteness and what it might mean for people to find themselves with claims to both in this historical moment (when black pride and solidarity are indispensable but white family branches are something people often *want* to and *can* acknowledge). As chapter 1 observes, social expectations and practices complicate multiracial identity formation because of a national racial history that has always pitted whiteness and blackness in opposition. Chapter 2 notes that whiteness is beginning to be transformed into something diverse and racialized and is therefore capable of accepting mixture and coexisting with blackness. And chapter 3 argues that having white parentage that claims (rather than disowns) one does not mean that one must surrender claims to black pride or solidarity when one identifies with white heritage as well. Taken together, chapters 2 and 3 demonstrate that both blackness and whiteness operate in terms of exclusivity. Both whiteness and blackness are homogenized and so variation is marginalized: one is either white or mixed just as one is either black or mixed.

What contemporary literature is beginning to explore is whether black and white can exist together outside the dichotomy of mixed and not-mixed, whether the terms of mixture can be changed so that black–white multiracial identity need not inherently impose a separation from blackness or whiteness. Contemporary writers are imagining how black–white identity/identities might negotiate a new type of identity formation in a society that has so much racial history reinforcing monoracial race concepts (and a separate category of mixture). And with this history in mind, contemporary literature does not propose monoracial identity or mulatto identity. Instead, this literature balances on the relational since no other option appears to exist. Ultimately, these writers are pulling at the threads that have held blackness and whiteness in dichotomous opposition, and while their efforts may or may not eventually contribute to the deterioration of the practice of race, for now they are most certainly trying to undo the binary.

| Chapter Four

Mixed Ethnicity
Multiracialism as Multicultural Identity

As in the earlier chapters, this chapter addresses the significance of others' expectations, individuals' needs or desires, and the social context of identification, but it shifts the focus of black–white mixture from race to ethnicity. It focuses on Heidi Durrow's *The Girl Who Fell from the Sky* because this novel does something with multiracialism that is in many ways dissimilar from Senna, Walker, Raboteau, and Harper, something rather unique among contemporary narratives of black–white multiracialism: it challenges not monoracialism but rather monoculturalism. Durrow uncouples two important aspects of identity—race and ethnicity—and draws our attention to the differences between them as well as the ways they both contribute to the identity of her mixed protagonist. By dissecting how identity can be formed and altered and how race and ethnicity operate in contemporary American society, Durrow's novel shows us new ways that multiracialism can help us better understand how we conceive of race, ethnicity, and (ethno)racial identities.

The Girl Who Fell from the Sky depicts Rachel's racial and ethnic development from her early childhood to adolescence. Along the way, her identity development is interrupted repeatedly by changes in parenting (including changes between white and black parental figures) and location (from Europe to America and from white-majority to black-majority communities). These changes in family structure and geography help to demonstrate how familial and social environments affect Rachel's identities; they also emphasize how she views her mixedness in terms of both race and ethnicity (largely as a result of the diversity in her communities and her experiences of parenting). When Rachel accepts a monoracial label and pursues not a multi*racial* identity but rather a multi*ethnic* identity, the novel challenges the common view that collapses ethnicity and race into one category. The novel does this in terms of both white and black identities since it refutes the idea that monoracialism leads necessarily to monoethnicity (because in this case, African Americanness is part—but not all—of Rachel's ethnicity despite being all of her racial identity) and questions the idea that ethnicity is also a racial label (because in this case, Danishness is part of her ethnicity but whiteness is none of her racial identity). In this way, Durrow's work scrutinizes beliefs about whiteness, blackness, and the links between race and ethnicity. Ultimately, *The Girl Who Fell from the Sky* offers another identity path for multiracial subjects as Durrow's protagonist explores her mixedness in the form of (cultural) ethnicity rather than (phenotypical) race.

Ethnicity and Race: Identity Formation and Terminology

Because this discussion of Durrow's text is so focused on the process by which Rachel develops her identity, this chapter will employ racial formation scholarship (to address the stages she goes through as she learns to navigate the social environments that affect her identity development). Before turning to the text itself, I will briefly outline some of the scholarship that the subsequent textual analysis will reference.

Ethnic and racial formation scholarship indicates that several important factors contribute to how an individual chooses to identify or is identified—or, in other words, how a functional identity is embodied by or ascribed to an individual. Chief among these factors are the role of parents and community and the social environments in which multiracial subjects find themselves. As the earlier chapters demonstrate, multiracials must contend with the social expectations of family and community as well as those of broader society: in order for social identity to function as such, it must be understood or otherwise recognized by those around the subject.[1] Indeed, as Hazel Rose Markus states, identities "are both private and public property—others have a say in who a person becomes."[2] That is, even when someone prefers to identify in certain ways, their identity will still be tied to how others see them. As Markus explains, since identity is "a combination" of "our *own* view of *ourselves* with *others' views* of us," it means that "sometimes, in some situations, these views converge; at other times or in other situations, they diverge."[3] As a result, it is not a simple task to declare one's identity—for an identity to function in any practical sense it must be recognized, understood, and acknowledged by at least part of one's family, community, and/or society. Thus, according to Miller and Buchanan, "A child's racial identity may be determined and influenced by his or her own self-label, the family's label, or labels imposed by society and may reflect a consensus-building process across self, family, and society's label."[4] For these reasons, it is perhaps unsurprising that multiracial identities are received positively in integrated and diverse communities and tend to produce negative results in monoracial communities, where pressures to maintain racial norms prevail.[5]

In general, family and community guidance can become essential to the development of, in sociological terms, healthy and functional identities for children with minority heritages or identities ("minority" in terms of numbers but also in terms of the ethnoracial hierarchy of the United States). Sociologists define three developmental stages: "early childhood" (ages four to six), when children tend to learn their identities from their families and develop "coping skills" if theirs are marginalized identities (i.e., non–white/Anglo); "middle childhood" (ages seven to eleven), when children's identities tend to be reinforced or challenged by their social environments; and "adolescence and early adulthood," when children's identities are shaped by broader community norms and individuals are more likely to begin associating with in-groups or other ethnoracial "reference groups."[6] For black–white multiethnic and/or multiracial subjects, these stages are complicated by the pressures of white majority culture and white supremacist racial hierarchies; as sociologists and psychologists note, subjects are most successful at avoiding what Lee Jenkins calls "identity conflicts"

and "maladaptive behavior" if they can develop black pride, black solidarity, black community, and what are commonly referred to as the
"survival skills" or "coping mechanisms" necessary to contend with
racism and white privilege.[7] Moreover, multiracial identity formation tends to be "not a static process . . . but an evolving social process
across the life span"; that is, multiracial "status" affects identity formation in ways that even minority monoethnic or monoracial "status" does not, since "the multiracial child's potential for choosing an
identity of one racial group reemerges at each developmental period."[8]

As this discussion and the previous chapters illustrate, black–white
multiracial identity formation is complicated and must take into account the effects of white supremacy, the importance of black pride,
and the overwhelming influence of family and society—two entities
that tend to let individuals down in minor and major ways. What this
chapter aims to do is complicate all of this further with ethnicity. As
Kwame Anthony Appiah points out, "The body is central to race, gender, and sexuality but not so central to class and ethnicity" because,
unlike ethnicity, "unless you are morphologically atypical for your
racial group, strangers, friends, officials are always aware of it in public and private contexts, always notice it, almost never let it slip from
view."[9] However, that Hispanic/Latinx ethnicity (which can currently be officially combined with any race) now seems likely to become
a racial rather than ethnic category on the American census demonstrates how difficult it is not only to separate race and ethnicity but
also to identify ethnicity (as a public and nonracial identity). American
society seems unable to understand ethnicity as an identity distinct
from race, in other words, and in many practical ways it has always
treated Hispanicness, the only officially recognized "ethnicity," as a
racial identity. In the case of black–white multiracialism, the importance of black pride and the struggle to assert a multiracial identity
that avoids white privilege make ethnicity either a lower priority or, as
this chapter will demonstrate, a way to access white heritage in terms
that are not racial. Ethnicity muddies the waters of race classification
(and both mono- and multiracial identity) by forcing us to consider
whether ethnicity is part of race or separate from it. For instance, if

black identity requires cultural fluency and a lack of it can make one insufficiently black—hence the slur "Oreo," which indicates a black "outside" and white "inside"—then blackness is certainly not simply an identity of phenotypical race. And if black identity requires cultural fluency but not necessarily black "race," then one could potentially be culturally—but not racially—black. That is, someone who is not black in appearance and/or ancestry could be ethnically black. (While it would be complicated by the conventional race concepts of white purity and one-drop blackness, the same thing could be proposed regarding white racial and white ethnic identities.) These concerns are outside of the scope of this project and require lengthy independent consideration, but they do suggest that the differences and connections between ethnicity and race are not as simple as we might think.

Here, it is important to be clear about the language this chapter employs. Certainly, "race" is a very contested term and its definition is hardly simple. Moreover, race is often discussed in terms of ethnicity. But for the purposes of the discussion in *this* chapter, I will treat race in the conventional terms of American race practices—namely, as a largely physiological concept. Thus, here, "race" has the very basic meaning of color and other phenotypical characteristics that have been racialized—something someone inherits through genes, we might say. Here "ethnicity," as is usually the case, has the basic meaning of taught culture—something someone assimilates through socialization (despite the fact that ethnicity is frequently tied to notions of inheritance or ancestral heritage, it is still acknowledged as something that can be transmitted—or not transmitted—to children, unlike race).[10]

Monoracial Multiethnic Identity:
Heidi Durrow's *The Girl Who Fell from the Sky*

Historically, the social practice of "passing" and the literary tradition of passing novels exhibit the ethnicity of racial identities alongside the phenotype of racial identities since racial passing hinges not only on appearance but also on the active performance of a race (that is, racial belonging is often solidified through convincing cultural fluency and behaviors). However, Durrow's text explores racialized ethnicity as something that can be claimed by individuals who do not always "match" in color and culture. Now more than ever, writers are exploring how racial identity is linked to culture and how racialized identities, such as blackness or whiteness, can be embodied or claimed through ethnicity rather than just physical appearance. For the multiracial Birdie in Danzy Senna's *Caucasia*, for instance, her blackness is more an identity of politics, culture, and family than phenotype—in fact, it is virtually never seen in her body. Similarly, in James McBride's *The Color of Water*, his mother's blackness is an identity of politics, family, and community rather than phenotypical or inherited race since she has no known black ancestry. Also, in *Black White and Jewish*, Rebecca Walker's shifts between WASP, Jewish, Latinx, and African American communities mean that her racial identity is often explicitly tied to culture and other ethnic signifiers even though her blackness is constantly visible in her body.

Like her contemporaries, Heidi Durrow explores phenotypical concepts of race and their impact on multiracial subjects in her novel *The Girl Who Fell from the Sky*. But Durrow is less interested than many of her fellow writers in depicting black–white multiracial identity. Rather, Durrow's text takes up quite specifically the issue of how prevailing concepts of race and culture manifest two distinct facets of identity. *The Girl Who Fell from the Sky* explores the relationship of race and ethnicity to notions of inheritance and whether race (in the phenotypical sense) and ethnicity (in the cultural sense) must mirror one another or might sometimes be considered independently. For the protagonist, her mother's Danishness is not simply defined by racial whiteness; rather, the Danishness she "inherits" from her mother is something she considers primarily an ethnic (rather than racial) part of her identity.

In Durrow's novel, Rachel is the child of an African American father and a white Danish mother who meet and then begin their family in Europe, where the father is stationed as a military officer. When Rachel is about ten years old, her mother leaves her father and moves the children to Chicago to be with a white American man. When Rachel's mother dies, Rachel is raised by her paternal grandmother and aunt in Portland, Oregon. The shifts in location and parenting are central to defamiliarizing race—that is, her ever-changing family structure and locale expose Rachel to a variety of racial practices among her various parental figures and the societies in which she lives. Because of the discontinuity in her life, Rachel is tasked with the ongoing process of determining how she might be identified or identify herself. Like many of her fellow literary multiracial subjects, Rachel is rarely perceived by others in ways that reflect how she wants to be perceived. But what is so unusual about Durrow's novel is that Rachel is not consumed with the desire to belong or to make herself "make sense" in a black-and-white world (that we see in the works of Senna, Walker, Raboteau, and Harper). Rather, Rachel is conscious of how her racial identity is being constructed around her and she accepts it willingly. Yet she resists the hegemonic power of race and refuses to let her racial identity dictate her ethnic identity. She agrees to a great extent to fulfill her society's perception of her as mono*racially* black but refuses to be mono*culturally* African American; instead, she insists that she is multiculturally African American and Danish.

As Rachel cycles through various parents—including her father, her mother, her mother's boyfriend, her grandmother, her aunt, and her aunt's fiancé—she is forced to consider her racial and ethnic identities critically. For children exposed to consistent messages about their race or culture, both become normalized and may go unexamined. But the variation in Rachel's life causes her to interrogate the views of any particular parent and allows her the rare opportunity to identify self-reflectively. Additionally, it is parenting, which nurtures black racial pride and black cultural fluency, that results in what sociologists call a "positive black identity," and in many ways Rachel achieves this "positive black identity" (even if it is not a totalizing or complete identity for her). Throughout her childhood, Rachel is bombarded with—at times inconsistent—information about her ethnic and racial identities. If, as sociologists and social workers argue, a child must be steered by the clear and positive guidance of parents in order to develop an "appropriate" identity, it is worth examining how Rachel's identity is aided or compromised by her various parents. Rachel's African American father, grandmother, aunt, and uncle-to-be offer very different approaches to African American ethnicity and, to differing degrees and in different ways, shape Rachel's development of an African American identity. But perhaps the most obvious would-be impediment to her development of a "positive black identity" is her white mother.

Any number of sociologists and laypeople recognize the social and political importance of sustained black culture in white-majority societies, both in the late twentieth century and now. Though one might argue that progressive, intelligent, and sensitive white parents are capable of providing access to black culture, developing "survival skills," and fostering what sociologists call a "positive black identity" in their black or multiracial children, Rachel's mother is not such a parent.[11] However, an important distinction between Rachel's mother, Nella, and other white American parents of African American children is that her failure stems not from her racial whiteness and the American norms that accompany it but rather from her foreignness. Part of the argument regarding the inappropriateness of white parents is the fact of their ignorance of the experience of being black and the difficulty they might have in overcoming often unnoticed white privilege to see the institutional or unconscious racism in their society—and this would apply equally to Nella. But Nella has none of what also concerns some sociologists about white parents—namely, a disinterest in black identity or culture and a naïve interest in "color blindness."[12] Nella's inability to parent her children is due to the fact that she is Danish and entirely unknowledgeable about American race practices or American racism. In fact, Roger, Rachel's father, must share some of the blame for Nella's inability to parent her children because he has refused to instruct her or the children in what he knows about race in the United States. As Rachel observes, "He never told us he was black. He never told us that we were" (Durrow, *The Girl Who Fell from the Sky*, 80). Though he wants to stay away from the United States and its racism, Roger nevertheless fails to fulfill what sociologists see as his parental role in his refusal to teach his children about racial pride, racial identity, and the "survival skills" necessary to navigate racial inequality. Nella acknowledges that "Roger always said it would be hard" but also says that he never explained why (23). Nella's ignorance is clear when she explains her lack of awareness of race or what race might "mean":

"I wasn't ever thinking he was black. When he said but you cannot be pregnant, we cannot get married, and when I said why not he said cause you are white and I am not. I did not know that was a problem. So many white women were dating NCOS with brown skin, and it was normal to me. I do not think of this thing. . . . Roger said I could not understand because Europa is not the same. He never wanted to come back to America" (123–24). Nella recognizes her mistake in leaving Europe, admitting, "America was not what I thought it was," and, "I think it sometimes that to come here was a mistake. I did not think it would be so hard" (23, 110). Ultimately, it is her ignorance of racial practices and race norms in the United States, not a refusal to respect her children's blackness, that proves to be Nella's undoing. If we consider that Rachel's "early childhood" stage of development is marked first by Roger's refusal to school her in black identity in any form and then by Nella's inability to provide sufficient guidance as a foreign white parent of multiracial children in the United States, Rachel's parents together offer little of the support that sociologists consider necessary for functional identity formation. When Nella takes the children to the United States without Roger, she is at a severe disadvantage as a parent with children at this stage of development since they look to her for guidance. As sociologists point out, most of a child's identity formation in early childhood comes from the family; without her father's interest in or, eventually, ability to parent her at this time, and then with only her mother's insufficient guidance available, Rachel has essentially no familial source of information guiding her identity development. Indeed, if it is "especially important that the parent be cognizant of the ways in which racial issues may affect [their] child" and that they "help their children by teaching them to recognize and value their racial identity and acknowledge the ways race affects their lives, positively and negatively," clearly neither of Rachel's parents helps her to develop a "positive" identity of any kind in Europe or in America.[13]

It appears that while Roger has hoped to avoid dealing with race and identity altogether, Nella would have been pleased to raise her children with a "positive black identity" had she been equipped to do so. It also appears that it is precisely her inability to do so that destroys her psychologically. In a sense, then, she has the right instincts—she desperately wants to "protect" her children and have her family be recognized as such. She also lacks any investment in white suprema-cy, which is evident in her devastation after she unknowingly utters a racist epithet. Mimicking her white boyfriend's language, she refers to her children as "jigaboos" before being corrected by Laronne, her African American employer:

> "Nigger. Nella, it means nigger."
> "Oh goodness. Oh my goodness," Nella had said. "Oh goodness, no—I didn't know. Oh, I knew about the other word . . ."
> "Nigger?" Laronne said it again as if she were preempting Nella from saying it.
> "Oh, that's a terrible word. I . . ."
> "It's the same thing." Laronne's voice had more anger in it than she meant.
> "I didn't know," Nella had said again, in almost a whisper. "Do you think, Laronne—Laronne do you think the kids know? Is it something you would just know . . . the word?"
> Laronne didn't know how to answer. "Nella, they know you love them."
> "But I don't ever want them to think—to think I'd let anything hurt them."
> "They know."
> "I want them to really know."[14]

Nella is hurt on multiple levels: she has said something hateful to her children, even if unknowingly; she did not know better than to pro-tect them from a racial slur; and she is failing to protect them, gener-ally speaking, and is, in fact, exposing them to racism in their own home through Doug, her boyfriend. As Miller and Buchanan point out, "Some psychologists believe that White families may struggle at help-ing a multiracial child effectively cope with racism because White par-ents have not had to develop the requisite survival skills to cope with race-related stressors that are more subtle in nature than overt acts of racism (for example, racial microaggressions)."[15] Here, Nella cannot even identify obvious racism or threats posed to her children, such as Doug's harmful language, let alone subtle prejudice. Thus, the incident helps Nella realize that she is far from capable of instilling "survival skills" in her children.

Indeed, Nella begins to recognize that despite her good intentions, she simply does not have the knowledge or capability to help her children navigate an unjust world. She has to ask Laronne about what her own children might know or not know because, unlike herself, Laronne does know what it is like to be black in America. The words she chooses emphasize this: "Is it something you would just know . . . the word?" (Durrow, *The Girl Who Fell from the Sky*, 156). Nella's use of the second-person pronoun suggests that she links her children and Laronne as "the same" in a way that she and her children are not. Nella is at first baffled when people look at her strangely when she is out with her children, and she is mystified when a woman seems to think she has adopted her children: "What does the woman not see? Robbie, the little brown *kys*. He looks like Roger—around the eyes, his nose. His mouth looks like me. Rachel has the same color eyes. They are more pretty for her. Ariel looks just like them when they were babys. More hair. They are my natural children. And look like it" (123–24). Where Americans simply see color and thus see her as unlike her children, Nella sees family resemblances. It is this inability to have her family recognized that she claims prevents her from protecting her children: "They're mine. If people can't see it, how can I keep them safe?" (104). But we might also interpret Nella's remarks as suggesting not only that she needs her children to be seen as hers but also that she cannot manage having them defined by their race (and thus as different from her). She understands that she is incapable of raising black children in the United States; she knows that for her to parent them successfully they cannot be seen only in terms of their race. In her more hopeful moments she insists, "I love them and will keep them safe. My children are one half of black. They are also one half of me. I want them to be anything. They are not just a color that people see" (157). But when she leads them up to the roof with plans to kill them and herself, it is because she has failed to "keep them safe" and understands she cannot protect her children against that which she cannot anticipate: she acknowledges she cannot control how her children are seen and treated and admits there will be more "dangers" that she "can't know" yet (260). In fact, she has so little hope of protecting her children that she feels killing them is the only sure way to prevent them from coming to harm in the United States: as Nella inches her family toward the edge of the roof in their last moments together, she tells her children that the "way people look at [them and the] things that people say" are precisely what that she "will protect [them] from" (260). Nella also acknowledges that the children are becoming somewhat distant from her. For instance, when she tries to comfort Rachel after Doug has become violent and used the word "nigger," Nella notices Rachel's expression and feels that she is "a step away—maybe that step is there forever" (243). She recognizes that the way her children are being racialized in America is driving her family apart. Ironically, it is the preservation of her family that motivates Nella to lead the children to the rooftop, as she says to them before taking them to their presumed deaths, "We will always be a family this way" (260). In killing herself and her children, Nella succumbs to her belief that racism and race concepts in America make both her family and, especially, her role as her children's mother unfeasible if not impossible.

Nella fails as a white mother of black children in the starkest and most tragic of ways. But her failure is not one of a white parent insensitive to the racism her children will face in the United States or unwilling to help her children foster "positive black identity." Rather, it is her *sensitivity* to the harm of racism and her *inability* to help her children (because of her racial illiteracy) that lead her to attempt to kill them and herself. Nella demonstrates that hers is not a willing or even unconscious denial of African American culture with respect to her children's identities. It is her foreignness—or, more accurately, her ignorance of what is to her a foreign American culture—that makes her an inadequate parent of African American children. Unlike the white American parents of black/multiracial children who are sometimes condemned as too oblivious to race and racism to parent appropriately, Nella is well aware of how American race practices make her parenthood such a challenging experience. It is important to notice that it is the social environment in the United States that causes the problem and not interracial families themselves. Nella's failure as a parent seems directly linked to the context in which she raises her children and not simply to her racial whiteness; the reader is left to wonder whether she could have succeeded in other circumstances or other places. That is to say, we are invited to see that the malady is rooted in America's race practices rather than Nella's parenting skills, in part if not entirely.[16]

Certainly, Nella is ill-equipped to guide her children to inhabit "positive black identity" and her husband is of no help—though, to be fair to Roger, he did not anticipate that Nella would be raising the children in the United States or that she would be doing it without him. The second father figure, Doug, is American; however, he is not only equally unhelpful but actually causes harm because he repeats the racism he has learned in America—including the epithets "jigaboo" and "nigger"—around the comprehending children. When they live in Turkey and Germany with both biological parents and in Chicago with their white mother and her white boyfriend, Rachel and her siblings lack the kind of parental guidance that social workers deem necessary for the formation of children's identities. But if African American parents might be considered most appropriate for black children (as they are by, for instance, the National Association of Black Social Workers), Rachel's grandmother ought to be successful at parenting Rachel. (Intriguingly, because he absents himself from Rachel's life once she leaves Europe, Roger's skills as a black parent are never tested in the context of the United States.) And indeed, Doris does seem to fulfill the racially appropriate parenting role: as soon as she arrives home in Portland with Rachel, she gives her granddaughter black Raggedy Ann and Andy dolls and addresses Rachel's hair, which has been neglected and is a "mess." In these two initial acts, Doris attends to Rachel's self-esteem by giving her black dolls and demonstrates her appropriateness as the parent of a black child by noticing that Rachel's hair has not been treated properly by her (white) mother. Doris and her daughter Loretta (Roger's sister) are committed parents to Rachel and are successful in teaching Rachel the African American culture lacking in her life so far. Interestingly, Rachel's shift from her white mother to her black grandmother and aunt seems to occur simultaneously with the sociological shift between the "phases" of early and middle childhood identity development—stages that can accompany significant shifts in racial identity under even ordinary circumstances. Notably, Rachel embarks on her middle-childhood phase, in which parental influence begins to be affected by the child's environment, while moving to her first black-majority community.

The shift in Rachel's parenting from her mother to her grandmother is significant, and Rachel is acutely aware that her racial identity is being remade. She calls herself the "new girl" and envisions herself as a kind of blank slate, a girl with no memory and no white mother. In her diary she begins each entry not with the date but with the number of days she has been the "new girl," and from "Day One" onward she becomes more and more culturally and racially African American. At first Rachel is confused about what makes her and other light-skinned children "black," noticing,

> There are fifteen black people in the class and seven white people. And there's me. There's another girl who sits in the back. Her name is Carmen LaGuardia, and she has hair like mine, my same color skin, and she counts as black. I don't understand how, but she seems to know.
>
> I see people two different ways now: people who look like me and people who don't look like me. (9)

However, as she learns more she begins to understand that her mother ("Mor") never taught her about how blackness is perceived; she becomes more fluent in how race is practiced in the United States and how she fits (and does not fit) into American concepts of race:

> I am light-skinned-ed. That's what the other kids say. And I talk white. I think new things when they say this. There are a lot of important things I didn't know about. I think Mor didn't know either. They tell me it is bad to have ashy knees. They say stay out of the rain so my hair doesn't go back. They say white people don't use washrags, and I realize now, at Grandma's, I do. They have a language I don't know but I understand. I learn that black people don't have blue eyes. I learn that I am black. I have blue eyes. I put all these new facts into the new girl. (10)

Here, Rachel demonstrates that she is consciously adapting to a set of social norms new to her. But Rachel's observations also suggest that she sees herself as a contradiction according to these social norms and signal an ambivalence about her racial identity that will endure for the rest of the novel.

Indeed, despite being the "new girl" to her grandmother, Rachel thinks to herself, "I am not the new girl. But I will pretend" (6). In much the same way that she is complicit in her grandmother's refusal to acknowledge Rachel's mother or past life by being the "new girl," Rachel is also complicit in her racialization as black despite her doubts. She does not understand her own categorization as black, or that of Carmen LaGuardia, someone she feels she resembles, but she does not challenge it. Similarly, she thinks that blue-eyed Vanessa Williams, the first black Miss America, "doesn't look black," is "white-looking," and even looks phenotypically like herself, but she never queries her grandmother's pride in claiming Williams as a representative of blackness (58). She notices silently that some people with black identity, such as Carmen, Williams, and her friend Brick, do not look black to her; that she notices they all look like herself suggests that she accepts the racial label of blackness without necessarily agreeing with it. Rachel even entertains a fantasy of having her schoolmates see her differently: "Everyone will see that the beautiful Carmen LaGuardia is just like me. She is no longer one of the fifteen [black students]. And I will no longer count myself as one" (69). Rachel acknowledges that the "outside" of herself—the self "that people see"—is not the same self that "is really [her]" (150). So while she knows that she is black, she also knows that this label is something of a misnomer (120). While Rachel's mixed appearance is occasionally acknowledged—by Brick, for instance, or her own boyfriend Jesse, who considers her "exotic," likens her to the "mulatto" population of Brazil, and says she is "black but not really"—others reinforce the blackness of her body through the unmistakable label of "nigger" (230, 233). Significantly, even when her peers question her racial authenticity, they do so in cultural terms (by criticizing her speech, in particular), not phenotypical terms (Drew's daughter Lakeisha, for instance, simply calls her "light"). She understands what racial blackness can and does encompass—including herself. For instance, she wonders about Brick's racial identity; judging him by his appearance, she thinks that he "could be black or Mexican or mixed like me" (202). With this remark, Rachel expresses that racial blackness not only incorporates mixedness but can also be an identity ascribed to or claimed by those who could just as easily be (or be seen as) another race altogether. Ultimately, she learns that she is racially "black" even if she disagrees with the label's application, but she knows that she has no obvious or easy alternative. When Anthony Miller attempts to proclaim Ojibway heritage in addition to his blackness and is mocked, Rachel wonders "if it's better to have people laugh at what [one is] or just not understand" (52). As a "new girl" in entirely new surroundings, she works hard to fit into the social structures around her and risks neither laughter nor misunderstanding.[17] She anticipates the inevitable questions about her identity and learns how to answer "the questions" satisfactorily. Her answers do not allow for the inheritance of her blue eyes or pale skin from her mother; instead of "explaining" herself (in the sense of having the freedom to self-identify), her answers are intended only to solidify and maintain her African American identity according to the standards of her new community: "I'm black. I'm from northeast Portland. My grandfather's eyes are this color. I've lived here mostly my whole life. I'm black. I'm black, I know" (148). Rachel is smart and a quick study, and before long she is fluent in African American racial and cultural norms and understands how she ought to identify herself: namely, as ethnically and racially African American.

While Rachel is genuinely enamored with African American culture—especially the Gospel tradition of her grandmother's African Methodist Episcopal (AME) church and Drew's blues music—and is genuinely proud of her black racial identity, it is clear to her that multiracial identity or any acknowledgment of her own racial whiteness would not be acceptable to those around her. She knows it is dangerous to claim whiteness among her African American classmates because they find whiteness suspect and a betrayal of black pride and solidarity (her peers have been properly schooled in "survival skills"). Rachel seems to think

of herself as racially white when she says, "The only black people I've
seen play tennis are Aunt Loretta and Pop. And they're related to white
people, to me" (28). But she shifts quickly to embody a black racial identity to protect her black status within her peer group, stating, "I don't
ever mention that I'm related to white people" (28). Accordingly, she
never tells any of her black peers that her mother is white; instead, she
tells Lakeisha that her mother is "light-skinned" (115). As a girl, Rachel
also faces a great deal of defensiveness among members of her own sex,
who must contend with the pressures of white beauty standards and the
tangle of race, gender, and sexuality in white supremacist society. Her
schoolmates, for instance, are resentful of her white-looking features
(especially when she straightens her already long hair), and one of Aunt
Loretta's friends comments that a black man as handsome as Roger was
bound to be "snatched up" by a white woman. Consequently, Rachel
must work to accommodate race norms rather than attempt to assert
some racial identity that no one will understand at best, and that most
would misunderstand as disloyal, shameful, and dangerous at worst.

However, at times Rachel finds her new life in race-obsessed America burdensome: some of her classmates tell her she wants to be white:
"They call me an Oreo. I don't want to be white. Sometimes I want to
go back to being what I was. I want to be nothing" (148). Freedom from
racial identity appeals to her because the politics of blackness and whiteness are so demanding, but her nostalgia for her childhood overlooks
the fact that regardless of where she lives or by whom she is raised, she
will eventually have to deal with matters of racial identity—matters
she did not have to face as a very young child. Nevertheless, her desire
to simply avoid the demands of race and racial identity in the United
States suggests that she is not particularly invested in the turf warfare
of race in America beyond an interest in social justice. Her desire to "be
nothing" reflects how much American race practices wear her down
and how she would rather be free of them than struggle to fit into them.

But fit she must, and as an adolescent Rachel is confident in her
black racial identity despite being told repeatedly that she "talks white"
and despite the fact that her only friend is white. In fact, her friendship
with Tracy is a sign of self-confidence since she admits, at first, that

"most of the time [she tries] not to let the black girls like Tamika see [her] talk to Tracy, because Tracy is a white girl. And the way they say that—*white girl*—it feels like a dangerous thing to be" (28). She is able to endure the menacing hatred and racial suspicions of virtually all of the African American girls at her school because of her own ability to tolerate grief but also because of the guidance of her black parents. Her grandmother coaches her about her beauty and her aunt coaches her about her academic success; consequently, they help her to be proud of the two things about herself that cause conflict with other black girls.

Thus, Rachel understands that her family is teaching her how to embody her black racial identity and she is comfortable doing so. However, while Doris might be successful in teaching Rachel about African American race and culture, she could be considered less successful in developing a "positive identity" in her granddaughter because of her beliefs about class and gender and also, at times, about blackness. She certainly instills racial self-respect in her granddaughter and teaches her that black people should strive to be independent and successful. She teaches Rachel about the value of racial pride and laments the transformation of their once "respectable" neighborhood into a ghetto: "It was the best of the best black folk living around here when I first come. And the rest of them hard workers, mostly from the shipyards—not like them kids ruinin things just to get some new sneakers. Look at us now" (159–60). But Rachel notices, "The way Grandma paints her dream for me, there's a low sky" (149). Doris teaches Rachel to value her looks, preserve her chastity, and pursue her education in order to marry well and get what she considers a "good" secretarial job like Loretta's, "an office job where she types and gets coffee or lunch for the boss" (34). It has not occurred to Doris that Loretta could be one of the people in power rather than one of their assistants or that she could be happy without a husband. In Rachel's eyes, her grandmother has old-fashioned ideas about gender and success that are not especially relevant to her because Doris is elderly, she lived in abject poverty in Texas in her youth, and she moved to Oregon during the Second Great Migration in an effort to pursue the promise of "Up North." Doris's education is also minimal, which she laments, saying to her well-read

granddaughter: "It's true. I don't know any of them books you be reading. . . . But I would of if they let me go to school. To that private school"
(34). Just as Doris's opportunities have been limited because of social
inequality, so too do her aspirations seem limited to younger generations. Despite the fact that Rachel considers her grandmother's dreams
to have a "low sky," she also recognizes that because her grandmother
works until her old age caring for white people, having to commute
for four hours a day and wear a uniform to do it, "Grandma's dream
is bigger than her life" (149). Rachel's sympathy aside, however, Doris's
"low sky" is still what she imagines for her daughter and granddaughter. In this way, then, Doris is as incapable as Nella of fostering in Rachel an especially "positive" identity—or at least the ambitious goals
that might accompany one—since Rachel finds inspiration in neither
of them. In fact, Rachel draws an explicit comparison between the
two women: she wonders if their failure to hope for more means that
"Grandma and Mor are two sides of the same coin" (149).

This similarity between Doris and Nella invites us to compare them
as mothers in other ways. Perhaps most significantly, they each socialize
Rachel in virtually opposite ways. Nella, because she has no knowledge
of American race concepts and has not even considered her children
as black, has raised Rachel with no particular racial identity (and thus
instilled no strategies for dealing with anti-black racism). Doris, on the
other hand, is well versed in American race practices and has learned
all too well the difference between black and white—a difference she
teaches Rachel and reinforces through Rachel's socialization as black.
In other words, Nella offers no guidance whereas Doris offers nothing but guidance. However, while Nella seems unable to help Rachel
formulate a racial identity or the necessary "survival skills," Doris's
enforcement of Rachel's black identity does not seem to improve Rachel's emotional or psychological health significantly, either. In fact,
Doris's refusal to allow Rachel to acknowledge her nonblack heritage
causes Rachel a lot of pain. Though it is difficult and perhaps unfair
to compare the two as mothers, considering Rachel's youth at the
time of Nella's death, the novel does not suggest that Rachel's black
identity or location in a black community guarantees psychological

health or feelings of social belonging. While Doris certainly cannot be blamed for the racism (external or internalized) to which Rachel is exposed (and harmed by), she can be held responsible for the hurt she causes her granddaughter by being so adamant that Rachel embrace blackness to the exclusion of all else.

The "positive" quality of the black identity that Doris teaches Rachel to embody is further complicated by the fact that Doris has assimilated white supremacist values through her class ambitions. No doubt because of her age, and perhaps also because of having been raised in the South, Doris has absorbed the messages of "racial uplift" that were prominent in her own and her parents' generations. Doris is compulsively concerned with appearing "respectable," but what she deems "respectable" seems largely to do with white middle-class values. For instance, she encouraged both of her children to play tennis when they were growing up, which Rachel observes "is one of the things that goes in the white category, along with classical music and golf" (28). Similarly, when Roger wanted to learn an instrument as a young man, she made him learn the piano rather than the banjo or harmonica he favored. Rachel puts it plainly when she says, "Grandma always wanted Pop and Aunt Loretta to know white things," and her grandmother's intentions seem to be not subversive but assimilationist (28). As a habitual collector of middle-class artifacts, Doris's acceptance of white normativity is most apparent in her belongings: "Like other volunteer sorters at the Salvation Army, Grandma sets aside the good stuff for herself. Good stuff is a silver spoon, or a china teacup with or without a matching plate, or a dress-up purse with four beads missing and a torn strap. Grandma has boxes of mismatched coffee cups and saucers and yards of corduroy, gingham, silk, and lace stuffed into dozens of drawers and boxes in the basement" (13). "Good stuff" is essentially white stuff. Doris and her best friend Verle discuss "the good things they found at the St. Vincent de Paul thrift store in the part of town where Grandma works," noting, "You can buy a whole bag of clothes for five dollars there. 'White people throw some valuable stuff away,' Miss Verle always says. 'Throws it out like it don't even matter'" (53). Despite being so poor that she has to buy day-old bread from the local Wonder Bread factory store, Doris strives to appear middle class or, at least, surrounds herself with the things that reflect her middle-class tastes.[18]

The items that she hoards are largely the discarded belongings of white people and are frequently actual white totems. For instance, when Doris unpacks her Christmas ornaments, Rachel notices their race:

> "Grandma, all of your angels are white," I say.
> "Angels are angels," Grandma says.
> "But they all have blue eyes and blond hair," I say. Grandma looks at her collection then really hard at me.
> "Angels ain't people," she says. Then Grandma makes a humph sound and leaves the room. (60)

Later, Rachel remarks that all of their holiday photos feature the Christmas tree in the background: "the tree is always right behind" the family members "with Grandma's angels and their bright white faces" hanging on the branches (60). The presence of these angels acts as a metaphor for the presence of whiteness in their lives: it is largely unnoticed (at least by Doris) and also acts as an observation from on high, a kind of judgmental keeper's gaze cast upon the family by white American society. That Rachel notices the angels' whiteness immediately while her grandmother has never noticed it indicates that Doris has not thought critically about the racialization of the items that decorate her home. Perhaps she has even taken for granted that angels would be white and has thus allowed white normativity to make her blind to the white supremacist racialization of the angelic. Similarly, when Loretta places fabric and artwork celebrating African culture around the house, Doris "doesn't like any of these things. She likes things respectable, she says" (78). When Loretta places a "statue of an Igbo goddess" alongside her mother's "porcelain figures of kings and queens," this juxtaposition of cultural artifacts demonstrates the way in which "respectability" is racialized in Doris's mind: in Doris's home, symbols of white colonial empire are respectable whereas black deities are not (78). Rather than having consciously accepted white supremacy, Doris seems to have simply never considered how her middle-class values embody white normativity or why she aspires to such norms. Doris seems also to have unthinkingly absorbed the white supremacist values that accompany her class values when, for instance, she gets Rachel's hair done before Sunday services because, she says, "None of those people want to see a pickaninny in they church" (96). She tries to prevent Rachel from fulfilling the racist stereotype of the "wild and woolly" African American child; however, in addition to using a racist term, she also explicitly accepts the racist values that make unstraightened hair something other than respectable.

Yet, we see that beneath her "respectability" Doris is still capable of racial consciousness and does tend to favor black pride over white middle-class respectability when forced to make a choice. For example, when Rachel begins to tan and grow dark, Doris's initial instinct to preserve her granddaughter's paleness undergoes a fundamental shift once Rachel points out the white supremacy at the root of colorism: "'Stay outta that sun. It'll make you dark and dusty,' she says. I tell her that she is perpetuating racist ideas from slavery. There's nothing wrong with being dark-skinned. Like Drew says, I tell her: black folks have to stick together. She doesn't like me to sass her. It's what her mother taught her and she's passing it on. But she hushes up then. The words 'dark' and 'dusty' only come out after she's [been drinking]. She's not proud when she says those things" (170). We can see, then, that although she does not welcome "sass," Doris listens when younger people point out that some of her views are the consequence of white supremacy that she has internalized. Doris wants to practice black pride and solidarity, and her challenge lies in overcoming the way she has been socialized to accept and strive for white norms. Like Rachel, she learns new ways of embodying—or becoming fluent in—African American culture.

That Rachel notices her grandmother's anti-black racism suggests that she is an astute student of race in the United States and demonstrates that she has developed a "positive black identity" that will stand up against racial denigration. It is in large part thanks to Loretta and her fiancé Drew—who also parents Rachel very explicitly, especially after Loretta dies, and who says repeatedly that Rachel is "like a daughter" to him—that Rachel has developed such an identity (169, 185). Drew is a drug and alcohol counselor with the Salvation Army who reads three

newspapers every morning; in short, he is well informed and politically progressive. He teaches Rachel about the importance of intellectual pursuits, to empathize with and help those in need, and to respect
herself enough to make wise life choices. Drew is also responsible for
getting Rachel interested in issues of racial equality and social justice,
and it is he who introduces Rachel to blues music by taking her to hear
Etta James sing. Like Drew, Loretta teaches Rachel to have racial pride,
self-respect, and black cultural awareness and encourages her to value her intellect. Loretta is the one who teaches Rachel to think about
the "long run" and work hard to achieve her goals. Ultimately, Loretta is the African American woman model for Rachel, who recognizes her as such: "Aunt Loretta is a black woman—the kind of woman
I will be" (98). Because Loretta is dark skinned, unlike her niece, Rachel's insistence that she will be "the kind of woman" Loretta is has
less to do with their outward appearances and more to do with the
inner strength, intelligence, and values they share. Rachel is never interested in what her grandmother values—namely, "gardening, good
deals, looking respectable, and being clean in pressed clothes" (33). But
she finds a kindred spirit in her aunt. As Rachel puts it, "Aunt Loretta
has something that maybe you could call class. It's not the made-up
kind like Grandma has, fake pearls and Sunday hats. . . . Aunt Loretta understands better than Grandma that reading a big book is more
classy than wearing fake pearls watching TV. I wish I knew a better
word for what I mean. On the days she's feeling fussy, Grandma calls
it 'High Falutin' and then she calls it 'white'—like the kids at school"
(33). Although the black girls at her school and even her grandmother
attempt to defend their own lack of interest in academia and ideas by
calling them "white," Rachel finds in Loretta a model for black interest in intelligence and education. Loretta's niece sees how smart she
is, how well-read she is, and how valuable both qualities are. Rachel
also sees the development of her mind as something specifically black
because, regardless of how others try to racialize education and intelligence as white, Loretta is proof that these qualities are also racialized as black. Loretta teaches her that "Good students aren't always
going to be popular with their peers. Those are her exact words. 'You

make them have to work harder'" (68). It is Loretta who exemplifies how being smart and studious does not make one "white" and thus shields Rachel from the message that she needs to shun school in order to achieve black identity.

It is perhaps for the very reason that Loretta and Drew are not interested in exemplifying middle-class normativity but are instead interested in education and political awareness that they are so successful at instilling in Rachel the kind of racial consciousness she develops and the confidence she needs to embrace her identity "positively." Instead of spending her energy being vigilant about appearances or striving for "things," Rachel is free instead to read Fanon and think critically about race. It is because of her intellectual development that she is able to analyze and assess the racial messages she is exposed to and, ultimately, decide for herself how she wants to express her ethnic and racial identities. It is because of the self-confidence, racial pride, and respect for ethnic culture that Loretta and Drew foster in her that Rachel is, ultimately, able to negotiate a "positive identity." It is noteworthy, to say the least, that Loretta is living with her mother when Rachel arrives. Rachel's experience would have been quite different had she been raised by Doris alone, and Rachel is quite bereft when Loretta leaves her—first when she moves out of Doris's house and then when she dies. Moreover, without Loretta, there would be no Drew to parent her, and his role as parent becomes very important as Doris ages and becomes an alcoholic. It is only with Loretta or Drew in the house that Rachel feels the sense of "home" that she had as a child.

Though Rachel does develop a "positive black identity" in that she is proud of and knowledgeable about racial blackness and African American culture, her overall identity is not entirely "positive" when she is living with her grandmother. That is, to have a "positive identity"—or, more specifically, an identity that fulfills what Rachel wants her identity to be—Rachel needs to be able to express her Danish culture. In the same way that social workers consider transracial parenting insufficient if children's minority cultures are not made available to them, Rachel needs those parenting her to allow her to explore what is, in her African American community in Portland, her minority Danish culture.

She does not seem interested in embracing a multiracial identity—that is, an identity that encompasses both black and white racial ancestries. She appears to be satisfied with identifying racially as black. But she is not satisfied with having her mother's ethnicity ignored in favor of African American ethnicity and so, in this sense, a multicultural identity is what is most "positive" for Rachel. Alternative formulations of identity in comparison with "positive black identity" have been recognized by some scholars. For instance, Barbara Tizard and Ann Phoenix point out that sociology tends to "reify racial identity as of unique importance to the individual" and tends to equate "positive black identity" with "positive identity."[19] But, Tizard and Phoenix argue, "This equation cannot be justified on the basis of existing research, and its theoretical basis is contentious. It also inevitably results in the neglect of other important social identities, such as gender, social class, occupation, peer and neighborhood groupings."[20] Durrow's novel reflects this logic in that Rachel senses that the exclusive racial and cultural identity of "African American" is too narrow for her and allows little room for her neglected Danish heritage; her Danishness becomes necessary to any "positive identity" (even if this identity is racially black).

While the still-practiced one-drop rule might for all intents and purposes make a multiracial child socially black, scholars of multiracialism argue that the child still ought to have the freedom to identify (racially and culturally) however she or he prefers. And in cases of white parenting of black or multiracial children, the availability of black culture and identity is considered essential for the child. Yet in terms of "inherited" ethnicity the question remains: Ought a white parent's ethnicity be made as available to a multiracial child as a black parent's? Doris does not give Rachel a choice: because she (understandably) resents Nella for killing all but one of her grandchildren, Doris does not encourage (and would not accept, we might assume) any kind of mixed identity in her granddaughter—whether racial or cultural. From holding her own black ancestor responsible for Rachel's blue eyes to never talking about Nella or including her in the photographic record of the family, Doris works to erase Nella from Rachel's body, family, and identity. Whether out of her own investment in blackness or her hatred of Nella (or both), Doris will not acknowledge Rachel's maternal inheritance—whether biological or ethnic—except to disparage it and hold it responsible for anything objectionable she sees in Rachel.

Recognition matters to Rachel—though not the kind of recognition that Doris offers—and this need for recognition is one that she shares in common with most multiracial and/or multiethnic figures. Recognition of identity lends it validity and makes socially functional what would otherwise be an exclusively personal sense of self. But Rachel's desire for recognition is also about having her family recognize and respect her relationship with her mother. Hypodescent laws during slavery and anti-miscegenation laws (the last of which were struck down by the Supreme Court in the 1967 *Loving v. Virginia* case) among other racist customs and laws have, throughout American history, made "family" monoracial and prevented the formation of family ties across the color line. As Kimberly DaCosta points out, "The normative family was constructed as monoracial. But more than that, in legally prohibiting interracial families, monoraciality was made a *necessary condition* of family."[21] Consequently, DaCosta argues, Americans have great difficulty seeing or conceiving of families that do not racially "match" even today.[22] It matters, then, that when her grandmother takes Rachel to the store, a shopkeeper says, "No mistakin you in the same family. Roger got some strong genes makin these babies," or that another time a woman says her eyes are "pretty," but then "look[s] at Aunt Loretta and Drew real funny" because she thinks Rachel is "stolen" (Durrow, *The Girl Who Fell from the Sky*, 15, 77). The recognition of family and the inheritance visible in the body are certainly significant factors in how families feel about themselves and how they function in society. In the same sense, how Rachel feels about herself and her relationship to her family are dependent upon her Danishness being recognized as part of her "inherited" identity. In the case of her mother, the family resemblance that matters is one of ethnicity, not genes.

Rachel's perception of what she inherits from her mother might be seen in the fact that she never identifies her mother as racially white to others but instead identifies her ethnically, as Danish. That said, to a certain degree, we see Rachel's desire to have her mother acknowledged

as her ancestor in the more straightforward signs of race/whiteness. Although she is not personally invested in whiteness itself and has no interest in having her racial or phenotypical whiteness recognized, when
her mother's whiteness is noticed in her body she feels that she is at
least being seen as her mother's daughter. When Brick looks at photographs of Rachel's African American family, for example, he notices
the family resemblance between Rachel and both Roger and Loretta.
He then remarks, "You must have your mom's eyes," in an uncommon
acknowledgment of Rachel's (presumably) white racial ancestry (214).
More important, Brick's remarks allow Rachel a rare instance of having her mother seen in her (bodily or otherwise). Similarly, when she
notices that Loretta does her hair for her in two braids and remarks
that this makes her look like her mother, who also wore two braids as
a child, it is significant that Loretta then opts to do her hair in an African American style and says, "You look like your grandmother spit
you out herself" (12). In making Rachel's blue eyes something she has
inherited from her father's side and in doing her hair to make her look
as though she is her grandmother's offspring, her black family is actively working to make her connection to themselves more evident and
her connection to her mother less evident. In the same way, their effort to teach African American culture to Rachel is, in part, an effort
to replace her Danish culture. Even though their intentions are good—
they care for Rachel, make her feel like family, and transmit their own
racial and cultural pride in every way they know—her black family remains uninterested in offering her the opportunity to develop Danish
identity. They are not trying to strike a balance between the Danish
culture she knew when she arrived in Portland and their own African
American culture; they are simply replacing the former with the latter.

Just as Rachel's white racial ancestry is ignored in favor of her black
ancestry, so too is her Danish heritage ignored in favor of her African
American ethnicity. In much the same way that the one-drop rule has
traditionally made multiracialism invisible (by relegating mixture to
one homogenizing yet heterogeneous black category), Rachel finds that
her assimilation of African American culture makes her Danishness
fade into invisibility. Her racialized appearance works as a metaphor for

her ethnicity: if Roger's racial blackness can "overwrite" Nella's racial whiteness in Rachel's body, so too can her father's African American ethnicity "overwrite" her mother's Danish ethnicity. As a black-looking person, Rachel is assumed to be conversant in African American culture, but no one would expect her to be fluent in Danish culture. Yet because this erasure of her Danishness is not simply an issue of how race is perceived in the United States but largely one of whether she has the opportunity to participate in Danish culture in America, it means that Rachel's ethnic identity is more susceptible to matters of whim than is her racial identity, which is assessed at a glance and guided by a particular national history of race classification.

Rachel's African American family members are certainly limited in terms of the kind of Danish culture they can offer her since they do not live near a Danish population and have no knowledge of the culture themselves. When Doris takes Rachel to the Wonder Bread store, Rachel notices that Danish food is something entirely out of reach: "They do not have *franskbrod*, or *rugbrod*, or *wienerbrod*, or any pastries with marzipan. They do not have the kind of bread Mor made" (15). Rachel's family could show an interest in her minority ethnicity and let her incorporate aspects of it into her life. Instead, Rachel senses that her Danishness and any reminder of her mother is off limits and she can only practice her Danish language with her white friend Tracy or around Drew when Doris is away. However, even then her Danishness is considered amusing, and neither Tracy nor Drew attempts to learn more about her culture and thereby encourage Rachel's ethnic identification with Danishness. Tracy "giggles" and says, "It sounds like you're talking Scooby-Doo language. Like I can almost understand" (59). Drew is simply politely indifferent: "He doesn't ask me why I hold the fork and knife in opposite hands while I eat. (It's the Danish way.) And when I say, '*Tak for mad*'—which is what you say after a meal—he says, 'Well, alright,' and smiles" (161). On a regular basis, Rachel can only whisper Danish words (so that her grandmother cannot hear them) in order to feel some kind of closeness with that part of her ethnicity: "At the AME Zion Church, when we sing holiday songs, beneath my breath I sing the Danish words. The choir is so loud no one can tell that during 'Silent Night' I sing *stille* and not 'still,' *hellige* and not 'holy.' I'm glad I remember these sounds" (58–59).

Rachel's pleasure in being able to remember Danish words emphasizes the fact that she is at risk of forgetting them. As a child, she fears that her new knowledge will crowd out what she already knows: "I have learned a lot of words since I came to Grandma's. *Dis, conversate, Jheri curl*. There are a lot more. And sometimes I feel those words taking up too much space. I can't remember how to say cotton in Danish or even the word for cloud. What if you can have only so many words in you at once? What happens to the other words?" (59). Her fear reflects that there is a form of substitution at work: one culture is taking over another. She is at risk of forgetting because there is no Danish culture in her life; instead, her ethnicity is strictly African American when she lives in Portland. Danish culture is something she recognizes as lacking in her life, an absence of something: "When Aunt Loretta says 'Mama,' I think of saying 'Mor' and how I don't get to say it anymore. I am caught in before and after time. Last-time things and firsts. Last-time things make me sad like the last time I called for Mor and used Danish sounds. I feel my middle fill up with sounds that no one else understands" (8). Here, the relationship between the two cultures is depicted in a more plainly competitive way: her "last-time things" (that is, Danish "things") are being lost because of the "first-time things" (that is, African American "things") she is learning.

As Charlotte Witt reminds us, family "inheritance" and "resemblance" are as much about the transmission of things other than genes as they are about biology (142–43). In Rachel's case, because she does not look like her mother in the eyes of those around her (a lesson Nella learns in Chicago), the only way she can produce an observable familial connection is through the culture that she has "inherited" by way of her mother's instruction. Rachel feels close to her mother not through phenotypically white people but through Danish ethnicity. For instance, when Jesse invites her to his mother's traditional Scandinavian dinner, it reminds Rachel of her mother: it is the smell of the food and the culinary decorations that are "familiar" and what make Rachel imagine "turn[ing] the corner and find[ing] Mor right there in the kitchen" (204). It is also Nella's accent that Rachel thinks is so important about her because, without it, she would "seem like any other white person you'd see" (115). The importance of language and the family connection it demonstrates is exemplified in Drew and his daughter because they share the same accent. Rachel even reflects that "it's funny how people can sound related" (113). Thus, Rachel is thrilled when she has the opportunity to speak some Danish with Jesse's mother, who is Norwegian by birth. But after listening to Jesse's mother explain that she is really "more American than Norwegian" because her family immigrated when she was a baby, Rachel realizes that the woman's Norwegian culture is something that is not a part of her everyday life and that their dinner of Scandinavian food is an exception to their routine (205). She recognizes that this is not what she wants; she wants to embrace her Danish ethnicity as part of her identity, not indulge in it as an occasional treat: "I don't want being Danish to be something that I can put on and take off. I don't want the Danish in me to be something time makes me leave behind" (205).

While her experience with Jesse's family helps Rachel recognize how she does *not* want to treat her multicultural identity, other experiences help her recognize other possibilities open to her. For instance, when Rachel watches Jesse and Brick interact, she notices that Jesse is fluent in African American culture. She is surprised that he knows what he knows and surprised that he exhibits African American culture so freely and without self-consciousness. Unlike Rachel, Jesse has read *Black Skin, White Masks* in its entirety, and Rachel observes, "[He] knows things about black people that only black people know—like what it means for a black girl's hair to 'go back.' The things I learned after I came to live with Grandma and Aunt Loretta. I'm surprised that someone would have told him. Had he actually asked?" (189). Jesse confounds Rachel's expectation that race and culture will "match." Ironically, it is she, not Jesse, who does not know how to respond to Brick's attempt to fist bump: "I am embarrassed because I don't know what to do. Do I knock his fist with my own? Hold out my hand, palm flat?" (191). Similarly, she laments, "[I] know that I am black, but I can't make the Gospel sound right from my mouth" (120). Her cultural fluency, then, is still incomplete because, other than Lakeisha (who only visits Portland occasionally), she has had no black friends her own age to teach her about African American culture. Her knowledge is not entirely up to date because of the age of her teachers at home. Being around Jesse and Brick helps Rachel recognize that she can, indeed, inhabit race and ethnicity differently than the way she has been taught. After spending time with the two young men, she says, "I forget that what you are—being black or being white—matters. Jesse makes me see there's a different way to be white. And Brick makes me see there's a different way to be black" (202). Near the close of the narrative, when Brick (the only person outside of her family who knows about her mother and siblings) holds her and looks into her face, she feels like someone is seeing all of her for the first time: "When he looks at me, it feels like no one has really seen me since the accident. In his eyes, I'm not the new girl. I'm not the color of my skin. I'm a story. One with a past and a future unwritten" (264). It is this story she wants reflected in her identity. She wants her identity to include her past, her ancestry, but not to determine her story for her—not to be a prescriptive identity.

Rachel's identity development reflects rather timeless concerns regarding the formation of marginalized identities, albeit with a twist. Since W. E. B. Du Bois developed the concept of "double consciousness" at the turn of the twentieth century sociologists have thought about how minority figures must develop their identities in the shadow of, yet become fluent in, "mainstream" white American culture. Today, sociologists and psychologists who study or counsel interracial families and multiracial individuals discuss the importance of "biculturalism" (that is, facility in more than one culture—usually nonwhite minority and white majority cultures).[23] Psychologists also discuss the importance of racial or ethnic "self-schema," which refers to when and how individuals value their in-group associations.[24] Rachel shifts from being "aschematic" (lacking a schema) when she lives in Europe with her parents and then with her mother in America in her early childhood to having a (black-oriented) schema once she enters her middle childhood with her grandmother in Portland. In her adolescence, however, which is the developmental phase during which multiracial subjects solidify their identities in ways that function in their social environments, Rachel develops a "dual-schema"—that is, she asserts a "racial or ethnic identity *as well as* . . . membership or engagement with larger or majority society."[25] However, Rachel's dual-schema / biculturalism is not the typical minority identity paired with fluency in mainstream white American culture. Rather, Rachel develops, in a sense, a dual-minority schema: one in which she has a (black) minority racial in-group and a (Danish) minority ethnic in-group. What is interesting about this dual-schema is that, in a way, it pivots the usual relationship of blackness to whiteness in that blackness becomes the "majority" group and Danishness becomes her "minority" group (both in terms of numbers and the cultural dominance of each group in her immediate surroundings). If Rachel were to develop a black–white multiracial identity, blackness would be the "other" to the dominant category of whiteness. But in *The Girl Who Fell from the Sky*, Danishness becomes "other"—not as racial whiteness but as a "foreign" ethnic category. While Rachel's African Americanness is certainly still a "minority" identity in relation to white America, it does become the dominant identity in her family's and community's perceptions of her. That is, it is her Danishness that she must struggle to assert alongside a black identity that could otherwise overpower it. In this sense, African Americanness has become the "mainstream" or dominant part of her identity, and her Danishness has become the "minority" or vulnerable part of her identity—especially since she has virtually no in-group of Danish ethnics available with whom to practice her Danish culture. She is aware of how her African Americanness must be protected in the face of white majority culture, but she is also aware that her Danishness must be protected from being swallowed by her African Americanness. In this sense, the multicultural identity that Rachel develops is still one fluent in white and black cultures but one that does not adhere to the hierarchical American racial model.

While Doris and Loretta exhibit a typical minority consciousness in juxtaposition to a white-majority culture that is largely unaware of the privilege it enjoys (at the expense of African Americans), and they develop a typical bicultural fluency in both mainstream white American culture and African American culture, neither Doris nor Loretta recognizes that their necessary black pride and solidarity (and the black identity they foster in Rachel) have a similar "majority" effect on Rachel's Danishness. They do not recognize the privilege that their black identities have (not economic or social as with white privilege, but privilege in terms of cultural and racial ubiquity and normalcy), and how it might prevent Rachel from developing a multiracial or multiethnic identity of her own. Like their community at large in Portland, they are primed by in-group normativity and low socioeconomic status to reinforce monoracial identity; they have a historic memory of and continued experience with double consciousness and white supremacy, and thus embody black pride, in part through monoracial identity. Consequently, it does not appear to occur to them that Rachel has any needs that are not met by an African American identity.

Sociologists and psychologists argue that in order for multiracial children to have positive identity formation, families must make a series of decisions that allow the children freedom to explore their heritages with significant support from their families and communities. Importantly, "most of these decisions require the parents to clarify their own values and goals; when parents come from different racial backgrounds, this clarification often involves recognition and resolution of conflicting values and goals around racial identity."[26] Significantly, none of Rachel's parental figures accomplishes these things (perhaps for understandable reasons). None of her white or black, American or Danish parental figures appears to address the possibility that Rachel may want to claim a mixed identity of some kind, and none takes on the responsibility of providing the support she would need to do so. In large part, her parental figures are limited by a lack of knowledge or understanding and also of the socioeconomic privilege that would allow them to expose her to the integrated middle-class communities that sociologists deem so important to developing healthy multiracial identities. In this sense, the novel emphasizes the way in which society itself needs to change if multiracialism is going to be widely understood—and thus functional—in its potential formulations. In other words, unconventional identities can only develop at the pace of change of social attitudes. At the same time, the novel demonstrates how Rachel is able to accommodate conventional identities yet insist upon an unconventional identity that satisfies her own needs. That is, she is able, despite the lack of familial support, to foster her own multiethnic identity and find a way to embody the ethnoracial heritages that she feels she needs to embrace as part of who she is. In doing so, she avoids the pitfalls of late twentieth-century multiracialism in that she is able to develop a "positive" identity rather than a pathological one—without the support of her family or community.[27] Though she has not yet developed a clearly defined public identity, she has sorted out for herself what matters to her and begun to practice her identity with the support of friends.

Her final "wish" in the last sentence of the novel is that her mother and siblings had "been a family that could fly."[28] In making such a wish, Rachel is fantasizing about being able to escape from the racialist society that she finds so constrictive and the racist society that defeated her mother. She wants to be unfettered by the particularities of American—or any—race practices. Her desire exhibits a naïve and youthful wish to escape that which confines her. But it also reflects her disinclination to simply accept unquestioningly the way her society organizes itself. Though she cannot escape them and therefore does negotiate and assimilate social norms, she does not do so without critical examination. Hers is a self-reflective existence and one in which she does not give up her claim to multiple ethnicities even as she accepts her black racial identity according to society's expectations. Her complex relationship to Danishness as a cultural and more specific identity than generic racial or phenotypical whiteness—along with her tentative and careful negotiation of African American identity as something that straddles culture and color—makes her identity difficult if not impossible to articulate or define. The fact that she never seems concerned about defining herself or being recognized in any certain way suggests not only that definition is not her chief concern but that identity is perhaps too slippery to pin down—or at least that identities cannot necessarily be defined in conventional terms. Her identity, which is not simply a "hybrid," monoracial, or monocultural one, defies normal understanding and labels and, in this way, eludes neat classification. Certainly, her identity seems "multi" or "mixed" in conventional terms, but the novel makes no attempt to specify how, exactly, she ought to be identified. In fact, Rachel explicitly challenges the new (for the time) label of "African American" itself as it applies not only to herself but also to other black Americans. This elusiveness in terms of definition or categorization is something that arises in a lot of recent multiracial texts, and so in this way Durrow participates in what is becoming a multiracial literary habit: negotiating and challenging existing categories of classification without offering a substitute. It might be said that this lack of a substitute is what makes multiracial literature like Durrow's a potential challenge to traditional identification practices. The terms that exist, the terms in current usage, are no longer sufficient to refer to contemporary mixed identities.

However, Durrow does something with Rachel's identity that is unlike the depictions of multiracial characters in the work of her contemporaries. In so many contemporary narratives of black–white multiracialism, beliefs about what we understand the categories of "black" and "white" to encompass are questioned. When multiracial figures opt to assert their claim to both blackness and whiteness, both of those race categories are destabilized because they are not normally conceived of as existing simultaneously in one identity. As the earlier chapters have demonstrated, throughout much of American history, blackness has been considered to be inherently mixed and something that absorbs whiteness like a sponge (due to hypodescent and the one-drop rule) while whiteness has been considered mythically "pure" and incapable of being combined with blackness without disappearing. Mixture is certainly as old as the concepts of "black" and "white" themselves, and as soon as it is its own race (such as the historical census race category of "mulatto" or the enduring ethnoracial label of "Creole"), mixture stands with (rather than in opposition to) conventional race concepts. It is by asserting a multiracial identity that is *both* black *and* white— both of these supposedly independent categories—that contemporary writers like Senna, Walker, Raboteau, and Harper ask us to rethink how we conceive of both black and white categories.

But Rachel actually seems to affirm—or at least go along with—the one-drop rule and the traditional concept of blackness as an all-encompassing monoracial identity. She does not try to assert any kind of white racial identity along with her black racial identity and allows the apparent whiteness in her body to simply be part of her black identity via the one-drop rule. Instead of interrogating African Americanness as a racial category, she challenges it as an ethnic category. The most subversive aspect of Rachel's identity is that she accepts a mono*racial* African American identity but not a mono*cultural* African American identity. Indeed, black race and black culture are extremely difficult to see as separate—this is why, to oversimplify a very complex issue, white people who exhibit black culture are frequently considered to be performers or appropriators of a culture that is not theirs and why, for instance, black people who do not exhibit what some consider "appropriate" black culture are accused of "acting white" or of being "Oreos." Culture and race are very difficult to uncouple, as we see in categories like Hispanic/Latinx and Jewish as well. Moreover, the text seems to be responding to the still prevalent belief that African American culture is necessary in black subjects in order for "appropriate" African American identity to form (this is the premise of the ABC sitcom *Black-ish*, for instance). Thus, because of this very deeply rooted perception of African American race and culture as synonymous, or the belief that black racial identity is only successful if it is matched to black cultural expression, Rachel's choices become a challenge to the status quo. She complicates the racial and ethnic implications of the "African American" label by asserting a black racial identity that is not exclusively African American culturally. Significantly, she simultaneously poses a potential challenge to the category of Danishness by claiming Danishness without claiming racial whiteness. The novel suggests that the most appropriate or "positive" identity for Rachel is not one that matches exclusively black culture to black race but rather one that links blended culture to one race. Most important, the fact that she does not assert a multiracial identity means that she is not simply identifying as African American *and* white (or Danish)—as biracial or half white/half black, as it were. Because Rachel draws this distinction between racial and cultural identity, she challenges views that see black identity

as encompassing both race and ethnicity and forces African Americanness to be broken down as an ethnoracial category. In Durrow's novel,
African Americanness is not, as in other multiracial literature, intact
or whole (in and of itself) while being part of a dual identity. To Rachel it is, instead, all of her race but only part of her culture. And so,
in this way, Durrow poses yet another set of questions about conventional ethnoracial categories. The shift from multiracialism (the focus
of so much black–white multiracial literature in the twenty-first century) to ethnic identity in *The Girl Who Fell from the Sky* continues to
pry open the (multi)racial discourse of the new century and broaden
the use of multiracialism to think through the complexities of identity and classification.

| Conclusion

The (Continuing) Work of Multiracial Literature

Emily Raboteau opens her novel *The Professor's Daughter* with a "Bernie-ism," a remark made by her protagonist's brother: "It is a privilege to be able to invent oneself. It is also a burden."[1] In many ways, Bernie's observation reflects the necessary act of self-definition at work in contemporary multiracial literature—an act that Toi Derricotte delineates when she explains the purpose of her autobiographical *The Black Notebooks*: "This book is about the search for a home, a safe home for all our complexities. . . . It is about not finding that home in the world, and having to invent that home in language."[2] Raboteau's Bernie and Derricotte seem to suggest that in addition to the need to find ways to represent multiracialism, representation in and of itself does particular and important work—a sentiment Paule Marshall furthers when she says, "Once you see yourself truthfully depicted, you have a sense of your right to be in the world."[3] Or, as Lise Funderburg explains, representation is valuable because "to become a part of the media landscape, to be recognized in images that are used to promote and illustrate, is to be conferred a certain legitimacy."[4] The comments of these writers and thinkers illustrate how contemporary literature is writing contemporary multiracialism into the American literary landscape and the American social imagination. The characterization of the representation of multiracial identity as a "burden" and yet a necessary step for recognition, validation, or "legitimacy" emphasizes that multiracial identity has not been adequately represented. The demand for recognition is no simple task, however. The need to "invent" one's depiction suggests that no existing frame of reference is sufficient. Indeed, the ways in which multiracial identities are being explored now require new language, new politics, and a new ideology. When Jayne O. Ifekwunigwe observes, "The story is old. Our testimonies are new," she recognizes that the "story" or existence of mixed race is not new but contemporary experiences and representations of mixed race are.[5] Part of the writing of multiracialism, then, is a departure from previous depictions of mixture and an effort, in fact, to reimagine (mixed) racial identities for new generations. And while the literature may not yet be able to represent the normalcy of mixed identities, it is beginning to make normal (in the sense of being more commonly seen and heard) representations of contemporary identities that are in conversation with but do not always adhere to conventional racial categories. Currently, multiracial identity is imagined in relation to history and as born out of that history, but in a way that attempts to move beyond that history and discard some of its limitations. This is a new political, social, and literary moment in which racial identity is capable of transforming.

What is occurring now, however, is early and difficult work. Writers at the turn of the millennium have not neatly articulated black–white multiracial identity. Instead, their texts explore how an articulation of such identity may be possible and out of what late twentieth-century history this opportunity arises. Contemporary literature, including the works of Walker, Senna, Raboteau, Harper, and Durrow, does not simply name multiracialness or propose that naming would be a simple task. On the contrary, these authors emphasize the impossibility of formulating multiracial identity that is independent from social context, and their hesitancy (or inability) to specifically define multiracial identity suggests that American discourse and ideology do not yet provide an adequate framework in which identity formulation can be completed tidily. The focus of these texts is less about labels and more about the struggle necessary to arrive at satisfying racial identities. That none of them really does arrive suggests not a failure on the part of the writers or characters but rather the sheer difficulty of the effort and the abundance of variables that make identification so fraught. This is not to say that these and other writers will not eventually articulate black–white identities or resist more overtly the pressure to be racially defined in the first place. Current writers are depicting the transition to a literature that might arrive at specified identities or articulate new ways of resisting classification; they are actively participating in the development of a racial awareness that will more readily accommodate multiracial identity.

But most significant, the inability or unwillingness of writers to attempt to name or define multiracial identity in terms similar to those we already know and use in conventional race practices identifies perhaps the most innovative aspect of contemporary writing. If these texts represent multiracial identity as vague, difficult to pin down, and impossible to name, it is because race is, in fact, just that slippery. In this political and social era some of the strings binding multiraciality to conventional racial thinking are being severed, and the perceived need to follow customary race practices is beginning to falter. Contemporary writers are not demolishing race—nor could they. But they have ushered in a new era—perhaps only the beginning of a long one—in which American culture is seeing new possibilities regarding what racial identities might encompass or not encompass and how race might work. Unlike previous literary depictions of multiracialism, which balanced on the very stable color line, new depictions blur that line. It is, perhaps, this "foggy" representation of race that best characterizes the subversive potential of contemporary literature.

Literature since the late nineties has ushered in a broad and diverse set of issues surrounding multiracialism, on which literature and commentary are already beginning to elaborate. Many texts of the past twenty years, including those I discuss at length, focus on a relatively narrow slice of multiracialism in that they depict American, monoracially identified, heterosexual parents who have biological children within marriage, raise those children together at least until adolescence (or thereabouts), tend to be of middle-class means, and are well-educated intellectuals or academics. Certainly issues of class, education, nationality, multiracialism, multiculturalism, nonbiological families, nonheterosexual families, and single or group parenting, among others, will affect (multi)racial identity. The texts I analyze already begin to complicate the abovementioned scenario with regard to sexuality, class, single parenting, and multiculturalism in particular, and still others add to the conversation of black–white mixture. For instance, Catherine E. McKinley's autobiography, *The Book of Sarahs: A Family in Parts* (2002), explores transracial adoption and its effect on McKinley's racial identity. And as chapter 4 discusses, Heidi Durrow's *The Girl Who Fell from the Sky* depicts the coming-of-age of a girl who hardly knows the experience of a nuclear family structure or of being coparented by white and black parents at once. Naomi Pabst's essays include analyses of her own experience of being born to a white Swedish American mother and black African American father in the United States, being raised in Alberta by a white Canadian mother and white German and first-generation Canadian father (who was born and raised in Kenya), and returning to the United States as an adult; she discusses how this has affected her understanding of race and her own racial identity. There are, too, anthologies of multiracial narratives that include or even focus on multiracialism without whiteness and thus explore the very different racial discourse of nonwhite, multicultural/multiethnic/multiracial families. Commentators are already calling for attention to be paid to same-sex parents of multiracial children (who may or may not have biological links to their children). Other scenarios are likely to arise as well, such as step-parenting, multiracial identification that arises from ancestral rather than parental racial identity, black monoracial families who adopt nonblack children but raise them to identify as black in some fashion, immigrant parents who have not been socialized to perceive race the way their American children will (and whose children might self-identify in ways entirely foreign to them), and other situations in which racial identity might have nothing to do with ancestry or "blood" but instead involve family, culture, and/or politics.

By asserting the need to think about racial identity beyond heteronormative nuclear families, scholars are also recognizing the complexity of modern social behavior. Simultaneously, they are recognizing

new generations that are being raised with an awareness of nonnormative sex, gender, sexuality, nationality, and race, who consequently
come to consider identity of any kind to be more flexible and transi-
tory than had earlier generations. For instance, in her introduction
to *To Be Real*, Rebecca Walker explains that fitting people into particular molds is growing more difficult:

> This way of ordering the world is especially difficult for a generation
> that has grown up transgender, bisexual, interracial, and knowing and
> loving people who are racist, sexist, and otherwise afflicted. We have
> trouble formulating and perpetuating theories that compartmental-
> ize and divide according to race and gender and all of the other signi-
> fiers. For us the lines between Us and Them are often blurred, and as a
> result we find ourselves seeking to create identities that accommodate
> ambiguity and our multiple positionalities: including more than ex-
> cluding, exploring more than defining, searching more than arriving.[6]

The present moment that Walker identifies is one in which conventional
ways of ordering people have become less appealing and less practical.
In fact, Walker has said that she identifies herself as multi- or biracial
"only because there has yet to be a way of breaking through the need
to racially identify and be identified by the culture at large."[7] Similarly, Danzy Senna explains in "Passing and the Problematic of Multiracial Pride" that she is increasingly less interested in racial labeling: "I'm
not so fixated on what I call myself or anybody else calls himself or herself. I think that identity politics (and all questions of racial pride) can
be a form of narcissism, and at their worst are a distraction from real
questions of power."[8] Senna does not propose a version of a raceless future, but she thinks of one when she begins to challenge the American
obsession with and maintenance of race classification. Where she used
to proclaim her identity even before being asked, Senna's attitude has
changed: "These days, when people ask me what I identify with, instead of giving them a simple one-word answer, I often turn the tables
and ask them why they want to know. I interrogate their interest in my
identity before answering. I ask them what each of my potential answers
would mean to them. I want people to think more about what they are

asking me."[9] Ultimately, Senna and Walker both voice a political challenge to not only how but also why Americans are categorized. They express an interest in breaking down the perceived need to classify (as opposed to eliminating the practice of classification) as well as a dedication to identifying in a politically responsible way in the meantime.

The heterogeneity of American blackness and whiteness is partly responsible for the urge to depart from conventional classificatory concepts that we see in Walker's and Senna's comments. The way in which racial identity has been inscribed by nation and ethnicity is beginning to alter the way blackness, in particular, is assessed in the United States. Current conversations about African Americanness argue about whether blackness creates belonging to the racial category or whether one has to have ancestors and personal connections to slavery and oppression in the United States to claim belonging.[10] This is an observation of a difference between the biological/phenotypical aspect of African Americanness and its cultural, ethnic, and national context. The distinction is evident when, for example, Barack Obama's blackness is questioned. Some consider his racial identity a (biological) race issue, since he had a white (biological) mother, but most who question his blackness do so on the basis of culture and history. His father was Kenyan, not American; Obama was raised in Hawaii and Indonesia, not in the continental United States; and he was raised by white family almost exclusively. It is because of his time spent within black communities in Chicago and his marriage to a woman whose ancestors were enslaved that some consider Obama's blackness validated as African American.[11] The way that Obama's blackness has been questioned—particularly by those who identify as African American—illustrates the need to refine the language involved in racial discourse and to acknowledge the broad variety of black identities. In "An Unexpected Blackness," for instance, Naomi Pabst observes that the discussion of figures like Obama suggests that the United States is increasingly going to need to recognize a difference between "black" and "African American." When the *New York Times* referred to Nelson Mandela as an African American, she explains, it demonstrated the need for a broad understanding of "black." She contends, "We need a model of blackness that is inclusive, that is expansive, that accounts for difference and diversity within race, that crosses national and international borders, and that takes for granted that blackness is rooted and routed within and outside the United States. We need a definition of blackness that is not 'geocentric' or 'American-centric' or 'African American-centric.'"[12] In Pabst's formulation, then, "black" is a diasporic and diverse umbrella term, and "African American" is a specific kind of black.

However, while Pabst argues about the need for an understanding of "black" that "retains the viability of blackness as a political category" through the concepts of "hybridity" and "diaspora," hers is still a discussion of hybridity within blackness—the heterogeneity of blackness— rather than the relationship of blackness and whiteness.[13] Similarly, what is telling about the criticism regarding Obama's "inauthentic" African Americanness is the fact that it maps his blackness through American black history and does not consider his whiteness. Though such debates often consider his mixedness, it is considered strictly in terms of biological race whereas his blackness is considered more broadly as racially, culturally, and ethnically inscribed. If African Americanness is about a national black history, what of the white portion of mixedness? According to the terms of the discussion, if African Americanness is intrinsically mixed with whiteness (racially), the origins of whiteness should matter. If it is important that one's blackness is American (located in an ancestral line that survived slavery) rather than not American (from an African parent, for instance), it would seem important to map one's whiteness similarly—for instance, whether the source of one's whiteness is from American ancestors as opposed to non-Americans (such as a white foreign or immigrant parent).

Some literature complicates the national inscription of whiteness even if those who question Obama's blackness neglect to do so. In Heidi Durrow's autobiographical contributions to Lise Funderburg's collection *Black, White, Other: Biracial Americans Talk About Race and Identity*, she describes moving to the United States as an adolescent after having been raised overseas and how her (cultural) African Americanness is lacking. In Durrow's novel, as I have discussed in chapter 4, the white immigrant mother never quite understands her African

American husband's fascination with their relationship when they marry and begin their family in Europe. When she moves to the United States she has an almost total ignorance of anti-black racism and cannot figure out how to raise and protect her now–African American children. For the protagonist, her connection to whiteness is figured largely as a connection to foreignness—namely Danishness. Though she does not like her African American grandmother's dismissal of her mother because of her mother's racial whiteness, she contextualizes her mother primarily in terms of her Danishness rather than her phenotypical whiteness. She misses the language and other aspects of the Danish culture and wants to maintain that connection instead of a purely generic white racial connection. Thus, in this sense, Durrow's novel helps draw attention to the national inflection of whiteness in the same way that Obama has brought attention to those nationalistic qualities of American blackness.

Acknowledging the whiteness in blackness is useful, but in relation to multiracial theory, race mixing cannot be an issue relegated to blackness alone. Ultimately, if multiracialness or blackness is not considered in relation to and as affecting whiteness, but instead as an issue of one's relatedness to or understanding of blackness, whiteness remains unaffected. While Pabst insists that recognizing diaspora and hybridity in blackness is indeed of critical importance for the future of racial discourse, Rainier Spencer warns that if done in such a way that it simply reaffirms black (pan)nationalism, this recognition will simultaneously and exhaustively reaffirm whiteness as monolithic. Whiteness, then, must be included in the reorganization of blackness in racial theory; blackness and whiteness must not be considered in isolation. Spencer argues in "New Racial Identities, Old Arguments" that the "essential barometer of whether race is breaking down in the United States is the status of racial whiteness," and thus alerts us to the need to maintain as critical an eye on whiteness as on blackness.[14] Or, as he asserts in *Reproducing Race*, "The future will be postracial only and precisely to the extent that it is postwhite. It is at best a mistake, and at worst a devious subterfuge, to suggest or otherwise imply that postraciality simply means postblackness, as if it is the lingering nature of blackness that is the problem. Rather, the lingering nature of blackness is merely a symptom of the deeper and originary problem, which is the ferocious tenaciousness of whiteness."[15] While there may be a need to discuss blackness in different ways than whiteness, such discussion will be limited so long as whiteness is not examined with similar vigor. As Leilani Nishime argues, "Making multiraciality central and explicit in critical analyses can help us understand the construction of racial categories within a larger racial system."[16] This is precisely why looking at blackness and whiteness equally is necessary in critical mixed race studies: black–white multiracialism necessitates an examination of its relationship to both blackness *and* whiteness. Without examining whiteness (or by examining multiracialness simply as a formulation of blackness), neither blackness nor whiteness is challenged as a concept. Additionally, we must scrutinize whiteness in order to maintain a socially responsible political stance; as Minelle Mahtani warns, "If multiraciality is to mean anything in a politically progressive sense, it must come to terms not only with its relationship to whiteness but also with how it has allowed a particular ongoing form of white supremacy to thrive."[17]

Whiteness is, as chapter 2 demonstrates, under intense scrutiny. But as white studies scholars themselves warn, whiteness must not be considered in isolation. For racial identity to be able to cross racial borders— of whiteness, in particular—identification must be theorized beyond "blood" or phenotype. Other factors that contribute to how someone identifies apart from a biological sense of race offer critical sites of analysis. Sociologists are already beginning to examine white parents of multiracial children and the ways in which their racial identities shift because of changes to their immediate communities and sociopolitical consciousnesses. These sociological studies also suggest that whites who marry and have children with black partners are identified differently by others who see them within the context of their interracial and multiracial families. The theorization of racial identification will have to broaden discussion beyond biology and inheritance to include culture explicitly. Choice will also have to expand from the "honoring both parents" discourse of multiracialism toward a broader consideration of race in relation to family, community, and culture. Literary efforts already anticipate this fruitful discussion with figures like Dan-zy Senna's Sandy and James McBride's mother. As I have noted earli-er, Sandy Lee proclaims, "It doesn't matter what your color is or what you're born into, you know? It matters who you choose to call your own."[18] In this sense, Sandy is able to claim allegiance to blackness and disavow allegiance to whiteness because of her choice of spouse, her de-votion to her children, her politics, and her chosen community. Simi-larly, Ruth McBride claims blackness through choice rather than birth: "When Malcolm X talked about 'the white devil' Mommy simply felt those references didn't apply to her. She viewed the civil rights achieve-ments of black Americans with pride, as if they were her own. And she herself occasionally talked about 'the white man' in the third person, as if she had nothing to do with him, and in fact she didn't, since most of her friends and social circle were black women from church."[19] Both women identify with blackness and are accepted into black communi-ties on the basis of their black political allegiance and their awareness and rejection of white privilege. The fact that Ruth can refer to "the white man" in a way that excludes herself suggests that the meaning of the phrase has to do with a white-supremacist-oriented sensibility—one which she, like Sandy, does not possess. It is this kind of engage-ment with identity politics that will help inform the development of (multi)racial theorization. The proclamations of figures like Sandy and Ruth—who assert that their whiteness cannot be taken for granted—gesture toward a potential transformation of thinking about racializa-tion and identity across the borders that have historically bound race practices in the United States.

Similarly, the way in which Obama has brought attention to the national, historical, geographical, ethnic, and cultural overtones of American racial ideology—or at least to American concepts of blackness—signals the broader scholarly movement toward transna-tional and transhistorical disciplinary approaches that has been ongo-ing in the academy. In fact, in an article on the "changing profession" of literary studies, Ralph Bauer points out that literary scholarship is look-ing beyond the conventional categories of nation with the explosion of hemispheric studies. Bauer's comments and the rise in transnational and transhistorical dissertations and books attest to the increased attention paid to theorizing literature and culture beyond national borders. It is not as simple as abandoning the concept of nation, though, since American race concepts are specific to a national history and a nationalized social discourse. For the same reason that I argue that applying theories of racial identity from the Caribbean or South America will not resolve *American* racial practices or offer *American* racial identities, I argue that nation must still figure prominently—if not centrally—in the theorization of American multiracialism and especially black–white identities. However, a diasporic sensibility can only enhance discussion of U.S. race concepts. The recent development of a conversation about what "African American" means is evidence that thinking through race and identity in the United States is something that can no longer be inward looking only. There is, after all, a push to go beyond a distinctly national conception of racial, historical, and national identity to consider, in one way or another, the changing character of the black population in the United States. And part of the discussion will also include the characterization of whiteness as well as multiracialness.

However, though the dialogue may be new, the ideas upon which this dialogue stands are not particularly new. It is important to remember that contemporary multiracial debate is contemporary primarily because of timing rather than innovation. As the introduction demonstrates, the "newness" of ideas about multiracialness has been perpetuated for generations. Naomi Pabst argues in "Blackness/Mixedness," "Problematizing narrow, exclusionary racialist thinking and critiquing the viability of a simple race-equals-community equation are long-standing practices, and where they are attended by proclamations of newness, of beginnings, they are proverbial reinventions of the wheel. For even if an explicitly mixed-race agenda or movement has certain novel elements, attempts to place in relief and mobilize around ever-present black/white categorical interconnections are age-old."[20] Additionally, she points out that thinkers have been critiquing (multi) racialism for centuries. Like other observers, she cites Frederick Douglass and W. E. B. Du Bois in particular as having tried to articulate complicated and important ideas about race, classification, culture, and human rights activism and problematize "racialist thinking, race pride, and race consciousness."[21] But she notes that instead of being properly heard, Douglass and Du Bois were accused of wanting to deny their blackness and/or wanting to be white because of their frank acknowledgement of multiple racial or ethnic ancestries. She notes further that, similarly, Jean Toomer "was dismayed that his elaborate scheme of recasting and complicating identity along heterogeneous lines inspired people . . . to conclude that he was merely denying his blackness and declaring himself white."[22] As Paul Spickard observes, Toomer felt he was "a man of multiple ancestries and identities in a nation that did not then recognize such multiplicity."[23] Indeed, race mixture is certainly not new and neither is commentary on race mixture. However, what is new is the historical and political moment in which such commentary can be expressed and thoughtfully received. If Douglass, Du Bois, and Toomer were expressing ideas too radical or inconvenient to be addressed appropriately in their own time, it could be argued that the time they needed has arrived.

In "Assessing Multiracial Identity Theory and Politics," Rainier Spencer proposes that recent academic work is beginning to ask "hard questions" of multiracial advocacy and scholars who sympathize with such advocacy, whom he characterizes as "emotion-charged and theory-challenged."[24] He argues that "we are currently witnessing the beginning stages" of critical mixed race studies—most of which, he says, is still overshadowed by "the continued dominance of uncritical popular media coverage."[25] He states that his article is a plea to help gear discussion toward *"meta-multiracial theory"* instead of the "naïve" and "sentimental" theorizing that still dominates multiracial discourse.[26] But, he states, constructive "meta-multiracial theory" is indeed being undertaken currently. Similarly, in her introduction to *'Mixed Race' Studies: A Reader*, Jayne O. Ifekwunigwe identifies three "ages" of multiracial discourse. First is the mostly nineteenth-century subscription to notions of racial homogeneity that she terms the "Age of Pathology." Second is the explosion of late twentieth-century writing on "mixed race," in which she includes Maria P. P. Root and Naomi Zack and that she and other scholars term the "Age of Celebration." Third is the more recent turn-of-the-millennium and twenty-first-century "multiracial" scholarship that deals with complex problems of categorization, structure, and agency in what she terms the "Age of Critique."[27] For both critics, multiracial theory is now in a phase of productive criticism.

It seems, then, that in the early twenty-first century, academia, popular discourse, and literary production are, together, taking a path toward producing a North American theorization of black–white multiracialism. Ultimately, if it is conceived of in a Gilroyesque "relational" way, multiracial identity invites a critique of the whole system of racial practice in the United States. While this new era of multiracial consciousness and debate will be tested over time, the development of its literature and the history of this debate will ultimately shape racial discourse and race relations in the United States. Deck Lee argues in *Caucasia* that "the mulatto in America functions as a canary in the coal mine. . . . The fate of the mulatto in history and in literature . . . will manifest the symptoms that will eventually infect the rest of the nation."[28] If Deck is to be believed, then the theorization and literary representation of black–white multiracialism will indicate the limits—broken and intact—of racial discourse in America.

Notes

Preface

1. For instance, Abby Ferber notes that "marriages between whites and non-black others are three times more likely than marriages between whites and blacks," and that in public opinion polls "black/white relations remain the most problematic." Ferber, "Creation of Whiteness," 49. Kim Williams's study of multiracial organizations found that while black–white interracial marriage is one of the less frequent interracial combinations, it is black–white couples that "*almost exclusively*" constitute the membership of multiracial organizations. K. Williams, "Linking the Civil Rights," 90. These trends suggest that black–white interracial relationships (and the offspring they produce) continue to trouble a society that has historically been obsessed with black–white relations more than any other transracial relationships.

Introduction

1. Williamson, *New People*, xiii.

2. Douglass, *Narrative of the Life*, 50; Chesnutt, *House behind the Cedars*, 59.

3. Toomer, *Wayward and the Seeking*, 121; Senna, *Symptomatic*, 155.

4. R. Spencer, *Reproducing Race*, 324.

5. It is worth noting that in *The Trouble with Diversity*, Walter Benn Michaels proposes turning away from race (and toward class) specifically in the interest of social justice. While I would agree with Michaels that class is one of the most urgent and widespread sources of inequality in American society today, I disagree with his narrow view of the irrelevancy of race in contemporary society and consider his view to lack engagement with systemic racism on the whole and the relationships between racism and class in particular. He overlooks how class inequality is a legacy of racism (and other forms of bias) in our society, the remnants of such biases in our social practices and laws, the continued application of biases in the governance of our society and its social structures, and the prevalence of unconscious biases against those with historical disadvantages.

6. Few critical mixed race studies scholars would now propose that multiracialism actively produces a "raceless" society. Generally speaking, scholarly discourse is at the practical stage of addressing how (or whether) multiracialism can or cannot function as an identity and how (or whether) it affects racialism. Multiracial discourse (both popular and scholarly) is discussed in detail in chapter 1.

7. Warren, *What Was American Literature?*, 141.

8. For a helpful analogy—of the "witch" identity and its functionality (rather than accuracy) in American culture—and a useful discussion of "social identities," see Appiah, "Does Truth Matter."

9. Popular usage of racial labels has gone through significant change, and I use historical language (including "colored" and "Negro") throughout this section to emphasize the evolution of black identity. I use terms like "miscegenation" and "mulatto" for the same purpose: to draw attention to historical beliefs about mixing and mixed race.

10. Korgen, *From Black to Biracial*, 9–10.

11. Korgen, *From Black to Biracial*, 10–11.

12. Korgen, *From Black to Biracial*, 11. Eileen Walsh points out that this system was confusing when the child of a free white woman and black man (whether free or not) was considered white and free, whereas the child of a free white father and black enslaved mother was considered black and enslaved. As Walsh states, "The obvious inconsistency of this classification system threatened to undermine the presumed biological basis of inferiority that formed the ideological lynchpin for the enslavement of African descendants. Further complications of this classification system became apparent with the growth in numbers of offspring whose status as free or enslaved could not be 'read' from looking at their bodies." Walsh, "Ideology," 221–22. That the strict regulation of white women's sexuality soon followed is no coincidence.

13. Talty, *Mulatto America*, 54; Johnston, *Race Relations in Virginia*, 173–74.

14. Korgen, *From Black to Biracial*, 11.

15. The policing of white women's bodies with such laws protected the "purity" of the white race (and set a precedent for regulating white women's sexuality for centuries) while assuring that white male sexual privilege (over all female bodies) would be protected. Such laws supported white supremacy and slavery in that "a mixed child in a white family threatened the slave system" but "another mulatto in the slave quarters was an economic asset, not a threat." Davis, *Who Is Black?*, 48. Ultimately, the antimiscegenation laws enacted in forty-one colonies or states between 1660 and 1960 were engineered to protect white purity—by preventing "mongrelisation"—and white economic and political interests. Kennedy, *Interracial Intimacies*, 18; Pascoe, "Miscegenation Law," 183. Miscegenation

was certainly a regular practice on slave plantations, but legal miscegenation through marriage (and the rights that went with it) could not be tolerated because it would have confused the racist racial dichotomy upon which slavery was based. For a particularly insightful discussion of gender, race, and marriage before and after the Civil War, see Pascoe, *What Comes Naturally*, part 1.

16. Fields, "Slavery, Race, and Ideology," 107.

17. Berlin, *Slaves Without Masters*, 3.

18. Williamson, *New People*, 24.

19. Williamson, *New People*, 2.

20. Daniel, *More Than Black?*, 5. For an in-depth discussion of the *gens de couleur libre*, the "tripartite" racial system in Louisiana, and the way in which the French and Spanish influenced the state's race practices for centuries, see Domínguez, *White by Definition*. See also Joan Martin, "*Plaçage.*"

21. Daniel, *More Than Black?*, 5.

22. Williamson, *New People*, 25–26, 9. The importance of class continues to be a critical issue. In the same way that mixture has been officially observed among wealthy classes but not among enslaved or poor classes throughout American history, class is implicated in the decision to identify and the ease of identifying as multiracial today. As Sika A. Dagbovie-Mullins points out, flexible identity is more easily explored by individuals with class privilege as opposed to those struggling with poverty. She quotes Danzy Senna's observation: "Racial fluidity, ambiguity, comes with privilege. . . . Take away Tiger Woods' money, his sports affiliations (put him on a basketball court in Harlem), take away his Stanford education, and let's see how fluid his racial identity is." Dagbovie-Mullins, *Crossing B(l)ack*, 126. As Senna's comments suggest, one's social position (in terms of wealth, education, power, or fame) affects how one identifies racially and whether one's preferences are accepted among peers.

23. Korgen, *From Black to Biracial*, 14–15.

24. Williamson, *New People*, 68.

25. Williamson, *New People*, 73.

26. Williamson, *New People*, 73.

27. Williamson, *New People*, 75.

28. Korgen, *From Black to Biracial*, 15.

29. Notably, the word "miscegenation" was invented in a parodic 1864 election pamphlet; despite the mocking tone of the pamphlet, "Americans adopted the term . . . with such alacrity that it would frame public debate over race, sex, and marriage for the next century." Pascoe, *What Comes Naturally*, 28. For an interesting discussion of the pamphlet, see Talty, *Mulatto America*, 70–74.

30. Williamson, *New People*, 66–67.

31. Korgen, *From Black to Biracial*, 15. Scientific racism proposed that the mixture of white and black was unnatural and degenerate. Mixed-race people were considered to possess a "confusion" of blood that resulted in moral degeneracy, physical grotesqueness, and mental inadequacy. This opinion of mixture was almost a complete reversal of the former opinion of mulattoes as having exceptional beauty and possessing the improvements that white blood offered over black, which resulted in Quadroon Balls where white men of means essentially shopped for multiracial lovers who were highly educated and socially refined.

32. Williamson, *New People*, 65. Interestingly, though the one-drop rule was used to eliminate the confusions that arose with race mixture, it could also be used in subversive ways. For instance, Stephan Talty argues that by the end of the eighteenth century, a small number of whites evaded anti-miscegenation laws by drinking drops of their partners' blood in order to establish their own blackness according to the "one drop" rule and thus make their marriages legal ones between two of the same (black) race. Talty, *Mulatto America*, 56–57.

33. Quoted in Williamson, *New People*, 66.

34. When mulattoes became black after the war, many Creoles resisted amalgamation with blacks and therefore maintained the confusion surrounding "colored" racial classification. However, after *Plessy v. Ferguson* (1896), which provided judicial support to the one-drop rule and segregation, other Creoles of color who had resisted association with blacks developed an alliance with blacks and fought for civil rights. Daniel, "Passers and Pluralists," 106.

35. DaCosta, "All in the Family," 37n22.

36. Pascoe, *What Comes Naturally*, 27–28, 85.

37. Williamson, *New People*, 2.

38. Hypodescent, the practice of assigning children the race of their least socially privileged ancestries, is the anthropological term for what the one-drop rule was doing. In white supremacist society, this meant that whiteness would never be granted to a child with a nonwhite parent. Because of hypodescent / the one-drop rule, once black ancestry was in a family all children were considered black regardless of any other factors. While hypodescent was used to oppress people (for instance, to keep the descendants of black people enslaved), by the twentieth century it had effectively created monoracial black identity (and the sense of community and political solidarity that went with it). It is because of this history that many scholars continue to defend the importance of monoracialism.

39. Williamson, *New People*, 56. Though by the twentieth century blackness had absorbed the privileged mulatto caste, the fact that light-skinned black people contributed so disproportionately to black political leadership signals the important social differences that accompanied color differences during the formation of

the modern American "black race." The economic, political, and social advantages of light skin were felt keenly then, and this connection between (light) color and privilege has continued to this day. Scholars in several disciplines study colorism in contemporary American culture and warn that the privileging of lightness (among Americans of all races, both consciously and unconsciously) affects every aspect of life, from beauty norms to hiring practices to income levels. As Naomi Pabst states, "The tangible disadvantages dark-skinned blacks confront should not be understated." Pabst, "Blackness/Mixedness," 199.

40. Korgen, *From Black to Biracial*, 18.

41. Zack, *Race and Mixed Race*, 114.

42. Nobles, *Shades of Citizenship*, appendix.

43. powell, "Colorblind Multiracial Dilemma," 147.

44. Williamson, *New People*, 112–13.

45. Williamson, *New People*, 125.

46. Williamson, *New People*, 114. Ironically, when the census stopped counting black–white mixed-race individuals in 1920, it began counting "half-breeds" of "native" and foreign mixed couples, using such labels as "Irish-American" and "German-American" in a division that used a particular notion of racial belonging. A few years later, the National Origins Act of 1924 would all but halt the immigration of "aliens" and thus also stop the coupling of American and foreign whites. Williamson, *New People*, 114. Naomi Zack notes that "before the 1920s white Anglo-Saxon Americans believed that Italian, Irish, and Polish immigrants were distinct races. No one would suggest that now." Zack, *Race and Mixed Race*, 165. By the end of the twentieth century, several Arab American organizations asked (unsuccessfully) for the census to be revised to switch them from the "white" category to a new "Middle Eastern" category for the purposes of civil rights protections. J. Spencer, *New Colored People*, 5; Omi and Winant, "Racial Formation Rules," 230. (Turnbull notes that Arab "whites" may soon be able to write in their "country of origin," though it is unclear if this change would also be one of racial categorization. Omi and Winant note that since 9/11, Arab American organizations have ceased lobbying for a racial designation since "the line between group recognition and racial profiling is a thin one." Omi and Winant, "Racial Formation Rules," 230.) Jon Michael Spencer also notes that the 1970 census was changed to include North Africans and Southwest Asians as "white." J. Spencer, *New Colored People*, 6. Similarly, Mike Hill observes that the "white" classification has officially included, at one time or another, "North Africans, Arabs and Jews, and all peoples from India and the Middle East. Hispanic, which would have been counted as part of a 'Mexican' race in 1930, but not so in 1940, was until 1960 subsumed under 'white.'" Hill, *After Whiteness*, 32. These observations

highlight both the historical obsession with white purity in the United States and the futility of such an obsession. Although whiteness itself has been guarded steadfastly, its definition has changed drastically. Thus, the "purity" of the whiteness being guarded is inherently questionable if the definition of whiteness shifts so easily and frequently.

47. Pascoe, *What Comes Naturally*, 10.

48. Quoted in Pascoe, *What Comes Naturally*, 271.

49. Pascoe, *What Comes Naturally*, 271.

50. Pascoe, "Miscegenation Law," 194.

51. Pascoe, *What Comes Naturally*, 296.

52. Romano, *Race Mixing*, 177. Intermarriage is still the focus of white supremacy in the United States, and recent events demonstrate the lasting effects (and existence) of racism in the country. After *Loving v. Virginia* invalidated antimiscegenation laws in 1967, some of the sixteen states that still had laws prohibiting interracial marriage moved to remove such laws from their statutes and constitutions so as to "not allow them to stand as 'ghosts of a racist past in cold print.'" Kennedy, *Interracial Intimacies*, 279. Yet, about 38 percent of voters in South Carolina and 40 percent in Alabama voted, as recently as 1998 and 2000, respectively, to keep anti-miscegenation laws on the books for symbolic purposes even though they had been legally unenforceable for over thirty years. Altman and Klinkner, "Measuring the Difference," 301–2.

53. Romano, *Race Mixing*, 177–78.

54. Romano, *Race Mixing*, 178–85.

55. For a detailed discussion of the acceptance of interracial marriage among both black and white populations, see Romano, *Race Mixing*, chap. 3. Notably, a 2013 Gallup poll demonstrated that 87 percent of Americans (specifically, 96 percent of African Americans and 84 percent of white Americans) "approve" of black–white intermarriage (as opposed to 4 percent in 1958), which reflects a monumental shift in social attitudes in the twenty-first century. Newport, "In U.S., 87% Approve."

56. J. Spencer, *New Colored People*, 3.

57. J. Spencer, *New Colored People*, 4.

58. Williamson, *New People*, 189. Loving Day is celebrated across the country, and organizers hope to make it a national holiday as a landmark case in civil rights history and as an aid for building "multicultural community." DaCosta, *Making Multiracials*, 86; Tanabe, "Celebrate Loving Day."

59. Korgen, *From Black to Biracial*, 22.

60. *Time* magazine's issue and the "Eve" cover image, which is an amalgamation of a number of photographs of women of various ethnoracial backgrounds,

are discussed widely in multiracial studies. As an indication of the cover image's status as a rallying point, it graces the cover of Ifekwunigwe's *'Mixed Race' Studies* and is reproduced in several other anthologies related to multiracialism. Most book-length discussions and edited collections of multiracialism include analyses of this *Time* cover and the accompanying article. For a particularly insightful discussion, see Roediger, *Colored White*, chap. 1. For a discussion of *Newsweek*'s similar attempt to define new American multiracialism, see Meacham, "New Face of Race."

61. The multiracial movement might be said to have originated when multiracial activist groups began forming in the 1970s, though the most vocal multiracial advocacy occurred in the last decade of the twentieth century, and most scholars consider the movement to be of the nineties. The Association of Multi-Ethnic Americans (AMEA), an umbrella organization for numerous small groups, was formed in 1988, and Project RACE (Reclassify All Children Equally) was founded in 1991. As representative voices of "the multiracial community," leaders from AMEA and Project RACE testified before Congress on census revision. For a succinct history of the relationship between these two specific groups, see Ibrahim, *Troubling the Family*, 9–13; for one of the multiracial movement, see Nobles, *Shades of Citizenship*, 129–45.

62. In 2000 and 2010, the census asked respondents to identify "ethnically" (as Hispanic or not Hispanic in origin) and then "racially." See "U.S. Census Bureau, "Hispanic Origin"; see also U.S. Census Bureau, "Race and Hispanic Origin: 2000" and "Race and Hispanic Origin: 2010." With the option to "indicate their racial mixture" by checking more than one box, respondents could choose from these race categories: "White, Black or African American, American Indian or Alaska Native, Asian, and Native Hawaiian or Other Pacific Islander." Additionally, respondents could select "Some other race" and fill in the space provided instead of/in addition to any of these categories. U.S. Census Bureau, "Race"; "Race and Hispanic Origin: 2010."

63. The new attitude toward multiracial identification is evident in the fact that the number of people who choose more than one race on the census is growing. According to the U.S. Census Bureau, 2.9 percent of respondents chose the "two or more races" category in 2010, up from 2.4 percent in 2000. These numbers reflect a notable increase in the number of self-identified multiracials between the 2000 and 2010 censuses. U.S. Census Bureau, "Race and Hispanic Origin: 2010," 4. The U.S. Census Bureau also identified that the combination of African American and white—the most popular category of mixed blackness and mixed whiteness in the most recent census, at over 20 percent of the "two or more races" population—more than doubled in number between 2000 and 2010. U.S. Census Bureau, "Race and Hispanic Origin: 2010," 4; "Black," 3. In the 2010 census, black/white mixture

was approximately 60 percent of the "black in combination" population (up from 50 percent in the 2000 census), and approximately 25 percent of the "white in combination" population (up from less than 16 percent in the 2000 census). U.S. Census Bureau, "Black," 3; "White," 3; "Race and Hispanic Origin: 2000."

64. Goldberg, "Made in the USA," 243.

65. The way in which census results are tabulated affects the resulting statistics and can be very political. For a succinct summary of the options debated in the census reform hearings and the method that was chosen, see Nobles, *Shades of Citizenship*, chap. 5.

66. Romano, *Race Mixing*, 172.

67. Spickard, "Obama Nation?," 347.

68. Spickard, "Obama Nation?," 341–42.

69. This discussion will focus on African American literary history. Though white authors have written and continue to write about black characters and black–white multiracialism with some frequency, much early writing by white Americans reflects (conscious or unconscious) racism and white supremacist anxieties about multiracialism and whiteness. It is through the work of black (and/or multiracial) American authors that we can best avoid the detour of pathology and instead focus on less distracted representations of racial mixture. Furthermore, since a significant portion of *Shades of Gray* has to do with multiracial identities paired with black racial pride and progressive political positions, it is important to be able to demonstrate the African American social and literary traditions out of which this contemporary moment has arisen.

70. Judith Berzon argues that white authors tended to depict the mixed character as someone who desires a white lover but suffers a "tragic" demise, whereas black authors tended to depict the mixed character as an unhappy passer who denies black people. Berzon states that "in the white version, the mulatto usually dies; in the black version, he is 'summoned back to his people by the spirituals, or their full-throated laughter, or their simple sweet ways.'" Berzon, *Neither White nor Black*, 63. The implication of Berzon's comments is that to white writers passing had to do with a desire to be nearer to whiteness (and that this was intolerable), while to black writers passing was a betrayal of black culture and community. Much of the criticism of passing and the "tragic mulatto" figure supports Berzon's interpretation, and this agreement ultimately reflects the general apprehension whites had about "invisible blackness" and white purity, as well as the strategy among blacks to combat white supremacy with racial pride. Importantly, then, while passing questions both the validity and successful application of the color line, both black and white perspectives reinforce the binary and hypodescent in the end.

71. In particular, Zackodnik, *Mulatta*; Raimon,"*Tragic Mulatta" Revisited*; and Carby, *Reconstructing Womanhood* take up conventional ways of interpreting the mulatta figure and subsequent critical forays into the discussion, as well as propose new ways of examining the character. For an especially helpful and thorough discussion of African American literary criticism and how it has and does treat the mixed race figure, aesthetics, and literary signifying practice, see Fabi, *Passing and the Rise*, chap. 5. See also Sollors, *Neither Black nor White*, chap. 8.

72. Narratives of passing, abandonment, and segregation dominate these texts. Prominent examples are: Shirlee Taylor Haizlip's *The Sweeter the Juice* (1994) and her follow-up *Finding Grace* (2004), in which she traces her ancestry after learning that branches of her family chose to pass; G. H. Williams's *Life on the Color Line* (1995) tells his story of being raised white in segregated 1950s Virginia until his parents divorced and his black father (who had been passing for Italian) took him to live with his black family; June Cross's *Secret Daughter* (2006) tells her story of being raised by her white mother in the 1950s until her undeniably black appearance prompted her mother to have her raised by a black family; Bliss Broyard's *One Drop* (2007) explores the black/Creole family history that her father, Anatole Broyard, hid for most of his life; and Gene Cheek's *Color of Love* (2005) tells his story of being separated from his mother as a young adolescent in the early 1960s after North Carolina's court system refused to allow his mother and her black partner custody of both her white son and the new couple's mixed child.

Notably, as Paul Spickard points out, "By far the majority of the books in the biracial biography boom are about people who mix Black and White ancestries. That is odd testimony to the degree to which the Black-White encounter holds centre stage in the American racial imagination despite the presence of many other important racial dynamics." Spickard, "Subject is Mixed Race," 87.

73. It is significant to note that the new utterances of multiracial identity at the turn of the millennium have been made consistently by or about children of parents of different races. This important factor in who articulates multiracial identity reflects not the newness of mixture but the newness of a particular ability to identify as mixed. Though there are always exceptions, part of what defines this new era is the scenario of (for the first time), legally wed interracial couples raising children who can racially self-identify both within a sociopolitical context of black pride and among white families that are more likely to accept black family members than in the past.

74. Dagbovie-Mullins, *Crossing B(l)ack*, 17.

75. Dagbovie-Mullins, *Crossing B(l)ack*, 2–3.

76. Elam, *Souls of Mixed Folk*, 23.

77. Elam, *Souls of Mixed Folk*, 21.

78. Elam, *Souls of Mixed Folk*, 21.

79. Elam, *Souls of Mixed Folk*, 21.

80. Elam, *Souls of Mixed Folk*, xiv.

81. Joseph, *Transcending Blackness*, 6–7.

82. Joseph, *Transcending Blackness*, 34.

83. Joseph, *Transcending Blackness*, 4.

84. Elam, *Souls of Mixed Folk*, 23.

85. Moya, "Another Way to Be," 484.

86. Moya, "Another Way to Be," 487–88.

1. "What Are You, Anyway?"

1. Walker, *Black White and Jewish*, 7.

2. Bowman, "Black Like Who?," 24.

3. L. Jones, *Bulletproof Diva*, 61.

4. While many wish to assert belonging to *more than one* ethnoracial group, others advocate that multiracialness be recognized as a *separate racial category*. The testimonies of various multiracial-advocacy leaders before Congress demonstrates that a number of prominent voices advocate multiraciality as a race (chief among them Susan Graham of Project RACE). That is, these activists identify (or advocate identification) as multiracial and do not identify (or advocate identification) with multiple conventional races. Some advocacy groups, such as Project RACE, lobby for a stand-alone multiracial option on government forms and the census. Project RACE's efforts have met with significant success at the state level and, as Melissa Nobles observes, helped force the question at the federal level (though the U.S. Census Bureau has opted for a "choose one or more" option instead of a "multiracial" category). Importantly, the Third Multiracial Leadership Conference of 1997 resulted in consensus surrounding the "check one or more" option rather than a "multiracial" category; Project RACE was the only organization at the conference that insisted upon a multiracial classification. Ibrahim, *Troubling the Family*, 11. Nevertheless, Nobles argues that the recent census reforms have settled the question of how the federal government will count multiracialism for the foreseeable future. Nobles, *Shades of Citizenship*, 144.

5. Because of the small but powerful lobby for a "multiracial" category, the political effects of changing the census continue to be debated. Before the changes were made to the 2000 census, many voiced concern that a multiracial category would deny the legal and political protection of minorities as well as the possibility of political mobilization and solidarity of ethnic or racial groups. This problem appears to have been solved by the "choose one or more" format and

the lack of a multiracial category; however, lobbying continues for a multiracial option, with success on local and state levels to date. The changes mean that Americans must still work within the state's classification system in that they must either choose a category that the state deems valid or deal with the often troubling issues surrounding the fill-in-the-blank "Some other race" option. But the changes also maintain the protection that minority groups have had under the former census because all minority selections are counted as such. For instance, if a person checks both "black" and "white," they are counted as "black" with regard to any civil rights protections or programs that require census information. The U.S. Census Bureau uses the "collapsing" method to produce its statistics; regarding how races are counted for the purposes of civil rights legislation, see Nobles, *Shades of Citizenship*, 163–70.

It should also be acknowledged that the debate surrounding whether multiracial individuals form a group is part of the legal argument used by some activist groups. If multiracials are an identifiable group, then the same arguments used for African Americans during the civil rights movement can also be used for multiracials' rights. For a discussion of the legal strategies of some multiracial organizations, see DaCosta, "Multiracial Identity."

6. For a helpful discussion of Tiger Woods's identity, see Nishime, *Undercover Asian*, chap. 3.

7. While some multiracial activists desire group recognition, such recognition could well come at the cost of existing groups. If multiracials are recognized exclusively as a group, choosing "multiracial" will indeed remove a person from all monoracial categories. This effect leads to polarizing views. Some argue that a multiracial label is important for self-esteem and thus advocate for a multiracial category rather than "choose one or more" or "other" options (that is, group formation should be used to the benefit of individuals' personal needs). Others argue that adding "multiracial" to a "choose one or more" option serves no purpose for civil rights monitoring of historically oppressed groups (that is, group identity should serve the purpose of rooting out discrimination on the basis of that identity).

8. For a detailed discussion of the potential for black racial pride and solidarity within multiracial identity, see chapter 3.

9. powell, "Colorblind Multiracial Dilemma," 147.

10. Walsh, "Ideology," 220.

11. Walsh, "Ideology," 231.

12. Walsh, "Ideology," 220.

13. Dalmage, *The Politics of Multiracialism*, 176.

14. Dalmage, *The Politics of Multiracialism*, 176.

15. Race has essentially been abandoned as a strictly biologically defined category. The work of anthropologist Franz Boas in the early decades of the twentieth century is credited with leading the (eventually successful) challenge against the prevailing scientific racism of the nineteenth century and shifting the working definition of race away from uncertain science. Pascoe, "Miscegenation Law," 188–89. However, scholarship a century later not only reminds readers of the (apparent) lack of biological race but also states that race is "socially constructed" and therefore subject to deep-rooted national and historical ideas about what determines race. Indeed, as Peggy Pascoe points out, Boas and other "culturalists" faced an uphill battle when they worked to change popular and legal opinion about race classification. Tellingly, as Pascoe further notes, American eugenics programs that "reproduced a modern racism that was biological in a particularly virulent sense" were producing research and influencing law and policy in profound ways "until at least World War II." Pascoe, "Miscegenation Law," 193. The change was slow: she notes that *Perez v. Lippold* (1947) was an early and somewhat irregular instance of a judge demonstrating "willingness to believe in the biological indeterminacy of race," but that by the time the Supreme Court ruled on *Loving v. Virginia* (1967), culturalist opinion about race had replaced eugenicist views, and both social scientists and biologists had largely abandoned arguments about biological race. Pascoe, "Miscegenation Law," 197, 201. Pascoe argues that the *Loving* decision "shows the distance twentieth-century American courts had traveled" and demonstrates how race was recognized not as the "all-encompassing phenomenon nineteenth-century racialist thinkers had assumed it to be." Pascoe, "Miscegenation Law," 202.

For astute discussions of the current intersection of genes, medicine, science, and race, see Nishime, *Undercover Asian*, chap. 7; and Roberts, *Fatal Invention*. Regarding the new and in many ways troubling trend of determining racial "origins" using DNA testing, see Nishime, *Undercover Asian*, chap. 7; Carter, *United States of the United Races*, chap. 7; Spickard, "Return of Scientific Racism?"; Nelson, *Social Life of DNA*; and Roberts, *Fatal Invention*, chap. 10.

16. While race is not biological in the sense that there is no gene for race and no way to discern racial makeup at such a level, the general overall understanding of race has to do with biology in that there are shared traits within inbred populations. Indeed, many point out that certain populations contain high rates of particular diseases and conditions, and so "racial" ancestry from one of these populations ought to be considered reason to be tested for such inherited medical conditions. However, since the genes for disease have to do with geography rather than modern race concepts, and since these populations do not necessarily

coincide with a particular culture's idea of race (such as "Mediterranean" or "West African"), this same example of disease demonstrates again the fact that racial groups are reliant on social ideology rather than biology. Furthermore, since there are no strict borders for populations and the human population is increasingly global rather than geographically isolated in groups, defining and discerning race based on inherited traits has become all the more difficult. As Joshua Glasgow points out, philosophers do argue about "races as biologically-identified reproductively isolated populations" and so demonstrate the "biology" of race at least philosophically or semantically. However, Glasgow points out, "This theory would mean that we'd have to talk about non-racial populations as if they were races, which threatens to divert our political and moral attention to race to the wrong targets." Glasgow, "Methodology of the Race Debate," 340. Ultimately, like intellectual discussions of sex and gender, discussions of race are more about culture than biology.

The philosophical analysis of race is concerned with the metaphysical or ontological conception of race and so, while fascinating, is not particularly relevant to my discussion because I am interested in how race functions in a practical sense regardless of how flawed our understandings of "race" are. It might be said, however, that the philosophical discussion should inform multiracial commentary since "race" is so frequently used in such a messy way. The precision with which some analytic philosophers approach race should help some commentators clarify their own arguments about what defines race. Furthermore, it is the philosophers who offer the most complete arguments about what "race" is.

17. Glasgow explains that "one of the most pressing questions about race at present is the normative question of whether race should be eliminated from, or conserved in, public discourse and practice. This normative question is often answered in part by appealing to the ontological status of race: if race is an illusion, then it should be eliminated, and if it is real, then it can be conserved. Thus, for many participants in this debate . . . , ontology constrains normativity." Glasgow, "Methodology of the Race Debate," 333–34. For a good multidisciplinary overview of the debate surrounding the "elimination" or "conservation" of race, see Kelly, Machery, and Mallon, "Race and Racial Cognition."

18. Glasgow, "Methodology of the Race Debate," 334.

19. R. Spencer, "New Racial Identities," 84.

20. R. Spencer, "New Racial Identities," 85.

21. R. Spencer, "New Racial Identities," 96–97.

22. R. Spencer, "New Racial Identities," 85–86.

23. R. Spencer, Challenging Multiracial Identity, 88.

24. R. Spencer, *Challenging Multiracial Identity*, 88.

25. J. Spencer, *New Colored People*, 61; R. Spencer, "New Racial Identities," 89.

26. Ironically, in "The Problem with the 'Mixed' Label," Susan Graham states, "One day I really thought about why 'mixed' annoys me so much. I realized that if a person isn't 'mixed,' what is he or she—*pure*? Wow. It sounds pretty neo-Nazi-Hitler-like to me. Do we really want to separate Americans into those who are pure and those who are mixed?" Despite offering no distinction between the meaning of "mixed race" and "multiracial" (she offers only an argument about the pejorative connotations of the former), she contradicts her own subscription to the purity of monoracialness and plurality of multiracialness.

27. Rainier Spencer, for example, argues repeatedly that multiracial activism has been largely uncritical. Erica Childs's study of online multiracial communities also demonstrates the proliferation of contradictory and problematic views like Graham's as well as a distinct anti-black sentiment that does not engage with even the basics of the issues at hand. Childs demonstrates, for instance, how the two largest and most frequently visited websites "specifically and repeatedly argue that white and black opposition is the same" and so, according to one site, white supremacist opposition is considered "no less dangerous" than black civil rights organizations' opposition. Childs, "Multirace.com," 154–55. Unlike these sites, which are run by multiracially identified individuals, groups run by monoracially identified parents (most often white middle-class mothers, statistically) tend to offer color-blind views on identity and therefore do not engage with the important issues of functional identity, white supremacy, racism, and civil rights. Childs notes that academics conducting research, the media, and legislators who want to learn more about multiracialism and hear from multiracials all turn to these sites and organizations for information. But, as she points out, the use of responses from participants in these sites as representative of all multiracial people and families is extremely misleading, because only those who subscribe to a very particular idea of multiracialism participate in such sites and organizations. Childs, "Multirace.com," 151. Regarding multiracial activist websites, see also Makalani, "Rejecting Blackness and Claiming Whiteness."

28. Graham, "Real World," 44.

29. Zack, "Mixed Black and White," 126.

30. Zack, *Race and Mixed Race*, 97.

31. R. Spencer, "Beyond Pathology and Cheerleading," 117.

32. Pabst, "Blackness/Mixedness," 202–3.

33. Elam, "2010 Census"; Elam, *Souls of Mixed Folk*, 14.

34. Elam, *Souls of Mixed Folk*, 14.

35. Dalmage, *Tripping*, 149.

36. Ferber, "Creation of Whiteness," 56.

37. R. Spencer, "Beyond Pathology and Cheerleading," 117.

38. Bost, *Mulattas and Mestizas*, 6.

39. Texeira, "New Multiracialism," 24.

40. Pabst, "Blackness/Mixedness," 203.

41. Daniel, *More Than Black?*, 174–75.

42. G. Reginald Daniel analyzes the cultural and theoretical discourses surrounding race and identifies the risks associated with the contemporary impulse to "transcend" race. Daniel argues instead that we need to pursue "racial transcendence" by acknowledging more complex and varied racial identities in a way that "does not dismiss the concept of race" itself but rather "interrogate[s] essentialist and reductionist notions of race and decenters racial categories by pointing out the ambiguity and multiplicity of identities." Daniel, *More Than Black?*, 179.

Though whiteness will be discussed in chapter 2, it is useful to point out here that the arguments against abolishing race more generally are also used against efforts to abolish whiteness specifically. As Howard Winant warns, "Efforts to *deconstruct* whiteness are more practical and more promising than attempts to abolish it." Winant, "White Racial Projects," 98. Any shift away from a direct engagement with the functioning of race (and white privilege) threatens to undermine awareness of and resistance to racism. Vigilance among multiracial advocates and white studies scholars must be maintained for the same reasons.

43. There is work being done on the implications of largely white, middle-class female leadership of and participation in multiracial advocacy groups. For particularly astute discussions, see K. Williams, "Linking the Civil Rights" and "Civil Rights Future"; Karis, "'I Prefer to Speak.'" For other insightful discussions of white motherhood in interracial families, see especially Twine, "White Mother" and Aanerud, "Legacy of White Supremacy." For an excellent in-depth analysis of the intersection of class, gender, and race in relation to multiracialism and the way it is discussed both publicly and academically, see Ibrahim, *Troubling the Family*, especially chap. 3.

In relation to color blindness, it is perhaps only fair to mention that there are other approaches to abolitionism. For instance, a white-led effort, centralized in the journal *Race Traitor* (with the motto: "Treason to whiteness is loyalty to humanity"), proposes engaging directly with (and refusing) whiteness rather than ignoring race in color blindness. See Garvey and Ignatiev, "Toward a New Abolitionism." However, *Race Traitor*'s approach to abolition is tricky for similar reasons. For instance, Howard Winant wonders, "Is whiteness so flimsy that it can be repudiated by a mere act of political will—or even by widespread and repeated acts aimed at rejecting white privilege? I think not." Winant, "White Racial Projects,"

107. Similarly, Paul Spickard points out that it not clear how the "'defection' from the White race" proposed in some scholarship "is to be accomplished, nor is it clear how one can disavow one's Whiteness and make it stick." Spickard, "What's Critical," 250. Furthermore, Margaret Andersen argues that it is a widespread problem in white studies that some analyses of whiteness engage insufficiently with racism and the entrenched practices of white supremacy, and instead focus too much on whiteness itself in an isolated way. This approach unusefully supposes, she argues, that "if white people were to abandon whiteness and change their minds, it would go away." Andersen, "Whitewashing Race," 30. *Race Traitor*'s arguments, Andersen claims, do not account for the economic and social practices that arose within and would continue to produce racial stratification. Anderson, "Whitewashing Race," 31. For commentaries on *Race Traitor*, see also Flores and Moon, "Rethinking Race, Revealing Dilemmas; and Alcoff, *Visible Identities*, 213–19."

44. powell, "Colorblind Multiracial Dilemma," 143.

45. Pascoe, *What Comes Naturally*, 313.

46. Pascoe, "Miscegenation Law," 204.

47. Connerly, *Creating Equal*, 3.

48. There is a considerable amount of ongoing scholarship surrounding "color-blind racism." In fact, most work that deals with multiracialism takes it up. Legal scholarship, in particular, examines the motivations, ambitions, and effects of color-blind policies and strategies and is essentially unanimous in condemning color blindness as contrary to the interests of civil rights and social equality. See, for instance, Bonilla-Silva, *Racism without Racists*; Bonilla-Silva, *White Supremacy and Racism*; Brown et al., *Whitewashing Race*; Carr, *"Color-Blind" Racism*; P. Williams, *Color-Blind Future*. For an astute assessment of how we might critique color blindness, see Harris, *"Whitewashing Race."* For excellent broad discussions of racialization, racism, and "color blindness," see Martinot, *Machinery of Whiteness*; and Martinot, *Rule of Racialization*.

49. Walsh, "Ideology," 220.

50. Pabst, "Blackness/Mixedness," 190.

51. L. Jones, *Bulletproof Diva*, 61–62. Graham's views reflect an ahistorical treatment of multiracialism: on the one hand, as Melissa Nobles points out, the arguments she made before Congress in favor of a "multiracial" category treated multiracialism as new and ignored the inclusion of the "mulatto" category in previous censuses. Nobles, *Shades of Citizenship*, 143. On the other hand, she campaigns to have historical figures like Langston Hughes taught as multiracial heroes. Her position regarding the census proposes that multiracialism is new, yet her position on education proposes that multiracialism has a long history;

in neither situation does Graham actually account for the sociopolitical change that mixedness and mixed identities have undergone over the course of history.

52. See, especially, Paul Spickard, "Power of Blackness"; Hutchinson, "Jean Toomer and American" and "Nella Larsen." (The last includes a thoughtful examination of Thadious Davis's authoritative work on Larsen and Charles R. Larson's work on Larsen and Toomer). Additionally, see Pabst, "Blackness/Mixedness"; Pfeiffer, *Race Passing*, chap. 4.

53. DaCosta, "Interracial Intimacies," 6.

54. Pabst, "Baby Janay," 39–40.

55. K. Williams, "Linking the Civil Rights," 81.

56. The response to Rachel Doležal is a case in point, though it is important to note that issues of authenticity and/or ancestry are key factors in the public criticism of her self-identification as black. It is also important to note that different political concerns arise depending on whether identities being claimed are white or nonwhite. That commentators have begun to discuss "transracial identity" in response to Doležal suggests that the new millennium does, indeed, offer a new context for thinking about racial identity and indicates that some interesting and complicated conversations about contemporary racial identities are still in their early stages.

57. Root, *Multiracial Experience*, xxiv.

58. Root, *Multiracial Experience*, xxiv.

59. Root, "Bill of Rights," 359.

60. Root has subsequently created the "Multiracial Oath of Social Responsibility," which essentially locates multiracial people within a historical and political context of racial identity and race relations but, like her "Bill of Rights," focuses more on how multiracial people need not be bound by social norms rather than offering a list of responsibilities for multiracial people. Rather, her "Oath" requires multiracials to "recognize the people" who have preceded them in multiracial activism; her lone stated social obligation is a general appeal to "fight all forms of oppression" primarily through an awareness of "prejudice."

61. Ifekwunigwe, *Scattered Belongings*, 17.

62. Root, *Multiracial Experience*, xxiii.

63. Quoted in Ifekwunigwe, *Scattered Belongings*, 17. Ellipses in original.

64. Quoted in Ifekwunigwe, *Scattered Belongings*, 17.

65. Senna, "The Mulatto Millennium," 23–27.

66. E. Lewis, *Fade*, 19.

67. E. Lewis, *Fade*, 25–26.

68. E. Lewis, *Fade*, 26.

69. E. Lewis, *Fade*, 31.

70. Ali, *Mixed-Race, Post-Race*, 2.

71. Rockquemore, Laszloffy, and Noveske, "It All Starts," 203.

72. Meyer, *Jubilee Journey*, 20.

73. Meyer, *Jubilee Journey*, 39, 106–7.

74. Meyer, *Jubilee Journey*, 166–67.

75. Meyer, *Jubilee Journey*, 167.

76. Meyer, *Jubilee Journey*, 263.

77. R. L. Lewis and Bell, "Negotiating Racial Identity," 251. This article contains a succinct history of sociological theories of identity formation, including black-oriented theories such as Nigrescence, which tend to consider identity as either socially ascribed or internally developed. Lewis and Bell see merit in considering identity formation as a nuanced process that relies both on acculturation and personal choice, and are consequently in favor of the complexity of the "intersectional model of identity." R. L. Lewis and Bell, "Negotiating Racial Identity," 253.

78. Maria Root's "50 Experiences of Racially Mixed People" lists common experiences of many multiracials, and the vast majority of her entries concern the judgement of others. For instance, others might deny multiracial identities or doubt a multiracial's authenticity or legitimacy, family might affect one's racial attitudes, and multiracials might simply be made to feel that they are oddities. Root's list helps to highlight the ways in which racial identity is shaped by social attitudes and the circumstances of everyday life.

79. L. Jones, *Bulletproof Diva*, 53–54.

80. Womack, *Post Black*, 70.

81. Joseph, *Transcending Blackness*, xv.

82. Markus, "Who Am I?," 364.

83. Markus, "Who Am I?," 365.

84. Elam, *Souls of Mixed Folk*, 125.

85. Raboteau, *Professor's Daughter*, 126.

86. DaCosta, "All in the Family," 20.

87. DaCosta, "All in the Family," 25.

88. Walker, *Black White and Jewish*, 36–37.

89. Walker, *Black White and Jewish*, 37.

90. Walker, *Black White and Jewish*, 306.

91. Lester, "Review," 137. Interestingly, Lester is identified exclusively as a Judaic studies scholar in the Judaic studies journal that published his review of Walker's autobiography, but he is also an African American studies scholar and a black Jew himself. The framing of his caustic response to Walker in terms of

his expertise on Judaic studies alone is intriguing considering Walker's discussion of the exclusionary practices of in-groups.

92. Walker, introduction to Prasad, *Mixed*, 17.

93. Walker, *Black White and Jewish*, 74.

94. Walker, *Black White and Jewish*, 307.

95. Walker, introduction to Prasad, *Mixed*, 15.

96. Walker, introduction to Prasad, *Mixed*, 17.

97. Walker, introduction to Prasad, *Mixed*, 18.

98. Young, "Black 'Like Me,'" 297.

99. Senna, *Caucasia*, 351.

100. Senna, *Caucasia*, 189.

101. Senna, *Caucasia*, 274.

102. Perhaps the most obvious historical example is the "marginal man" sociological theory, developed in the late 1920s, which posits that multiracials are socially problematic and doomed to misfortune. As Sika A. Dagbovie-Mullins points out, this theory is still employed in recent scholarship despite its obvious stereotyping and outdatedness. Dagbovie-Mullins, *Crossing B(l)ack*, 121. She also points out that as recently as 2009, a judge in Louisiana refused to marry an interracial couple out of concern for potential children, Dagbovie-Mullins, *Crossing B(l)ack*, 122.

103. Mercer, *Welcome to the Jungle*, 292.

2. Wonders of the Invisible Race

1. Spaulding, "Go-Between People," 99.

2. Morrison, *Playing in the Dark*, xii.

3. Ferber, *White Man Falling*, 4.

4. Bhabha, "Third Space," 208.

5. Though Hill himself is a more careful commentator than his book cover suggests, his proposal that we are living in "after whiteness eve," in which whiteness is in an "agitated" state, and his desire to consider what the future might hold seems to avoid doing the work of getting to that future. Hill, *After Whiteness*, 1, 8.

Additionally, it should be acknowledged that a large number of multiracial advocates do, in one way or another, consider multiracialism as leading to the abolition of race (and thus the end of whiteness). Whether this will ever be possible in the United States, it seems risky to approach such a prospect by considering whiteness as overwritten by multiracialism, since this stance does nothing to challenge conceptions of whiteness (as pure)—a challenge that is likely critical to overcoming white supremacy. Rather, such a stance reinforces the unracialness of whiteness and the racialness of nonwhiteness and presumes to solve the problem of white supremacy through a population reformation. As David Roediger argues convincingly in *Colored White*, American history suggests that racial oppression can only be overcome with political struggle, not by intermarriage and demographic shifts. Tellingly, the racial group that was least likely to declare more than one race on the 2010 census was "white." U.S. Census Bureau, "Race and Hispanic Origin: 2010," 10. In cases when the children of interracially married parents are classified as a single race, "white" is the least likely category to be assigned. Bratter, "Will 'Multiracial' Survive," 825. What this census data suggests is that hypodescent and notions of white purity are still overwhelming forces in American race practices.

6. Ibrahim, "Canary," 156, 155.

7. Ibrahim, "Canary," 170.

8. Elam, *Souls of Mixed Folk*, 14.

9. Babb, *Whiteness Visible*, 20.

10. Jacobson, *Whiteness of a Different*, 22.

11. Babb, *Whiteness Visible*, 16–19.

12. Babb, *Whiteness Visible*, 18.

13. Roediger, *Abolition of Whiteness*, 186.

14. Roediger, *Abolition of Whiteness*, 185–86.

15. Roediger, *Abolition of Whiteness*, 186.

16. Roediger, *Abolition of Whiteness*, 186.

17. Painter, *History of White People*, 134.

18. Jacobson, *Whiteness of a Different*, 40. In his "Observations Concerning the Increase of Mankind," Franklin famously stated that Spaniards, Italians, Russians, Swedes, Germans, and the French were of "a swarthy complexion" and counted the Saxons and English exclusively as the vast majority of the earth's "white people."

19. Nell Painter insists that the importance of religion must not be lost in understanding white racial construction in the United States and points out that most Irish immigration before 1820 consisted of Protestant Irish from the north, who "fairly easily incorporated into American society." However, the potato famine and consequent influx of poor Catholic Irish immigrants after 1830 roused nativist rhetoric in American politics and prompted the Protestant Irish to relabel themselves "Scotch Irish" to distinguish themselves as more appropriately American. Painter, *History of White People*, 133. For an in-depth discussion of anti-Catholic sentiment in American (specifically, British American) history, see Painter, *History of White People*, chap. 3.

20. Jacobson, *Whiteness of a Different*, 23–24.

21. Jacobson, *Whiteness of a Different*, 24–25.

22. Jacobson, *Whiteness of a Different*, 22.

23. Hanley-López, *White by Law*, 1.

24. Jacobson, *Whiteness of a Different*, 22.

25. Painter, *History of White People*, 107.

26. Frankenberg, "Mirage," 75.

27. Roediger, *Abolition of Whiteness*, 190–92.

28. Painter, *History of White People*, 143.

29. Burns, *Civil War*; Painter, *History of White People*, 143.

30. Though most commentators are careful not to equate white ethnic oppression to that suffered by black Americans, early American writing demonstrates that the groups shared some things in common—at least before white racial awareness led to the protection of poor whites from the same level of degradation visited upon blacks. See, for instance, Babb, *Whiteness Visible*, chap. 1 and Korgen, *From Black to Biracial*, chap. 1.

31. Painter, *History of White People*, 256. Along with nonwhite racial groups, some of these "degenerate families" were victims of the eugenics-era forced sterilization efforts of the late nineteenth- and early twentieth-century United States. For instance, see Painter, *History of White People*, chap. 19.

32. Roediger, *Abolition of Whiteness*, 192.

33. Roediger, *Abolition of Whiteness*, 189.

34. Roediger, *Abolition of Whiteness*, 189–90.

35. Roediger, *Abolition of Whiteness*, 187–88.

36. Jacobson, *Whiteness of a Different*, 93–94.

37. Roediger, *Abolition of Whiteness*, 190.

38. Roediger, *Abolition of Whiteness*, 190.

39. Gallagher, "White Racial Formation," 8.

40. Gallagher, "White Racial Formation," 10.

41. Cornell and Hartmann, *Ethnicity and Race*, 18.

42. Gallagher, "Playing," 157.

43. Babb, *Whiteness Visible*, 41.

44. Anderson, "Whitewashing Race," 26.

45. Ruth Frankenberg cites white studies scholar Richard Dyer as articulating an "early and influential" version of the un/markedness idea in the late eighties—it is a concept that frequently arises in white studies. Frankenberg, "Mirage," 93n7.

46. Schlossberg, "Rites of Passing," 5.

47. Evelyn Alsultany, for instance, points out that ethnicity and culture are read as signs of racial difference within American society; while she is racially white in the United States, as a (Muslim) Arab and Latina she is rarely recognized as white in mainstream American culture. Alsultany, "Toward a Multiethnic Cartography," 143–44. The difficulty in discerning and articulating the

similarities and differences of whiteness largely has to do with the "universality" and generic quality of American whiteness, which is tied to concepts of nation and specifically American concepts of whiteness formed through white British and European Christian immigration. Whiteness is defined by its Western European origins, Judeo-Christianity, the English language, and the culture that has arisen from the blending of these groups and their cultures into one *American* white race.

48. Babb, *Whiteness Visible*, 42–43.

49. Frankenberg, "Mirage," 73.

50. Frankenberg, "Mirage," 81.

51. Frankenberg, *White Women, Race Matters*, 6.

52. Quoted in Roediger, *Abolition of Whiteness*, 12, 183.

53. Doane, "Rethinking Whiteness Studies," 7.

54. In the literary world, the increase in fictional and nonfictional representations of multiracial experience is echoed by increased literary criticism that takes up the call of white studies. Including Babb's, a considerable number of scholarly books that specifically address whiteness in American literature have been published since the late 1990s. (The academy has, in a sense, simply caught up with African American writers who thought critically about whiteness a century earlier—see, for instance, Roediger's collection, *Black on White*).

55. Morrison, *Playing in the Dark*, xii.

56. Babb, *Whiteness Visible*, 15–16.

57. Though earlier writers were certainly able to conceive of race and racial identity beyond their particular social contexts, the relationship between literature and the society from which it arises and in which it is received has to be acknowledged. George Hutchinson's and Naomi Pabst's discussions of Jean Toomer, for instance, demonstrate how common it was for Toomer's vision to be misunderstood or underestimated. Hutchinson, "Jean Toomer," 230; Pabst, "Blackness/Mixedness," 185. Since racial identity is such a socially dependent concept, literary explorations of race are still, at least to some degree, reliant on the "race literacy" (to borrow Rebecca Aanerud's phrase) of their audiences.

58. Senna, *Caucasia*, 12.

59. Senna, *Caucasia*, 7.

60. Michele Hunter, "Revisiting the Third Space," 303.

61. Senna, *Caucasia*, 36.

62. Senna, *Caucasia*, 37.

63. Dagbovie, "Fading to White," 102.

64. Senna, *Caucasia*, 63.

65. Senna, *Caucasia*, 79, 78.

66. Senna, *Caucasia*, 78 (emphasis added).

67. Senna, *Caucasia*, 78.

68. Dagbovie, "Fading to White," 101.

69. Dagbovie, "Fading to White," 104.

70. Senna, *Caucasia*, 1.

71. Senna, *Caucasia*, 1.

72. Senna, *Caucasia*, 108.

73. Mather serves as a symbol of intolerance, abusive power, and persecution, and he is an ancestor whom Birdie's grandmother is proud to call her own. However, Birdie also calls Mather an "octoroon dandy," which casts doubt on the white purity of her mother's aristocratic family and its self-made mythology, and hints at the hypocrisy of white supremacist tradition in the United States. Senna references Mather's famous work *The Wonders of the Invisible World* in her novel, and it is this same work that inspires this chapter's title.

74. Michele Hunter, "Revisiting the Third Space," 309.

75. Harrison-Kahan, "Passing for White," 22.

76. Sacks, "How Did Jews," 395.

77. Roediger, *Abolition of Whiteness*, 184.

78. Roediger, *Abolition of Whiteness*, 184.

79. Greenberg, *Troubling the Waters*, 11.

80. Greenberg, *Troubling the Waters*, 12.

81. Greenberg, *Troubling the Waters*, 12.

82. Itzkovitz, "Passing Like Me," 45.

83. Itzkovitz, "Passing Like Me," 47.

84. Schlossberg, "Rites of Passing," 2.

85. Itzkovitz, "Passing Like Me," 45.

86. Itzkovitz, "Passing Like Me," 47.

87. Senna, *Caucasia*, 110.

88. Senna, *Caucasia*, 119.

89. Senna, *Caucasia*, 111.

90. Senna, *Caucasia*, 111.

91. Ibrahim, "Canary," 160.

92. Senna, *Caucasia*, 119.

93. Senna, *Caucasia*, 198.

94. Senna, *Caucasia*, 209–10.

95. Harrison-Kahan, "Passing for White," 31.

96. Harrison-Kahan, "Passing for White," 31.

97. Rummell, "Rewriting the Passing Novel," 12.

98. Rummell, "Rewriting the Passing Novel," 1.

99. Senna, *Caucasia*, 353.

100. Harrison-Kahan, "Passing for White," 32.

101. Harrison-Kahan, "Passing for White," 32.

102. Walker's use of Hispanicness is interesting since it is both a racial and non-racial label; like blackness, it is a homogeneous category that itself houses broad heterogeneity. "Hispanic"—which was created in the United States and is not used outside of North America—is knowingly used to identify a broad swath of ethnic and national backgrounds as one ethnoracial group and has, so far (though this might change in the 2020 census when "Hispanic" may turn into a "race" category), been treated officially as an ethnic label only. That said, Hispanicness is often considered an (ethno)racial identity and is in common practice treated like any other racialized identity. Nathan Glazer notes, "When we are informed of the racial or ethnic composition of a school or a city, it is generally broken down into the categories white, black, Hispanic, and, if there are enough of them, Asian." Glazer, "Future of Race," 74. In fact, one could draw a comparison between "Asian" and "Hispanic" since "Asian" is an American racial designator that collapses or ignores cultural, national, and ethnic differences as well as, to most Asians, racial differences (although, for that matter, so do—or did—the categories "white" and "black"). "Hispanic," like "Asian," is a label that "*others* as it unites, marginalizes as it generalizes, stereotypes as it aggregates. It purports to extend specific identity to an entire subcontinent." Goldberg, "Made in the USA," 245.

103. Walker, *Black White and Jewish*, 205.

104. Walker, *Black White and Jewish*, 202–3.

105. Harrison-Kahan, "Passing for White," 37.

106. Walker, *Black White and Jewish*, 211–12.

107. Walker, *Black White and Jewish*, 202.

108. Harrison-Kahan, "Passing for White," 37.

109. Walker, *Black White and Jewish*, 89.

110. Walker, *Black White and Jewish*, 89.

111. Harrison-Kahan, "Passing for White," 38.

112. In her introduction to Prasad, *Mixed*, Walker identifies her autobiography's title as *Black, White, and Jewish*; however, the actual book cover, title page, and spine include neither comma.

113. Pabst, "Blackness/Mixedness," 209n1.

114. Pabst, "Blackness/Mixedness," 200–201.

3. "Black Like Me"

1. Birdie says twice that a mixed person is "black like me." Senna, *Caucasia*, 189, 353.

2. Senna, "Passing and the Problematic," 86.

3. Dagbovie-Mullins, *Crossing B(l)ack*, 76.

4. Marable, "Race, Identity, and Political Culture," 295.

5. Shelby, *We Who Are Dark*, 3–4.

6. Shelby, *We Who Are Dark*, 4.

7. Quoted in Lowe, *Immigrant Acts*, 75.

8. Funderburg, *Black, White, Other*, 14.

9. Dagbovie-Mullins, *Crossing B(l)ack*, 14.

10. E. Lewis, *Fade*, 18.

11. Margaret Hunter, "Light, Bright," 24.

12. Margaret Hunter, "Light, Bright," 24.

13. Margaret Hunter, "Light, Bright," 35.

14. Senna, "Passing and the Problematic," 84.

15. Leverette, "Re-visions of Difference," 111.

16. Nishime, *Undercover Asian*, 48.

17. Nishime, *Undercover Asian*, 48.

18. Ironically, when the body *is* "black enough" to be "seen" as black (or as mixed), the interpretive potential of race and the ability to self-identify become difficult for a different set of reasons. For instance, Cole has no choice but to embody a black (and/or mixed) identity, whereas Birdie is capable of being perceived as black or nonblack in different moments. Because Cole's blackness is visible, it cannot be "unseen." As Tru Leverette puts it, Birdie's "'freedom' of performativity is not allowed for individuals with more precisely determined phenotypes—such as Cole and Deck." Leverette, "Re-visions of Difference," 117.

19. L. Jones, *Bulletproof Diva*, 29.

20. Pabst, "Blackness/Mixedness," 205.

21. Piper, "Passing for White," 246, 234.

22. Piper, "Passing for White," 235.

23. Derricotte, *Black Notebooks*, 141.

24. Derricotte, *Black Notebooks*, 112.

25. The slur "Oreo" in the United States (and "Bounty Bar" in Britain) emphasizes the importance of cultural fluency in the authentication of blackness (since being black on the outside but "white in the middle" is an accusation of lacking black culture or the sensibility to match—or authenticate—black appearance). While appearance is important and a prominent concern in contemporary mixed-race literature, it is certainly not the only factor in establishing an "authentic" black identity.

26. Funderburg, *Black, White, Other*, 15.

27. L. Jones, *Bulletproof Diva*, 31.

28. Senna, "Passing and the Problematic," 85.

29. Senna, "Passing and the Problematic," 85.

30. Lisa Jones resists multiracial identity and considers her black identity a political choice. She makes clear that she has a white mother, is "ethnically" African American, and is "politically" a "person of color." L. Jones, *Bulletproof Diva*, 54. Indeed, self-identifying is complicated by the fact that multiracialism is overwhelmingly about a personal sense of self and a reflection of individual heritages and family situations (even though some multiracial activists argue for multiracial community). Like other scholars, Paul Spickard points out that many people are monoracially committed to a community or group and that their multiracial identity is something personal. Spickard states, "Many multiracial activists are in practical fact committed to the needs of the communities of color to which they have connections, but their multiracial claim is essentially an individualistic concern." Spickard, "Does Multiraciality Lighten?," 293. With this in mind, it is not a contradiction when an individual like Lisa Jones identifies as a "racially mixed Black person" in that she is mixed and acknowledges it as part of her personal identity but also asserts that she has made a political choice to be publicly and unambiguously African American. Spickard, "Subject is Mixed Race," 79.

31. I am employing the distinction Lawrence Grossberg makes between "individual identities" and the "social categories (of difference) within which individuals are placed." Grossberg, "Identity and Cultural Studies," 91.

32. Pabst, "An Unexpected Blackness," 115.

33. Pabst, "An Unexpected Blackness," 115.

34. Pabst, "An Unexpected Blackness," 115.

35. Pabst, "Blackness/Mixedness," 189.

36. Pabst, "Blackness/Mixedness," 208.

37. Pabst, "Blackness/Mixedness," 208.

38. Gilroy, *Against Race*, 268.

39. Gilroy, *Against Race*, 268.

40. Pabst, "An Unexpected Blackness," 116.

41. Pabst, "Blackness/Mixedness," 205.

42. Raboteau, *Professor's Daughter*, 230.

43. Walker, *Black White and Jewish*, 204.

44. Streeter, *Tragic No More*, 40.

45. "Redbone" is, presumably not coincidentally, also a term for multiracials and has been used pejoratively, though not always.

46. Rummell, "Rewriting the Passing Novel," 4.

47. Cape Verde is a Portuguese-colonized archipelago off the cost of West Africa, which suggests that Maria is acknowledging a multiracial background and thereby explaining why her (black) brother looks like Birdie (and thus that Birdie's multiracialness is acceptable as black).

48. Harrison-Kahan, "Passing for White," 43.

49. Senna, *Caucasia*, 242.

50. Senna, *Caucasia*, 245.

51. Harrison-Kahan, "Passing for White," 43.

52. S. Jones, "Tragic No More?," 95.

53. Senna, *Caucasia*, 351.

54. Young, "Black 'Like Me,'" 297.

55. Harrison-Kahan, "Passing for White," 41.

56. Harrison-Kahan, "Passing for White," 40.

57. Harrison-Kahan, "Passing for White," 40; Walker, *Black White and Jewish*, 200.

58. Thompson and Tyagi, *Names We Call Home*, xii.

59. Smith and Watson, *Reading Autobiography*, 189.

60. Smith and Watson, *Reading Autobiography*, 189–90.

61. Smith and Watson, *Reading Autobiography*, 172.

62. Tessman, "Racial Politics of Mixed," 280.

63. Rockquemore, "Deconstructing Tiger Woods," 128.

64. While some multiracials and activists do subscribe to the notion of multiracialness as a race, most contemporary literature—including the works of Harper, Senna, Raboteau, and Walker—does not. See the introduction for a discussion of multiracialism as a new race (socially and politically).

65. Gilroy, *Against Race*, 275.

66. Michele Hunter, "Revisiting the Third Space," 304.

67. Michele Hunter, "Revisiting the Third Space," 302.

68. Michele Hunter, "Revisiting the Third Space," 304.

69. Tessman, "Racial Politics of Mixed," 289.

70. My claim that hybridity forms new "races" while multiracialness does not is meant to suggest that certain hybrid identities constitute, for all intents and purposes, "races." While a "race" like mestiza is inherently a combination of "races," it is still a category that conjures the belonging, specificity, and even borders of any conventional "race" classification. My argument is that while "multiracial" might itself be a name or category, it does not necessarily duplicate the qualities that form a "race." My use of "race" is thus meant to refer to a particular set of qualities.

71. Margaret Hunter, "Light, Bright," 25.

4. Mixed Ethnicity

1. I employ Kwame Anthony Appiah's term "social identity" here to signify the scenario in which a given identity is observed in and makes sense to a given society.

2. Markus, "Who Am I?," 365.

3. Markus, "Who Am I?," 368.

4. Miller and Buchanan, "Growing Up Multiracial," 141.

5. Miller and Buchanan, "Growing Up Multiracial," 146–47. Sociologists and social psychologists who work in racial formation studies tend to agree about this correlation, and some even counsel interracial families to ensure that their multiracial children are raised in integrated communities that practice multiracialism language in order to offer positive contexts in which children can develop the identities they want. What is evident in this scholarship is not only that a receptive social environment is essential for children to have unobstructed and positive experiences developing their multiracial identities but that class plays a significant role in a child's ability to form a multiracial identity. In fact, multiple sociological studies have demonstrated that class reflects the degree to which a given family or community will acknowledge multiracial identities. Families of low socioeconomic status tend to reinforce monoracial identities while families of higher socioeconomic status tend to be more willing to accept or foster multiracial identities. For a brief summary of these studies, see Miller and Buchanan, "Growing Up Multiracial."

6. Miller and Buchanan, "Growing Up Multiracial," 151–55; Miller and Rotheram-Borus, "Growing Up Biracial," 154–59.

7. Jenkins, "African American Identity."

8. Miller and Buchanan, "Growing Up Multiracial," 151.

9. Appiah and Gutmann, *Color Consciousness*, 80.

10. Many scholars of race and ethnicity draw similar distinctions, but these terms do not necessarily mean the same things to all scholars or in all circumstances. I make an effort here to outline exactly how I use the terms in this particular discussion.

11. For an especially thoughtful essay on the potentially "successful" white parenting of black children, see Sally Haslanger, "You Mixed?"

12. Color blindness is a major issue in multiracial discourse and one that has serious and often unfortunate consequences, as I discuss in chapter 1.

13. Miller and Buchanan, "Growing Up Multiracial," 159.

14. Durrow, *Girl Who Fell*, 155–56. Ellipses in original.

15. Miller and Buchanan, "Growing Up Multiracial," 146.

16. In this sense, Durrow's novel suggests that instead of adapting to inequality (by, for instance, obstructing the formation of interracial families), society has to change to adapt to the social realities of the contemporary era. Moreover, that Rachel's life is hardly made easier when she has a black "mother" rather than a white one illustrates how parenting is not necessarily an effective way to deal with American racism.

17. Anthony Miller becomes an interesting figure against which to compare Rachel. Anthony's Ojibway heritage is treated as a purely racial identity (in so far as this particular conversation treats "race" as a category of genes/phenotype) as opposed to a cultural one. Anthony knows he has Ojibway ancestors but does not claim Ojibway cultural fluency. Similarly, Rachel looks for signs of his Ojibway ancestry in his facial features, not in his ethnic knowledge. While Rachel sees Danishness in her body in a similar fashion, she lets go of the physical/racial signs of her mother in her body due to the pressure of her black family and community. Instead, she comes to focus on her Danishness as a cultural part of herself.

In this sense, Anthony and Rachel complicate the assumption that racial and cultural identities will coincide. Gina Samuels argues that "an individual's choice of racial label is not a proxy for his or her cultural experiences or background. It is also important to note that people who are multiracial are not automatically multicultural; not all multiracial people have had access to their cultures of origin as children or even as adults." Samuels, "Beyond the Rainbow," 39. Or, to put it another way, "inheriting" ethnicity is less straightforward than "inheriting" race since ethnicity necessarily requires an active transmission of cultural knowledge—something Anthony lacks regarding his Ojibway heritage and something Rachel possesses regarding her Danish heritage.

18. Considering Doris's interest in "respectability" and social striving, it is interesting that she does not pressure Rachel to join the Jack and Jill—a social club that grooms African American children for middle- and upper-class lifestyles. In fact, none of the novel's three references to the Jack and Jill has anything to do with her, the character most likely to appreciate the elite organization's goals. However, the fact that, at the time, the club was governed by well-educated and often professional mothers and required an invitation to join reminds us of how Doris's ambitions are always going to be limited. While her own economic and social status would disqualify her from participating in the Jack and Jill, the Jack and Jill would quite possibly offer her daughter or granddaughter access to a level of social privilege that Doris would not even imagine (but would desire) for her family.

19. Tizard and Phoenix, "Black Identity," 99.

20. Tizard and Phoenix, "Black Identity," 99.

21. DaCosta, "All in the Family," 28.

22. DaCosta, "All in the Family," 22.

23. For discussions of "biculturalism" and the importance of diverse social environments, see Markus, "Who Am I?"; Jenkins, "African American Identity"; Miller and Buchanan, "Growing Up Multiracial."

24. Markus, "Who Am I?," 381.

25. Markus, "Who Am I?," 382.

26. Miller and Buchanan, "Growing up Multiracial," 159.

27. In the mid-twentieth century it was commonly held—popularly as well as sociologically—that multiracial identities were largely negative ones. Since this negativity was the result of monoracialist expectations and racism (which made interracial relationships taboo), it is unsurprising that multiracial identities are rapidly becoming disassociated with pathology. As society becomes more tolerant of ideas about racial equality and therefore of interracial families, it becomes more receptive to multiracial identities.

28. Durrow, *Girl Who Fell*, 264.

Conclusion

1. Raboteau, *Professor's Daughter*, 1.

2. Derricotte, *Black Notebooks*, 19.

3. Marshall made this statement in a 1992 National Public Radio interview; quoted in Funderburg, *Black, White, Other*, 9.

4. Funderburg, *Black, White, Other*, 12.

5. Ifekwunigwe, *Scattered Belongings*, 50.

6. Walker, *To Be Real*, xxxiii.

7. Walker, quoted in Washington, "Obama's True Colors."

8. Senna, "Passing and the Problematic," 86.

9. Senna, "Passing and the Problematic," 86.

10. There is work being done on African and Caribbean immigrants and the ways in which their blackness complicates and relates to African American blackness. See, for instance, Kobina Aidoo's documentary *The Neo-African-Americans* or Yoku Shaw-Taylor and Steven A. Tuch's edited collection, *The Other African Americans.* For a list of scholarship on the topic, see also Spickard, "Obama Nation?," 363n10.

11. Interestingly, the "Changing Perception of 'Mixed Race'" section of Paul Taylor's study for the Pew Research Center "The Next America" demonstrates that 52 percent of Americans see Obama as "mostly mixed" while only 27 percent see him as "mostly black." Notably, more whites and Hispanics see him as mixed than blacks do—the majority of blacks see him as black. For a particularly

astute assessment of popular perception of Obama's racial identity, see Dagbovie-Mullins, *Crossing B(l)ack*, 5–10. Regarding public accusations that Obama is not black enough, see the introduction to Nyong'o, *Amalgamation Waltz*. See also Carter, *United States of the United Races*, chap. 7.

12. Pabst, "An Unexpected Blackness," 117.

13. Pabst, "An Unexpected Blackness," 113.

14. R. Spencer, "New Racial Identities," 98.

15. R. Spencer, *Reproducing Race*, 325

16. Nishime, *Undercover Asian*, xvii–xviii.

17. Mahtani, *Mixed Race Amnesia*, 248.

18. Senna, *Caucasia*, 74.

19. McBride, *Color of Water*, 32.

20. Pabst, "Blackness/Mixedness," 181–82.

21. Pabst, "Blackness/Mixedness," 182.

22. Pabst, "Blackness/Mixedness," 185.

23. Spickard, "Obama Nation?," 344.

24. R. Spencer, "Assessing Multiracial Identity Theory," 358.

25. R. Spencer, "Assessing Multiracial Identity Theory," 358.

26. R. Spencer, "Assessing Multiracial Identity Theory," 360–61.

27. Ifekwunigwe, '*Mixed Race' Studies*, 8.

28. Senna, *Caucasia*, 335.

Bibliography

Aanerud, Rebecca. "Fictions of Whiteness: Speaking the Names of Whiteness in U.S. Literature." In Frankenberg, *Displacing Whiteness*, 35–59.

———. "The Legacy of White Supremacy and the Challenge of White Antiracist Mothering." *Hypatia* 22, no. 2 (2007): 20–38.

Adams, Jenoyne. *Resurrecting Mingus: A Novel.* New York: Washington Square Press, 2001.

"Adversity.Net Home Page." Adversity.Net. Accessed June 19, 2010.

Ahad, Badia Sahar. "'Wonders of the Invisible World': Psychoanalysis and Border Identities in the Novels of Nella Larsen, Ralph Ellison and Danzy Senna." PhD diss., University of Notre Dame, 2004. ProQuest (3121044).

Ahmed, Sara. "'She'll Wake Up One of These Days and Find She's Turned into a Nigger': Passing through Hybridity." In *Performativity and Belonging*, edited by Vikki Bell, 87–106. London: SAGE, 1999.

Aidoo, Kobina, dir. *The Neo-African-Americans.* River Densu LC, 2008. DVD.

Alcoff, Linda Martin. *Visible Identities: Race, Gender, and the Self.* New York: Oxford University Press, 2006.

Alex-Assensoh, Yvette M., and Lawrence J. Hanks, eds. *Black and Multiracial Politics in America.* New York: New York University Press, 2000.

Ali, Suki. *Mixed-Race, Post-Race: Gender, New Ethnicities and Cultural Practices.* New York: Berg, 2003.

Alsultany, Evelyn. "Toward a Multiethnic Cartography: Multiethnic Identity, Monoracial Cultural Logic, and Popular Culture." In Kwan and Speirs, *Mixing it Up*, 141–62.

Altman, Micah, and Philip A. Klinkner. "Measuring the Difference between White Voting and Polling on Interracial Marriage." *Du Bois Review: Social Science Research on Race* 3, no. 2 (2006): 299–315.

"American Civil Rights Institute." American Civil Rights Institute (ACRI). Accessed June 19, 2010. http://acri.org.

Andersen, Margaret L. "Whitewashing Race: A Critical Perspective on Whiteness." In Doane and Bonilla-Silva, *White Out*, 21–34.

Anzaldúa, Gloria. *Borderlands/La Frontera: The New Mestiza*. 2nd ed. San Francisco: Aunt Lute Books, 1999.

Appiah, Kwame Anthony. "Identity, Authenticity, Survival: Multicultural Societies and Social Reproduction." In Gutmann, *Multiculturalism*, 149–64.

———. "Does Truth Matter to Identity?" In Gracia, *Race or Ethnicity?*, 19–44.

Appiah, Kwame Anthony, and Amy Gutmann. *Color Conscious: The Political Morality of Race*. Princeton NJ: Princeton University Press, 1996.

Arboleda, Teja. *In the Shadow of Race: Growing Up As a Multiethnic, Multicultural, and "Multiracial" American*. Mahwah NJ: Lawrence Erlbaum, 1998.

Azoulay, Katya Gibel. *Black, Jewish, and Interracial: It's Not the Color of Your Skin, but the Race of Your Kin, and Other Myths of Identity*. Durham NC: Duke University Press, 1997.

Babb, Valerie. *Whiteness Visible: The Meaning of Whiteness in American Literature and Culture*. New York: New York University Press, 1998.

Bailey-Williams, Nicole. *Floating: A Novel*. New York: Broadway Books, 2004.

Baker, Peter, and Sheryl Gay Stolberg. "Saluting a Dream, and Adapting It for a New Era." *New York Times*, August 28, 2013.

Bartholet, Elizabeth. "Where Do Black Children Belong? The Politics of Race Matching in Adoption." *University of Pennsylvania Law Review* 139, no. 5 (1991): 1163–256.

Bauer, Ralph. "Hemispheric Studies." PMLA 124, no.1 (2009): 234–50.

Bell, Derrick. *Faces at the Bottom of the Well: The Permanence of Racism*. New York: Basic Books, 1992.

Berlin, Ira. *Slaves Without Masters: The Free Negro in the Antebellum South*. Oxford: Oxford University Press, 1974.

Berzon, Judith. *Neither White nor Black: The Mulatto Character in American Fiction*. New York: New York University Press, 1978.

Bhabha, Homi K. "The Third Space: Interview with Homi Bhabha." In *Identity: Community, Culture, Difference*, edited by Jonathan Rutherford, 207–21. London: Lawrence & Wishart, 1990.

Bibb, Henry. *Narrative of the Life and Adventures of Henry Bibb, an American Slave*. 1949. In *I Was Born a Slave: An Anthology of Classic Slave Narratives; 1849–1866*, edited by Yuval Taylor, 1–101. The Library of Black America 2. Chicago: Lawrence Hill Books, 1999.

Black-ish. Season One. ABC Studios. 2015. DVD.

Bonilla-Silva, Eduardo. *Racism without Racists: Color-Blind Racism and the Persistence of Racial Inequality in the United States*. 3rd ed. Lanham MD: Rowman & Littlefield, 2010.

———. *White Supremacy and Racism in the Post-Civil Rights Era.* Boulder CO: Lynne Rienner, 2001.

Bost, Suzanne. *Mulattas and Mestizas: Representing Mixed Identities in the Americas, 1850–2000.* Athens: University of Georgia Press, 2003.

Boudreau, Brenda. "Letting the Body Speak: 'Becoming' White in *Caucasia*." *Modern Language Studies* 32, no.1 (2002): 59–70.

Bowman, Elizabeth Atkins. "Black Like Who?" *Black Issues Book Review* 3, no.1 (2001): 24–27.

Bradshaw, Carla K. "Beauty and the Beast: On Racial Ambiguity." In Root, *Racially Mixed People*, 77–88.

Bratter, Jenifer. "Will 'Multiracial' Survive to the Next Generation? The Racial Classification of Children of Multiracial Parents." *Social Forces* 86, no. 2 (2007): 821–49.

Brennan, Jonathan, ed. *Mixed Race Literature.* Redwood City CA: Stanford University Press, 2002.

Browder, Laura. *Slippery Characters: Ethnic Impersonators and American Identities.* Chapel Hill: University of North Carolina Press, 2000.

Brown, Michael K., Martin Carnoy, Elliott Currie, Troy Duster, David B. Oppenheimer, Marjorie M. Shultz, and David Wellman. *Whitewashing Race: The Myth of a Color-Blind Society.* Berkeley: University of California Press, 2003.

Brown, Rosellen. *Half a Heart.* New York: Picador, 2000.

Brown, William Wells. *Clotelle; or, The Colored Heroine: A Tale of the Southern States.* 1867. Miami FL: Mnemosyne, 1969.

———. *Clotel; or, The President's Daughter.* 1853. Boston: Bedford/St. Martin's, 2000.

Broyard, Bliss. *One Drop: My Father's Hidden Life; A Story of Race and Family Secrets.* New York: Little, Brown, 2007.

Brunsma, David L., ed. *Mixed Messages: Multiracial Identities in the "Color-Blind" Era.* Boulder CO: Lynne Rienner, 2006.

Burns, Ken, dir. *The Civil War.* PBS Home Video, 1990. 9 vols. DVD.

Butler, Judith. "Performative Acts and Gender Constitution: An Essay in Phenomenology and Feminist Theory." In *Writing on the Body: Female Embodiment and Feminist Theory*, edited by Katie Conboy, Nadia Medina, and Sarah Stanbury, 401–17. New York: Columbia University Press, 1997.

Callahan, Cynthia. *Kin of Another Kind: Transracial Adoption in American Literature.* Ann Arbor: University of Michigan Press, 2011.

Campbell, Bebe Moore. *Your Blues Ain't Like Mine.* New York: G. P. Putnam's Sons, 1992.

Camper, Carol, ed. *Miscegenation Blues: Voices of Mixed Race Women.* Toronto: Sister Vision, 1994.

Carby, Hazel. *Reconstructing Womanhood: The Emergence of the Afro-American Woman Novelist.* New York: Oxford University Press, 1987.

Carr, Leslie G. *"Color-Blind" Racism.* Thousand Oaks CA: SAGE, 1997.

Carter, Greg. *The United States of the United Races: A Utopian History of Racial Mixing.* New York: New York University Press, 2013.

Cheek, Gene. *The Color of Love: A Mother's Choice in the Jim Crow South.* Guilford CT: Lyons Press, 2005.

Chen, Fu-Jen. "Postmodern Hybridity and Performing Identity in Gish Jen and Rebecca Walker." *Critique: Studies in Contemporary Fiction* 50, no. 4 (2009): 337–96.

Cheng, Vincent J. *Inauthentic: The Anxiety over Culture and Identity.* New Brunswick NJ: Rutgers University Press, 2004.

Chesnutt, Charles Waddell. *The House behind the Cedars.* 1900. New York: Modern Library, 2003.

Childs, Erica Chito. "Black and White: Family Opposition to Becoming Multiracial." In Brunsma, *Mixed Messages*, 233–46.

———. *Fade to Black and White: Interracial Images in Popular Culture.* Lanham MD: Rowman & Littlefield, 2009.

———. "Multirace.com: Multiracial Cyberspace." In Dalmage, *Politics of Multiracialism*, 143–59.

Chrisman, Laura. "Introduction to 'The Politics of Biracialism'." *Black Scholar* 39, no. 3/4 (2009/10): 2–3.

Collins, Patricia Hill. *Black Feminist Thought: Knowledge, Consciousness, and the Politics of Empowerment.* 2nd ed. New York: Routledge, 2000.

Connerly, Ward. *Creating Equal: My Fight against Race Preferences.* San Francisco: Encounter Books, 2000.

Cornell, Stephen, and Douglas Hartmann. *Ethnicity and Race: Making Identities in a Changing World.* Thousand Oaks CA: Pine Forge, 1998.

Craft, William, and Ellen Craft. *Running a Thousand Miles for Freedom: The Escape of William and Ellen Craft from Slavery.* 1860. Athens: Brown Thrasher Books, an imprint of University of Georgia Press, 1999.

Cross, June. *Secret Daughter: A Mixed-Race Daughter and the Mother Who Gave Her Away.* New York: Viking, 2006.

Cuomo, Chris J., and Kim Q. Hall, eds. *Whiteness: Feminist Philosophical Reflections.* Lanham MD: Rowman & Littlefield, 1999.

DaCosta, Kimberly McClain. "All in the Family: The Familial Roots of Racial Division." In Dalmage, *Politics of Multiracialism*, 19–41.

———. "Interracial Intimacies, Barack Obama, and Politics of Multiracialism." *Black Scholar* 39, no. 3/4 (2009/10): 4–12.

———. *Making Multiracials: State, Family, and Market in the Redrawing of the Color Line.* Redwood City CA: Stanford University Press, 2007.

———. "Multiracial Identity: From Personal Problem to Public Issue." In Winters and DeBose, *New Faces*, 68–84.

Dagbovie-Mullins, Sika A. *Crossing B(l)ack: Mixed-Race Identity in Modern American Fiction and Culture.* Knoxville: University of Tennessee Press, 2013.

Dagbovie, Sika Alaine. "Black Biracial Crossing: Mixed Race Identity in Modern Literature and Culture." PhD diss., University of Illinois at Urbana-Champaign, 2004. ProQuest (3153282).

———. "Fading to White, Fading Away: Biracial Bodies in Michelle Cliff's *Abeng* and Danzy Senna's *Caucasia*." *African American Review* 40, no. 1 (2006): 93–109.

Dalmage, Heather M. "'Mama, Are You Brown?': Multiracial Families and the Color Line." In Herring, Keith, and Horton, *Skin Deep*, 82–98.

———, ed. *The Politics of Multiracialism: Challenging Racial Thinking.* Albany: State University of New York Press, 2004.

———. "Protecting Racial Comfort, Protecting White Privilege." In Dalmage, *Politics of Multiracialism*, 203–18.

———. *Tripping on the Color Line: Black-White Multiracial Families in a Racially Divided World.* New Brunswick NJ: Rutgers University Press, 2000.

Daniel, G. Reginald. "Beyond Black and White: The New Multiracial Consciousness." In Root, *Racially Mixed People*, 333–41.

———. *More Than Black? Multiracial Identity and the New Racial Order.* Philadelphia: Temple University Press, 2002.

———. "Passers and Pluralists: Subverting the Racial Divide." In Root, *Racially Mixed People*, 91–107.

———. "Race, Multiraciality, and Barack Obama: Toward a More Perfect Union?" *Black Scholar* 39, no. 3/4 (2009/10): 51–62.

Daniel, G. Reginald, and Josef Manuel Castañeda-Liles. "Race, Multiraciality, and the Neoconservative Agenda." In Brunsma, *Mixed Messages*, 125–45.

Daniels, Lucy. *The Eyes of the Father.* New York: iUniverse, 2005.

Davis, Angela Y. "Black Nationalism: The Sixties and the Nineties." In Dent, *Black Popular Culture*, 317–24.

Davis, F. James. "Defining Race: Comparative Perspectives." In Brunsma, *Mixed Messages*, 15–31.

———. "The Hawaiian Alternative to the One-Drop Rule." In Zack, *American Mixed Race*, 115–31.

———. *Who Is Black? One Nation's Definition.* University Park: Pennsylvania State University Press, 1991.

Dawkins, Marcia Alesan. *Clearly Invisible: Racial Passing and the Color of Cultural Identity.* Waco TX: Baylor University Press, 2012.

Delgado, Richard, and Jean Stefancic, eds. *Critical White Studies: Looking behind the Mirror.* Philadelphia: Temple University Press, 1997.

Dent, Gina, ed. *Black Popular Culture.* Seattle: Bay Press, 1992.

Derricotte, Toi. *The Black Notebooks: An Interior Journey.* New York: W. W. Norton, 1997.

Diehl, Kim. "Power of the Periphery." In Trenka, Oparah, and Shin, *Outsiders Within,* 31–37.

Doane, [Ashley] Woody. "Rethinking Whiteness Studies." In Doane and Bonilla-Silva, *White Out,* 3–18.

Doane, Ashley "Woody," and Eduardo Bonilla-Silva, eds. *White Out: The Continuing Significance of Racism.* New York: Routledge, 2003.

Domínguez, Virginia R. *White by Definition: Social Classification in Creole Louisiana.* New Brunswick NJ: Rutgers University Press, 1986.

Douglass, Frederick. *Narrative of the Life of Frederick Douglass, an American Slave.* 1865. New York: Penguin, 1986.

Dreisinger, Baz. *Near Black: White-to-Black Passing in American Culture.* Amherst: University of Massachusetts Press, 2008.

Durrow, Heidi. *The Girl Who Fell from the Sky.* Chapel Hill NC: Algonquin Books, 2010.

Dyer, Richard. *White.* New York: Routledge, 1997.

Edles, Laura Desfor. "'Race,' 'Ethnicity,' and 'Culture' in Hawai'i: The Myth of the 'Model Minority' State." In Winters and DeBose, *New Faces,* 222–46.

Elam, Michele. "2010 Census: Think Twice, Check Once." *Huffington Post,* May 8, 2010. Updated May 25, 2010. https://www.huffingtonpost.com/michele-elam/2010-census-think-twice-c_b_490164.html.

———. "The 'Ethno-Ambiguo Hostility Syndrome': Mixed Race, Identity, and Popular Culture." In Markus and Moya, *Doing Race,* 528–44.

———. "Passing in the Post-Race Era: Danzy Senna, Philip Roth, and Colson Whitehead." *African American Review* 41, no. 4 (2007): 749–68.

———. *The Souls of Mixed Folk: Race, Politics, and Aesthetics in the New Millennium.* Redwood City CA: Stanford University Press, 2011.

Ellison, Ralph. *Invisible Man.* 1952. New York: Vintage International, 1995.

Erkkilä, Betsy. *Mixed Bloods and Other Crosses: Rethinking American Literature from the Revolution to the Culture Wars.* Philadelphia: University of Pennsylvania Press, 2005.

Essed, Philomena, and David Theo Goldberg, eds. *Race Critical Theories: Text and Context.* Malden MA: Blackwell, 2002.

Fabi, M. Giulia. *Passing and the Rise of the African American Novel.* Urbana: University of Illinois Press, 2001.

Fauset, Jessie Redmon. *Plum Bun: A Novel Without a Moral.* 1929. Boston: Beacon Press, 1990.

Ferber, Abby L. "Defending the Creation of Whiteness: White Supremacy and the Threat of Interracial Sexuality." In Dalmage, *Politics of Multiracialism*, 43–57.

———. *White Man Falling: Race, Gender, and White Supremacy.* Lanham MD: Rowman & Littlefield, 1998.

———. "White Supremacists in the Color-Blind Era: Redefining Multiracial and White Identities." In Brunsma, *Mixed Messages*, 147–59.

Ferrante, Joan, and Prince Brown, Jr., eds. *The Social Construction of Race and Ethnicity in the United States.* New York: Longman, 1998.

Fields, Barbara Jeanne. "Slavery, Race, and Ideology in the United States of America." *New Left Review* 181 (1990): 95–118.

Flores, Lisa A., and Dreama G. Moon. "Rethinking Race, Revealing Dilemmas: Imagining a New Racial Subject in *Race Traitor.*" *Western Journal of Communication* 66, no.2 (2002): 181–207.

Fogg-Davis, Hawley. *The Ethics of Transracial Adoption.* Ithaca NY: Cornell University Press, 2002.

Fojas, Camilla. "The Biracial Baby Boom and the Multiracial Millennium." In Kina and Dariotis, *War Baby / Love Child*, 225–29.

Frankenberg, Ruth, ed. *Displacing Whiteness: Essays in Social and Cultural Criticism.* Durham NC: Duke University Press, 1997.

———. "Local Whitenesses, Localizing Whiteness." Introduction to Frankenberg, *Displacing Whiteness*, 1–33.

———. "The Mirage of an Unmarked Whiteness." In Rasmussen, *Making and Unmaking*, 72–96.

———. "'When We are Capable of Stopping, We Begin to See': Being White, Seeing Whiteness." In Thompson and Sangeeta, *Names We Call Home*, 3–17.

———. *White Women, Race Matters: The Social Construction of Whiteness.* Minneapolis: University of Minnesota Press, 1993.

Franklin, Benjamin. "Observations Concerning the Increase of Mankind." *Founders Online*, National Archives. Last modified February 1, 2018. http://founders.archives.gov/documents/Franklin/01-04-02-0080.

Fredrickson, George M. "Beyond Race? Ideological Color Blindness in the United States, Brazil, and South Africa." In Stokes, Meléndez, and Rhodes-Reed, *Race in 21st Century*, 59–72.

Friedman, Murray. *What Went Wrong? The Creation and Collapse of the Black-Jewish Alliance.* New York: Free Press, 1995.

Funderburg, Lise. *Black, White, Other: Biracial Americans Talk About Race and Identity.* New York: William Morrow, 1994.

Gaffney, Stuart, and Ken Tanabe. "Loving Days: Images of Marriage Equality Then and Now." In Kina and Dariotis, *War Baby / Love Child*, 230–42.

Gallagher, Charles A. "Color Blindness: An Obstacle to Racial Injustice?" In Brunsma, *Mixed Messages*, 103–16.

———. "Playing the White Ethnic Card: Using Ethnic Identity to Deny Contemporary Racism." In Doane and Bonilla-Silva, *White Out*, 145–58.

———. "Racial Redistricting: Expanding the Boundaries of Whiteness." In Dalmage, *Politics of Multiracialism*, 59–76.

———. "White Racial Formation: Into the Twenty-First Century." In Delgado and Stefancic, *Critical White Studies*, 6–11.

Garvey, John, and Noel Ignatiev. "Toward a New Abolitionism: A *Race Traitor* Manifesto." In *Whiteness: A Critical Reader*, edited by Mike Hill, 346–49. New York: New York University Press, 1997.

Gilroy, Paul. *Against Race: Imagining Political Culture Beyond the Color Line.* Cambridge MA: Harvard University Press, 2001.

Ginsberg, Elaine K, ed. *Passing and the Fictions of Identity.* Durham NC: Duke University Press, 1996.

Glasgow, Joshua. "On the Methodology of the Race Debate: Conceptual Analysis and Racial Discourse." *Philosophy and Phenomenological Research* 76, no. 2 (2008): 333–58.

Glazer, Nathan. "The Future of Race in the United States." In Stokes, Meléndez, and Rhodes-Reed, *Race in 21st Century*, 73–78.

Goldberg, David Theo. "Made in the USA: Racial Mixing 'n Matching." In Zack, *American Mixed Race*, 237–55.

Gracia, Jorge J. E., ed. *Race or Ethnicity? On Black and Latino Identity.* Ithaca NY: Cornell University Press, 2007.

———. "Racial and Ethnic Identity?" Gracia, *Race or Ethnicity?*, 45–77.

Graham, Susan. "Articles from the Director." Project RACE. Updated January 20, 2009. http://www.projectrace.com/about_us/archives/from-the-director/.

———. "Grassroots Advocacy." In Zack, *American Mixed Race*, 185–89.

———. "The Real World." In Root, *Multiracial Experience*, 37–48.

Grassian, Daniel. "Passing into Post-Ethnicity: A Study of Danzy Senna's *Caucasia.*" *Midwest Quarterly* 47, no. 4 (2006): 317–35.

Graves, Joseph L., Jr. *The Race Myth: Why We Pretend Race Exists in America.* New York: Dutton, 2004.

Greenberg, Cheryl Lynn. *Troubling the Waters: Black-Jewish Relations in the American Century.* Princeton NJ: Princeton University Press, 2006.

Griffin, John Howard. *Black Like Me.* 1960. New York: New American Library, 2003.

Grimes, William. *Life of William Grimes, the Runaway Slave.* 1825. In *I Was Born a Slave: An Anthology of Classic Slave Narratives, 1770–1849,* edited by Yuval Taylor, 181–233. The Library of Black America 1. Chicago: Lawrence Hill Books, 1999.

Grossberg, Lawrence. "Identity and Cultural Studies: Is That All There Is?" In Hall and du Gay, *Questions of Cultural Identity,* 87–107.

Gubar, Susan. *Racechanges: White Skin, Black Face in American Culture.* New York: Oxford University Press, 1997.

Guevarra, Rudy P., Jr. *Becoming Mexipino: Multiethnic Identities and Communities in San Diego.* New Brunswick NJ: Rutgers University Press, 2012.

Gutmann, Amy, ed. *Multiculturalism: Examining the Politics of Recognition.* Princeton: Princeton University Press, 1994.

Haizlip, Shirlee Taylor. *Finding Grace: Two Sisters and the Search for Meaning Beyond the Color Line.* New York: Free Press, 2004.

———. *The Sweeter the Juice: A Family Memoir in Black and White.* New York: Touchstone, 1994.

Hall, Stuart. "What is this 'Black' in Black Popular Culture?" In Dent, *Black Popular Culture,* 21–33.

———. "Who Needs 'Identity'?" Introduction to Hall and du Gay, *Questions of Cultural Identity,* 1–17.

Hall, Stuart, and Paul du Gay, eds. *Questions of Cultural Identity.* London: SAGE, 1996.

Haney-López, Ian F. *White by Law: The Legal Construction of Race.* New York: New York University Press, 1996.

Harper, Frances E. W. *Iola Leroy; or, Shadows Uplifted.* 1892. Boston: Beacon Press, 1987.

Harper, Rachel. *Brass Ankle Blues: A Novel.* New York: Touchstone, 2006.

Harris, Cheryl I. "*Whitewashing Race:* Scapegoating Culture." Review of *Whitewashing Race: The Myth of a Color-Blind Society* by Michael K. Brown. *California Law Review* 94, no. 3 (2006): 907–43.

Harrison-Kahan, Lori. "Passing for White, Passing for Jewish: Mixed Race Identity in Danzy Senna and Rebecca Walker." *MELUS* 30, no. 1 (2005): 19–48.

Haslanger, Sally. "You Mixed? Racial Identity Without Racial Biology." In Haslanger and Charlotte Witt, *Adoption Matters,* 265–90.

Haslanger, Sally, and Charlotte Witt, eds. *Adoption Matters: Philosophical and Feminist Essays.* Ithaca NY: Cornell University Press, 2005.

Henry, Neil. *Pearl's Secret: A Black Man's Search for His White Family.* Berkeley: University of California Press, 2001.

Herring, Cedric, Verna M. Keith, and Hayward Derrick Horton, eds. *Skin Deep: How Race and Complexion Matter in the "Color-Blind" Era*. Chicago: University of Illinois Press, 2004.

Hill, Mike. *After Whiteness: Unmaking an American Majority*. New York: New York University Press, 2004.

Homans, Margaret. "Adoption and Essentialism." *Tulsa Studies in Women's Literature* 21, no. 2 (2002): 257–74.

hooks, bell. *Black Looks: Race and Representation*. Boston: South End, 1992.

———. "Postmodern Blackness." In Natoli and Hutcheon, *Postmodern Reader*, 510–18.

———. *Yearning: Race, Gender, and Cultural Politics*. 1990. Toronto: Between the Lines, 1992.

Horsman, Reginald. *Race and Manifest Destiny: The Origins of American Racial Anglo-Saxonism*. Cambridge MA: Harvard University Press, 1981.

HoSang, Daniel Martinez, Oneka LaBennett, and Laura Pulido, eds. *Racial Formation in the Twenty-First Century*. Berkeley: University of California Press, 2012.

Hughes, Langston. *The Collected Poems of Langston Hughes*. Edited by Arnold Rampersad. New York: Knopf, 1994.

———. *Mulatto: A Tragedy of the Deep South*. 1935. In *The Collected Works of Langston Hughes*, edited by Leslie Catherine Sanders, 5:17–50. Columbia: University of Missouri Press, 2002.

Hunter, Margaret. "Light, Bright, and Almost White: The Advantages and Disadvantages of Light Skin." In Herring, Keith, and Horton, *Skin Deep*, 22–44.

Hunter, Michele. "Revisiting the Third Space: Reading Danzy Senna's *Caucasia*." In *Literature and Racial Ambiguity*, edited by Teresa Hubel and Neil Brooks, 297–316. Amsterdam, Netherlands: Rodopi, 2002.

Hurston, Zora Neale. *Dust Tracks on a Road*. 1942. New York: Harper Perennial, 1996.

———. *Their Eyes Were Watching God*. 1937. New York: Perennial Classics, 1998.

Hutchinson, George. "Jean Toomer and American Racial Discourse." *Texas Studies in Literature and Language* 35, no. 2 (1993): 226–50.

———. "Nella Larsen and the Veil of Race." *American Literary History* 9, no. 2 (1997): 329–49.

Ibrahim, Habiba. "Canary in a Coal Mine: Performing Biracial Difference in *Caucasia*." *Literature Interpretation Theory* 18, no. 2 (2007): 155–72.

———. "Toward Black and Multiracial 'Kinship' After 1997, or How a Race Man Became 'Cablinasian.'" *Black Scholar* 39, no. 3/4 (2009/10): 23–31.

———. *Troubling the Family: The Promise of Personhood and the Rise of Multiracialism*. Minneapolis: University of Minnesota Press, 2012.

Ifekwunigwe, Jayne O., ed. *'Mixed Race' Studies: A Reader.* New York: Routledge, 2004.

———. "Re-Membering 'Race': On Gender, 'Mixed Race' and Family in the English-African Diaspora." In Parker and Song, *Rethinking 'Mixed Race,'* 42–64.

———. "Rethinking 'Mixed Race' Studies. Introduction to Ifekwunigwe, *'Mixed Race' Studies,* 1–29.

———. *Scattered Belongings: Cultural Paradoxes of "Race," Nation and Gender.* London: Routledge, 1999.

Itzkovitz, Daniel. "Passing Like Me: Jewish Chameleonism and the Politics of Race." In Sánchez and Schlossberg, *Passing,* 38–63.

Jacobson, Matthew Frye. *Whiteness of a Different Color: European Immigrants and the Alchemy of Race.* Cambridge MA: Harvard University Press, 1998.

Jeffries, Hasan Kwame. *Bloody Lowndes: Civil Rights and Black Power in Alabama's Black Belt.* New York: New York University Press, 2009.

Jenkins, Lee. "African American Identity and Its Social Context." In Salett and Koslow, *Race, Ethnicity, and Self,* 63–88.

Jerng, Mark C. *Claiming Others: Transracial Adoption and National Belonging.* Minneapolis: University of Minnesota Press, 2010.

Johnson, Charles. *Oxherding Tale: A Novel.* New York: Scribner, 1982.

Johnson, James Weldon. *The Autobiography of an Ex-Colored Man.* 1912. New York: Vintage, 1989.

Johnson, Kevin R., ed. *Mixed Race America and the Law: A Reader.* New York: New York University Press, 2003.

Johnson, Mat. *Loving Day: A Novel.* New York: Spiegel & Grau, 2015.

Johnston, James Hugo. *Race Relations in Virginia & Miscegenation in the South: 1776–1860.* Amherst: University of Massachusetts Press, 1970.

Jones, Gayl. *Corregidora.* Boston: Beacon Press, 1975.

Jones, Lisa. *Bulletproof Diva: Tales of Race, Sex, and Hair.* New York: Anchor Books, 1994.

———. "She Came with the Rodeo (An Excerpt)." In Walker, *To Be Real,* 253–65.

Jones, Patricia. *The Color of Family: A Novel.* New York: Avon Trade, 2004.

Jones, Suzanne W. *Race Mixing: Southern Fiction since the Sixties.* Baltimore MD: Johns Hopkins University Press, 2004.

———. "Tragic No More? The Reappearance of the Racially Mixed Character." In *American Fiction of the 1990s: Reflections of History and Culture,* edited by Jay Prosser, 89–103. London: Routledge, 2008.

Joseph, Ralina. "Performing the Twenty-First Century Tragic Mulatto." Review of *Black White and Jewish: Autobiography of a Shifting Self* by Rebecca Walker. *Black Scholar* 39, no. 3/4 (2009/10): 13–22.

————. *Transcending Blackness: From the New Millennium Mulatta to the Exceptional Multiracial.* Durham NC: Duke University Press, 2013.

Karis, Terri A. "'I Prefer to Speak of Culture': White Mothers of Multiracial Children." In Dalmage, *Politics of Multiracialism*, 161–76.

Kawash, Samira. *Dislocating the Color Line: Identity, Hybridity, and Singularity in African-American Literature.* Redwood City CA: Stanford University Press, 1997.

Kein, Sybil, ed. *Creole: The History and Legacy of Louisiana's Free People of Color.* Baton Rouge: Louisiana State University Press, 2000.

Kelly, Daniel, Edouard Machery, and Ron Mallon. "Race and Racial Cognition." In *The Moral Psychology Handbook*, edited by John M. Doris, 433–72. Oxford: Oxford University Press, 2010.

Kennedy, Randall. *Interracial Intimacies: Sex, Marriage, Identity, and Adoption.* New York: Pantheon, 2003.

Kina, Laura, and Wei Ming Dariotis, eds. *War Baby / Love Child: Mixed Race Asian American Art.* Seattle: University of Washington Press, 2013.

Korgen, Kathleen Odell. *From Black to Biracial: Transforming Racial Identity among Americans.* Westport CT: Praeger, 1998.

Kwan, SanSan, and Kenneth Speirs, eds. *Mixing It Up: Multiracial Subjects.* Austin: University of Texas Press, 2004.

Lal, Barbara Ballis. "Learning to Do Ethnic Identity: The Transracial/Transethnic Adoptive Family as Site and Context." In Parker and Song, *Rethinking 'Mixed Race,'* 154–72.

Larsen, Nella. *Passing.* 1929. Edited by Deborah E. McDowell. New Brunswick NJ: Rutgers University Press, 1986.

————. *Quicksand.* 1928. Edited by Deborah E. McDowell. New Brunswick NJ: Rutgers University Press, 1986.

Lazarre, Jane. *Beyond the Whiteness of Whiteness: Memoir of a White Mother of Black Sons.* Durham NC: Duke University Press, 1996.

Lee, James Kyung-Jin. "The Transitivity of Race and the Challenge of the Imagination." In HoSang, LaBennett, and Pulido, *Racial Formation*, 48–54.

Lemire, Elise. *"Miscegenation": Making Race in America.* Philadelphia: University of Pennsylvania Press, 2002.

Lester, Julius. Review of *Black, White and Jewish: Autobiography of a Shifting Self* by Rebecca Walker. *Shofar* 22, no. 1 (2003): 136–37.

Leverette, Tru. "Re-visions of Difference in Danzy Senna's *Caucasia*." *Obsidian III* 12, no. 1 (2011): 110–27.

Lewis, Elliott. *Fade: My Journeys in Multiracial America.* New York: Carroll & Graf, 2006.

Lewis, R. L'Heureux, and Kanika Bell. "Negotiating Racial Identity in Social Interactions." In Brunsma, *Mixed Messages*, 249–65.

Lipsitz, George. *The Possessive Investment in Whiteness: How White People Profit from Identity Politics*. Rev. ed. Philadelphia: Temple University Press, 2006.

Lowe, Lisa. *Immigrant Acts: On Asian American Cultural Politics*. Durham NC: Duke University Press, 1996.

Mahtani, Minelle. *Mixed Race Amnesia: Resisting the Romanticization of Multiraciality*. Vancouver: University of British Columbia Press, 2014.

Makalani, Minkah. "Rejecting Blackness and Claiming Whiteness: Antiblack Whiteness in the Biracial Project." In Doane and Bonilla-Silva, *White Out*, 81–94.

Marable, Manning. *Beyond Black and White: Transforming African-American Politics*. London: Verso, 1995.

———. "Race, Identity, and Political Culture." In Dent, *Black Popular Culture*, 292–302.

Markus, Hazel Rose. "Who Am I? Race, Ethnicity, and Identity." In Markus and Moya, *Doing Race*, 359–89.

Markus, Hazel Rose, and Paula M. L. Moya, eds. *Doing Race: 21 Essays for the 21st Century*. New York: W. W. Norton, 2010.

Martin, Joan M. "*Plaçage* and the Louisiana *Gens de Couleur Libre*: How Race and Sex Defined the Lifestyles of Free Women of Color." In Kein, *Creole*, 57–70.

Martinot, Steve. *The Machinery of Whiteness: Studies in the Structure of Racialization*. Philadelphia: Temple University Press, 2010.

———. *The Rule of Racialization: Class, Identity, Governance*. Philadelphia: Temple University Press, 2003.

McBride, James. *The Color of Water: A Black Man's Tribute to His White Mother*. New York: Riverhead Books, 1996.

McGuire, Danielle L. *At the Dark End of the Street: Black Women, Rape, and Resistance—a New History of the Civil Rights Movement from Rosa Parks to the Rise of Black Power*. New York: Alfred A. Knopf, 2010.

McIntosh, Peggy. "White Privilege and Male Privilege: A Personal Account of Coming to See Correspondences through Work in Women's Studies." In Delgado and Stefancic, *Critical White Studies*, 291–99.

McKinley, Catherine E. *The Book of Sarahs: A Family in Parts*. New York: Counterpoint, 2002.

Meacham, Jon. "The New Face of Race." *Newsweek*, September 18, 2000.

Mercer, Kobena. *Welcome to the Jungle: New Positions in Black Cultural Studies*. New York: Routledge, 1994.

Meyer, Carolyn. *Jubilee Journey: A Novel.* Orlando FL: Houghton Mifflin Harcourt, 1997.

Michaels, Walter Benn. *The Trouble with Diversity: How We Learned to Love Identity and Ignore Inequality.* New York: Metropolitan Books, 2006.

Miller, Robin Lin, and Mary Jane Rotheram-Borus. "Growing Up Biracial in the United States." In Salett and Koslow, *Race, Ethnicity, and Self,* 143–69.

Miller, Robin Lin, and NiCole T. Buchanan. "Growing Up Multiracial in the United States." In Salett and Koslow, *Multicultural Perspectives,* 139–67.

Mills, Charles W. *Blackness Visible: Essays on Philosophy of Race.* Ithaca NY: Cornell University Press, 1998.

Moniz, Jeffrey, and Paul Spickard. "Carving Out a Middle Ground: The Case of Hawai'i." In Brunsma, *Mixed Messages,* 63–81.

Moore, Geneva Cobb. "*Caucasia*'s Migrating Bodies: Lessons in American History and Postmodernism." *Western Journal of Black Studies* 36, no. 2 (2012): 108–18.

Morrison, Toni. *Playing in the Dark: Whiteness and the Literary Imagination.* 1992. New York: Vintage, 1993.

Moya, Paula M. L. "Another Way to Be: Women of Color, Literature, and Myth." In Markus and Moya, *Doing Race,* 483–508.

Nakashima, Cynthia L. "An Invisible Monster: The Creation and Denial of Mixed-Race People in America." In Root, *Racially Mixed People,* 162–78.

National Association of Black Social Workers. "Preserving African American Families: Research and Action Beyond the Rhetoric." April 1991. https://c
.ymcdn.com/sites/nabsw.site-ym.com/resource/collection/0D2D2404-77EB
-49B5-962E-7E6FADBF3D0D/Preserving_African_American_Families.pdf.

Natoli, Joseph, and Linda Hutcheon. *A Postmodern Reader.* Albany: State University of New York Press, 1993.

Nelson, Alondra. *The Social Life of DNA: Race, Reparations, and Reconciliation after the Genome.* Boston: Beacon Press, 2016.

"The New Face of America: How Immigrants Are Shaping the World's First Multicultural Society." Special issue, *Time Magazine,* Fall 1993.

Newport, Frank. "In U.S., 87% Approve of Black-White Marriage, vs. 4% in 1958." Gallup. Updated July 25, 2013. http://news.gallup.com/poll/163697/approve
-marriage-blacks-whites.aspx.

Nishime, Leilani. *Undercover Asian: Multiracial Asian Americans in Visual Culture.* Urbana: University of Illinois Press, 2014.

Njeri, Itabari. *The Last Plantation: Color, Conflict, and Identity; Reflections of a New World Black.* Boston: Houghton Mifflin, 1997.

Nobles, Melissa. *Shades of Citizenship: Race and the Census in Modern Politics.* Redwood City CA: Stanford University Press, 2000.

Nyong'o, Tavia. *The Amalgamation Waltz: Race, Performance, and the Ruses of Memory.* Minneapolis: University of Minnesota Press, 2009.

O'Hearn, Claudine Chiawei, ed. *Half and Half: Writers on Growing Up Biracial and Bicultural.* New York: Pantheon, 1998.

Omi, Michael. "Racialization in the Post-Civil Rights Era." In *Mapping Multiculturalism*, edited by Avery F. Gordon and Christopher Newfield, 178–86. Minneapolis: University of Minnesota Press, 1996.

Omi, Michael, and Howard Winant. *Racial Formation in the United States.* 3rd ed. New York: Routledge, 2015.

———. "Racial Formation Rules: Continuity, Instability, and Change." In HoSang, LaBennett, and Pulido, *Racial Formation*, 222–40.

Pabst, Naomi. "An Unexpected Blackness." *Transition* 100, no. 1 (2008): 112–32.

———. "Baby Janay and Naomi Pabst: Negotiating Race Mixing, Adoption, and Transnationality." *Black Scholar* 39, no. 3/4 (2009/10): 33–40.

———. "Blackness/Mixedness: Contestations over Crossing Signs." *Cultural Critique* 54, no. 1 (Spring 2003): 178–212.

Painter, Nell Irvin. *The History of White People.* New York: W. W. Norton, 2010.

Parker, David, and Miri Song, eds. *Rethinking 'Mixed Race.'* London: Pluto, 2001.

Pascoe, Peggy. "Miscegenation Law, Court Cases, and Ideologies of 'Race' in Twentieth-Century America." In Sollors, *Interracialism*, 178–204.

———. *What Comes Naturally: Miscegenation Law and the Making of Race in America.* Oxford: Oxford University Press, 2009.

Patton, Sandra. *Birth Marks: Transracial Adoption in Contemporary America.* New York: New York University Press, 2000.

Paulin, Diana Rebekkah. *Imperfect Unions: Staging Miscegenation in U.S. Drama and Fiction.* Minneapolis: University of Minnesota Press, 2012.

Pellegrini, Gino Michael. "Creating Multiracial Identities in the Work of Rebecca Walker and Kip Fulbeck: A Collective Critique of American Liberal Multiculturalism." *MELUS* 38, no. 4 (2013): 171–90.

Perlmann, Joel, and Mary C. Waters, eds. *The New Race Question: How the Census Counts Multiracial Individuals.* New York: Russell Sage Foundation, 2002.

Pfeiffer, Kathleen. *Race Passing and American Individualism.* Amherst: University of Massachusetts Press, 2003.

Piper, Adrian. "Passing for White, Passing for Black." In Ginsberg, *Passing and the Fictions of Identity*, 234–69.

powell, john a. "The Colorblind Multiracial Dilemma: Racial Categories Reconsidered." In Torres, Mirón, and Inda, *Race, Identity, and Citizenship*, 141–57.

Prasad, Chandra, ed. *Mixed: An Anthology of Short Fiction on the Multiracial Experience.* New York: W. W. Norton, 2006.

Raboteau, Emily. "Bernie and Me." *Callaloo* 25, no. 2 (2002): 367–80.

———. "From *The Mantra of the Dove*." *Callaloo* 30, no. 3 (2007): 718–20.

———. "Mrs. Turner's Lawn Jockeys." In Prasad, *Mixed*, 69–81.

———. *The Professor's Daughter: A Novel*. New York: Henry Holt, 2005.

———. "Rash." *The Missouri Review* 27, no. 3 (2004): 186–205.

———. "Respiration." *Callaloo* 26, no. 1 (2003): 23–25.

Raimon, Eve Allegra. *The "Tragic Mulatta" Revisited: Race and Nationalism in Nineteenth-Century Antislavery Fiction*. New Brunswick NJ: Rutgers University Press, 2004.

Rasmussen, Birgit Brander, Eric Klinenberg, Irene J. Nexica, and Matt Wray, eds. *The Making and Unmaking of Whiteness*. Durham NC: Duke University Press, 2001.

Reddy, Maureen T. *Crossing the Color Line: Race, Parenting, and Culture*. New Brunswick NJ: Rutgers University Press, 1994.

Rees, Richard W. *Shades of Difference: A History of Ethnicity in America*. Lanham MD: Rowman & Littlefield, 2007.

Roberts, Dorothy. *Fatal Invention: How Science, Politics, and Big Business Re-create Race in the Twenty-first Century*. New York: The New Press, 2011.

Rockquemore, Kerry Ann. "Deconstructing Tiger Woods: The Promise and the Pitfalls of Multiracial Identity." In Dalmage, *Politics of Multiracialism*, 125–41.

Rockquemore, Kerry Ann, and David L. Brunsma. *Beyond Black: Biracial Identity in America*. Thousand Oaks CA: SAGE, 2002.

Rockquemore, Kerry Ann, Tracey Laszloffy, and Julia Noveske. "It All Starts at Home: Racial Socialization in Multiracial Families." In Brunsma, *Mixed Messages*, 203–16.

Roediger, David R. *Black on White: Black Writers on What It Means to Be White*. New York: Schocken Books, 1998.

———. *Colored White: Transcending the Racial Past*. Berkeley: University of California Press, 2002.

———. *How Race Survived US History: From Settlement and Slavery to the Obama Phenomenon*. London: Verso, 2008.

———. *Towards the Abolition of Whiteness: Essays on Race, Politics, and Working Class History*. London: Verso, 1994.

———. *The Wages of Whiteness: Race and the Making of the American Working Class*. Rev. ed. London: Verso, 2007.

———. *Working Toward Whiteness: How America's Immigrants Became White; The Strange Journey from Ellis Island to the Suburbs*. New York: Basic Books, 2005.

Roland, Alan. "Identity, Self, and Individualism in a Multicultural Perspective." In Salett and Koslow, *Multicultural Perspectives*, 11–24.

Romano, Renee C. *Race Mixing: Black-White Marriage in Postwar America*. Cambridge MA: Harvard University Press, 2003.

Root, Maria P. P. "50 Experiences of Racially Mixed People." *The Multiracial Child Resource Book: Living Complex Identities*. Seattle: Mavin Foundation, 2003. http://www.drmariaroot.com/doc/50Experiences.pdf.

———. "A Bill of Rights for Racially Mixed People." 1996. In Essed and Goldberg, *Race Critical Theories*, 355–68.

———. "Five Mixed-Race Identities: From Relic to Revolution." In Winters and DeBose, *New Faces*, 3–20.

———. "The Multiracial Contribution to the Psychological Browning of America." In Zack, *American Mixed Race*, 231–36.

———. "The Multiracial Experience: Racial Borders as a Significant Frontier in Race Relations." Introduction to *The Multiracial Experience*, xiii–xxviii.

———, ed. *The Multiracial Experience: Racial Borders as the New Frontier*. Thousand Oaks CA: SAGE, 1996.

———. "Multiracial Oath of Social Responsibility." http://www.drmariaroot.com/doc/OathOfSocialResponsibility.pdf.

———, ed. *Racially Mixed People in America*. Newbury Park CA: SAGE, 1992.

———. "Reflections on 'A Bill of Rights for Racially Mixed People.'" In Essed and Goldberg, *Race Critical Theories*, 513–16.

———. "Within, Between, and Beyond Race." In Ifekwunigwe, *'Mixed Race' Studies*, 143–48.

Ross, Fran. *Oreo*. Boston: Northeastern University Press, 1974.

Rossi, Jennifer Christianna. "Souls across Spaces: Ambiguity as Resistance and a New Generation of Black Women Writers." PhD diss., State University of New York, 2003. ProQuest (3102398).

Rothman, Barbara Katz. *Weaving a Family: Untangling Race and Adoption*. Boston: Beacon Press, 2005.

Rummell, Kathryn. "Rewriting the Passing Novel: Danzy Senna's *Caucasia*." *Griot* 26, no. 2 (2007): 1–11.

Russell, Elizabeth, ed. *Caught between Cultures: Women, Writing & Subjectivities*. Amsterdam NL: Rodopi, 2002.

Sacks, Karen Brodkin. "How Did Jews Become White Folks?" In Delgado and Stefancic, *Critical White Studies*, 395–401.

Salett, Elizabeth Pathy, and Diane R. Koslow, eds. *Multicultural Perspectives on Race Ethnicity and Identity*. Washington DC: NASW Press, 2015.

———. *Race, Ethnicity, and Self: Identity in Multicultural Perspective*. Washington: NMCI, 1994.

Salzman, Jack, and Cornel West, eds. *Struggles in the Promised Land: Toward a History of Black-Jewish Relations in the United States*. New York: Oxford University Press, 1997.

Samuels, Gina Miranda. "Beyond the Rainbow: Multiraciality in the 21st Century." In *Our Diverse Society: Race and Ethnicity—Implications for 21st Century American Society*, edited by David W. Engstrom and Lissette M. Piedra, 37–64. Washington DC: NASW Press, 2006.

Sánchez, María Carla, and Linda Schlossberg. *Passing: Identity and Interpretation in Sexuality, Race, and Religion*. New York: New York University Press, 2001.

Scales-Trent, Judy. *Notes of a White Black Woman: Race, Color, Community*. University Park: Pennsylvania State University Press, 1995.

Schlossberg, Linda. "Rites of Passing." Introduction to Sánchez and Schlossberg, *Passing*, 1–12.

Schultermandl, Silvia. "'What Am I, Anyhow?': Ethnic Consciousness, Matrilineage and the Borderlands-Within in Maxine Hong Kingston's and Rebecca Walker's Autobiographies." In *Close Encounters of an Other Kind: New Perspectives on Race, Ethnicity and American Studies*, edited by Roy Goldblatt, Jopi Nyman and John A. Stotesbury, 3–17. Joensuu, Finland: University of Joensuu, 2005.

Schultz, Debra L. *Going South: Jewish Women in the Civil Rights Movement*. New York: New York University Press, 2001.

Schuyler, George S. *Black No More*. 1931. New York: Modern Library, 1999.

Senna, Danzy. "The Africana QA: Danzy Senna." Interview by Rebecca Weber. Africana. July 6, 2004. http://www.africana.com (site discontinued). https://www.rebeccalweber.com/danzy/.

———. *Caucasia: A Novel*. New York: Riverhead Books, 1998.

———. "An Interview with Danzy Senna." By Claudia M. Milian Arias. *Callaloo* 25, no. 2 (2002): 447–52.

———. "The Mulatto Millennium." In O'Hearn, *Half and Half*, 12–27.

———. "Passing and the Problematic of Multiracial Pride (or, Why One Mixed Girl Still Answers to Black)." In *Black Cultural Traffic: Crossroads in Global Performance and Popular Culture*, edited by Harry J. Elam, Jr. and Kennell Jackson, 83–87. Ann Arbor: University of Michigan Press, 2005.

———. "Resemblance." *Callaloo* 30, no. 3 (2007): 769–87.

———. *Symptomatic*. New York: Riverhead Books, 2004.

———. "To Be Real." In Walker, *To Be Real*, 5–20.

———. "Triad." In Prasad, *Mixed*, 309–24.

———. *Where Did You Sleep Last Night? A Personal History*. New York: Farrar, Straus & Giroux, 2009.

Sexton, Jared. *Amalgamation Schemes: Antiblackness and the Critique of Multiracialism.* Minneapolis: University of Minnesota Press, 2008.

Shanley, Mary Lyndon. "Transracial and Open Adoption: New Forms of Family Relationships." In *Family in Transition*, 12th ed., edited by Arlene S. Skolnick and Jerome H. Skolnick, 255–62. Boston: Allyn and Bacon, 2003.

Shaw-Taylor, Yoku, and Steven A. Tuch, eds. *The Other African Americans: Contemporary African and Caribbean Immigrants in the United States.* Lanham MD: Rowman & Littlefield, 2007.

Sheffer, Jolie A. *The Romance of Race: Incest, Miscegenation, and Multiculturalism in the United States, 1880–1930.* New Brunswick NJ: Rutgers University Press, 2013.

Shelby, Tommie. *We Who Are Dark: The Philosophical Foundations of Black Solidarity.* Cambridge MA: Belknap Press of Harvard University Press, 2005.

Simon, Rita J, and Howard Altstein. *Transracial Adoptees and Their Families: A Study of Identity and Commitment.* New York: Praeger, 1987.

Smedley, Audrey. *Race in North America: Origin and Evolution of a Worldview.* 2nd ed. Boulder CO: Westview, 1999.

Smith, Sidonie, and Julia Watson. *Reading Autobiography: A Guide for Interpreting Life Narratives.* Minneapolis: University of Minnesota Press, 2001.

Sollors, Werner, ed. *Interracialism: Black-White Intermarriage in American History, Literature, and Law.* Oxford: Oxford University Press, 2000.

———. *Neither Black nor White yet Both: Thematic Explorations of Interracial Literature.* New York: Oxford University Press, 1997.

———. "Obligations to Negros Who Would Be Kin If They Were Not Negro." *Daedalus* 140, no. 1 (2011): 142–53.

Spaulding, Carol Roh. "The Go-Between People: Representations of Mixed Race in Twentieth-Century American Literature." In Zack, *American Mixed Race*, 97–112.

Spencer, Jon Michael. *The New Colored People: The Mixed-Race Movement in America.* New York: New York University Press, 1997.

Spencer, Rainier. "Assessing Multiracial Identity Theory and Politics: The Challenge of Hypodescent." *Ethnicities* 4, no. 3 (2004): 357–79.

———. "Beyond Pathology and Cheerleading: Insurgency, Dissolution, and Complicity in the Multiracial Idea." In Dalmage, *Politics of Multiracialism*, 101–24.

———. "Census 2000: Assessments in Significance." In Winters and DeBose, *New Faces*, 99–110.

———. *Challenging Multiracial Identity.* Boulder CO: Lynne Rienner, 2006.

———. "New Racial Identities, Old Arguments: Continuing Biological Reification." In Brunsma, *Mixed Messages*, 83–102.

———. *Reproducing Race: The Paradox of Generation Mix.* Boulder CO: Lynne Rienner, 2011.

————. *Spurious Issues: Race and Multiracial Identity Politics in the United States.* Boulder CO: Westview, 1999.

Spencer, Stephen. *Race and Ethnicity: Culture, Identity and Representation.* New York: Routledge, 2006.

Spickard, Paul R. "Does Multiraciality Lighten? Me-Too Ethnicity and the Whiteness Trap." In Winters and DeBose, *New Faces*, 289–300.

————. "The Illogic of American Racial Categories." In Root, *Racially Mixed People*, 12–23.

————. *Mixed Blood: Intermarriage and Ethnic Identity in Twentieth-Century America.* Madison: University of Wisconsin Press, 1989.

————. "Obama Nation? Race, Multiraciality, and American Identity." In Spickard, *Race in Mind*, 330–75.

————. "The Power of Blackness: Mixed-Race Leaders and the Monoracial Ideal." In Spickard and Daniel, *Racial Thinking*, 103–23.

————. *Race in Mind: Critical Essays.* Notre Dame IN: University of Notre Dame Press, 2015.

————. "The Return of Scientific Racism? DNA Ancestry Testing, Race, and the New Eugenics Movement." Spickard, *Race in Mind*, 142–73.

————. "The Subject is Mixed Race: The Boom in Biracial Biography." Parker and Song, *Rethinking 'Mixed Race,'* 76–98.

————. "What's Critical about White Studies." Spickard and Daniel, *Racial Thinking*, 248–74.

Spickard, Paul, and G. Reginald Daniel, eds. *Racial Thinking in the United States: Uncompleted Independence.* Notre Dame IN: University of Notre Dame Press, 2004.

Spickard, Paul, and Ingrid Dineen-Wimberley. "It's Not That Simple: Multiraciality, Models, and Social Hierarchy." In Spickard, *Race in Mind*, 308–29.

Spillers, Hortense J. "Notes on an Alternative Model—Neither/Nor." In *Black, White, and In Color: Essays on American Literature and Culture*, 301–18. Chicago: University of Chicago Press, 2003.

Squires, Catherine. *Dispatches from the Color Line: The Press and Multiracial America.* Albany: State University of New York Press, 2007.

Staub, Michael E. *Torn at the Roots: The Crisis of Jewish Liberalism in Postwar America.* New York: Columbia University Press, 2002.

————, ed. *The Jewish 1960s: An American Sourcebook.* Lebanon NH: Brandeis University Press, 2004.

Stokes, Curtis, Theresa Meléndez, and Gernice Rhodes-Reed, eds. *Race in 21st Century America.* East Lansing: Michigan State University Press, 2001.

Streeter, Caroline A. *Tragic No More: Mixed-Race Women and the Nexus of Sex and Celebrity.* Amherst: University of Massachusetts Press, 2012.

Sundquist, Eric J. *Strangers in the Land: Blacks, Jews, Post-Holocaust America.* Cambridge MA: Belknap Press of Harvard University Press, 2005.

Sundstrom, Ronald R. *The Browning of America and the Evasion of Social Justice.* Albany: State University of New York Press, 2008.

Talty, Stephan. *Mulatto America: At the Crossroads of Black and White Culture; A Social History.* New York: HarperCollins, 2003.

Tanabe, Ken. "Celebrate Loving Day in June." Lovingday.org. Accessed August 3, 2010. http://lovingday.org.

Taylor, Charles. "The Politics of Recognition." In Gutmann, *Multiculturalism,* 25–74.

Taylor, Paul. "The Next America." Pew Research Center. April 10, 2014. http://www.pewresearch.org/next-america/#Two-Dramas-in-Slow-Motion.

Tessman, Lisa. "The Racial Politics of Mixed Race." *Journal of Social Philosophy* 30, no. 2 (1999): 276–94.

Texeira, Mary Thierry. "The New Multiracialism: An Affirmation of or an End to Race As We Know It?" In Winters and DeBose, *New Faces,* 21–37.

Thompson, Becky, and Sangeeta Tyagi, eds. *Names We Call Home: Autobiography on Racial Identity.* New York: Routledge, 1996.

Thompson, Maxine S., and Verna M. Keith. "Copper Brown and Blue Black: Colorism and Self Evaluation." In Herring, Keith, and Horton, *Skin Deep,* 45–64.

Thurman, Wallace. *The Blacker the Berry.* 1929. Mineola NY: Dover, 2008.

Tizard, Barbara, and Ann Phoenix. "Black Identity and Transracial Adoption." In *In the Best Interests of the Child: Culture, Identity, and Transracial Adoption,* edited by Ivor Gaber and Jane Aldridge, 89–102. London: Free Association Books, 1994.

Toomer, Jean. *Cane.* 1923. New York: Liveright, 1975.

———. *The Wayward and the Seeking: A Collection of Writings by Jean Toomer.* Edited by Darwin T. Turner. Washington DC: Howard University Press, 1980.

Torres, Rodolfo D., Louis F. Mirón, and Jonathan Xavier Inda, eds. *Race, Identity, and Citizenship: A Reader.* Malden MA: Blackwell, 1999.

Trenka, Jane Jeong, Julia Chinyere Oparah, and Sun Yung Shin, eds. *Outsiders Within: Writing on Transracial Adoption.* Cambridge MA: South End, 2006.

Turnbull, Lornet. "Latinos May Get Own Race Category on Census Form." *The Seattle Times,* August 30, 2012. https://www.seattletimes.com/seattle-news/latinos-may-get-own-race-category-on-census-form/.

Twine, France Winddance. "The White Mother: Blackness, Whiteness, and Interracial Families." *Transition,* no. 73 (1997): 144–54.

U.S. Census Bureau. "The Black Population 2010." Census Brief. Updated September 2011.

———. "Hispanic Origin." "About" page. Updated March 7, 2018. https://www.census.gov/topics/population/hispanic-origin/about.html.

———. "Overview of Race and Hispanic Origin: 2000." Census Brief. Updated March 2001. https://www.census.gov/prod/2001pubs/cenbr01-1.pdf.

———. "Overview of Race and Hispanic Origin: 2010." Census Brief. Updated March 2011. https://www.census.gov/prod/cen2010/briefs/c2010br-02.pdf.

———. "Race." "About" page. Updated January 2018. https://www.census.gov /topics/population/race/about.html.

———. "The White Population: 2010." Census Brief. Updated September 2011. https://www.census.gov/prod/cen2010/briefs/c2010br-05.pdf.

Valdes, Francisco, Jerome McCristal Culp, and Angela P. Harris, eds. *Crossroads, Directions, and a New Critical Race Theory*. Philadelphia: Temple University Press, 2002.

Van Tassel, Emily Field. "'Only the Law Would Rule between Us': Antimiscegenation, the Moral Economy of Dependency, and the Debate over Rights after the Civil War." In Delgado and Stefancic, *Critical White Studies*, 152–56.

Wald, Gayle Freda. *Crossing the Line: Racial Passing in Twentieth-Century U.S. Literature and Culture*. Durham NC: Duke University Press, 2000.

Walker, Rebecca. *Black White and Jewish: Autobiography of a Shifting Self*. New York: Riverhead Books, 2001.

———. Introduction to Prasad, *Mixed*, 13–18.

———, ed. *To Be Real: Telling the Truth and Changing the Face of Feminism*. New York: Anchor Books, 1995.

Wall, Natalie. "Passing, Performance, and Perversity: Rewriting Bodies in the Works of Lawrence Hill, Shani Mootoo, and Danzy Senna." *49th Parallel* 26, no. 1 (Autumn 2011).

Walsh, Eileen T. "Ideology of the Multiracial Movement: Dismantling the Color Line and Disguising White Supremacy?" In Dalmage, *Politics of Multiracialism*, 219–35.

Warren, Kenneth W. *What Was American Literature?* The W. E. B. Du Bois Lectures. Cambridge MA: Harvard University Press, 2012.

Washington, Jesse. "Obama's True Colors: Black, White . . . or Neither?" December 13, 2008. http://www.jessewashington.com/obamas-not-black.html.

Watson, Reginald. "The Changing Face of Biraciality: The White/Jewish Mother as Tragic Mulatto Figure in James McBride's *The Color of Water* and Danzy Senna's *Caucasia*." *Obsidian III* 4, no. 1 (2002): 101–13.

Webb, Frank J. *The Garies and Their Friends*. 1857. Baltimore MD: Johns Hopkins University Press, 1997.

White, Walter. *Flight: A Novel*. 1926. New York: Negro Universities Press, 1969.

Wiegman, Robyn. *Object Lessons*. Durham NC: Duke University Press, 2012.

Williams, Gregory Howard. *Life on the Color Line: The True Story of a White Boy Who Discovered He Was Black.* New York: Plume, 1995.

Williams, Kim M. "From Civil Rights to the Multiracial Movement." In Winters and DeBose, *New Faces*, 85–98.

———. "Linking the Civil Rights and Multiracial Movements." In Dalmage, *Politics of Multiracialism*, 77–97.

———. *Mark One or More: Civil Rights in Multiracial America.* Ann Arbor: University of Michigan Press, 2006.

———. "Multiracialism and the Civil Rights Future." *Daedalus* 134, no. 1 (2005): 53–60.

Williams, Patricia J. *Seeing a Colour-Blind Future: The Paradox of Race.* London: Virago, 1997.

Williamson, Joel. *New People: Miscegenation and Mulattoes in the United States.* 1980. Baton Rouge: Louisiana State University Press, 1995.

Wilson, George, and Jomills Braddock. "Analyzing Racial Ideology: Post-1980 America." In *Postmodernism and Race*, edited by Eric Mark Kramer, 129–43. Westport CT: Praeger, 1997.

Winant, Howard. "White Racial Projects." In Rasmussen, *Making and Unmaking*, 97–112.

Winters, Loretta I., and Herman L. DeBose, eds. *New Faces in a Changing America: Multiracial Identity in the 21st Century.* Thousand Oaks: SAGE, 2003.

Witt, Charlotte. "Family Resemblances: Adoption, Personal Identity, and Genetic Essentialism." In Haslanger and Witt, *Adoption Matters*, 135–45.

Wright, Jeni C. "Love is Colorblind: Reflections of a Mixed Girl." In Trenka, Oparah, and Shin, *Outsiders Within*, 27–30.

Womack, Ytasha L. *Post Black: How a New Generation Is Redefining African American Identity.* Chicago: Lawrence Hill Books, 2010.

Young, Hershini Bhana. "Black 'Like Me': (Mis) Recognition, the Racial Gothic, and the Post-1967 Mixed-Race Movement in Danzy Senna's *Symptomatic.*" *African American Review* 42, no. 2 (Summer 2008): 287–305.

Zack, Naomi, ed. *American Mixed Race: The Culture of Microdiversity.* Lanham MD: Rowman & Littlefield, 1995.

———. "American Mixed Race: The United States 2000 Census and Related Issues." In Kwan and Speirs, *Mixing It Up*, 13–30.

———. "Black, White, and Gray: Words, Words, Words." 1993. In Ifekwunigwe, *'Mixed Race' Studies*, 153–57.

———. "Different Forms of Mixed Race: Microdiversity and Destabilization." In Stokes, Meléndez, and Rhodes-Reed, *Race in 21st Century*, 49–58.

———. "Life After Race." In Zack, *American Mixed Race*, 297–307.

———. "Mixed Black and White Race and Public Policy." *Hypatia* 10, no. 1 (1995): 120–32.

———. "My Racial Self over Time." In Camper, *Miscegenation Blues*, 20–27.

———. Preface to Kwan and Speirs, *Mixing It Up*, ix–xii.

———. *Race and Mixed Race*. Philadelphia: Temple University Press, 1993.

———. "White Ideas." In Cuomo and Hall, *Whiteness*, 77–84.

Zackodnik, Teresa C. *The Mulatta and the Politics of Race*. Jackson: University Press of Mississippi, 2004.

Index

culture, black: and black authenticity, 152, 159–60, 182–85, 218–19, 229, 250; and ethnicity, 239, 244, 251; learning about, 114, 157, 158, 171–73, 179, 184, 199, 222–32, 236, 237, 241, 244–45; in literature, 154, 155, 177; of Rebecca Walker, 195, 198; symbols of, 186–87, 235. *See also* speech

DaCosta, Kimberly, 59, 83, 240
Dagbovie-Mullins, Sika A., 25, 28, 114, 146, 148, 194, 269n22, 285n102
Dalmage, Heather, 42, 53
Daniel, G. Reginald, 8, 55, 281n42
Danish ethnicity: literature about, 34, 259–60; and race practices, 222–23, 242–44; and racial identity, 216, 221, 239, 246, 250; recognition of, 240–41, 295n17. *See also* ethnicity
Davis, Angela, 147
Declaration of Independence, 101–2
Derricotte, Toi, 151, 253
The Diary of Anne Frank (Frank), 142
discrimination, reverse, 57. *See also* racism
Doane, Ashley, 108
Doležal, Rachel, 283n56
double consciousness, 245, 247
doubleness, 68
Douglass, Frederick, 1, 263–64
Du Bois, W. E. B., 11, 59, 245, 263–64
Durrow, Heidi: autobiography of, 259; *The Girl Who Fell from the Sky*, 30–31, 215–53; multiracial representation by, 23, 33–34, 254; and racial classification, 249; and racial identity, 256
Dyer, Richard, 287n45

Ebony, 114
economy, 99, 101, 102, 127
education, 119, 198, 200, 232–33, 236–38, 255–56. *See also* culture, black: learning about
Elam, Michele, 25–26, 28, 52–53, 74, 99
Ellis, Trey, 25
England, 99–101, 103, 104, 291n25
ethnicity: of African Americans, 34, 241–43, 246, 250–51, 256, 259–60; choosing of, 130, 244, 246; in literature, 30, 262–63; mixedness of, 213; and monoculturalism, 215; and physical appearance, 73–76, 230, 240–42, 295n17; and racial identity, 6, 32–34, 50–51, 151, 217–20, 223, 238–39, 244–48, 255–60, 287n47; of Rebecca Walker, 84, 204; terminology of, 219, 290n102, 294n10; in U.S. Census, 271n46, 290n102; and whiteness, 97, 100–106, 116, 117, 125, 128–29, 142.

See also cultural identity; Danish ethnicity; immigration; nationalism
Ethnicity and Race (Cornell and Hartmann), 105
eugenics, 104, 278n15, 287n31
Europe: African American ancestry in, 46, 152; American settlers from, 99, 100, 101, 103, 126, 286n18, 287n47; race mixing in, 1, 222–23; racial identity in, 82, 86, 259–60
European bildungsroman, 74, 208–9

Fade (Lewis), 66–67, 148
families. *See* multiracial families
Fauset, Jessie Redmon, 23, 128
Ferber, Abby, 53, 97, 108, 267n1
Ferguson, Plessy v., 270n34
"50 Experiences of Racially Mixed People," 284n78
Finding Grace (Haizlip), 275n72
Flight (White), 22, 23, 128
France, 8
Frankenberg, Ruth, 102, 107–8, 287n45
Franklin, Benjamin, 101, 286n18
Funderburg, Lise, 253, 259
Fusco, Coco, 108

Gallagher, Charles, 105
Gallup poll, 272n55
The Garies and Their Friends (Webb), 21
gender: and blackness, 172, 197–98; and civil rights, 102; and positive black identity, 232, 239; role-playing, 191–92, 204; and whiteness, 119. *See also* sexuality; women
Gilroy, Paul, 155, 211
Gingrich, Newt, 56, 57
The Girl Who Fell from the Sky (Durrow): racial identity in, 219–51; study of, 30–31, 215–16; terminology in, 216–19
Glasgow, Joshua, 44–45, 278n16, 279n17
Glazer, Nathan, 290n102
Goldberg, David Theo, 17
Graham, Susan, 48–50, 54, 59, 276n4, 280n26, 282n51
Greenberg, Cheryl, 126–27
Grossberg, Lawrence, 292n31

hair, 167–69, 178–81, 227, 236, 241, 244. *See also* racial identity: and physical appearance
Haizlip, Shirlee, 275n72
Half a Heart (Brown), 125
half-breed label, 182–83, 200, 271n46

To order or obtain more information on these or other
University of Nebraska Press titles, visit nebraskapress.unl.edu.

CPSIA information can be obtained
at www.ICGtesting.com
Printed in the USA
LVHW04*1746171018
593926LV00006B/124/P